To Be a
Redemptorist
Today

TO BE A REDEMPTORIST TODAY

Reflections on the Redemptorist Charism

Noel Londoño B., C.Ss.R., General Editor

LIGUORI
PUBLICATIONS

Liguori, Missouri

Published by Liguori Publications
Liguori, Missouri

Library of Congress Cataloging-in-Publication Data

To be a Redemptorist today : reflections on the Redemptorist charism / Noel Londoño B., general editor. — 1st ed.
    p.   cm.
  Includes bibliographical references.
  ISBN 0-7648-0052-3
  1. Redemptorists—Biography. 2. Redemptorists—Spiritual life. 3. Spiritual biography. I. Londoño B., Noel.
BX 4020.Z7T6   1996
255'.64—dc20   96-26511

Printed in the United States of America
99 98 97 96   4 3 2 1
First Edition

CONTENTS

THE DIMENSIONS OF THE CHARISM

THE CHARISM IN PRACTICE

INTRODUCTION

Noel Londoño B., C.Ss.R.
Province of Bogotá

ALTHOUGH HE WAS BORN three hundred years ago in Italy, Alphonsus Liguori is a saint with universal appeal. His life, his writings, and his religious Congregation have been a gift of God the Father to the whole Church, serving as a special reminder of the privileged way in which Christ reveals himself in the face of those most abandoned.

Given the fact that the missionary Institute founded by Alphonsus now is spread across seventy-four nations of the world, it seemed opportune to reexamine the principal elements of its charism. The celebration of the tercentenary of the birth of their founder provides the occasion for Redemptorists—priests, brothers, and students—as well as the laity, who stand shoulder to shoulder with them in the work of evangelization, to offer this charism anew to the faithful. Such was the inspiration for this book, which from the very beginning was conceived as an approach to the wellspring of our proper charism, so that we might drink deeply from this source of Redemptorist spirituality.

From this initial stimulus followed the task of deciding which aspects of the charism should be developed. The General Commission on Redemptorist spirituality proposed three broad categories: The Sources of Our Charism, The Dimensions of the Charism, and The Charism in Practice, defining as it did the contents of the respective chapters. The Commission also gave consideration to the authors who could represent the vast spectrum of geography, languages, and pastoral ministries in the Congregation. Even so, as it made its selection, the Commission was conscious of excluding many potential themes and valuable collaborators. But choices had to be made. It also seemed advisable to avoid an overly scholarly style, giving preference instead to highlighting the expansive array of experiences of real Redemptorists. There will be other books that will define the charism; here we want to describe it through our own personal history.

Through the good offices of the General Government, contact was made with the authors. All responded positively to the proposal. Ultimately, only Father João Felix, an Angolan Redemptorist still living the trials of civil war in his homeland, could not finish his contribution. His absence among the authors serves to remind us of the confreres who continue to suffer for the Gospel.

Many have contributed to the progress of this book: authors, translators, editors, typists. Only with their help has it been possible to produce simultaneously editions in Spanish, English, Portuguese, Italian, German, and Polish. We are sincerely grateful to these, our collaborators.

There was a quote from the prophet Isaiah which was a favorite of Saint Alphonsus: "You will draw water joyfully from the springs of salvation" (Isaiah 12:3). He made frequent reference to it in his writings on the Incarnation and the passion of Jesus Christ, proposing the Christian life as an ongoing approach to the source of life, which is Christ himself. The quotation captures the purpose of this book, an attempt to fix the sources which have constituted the Redemptorists as a religious congregation. With the guidance of the Spirit, we can continue to draw water from this saving spring, which is Christ the Redeemer, and joyfully share it with one another and the world.

Finally, it is worthwhile to recall the advise of Saint Bernard of Clairvaux: "Drink from your own well." According to the saint, each Christian must drink from his own well, that is, from the living tradition of the community which has given birth to him for Christ. We hope that the readers who are about to explore this work will themselves drink of the Spirit of this particular well, slaking their thirst at the fount of the Redeemer.

NOEL LONDOÑO B., C.Ss.R.
EDITOR

THE SOURCES
OF OUR CHARISM

1

THE REDEMPTORIST CHARISM AND THE SPIRIT OF THE RISEN ONE

F. X. Durrwell, C.Ss.R.
Province of Strasbourg
Translated by Donald Miniscalco, C.Ss.R.
Province of Baltimore

1. Why Did I Become a Redemptorist?

I wanted to become a missionary, so I entered the Congregation without being familiar with it. The Lord wanted it. That is also the reason I remain within the Congregation. There is nothing interesting or valuable to say about my personal life. Whatever I might say about myself could only be as refers to Christ, the Savior. I seek to take hold of his mystery, which is also the mystery of the Congregation.

During the novitiate and studendate, our teachers, faithful to the Constitutions then in force, taught that a Redemptorist strives for a double goal: the first is common to all religious-personal sanctification; the second, proper to the Congregation, the proclamation of the Gospel especially to the poor. It was said that the two goals were united because, to be effective, the apostle had to be animated by personal sanctity.

The Christology taught at that time was divided into two tracts: *De Verbo Incarnato* and *De Christo Redemptore*. The first studied the mystery of Christ, the God-man; the second studied the mystery of his work. The first had no allusion to the second. Nonetheless, a bond united the two tracts: in order for the salvific work of Christ to be efficacious, in order for him to pay the infinite price of redemption, it was necessary that his action be infinitely holy, which it indeed was by reason of his being the Incarnate Word.

An analogy existed between the double goals of the Congregation and the Christology of the times. Later, I understood that the Incarnation and the Redemption constitute one unique mystery. Consequently, it seemed to me that the Congregation should pursue one unique goal: to prolong the unique mystery of Christ in the world.

This is how I arrived at that conclusion. I was in the last year of the studendate (1936–1937). I knew I would continue my studies at the Biblicum in Rome. Naively, I had already chosen a subject for my doctoral thesis: the problem of evil in the Bible! That year we were in the second part of the tract on Christology, the tract on Redemption. In those days, only the passion of Jesus was considered salvific, because it was the price Christ paid for our redemption. The Resurrection was viewed only in its apologetic aspect as a proof of the faith. However, one morning, our very competent dogma professor, Father Dillenschneider, devoted an hour to the salvific role of the Resurrection. "It is neither meritorious nor expiatory. It is the personal recompense given to Jesus. For us, the Resurrection has an exemplary role since it is the model of our justification; furthermore, it is the efficient cause of the resurrection of the dead." Saint Thomas had said the same.

That morning, I sensed that the Resurrection of Jesus is more than that, much more. I went off to Rome. I quickly forgot the subject I had chosen for my thesis, but the question of the Resurrection would not leave me. I searched. I kept asking. A professor at the Biblicum told me: "Devote yourself to the Old Testament. There's nothing more to discover in the New." I remained firm. At that time I did not know the works of O. Casel—fortunately. I had to refer to another teacher, the only one capable of instructing me, the Holy Scripture.

In 1938, I enrolled in the course of Romans by Father Merk in the hope of finding the meaning of Romans 4:25: "Delivered over for our sins, raised for our justification." Most Protestants, following Saint Augustine, explained this text to mean that the Resurrection is the foundation of the faith by which we are justified. According to Saint Thomas and the majority of Catholic authors, the Resurrection is the exemplary cause of our justification. I was sure that neither one presented the whole meaning of this text. After some months we came to Romans 4:25. "This text does not present any difficulty," said the professor. "Christ died for the expiation of our sins, raised so as to be the model of our justification." My disappointment was great....

In August 1939, I understood that Jesus is risen in the power of the Holy Spirit, that he was transformed in this power of the Spirit so as to become himself a life-giving spirit (1 Corinthians 15:45). Today every good theologian knows that. At that time, however, it was new. For me, it was a dawning, already decisive.

War broke out at the beginning of September 1939 so I had to discontinue my studies, but in mid December I could return to Rome. Feverishly, I prepared a paper for Father Merk on the Resurrection of Jesus as the outpouring of the Holy Spirit upon him and upon the world. A question remained, however; since Jesus is our Savior by his death—the faith said this forcefully—what is the relation between his death and this Resurrection which is the outpouring of the Holy Spirit? Without an answer to this question, my problem about the salvific role of the Resurrection would remain unanswered. I asked the Lord to give me the answer soon because, from day to day, the military authorities might recall me to France.

One morning in February 1940, during thanksgiving after Mass—according to the Constitutions, we spent a half hour in prayer—I read Galatians 4:1–7. Although I must have read this text a hundred times without ever finding the answer to my question, that morning I grasped the sense that underlies these verses. I understood that *the redemption of the world is accomplished in the person of Jesus.* In his death to "the flesh" and his resurrection in the Spirit of divine sonship, *he has become the eschatological salvation in his own person.* The Redemption is nothing else than the personal mystery of the man Jesus, who, by the power of the Spirit, rises through his death to the fullness of sonship. It was a moment of light.

I had been taught that Christ had *obtained* salvation for men, acquiring by his passion the merits which the Church then must "apply." Now I saw that he has *become* salvation himself. "He has become for us... redemption" (1 Corinthians 1:30). This salvation is extended because Christ comes—"I go away and I come to you" (John 14:28)—communicates himself, and takes men into himself. The role of the Church is not to distribute merits, but to be the mediator of Christ's presence to and communion with the world.

A synthesis rapidly coalesced around this central truth. I brought my paper to the professor but, before I could learn what he thought of it, I had to report for the military service. After much wandering during the war and postwar period, I was able to publish a book: *The Resurrection of Jesus,*

Mystery of Salvation (1950). It expressed what I had grasped that morning in February 1940.

At that time I was perfect of students. In our French provinces, then flourishing, we were asking: What is the specific identity of the Congregation within the Church? I replied: Our specificity lies in what is common and essential to the whole Church. If we are to identify ourselves aside from the course of our history, it is in the measure in which we are consecrated uniquely to what is essential. Like the whole Church, the Congregation has the mission of being the mediator, particularly among the poor, of this Christ, the Good News of the world.

In 1952 or 1953, Father Buys, the superior general, entrusted to Father Buckers of the Cologne Province the work of preparing a directory for the novices of the Congregation. I studied the historical sources available. There I discerned two currents. It seemed that the first reflected the thought of Monsignor Tommaso Falcoia and still was being expressed in the distinction between the two goals of the Congregation. The second current came to the fore more and more clearly as Saint Alphonsus withdrew from the influence of Falcoia. The saint expresses it himself forcefully in the petition addressed to Benedict XIV: "The end of this Institute is to unite priests...whose *sole* purpose is to follow the example of our Lord Jesus Christ by preaching the Word of God to the poor, as He said of himself: 'He has send me to bring good news to the poor.' "

I discovered in this way the same unity in the mission of the Congregation as in the mystery of Christ the Savior. The mystery of Redemption is the very same mystery as that of Jesus, who, in the power of the Spirit, by his death and resurrection, attained the fullness of sonship, which properly is his for the sake of humanity. The mission of the Congregation and of the entire Church is to prolong and spread this unique mystery of salvation in the world. Personal sanctification and mission are only one: God has chosen us to be coworkers with his Son "in the salvation of souls...this vocation to the apostolate is the manifest sign of our predestination."[1] Moreover, the Constitutions of 1764 say: Congregati nostri...veluti Jesu Christi in magno redemptionis negotio adjutores atque socii et administri vocati sunt.[2] Our unique vocation, like that of the apostles who founded the Church, is "to be with Christ and to be sent to preach" (Mark 3:14). To be with Christ and to be sent forth are one.

Father Buys died in 1953 and his project was buried with him. However, I had the chance to present my research before an assembly of future capitulars preparing for the General Chapter of 1967.[3] Two confreres who are dear to me, Father Paul Hitz (+1974) and Father Domenico Capone, who shared these ideas, saw them reach fulfillment in the Constitutions of the General Chapter.[4]

2. The Resurrected Spirit

In the petition addressed to Benedict XIV, Saint Alphonsus likens the goal of the Congregation to the mission which Jesus defined in his discourse at the synagogue in Nazareth: "The Spirit of the Lord is upon me, because he has anointed me….He has sent me to bring the Good News to the poor…to proclaim a year of favor of the Lord" (Luke 4:18f).

Jesus "stood to do the reading" (Luke 4:16). Contrary to the custom (Acts of the Apostles 13:15), he takes the initiative. His authority comes from on high; he is sent by him who anointed him with the Holy Spirit. When Jesus rises to announce the Good News, it is realized: "Today, this scripture has been fulfilled in your hearing" (Luke 4:21). Jesus will repeat the same thing later on: "The law and the prophets reach unto John; since then the Good News of the kingdom is proclaimed" and is realized in its proclamation (Luke 16:16). Because it is not merely a verbal proclamation, "the year of favor" actually begins from that moment, the *copiosa redemptio* is at work for the liberation of the oppressed. Salvation comes in the coming of Jesus.

According to Mark 1:15, Jesus inaugurates his ministry by proclaiming the arrival of the kingdom of God. According to Luke 4:16, this kingdom comes in the person of Jesus who proclaims it. To those who demand signs of the coming of the kingdom, Jesus replies: "No sign will be given to it except the sign of Jonah" (Luke 11:29). Jesus, whose preaching is parallel to that of Jonah, is the manifestation of the coming of the kingdom. The good news comes in Jesus, who proclaims it: "Behold, the kingdom of God is in your midst" (Luke 17:21).

All of this has meaning for the Congregation, whose charism is to "continue" Christ. In the person of the apostle united to Christ and in his activity, God brings to realization the *copiosa redemptio*.

Saint Alphonsus does not cite the beginning of the text of Isaiah, proclaimed by Jesus, which is essential: "The Spirit of the Lord is upon me." The theology of those times was unaware of the role of the Spirit in the work of salvation just as it was unaware of the meaning of the Resurrection. It held that everything was brought about by Jesus' sufferings being

weighed on the scale of divine justice. However, without the Spirit, who is
the anointing, Jesus would not even be the Messiah, that is to say the Anointed
of God. Jesus would not as man be the Son of God, because it is in the Holy
Spirit that God begot him at the beginning of his human existence (Luke
1:35), lead him throughout his life (John 1:33f), and through his death to
the fullness of sonship (Acts of the Apostles 13:33; Romans 1:4) when he
raised him in the fullness of the Spirit (cf. Romans 8:11). Nor would Jesus
be the Savior, since it is in the Holy Spirit that he has offered himself to
God (Hebrews 9:14) and is raised. The Savior would not be sent into the
world as bearer of salvation because the consecration (by anointing in the
Spirit) and the sending into the world (cf. John 10:36) are inseparable. "The
Spirit of the Lord is upon me because he has anointed me; he has sent me to
bring good news to the poor."

Would the Redemptorist be able to "continue" Christ if he is not filled
with the Holy Spirit of Christ? Today when the Congregation is living in a
difficult period, the primary need is that it be open to the Holy Spirit, without whom it cannot continue Christ the Savior.

The sermon at Nazareth was both a program and a prelude. The admiration of the people of Nazareth for the "words of grace"—indeed they
are words of grace because they are the words of God (cf. Acts of the Apostles
14:3; 20:32)—turns into violent anger. They make an attack upon the life
of their compatriot, but "he, passing through the midst of them, went away"
(20:30). He escapes death. This episode is emblematic of the entire ministry of Jesus and announces his death and Resurrection.

In his *pascha* of death and glory, Jesus has "become for us...
redemption" (1 Corinthians 1:30). He has sacrificially offered himself to
the Father in the Holy Spirit (Hebrews 9:14); he is raised by the Spirit (Romans 8:11) through the power of God (2 Corinthians 13:4), who is the Spirit
and by the glory of God (Romans 6:4), who is the Spirit. The paschal anointing of the Spirit makes Jesus the Messiah: "God has made him both Lord
and Messiah, this Jesus whom you crucified" (Acts of the Apostles 2:36).
The mystery of his sonship in the Spirit expands to reach its fullness: "Declared to be Son of God with power according to the spirit of holiness by
resurrection from the dead" (Romans 1:4). In the power of the Spirit, Jesus
is Messiah, Son of God, Savior, and Good News spreading throughout the
world.

From the time of his earthly life, Jesus is "the one who is sent," the
one who brings the good news because he is anointed by the Spirit (Luke

4:18). Risen in the plenitude of the Spirit, his being sent is henceforth universal: "God has raised up his servant and sends him to you (Acts of the Apostles 3:26; cf. 26:23). Jesus had said: "From now on you will see the Son of Man coming…" (Matthew 26:64), "I am going away, and I am coming to you" (John 14:28). "Given life in the Spirit" (1 Peter 3:18), transformed so as to become himself "life-giving spirit" (1 Corinthians 15:45)—that is to say, a being totally communicating himself—Jesus is "the apostle" of God (Hebrews 3:1), his universal envoy.

How does he come into the world now that he is at the Father's side? He is no longer visible or audible in himself, but he raises up a visible and audible presence in the world by means of the Church, the apostles, the proclamation of the gospel, and the sacraments.

The apostolate is not a postpaschal activity, a second act joined to and completing the paschal mystery. The entire mystery is accomplished in the paschal Christ, who is the Alpha and Omega of salvation. The paschal mystery, which is personal to Christ, is destined for us—"for us he died and rose again" (2 Corinthians 5:15)—and becomes effectively our own by our communion with Christ. The apostles are not successor to Christ; they "continue" him. They are sacraments of Christ in his redemptive action, his expansion in the world: "Christ lives in me" (Galatians 2:20), speaks in me (2 Corinthians 13:3); "I speak in Christ" (2 Corinthians 2:17). Saint Augustine says: "Christ who preaches Christ"[5] by means of the Church which is his body.[6]

Saint Paul was aware of being like a sacrament of the paschal Christ: "We always carry everywhere in the body the death of Jesus, so that the life of Jesus also may be made visible in our bodies" (2 Corinthians 4:10). The Redemptorist allows himself to be taken up into Christ who "has become redemption" (cf. 1 Corinthians 1:30). He continues not just a work that was inaugurated in the past, but Christ himself in his eternal mystery of salvation.[7]

In this way, the apostle is witness to the risen One; he does not only proclaim that he knows of the risen One, he is the mediator of his resurrection in the world, a meeting point between Christ and men. He belongs to Christ, who is at the same time the savior and the salvation, which extends to all the world. Living in intimate communion with him—"Simon son of John, do you love me?" (John 21:15)—is essential to the apostolate. Saint Alphonsus, the Redemptorist par excellence, lived in passionate friendship with Jesus. "He called to him those whom he wanted…so that they might be with him and be sent forth" (Mark 3:13f).

To be sent forth while being with him whom the Father raised from the dead and sent forth into the world: "As the Father has sent me, so I send you" (John 20:21). To live in communion with Christ, to sanctify oneself, and to be an apostle are one and the same thing. "He who is called to the Congregation of the Most Holy Redeemer will never be a true continuator of Jesus Christ nor ever become holy if he does not fulfill the purpose of his vocation or does not have the spirit of the Institute which is to save souls most deprived of spiritual help."[8]

The sending forth of the apostle, as of Christ, is the work of the Holy Spirit. Jesus told them: "'As the Father has sent me, so I send you.' Having said this, he breathed on them and said: 'Receive the holy Spirit'" (John 20:21–22). "Having said this"—so that it would be realized—"he breathed on them." He communicated to them the Spirit by whose power he himself is sent. The Holy Spirit is the dynamism of the Congregation's apostolic mission.

By saying, "Receive the holy Spirit," Jesus signifies that the Spirit is given to the apostles. Yet they must receive him, open themselves to this gift. Without ceasing, the Congregation must ask itself if it is sufficiently open to the breath of the Spirit.

It is by prayer that man opens himself to the gift of God, "Your Father in heaven will give his Spirit to those who ask him" (Luke 11:13). The Church prepares herself in prayer to receive the Breath of Pentecost. In the loving contemplation of Christ the Savior, and in intense communion with him in the sacrament of the Eucharist, Saint Alphonsus drank of "waters of the Spirit" which spring from the pierced side of Jesus (cf. John 7:37–39; 19:34). In the name of its apostolic vocation, the Congregation must be an assembly of prayer in the world. Indeed, such is the duty of the entire Church.

"With Mary, the mother of Jesus," the disciples prepared to receive the Breath of Pentecost (Acts of the Apostles 1:14). In recounting the death of Jesus, the evangelist writes: "He bowed his head and gave up his spirit [or the Spirit]" (John 19:30). The same word has a double significance, a familiar literary procedure of the evangelist (3:14; 8:28; 12:32f). At one and the same time, he speaks of Jesus, who dies, and of Jesus, who in his mystery of death and glory, breathes forth the Spirit to his disciples. Toward whom does he bow his head? Upon whom does the Breath descend? "Near the cross of Jesus stood his mother and the disciple whom Jesus loved." In Saint John's eyes, Mary represents the Church. Upon her and upon the disciple who welcomes Mary (and the Church) as mother, the

Breath of God comes. The Spirit rests upon the Congregation, which welcomes Mary and the Church as its beloved Mother. Marian devotion and fidelity to the Church is a mark of the Holy Spirit impressed upon the Congregation.

Having said "receive the holy Spirit," Jesus adds, "If you forgive the sins of any, they are forgiven them, if you retain the sins of any, they are retained" (John 20:22f). The Holy Spirit is the forgiveness of all sins because he is the holiness of God. Jesus "takes away the sin of the world" because he is the holy paschal lamb within whom the Spirit dwells (John 1:29,33) and who allows himself to be sanctified (John 17:19) by his death. Enriched by the Spirit, the Church, and in her the Congregation, has power to forgive sins, *all* sins. "To forgive and to hold bound," this opposition of contraries signifies the totality of power.[9] Neither Christ (John 3:17) nor the Church is commissioned to hold sins bound. The charism of the Congregation is *copiosa redemptio*, the charism of an limitless power of mercy such as Saint Alphonsus practiced.

This charism extends to the moral and pastoral theology that is proper to the Congregation in following its founder. This theology has as its object the human person and not merely being and the laws of being. The human person must be understood as the crown of being. The laws of being must be considered as at the service of the human person. My study of Christology has taught me that redemption is identifiable as the personal mystery of Jesus; that the Holy Spirit everywhere plays a personalizing role[10]; and that the theologian must let himself be guided in everything by a personalist mode of thought. I was happy to note that the moral theology of the Congregation has this personalist character. In this as well one can discern and seal of the Spirit of the risen Christ imprinted upon the Congregation.

The text of John 20:21–23, which gives the power to forgive sins, is paralleled by Luke 24:44–47, which establishes the mission to convert the world: "Thus it is written, that the Messiah is to suffer and to rise from the dead on the third day, and that repentance and forgiveness of sins is to be proclaimed to all nations....I am sending upon you [the Spirit whom] what my Father promised." The Holy Spirit is the forgiveness of sins because he is the power of conversion and sanctification. Forgiveness of sins lies within the grace which converts the sinner and sanctifies him. Because of the Spirit that Christ breathes upon it, the Congregation has the mission of conversion: "Redemptorists are apostles of conversion" (Constitution 11). The Congregation must welcome this dynamic of conversion first of all for its own self. In this way, it can "continue" Christ, who has become "a life-giving spirit" (1 Corinthians 15:45), the power of sanctification.

All this—the call to conversion and the forgiveness of sins—is part of the Good News entrusted to one upon whom the Spirit rests: "The Spirit of the Lord is upon me....He has sent me to proclaim the good news" (Luke 4:18). Luke 24:44–47 and John 20:21ff mean essentially the same as Matthew 28:20 and Acts of the Apostles 1:8, where Jesus gives the mission of evangelizing all peoples. The apostles are "established...to be sent to preach" (Mark 3:13f). Risen in the Holy Spirit, Jesus has become in his person the Good News, which is both proclaimed and actualized in the world. He raises himself in the power of the Spirit and brings the resurrection into the world under the form of the Word, which the Breath of God carries. In the Bible, the Word of God and the Breath of God are inseparable. Jesus is inseparable from the Spirit, in whom he is the Son, in whom he is raised up and sent. Through the apostles, he comes into the world under the form of the Word which the Spirit inspires. The Word is a universal sacrament of the coming of Christ in the power of the Spirit.[11] "Our gospel has been preached to you...with power, with the Holy Spirit and great fullness" (1 Thessalonians 1:5) The Spirit of the risen One makes those who "continue" Christ into men of the Word. "Our mission in the Church is the explicit proclamation of the Word with the aim of conversion" (Constitution 10).

In John 20:22f, the Council of Trent saw the foundation of the sacrament of penance. Although the text is far more extensive and encompasses the entire mission of evangelization, the Council's insight into its meaning is very significant. "Your sins are forgiven" is an integral part of the Good News brought to the poor in the power of the Spirit. Saint Alphonsus's example and the history of the Congregation show that the sacrament of penance is part of the gift bestowed upon the Congregation in its mission among the poor.

In the sermon at Nazareth, Jesus declares himself to be sent to the poor in the power of the Holy Spirit. Risen in the fullness of the Spirit, Jesus no longer speaks of a "preferential option" for the poor; the gospel of the resurrection is addressed to all men. However, the discourse at Nazareth is a plan of action and its affirmation always remains of value. If the paschal gospel is destined for all men, that is precisely because all are poor, all are beings-oriented-toward-death, for whom the resurrection of Jesus is the good news of their liberation.

However, some are particularly poor and because of this the gospel is

ValYOU Award Nomination Form
Value of the Month: Dependability

Name of person honoring the Value: _____

How value was demonstrated:

Date: _____

Submitted by: _____

addressed to them. The riches of the paschal mystery are destined for them by preference because this mystery is that of Jesus in the extreme poverty of the death from which he is risen. Jesus is sent, first of all, to those whom his *kenosis* has made him closest. The Holy Spirit, by whose power Jesus is "saved from death" (cf. Hebrews 5:5), is infinite love (Romans 5:5). True love is humble; infinite humility because he is infinite. The Spirit is called the humility of God, the "Father of the poor." God, who in all things works according to his Spirit, has a preference for the poor: "Blessed are the poor! The kingdom of God is theirs" (Luke 6:20). He is pleased in them; he reveals himself to the little ones (Luke 10:21). He reveals himself above all to Jesus (Luke 10:22), who is, par excellence, the little one of the Father. Animated by this Spirit, Jesus is "gentle and humble in heart" (Matthew 11:29); "I will put my Spirit upon him…he will not wrangle or cry aloud…a bruised reed he will not break, the smoldering wick he will not extinguish" (Matthew 12:18–20).

"He has sent me to bring the good news to the poor" applies even more than at his discourse at Nazareth to Jesus, the risen One, because, from now on, the fullness of the Spirit is in him.

The Congregation must "continue" Christ because he is glorified in his *kenosis*, because of the Spirit of divine humility toward the poor, to whom we are sent in "simplicity of life and word" (Constitution 20). Our apostolate will always be devoid of human glory. We must make our choice: the Congregation perhaps will never be an illustrious religious order. We belong to the world of lowly people, "in glory and in dishonor…unknown yet well known." (2 Corinthians 6:8f). I've always thought that a veil over the Congregation hides its true glory from the eyes of the world. Its true glory is that of God which shines from the cross of Christ (Galatians 6:14). The Holy Spirit is, at one and the same time, the humility of God and "the Spirit of glory" (1 Peter 4:14). The charism of the Congregation is to "continue" Christ, who in his *kenosis* is risen by the power of the Spirit.

Notes

1. Cited from C. Dilgskron, *Leben des heiligen Bischofs und Kirchenlehrers Alphonsus Maria de Liguori.* Regensburg: Pustet, 1887. Tome I, p. 506.
2. Constitutions of 1764, n. 42. Cf. Constitutions of 1984, n. 2.
3. This meeting was held at Delemont, Switzerland, from July 30 to August 6, 1966.

4. A part of my research, which goes back to 1952 and was presented to the meeting at Delemont in 1966, was published by the Secretariat of Formation in 1977.

5. Saint Augustine, *In Joh. tract.* 47,3. CCL 36, 405

6. Saint Augustine, *Sermo 354, 1.* PL 39, 1563. "It is Christ who preaches Christ, the body which preaches the Head.

7. It is in this very strong sense that the former Constitution 40 must be understood: *Missiones nil aliud sunt nisi continuata Redemptio quam Filius Dei perpetuo, ope ministrorum suorum, in mundo operatur.*

8. Saint Alphonsus, *The True Redemptorist.*

9. Cf. Mark 3:4.

10. See especially my books—*L'Esprit Saint de Dieu* and *Le Pere, Dieu en son mystere.*

11. The preached Word is not counted among the seven individual sacraments perhaps because it is a universal sacrament.

2

To Preach Good News to the Poor: Luke 4:18

Denis McBride, C.Ss.R.
Province of London

1. Beginnings

Why do we do the things we do? How have we ended up where we are today? Looking back twenty-eight years to uncover why I chose the Redemptorist road as a way to life is proving to be an exercise in creative memory. Reviewing our past, we like to believe that our choices were free of desperation or compulsion, we want to believe that who we are is the fruit of high-minded decisions inspired by God and his angels. Our need for narrative sense makes us impose a pattern on the fitfulness of the past, so that it all reads like a sensible story. We can all rewrite our infancy narratives to build a ground of explanation for who we have turned out to be. Saint Paul wrote to the Galatians: "God specially chose me when I was still in my mother's womb, called me through his grace...." If God chose Paul while he was in his mother's womb, it took some time for the accomplished persecutor to catch up with his missionary beginning.

When we listen to stories of priests leaving the active priesthood, we hear them reinterpret the past in a new way. The old clarity has gone, life has taken a new turn, and that makes us hesitant in being dogmatic about our own story. We begin to wonder. Maybe the only way God can work is through the ordinary experience of attraction and want, drive and commitment. What else is there to work with? Certainly when these *natural* qualities disappear, we begin to wonder about *religious* vocation. We smother life's untidiness in theological language, the danger being that we end up saying nothing real at all.

Once upon a time I met a man in a Redemptorist habit who impressed me. He came to give a retreat at the college, a junior seminary in Scotland, where I was training for the secular priesthood. I was sixteen at the time. We greeted his arrival with the tired cynicism of youth, expecting to be bored by more religion. He was a surprise. His enormous natural gifts were put at the service of preaching the Gospel, and he succeeded in helping us believe that the Gospel could make a difference to the way we breathed and behaved. He didn't seem like other priests—tame and institutionalized— he appeared wild and free. When they were stuck teaching geography and mathematics in a seminary, he was wandering the country preaching the Good News. I was not only impressed by him, I wanted to be like him.

Nothing happened for a while. At the end of the school year, my form-master told me that I was being asked to leave: my academic work had not been up to standard; I was a lazy student, interested only in sports; I had been caught too often wasting my study periods reading fiction instead of doing my assignments. All this, I must admit, was perfectly true, but the rejection was hard to accept. I still believed, against the evidence, that I had the makings of a priest. The desire was still alive and well. My form-master knew I was impressed by the visiting Redemptorist. The Archdiocese of Glasgow did not want me but perhaps the Redemptorists might have room for the likes of me.

Rejection was my driving force for becoming a Redemptorist. I'm not sure what a psychiatrist or an angel would think about that as a nurturing ground for a religious vocation, but rejection, together with my desire to be a priest, impelled me into the Congregation. When I applied, I was interviewed and accepted—provided I first spent a year at a college in Wales because I was too young to enter the novitiate. I enjoyed that year enormously: the studies were easy and the freedom was cosmic compared to the junior seminary. I felt happy because I was on the road to becoming like the Redemptorist priest I had met once upon a time.

2. Staying On

That Redemptorist left the priesthood and is now married with grownup children. The dedication that he lived as a Redemptorist is now transferred to his work as a college lecturer and pastoral worker. He has moved on, but he serves the Church with the same energy and commitment that gives life to many people. I have stayed on, strenuously hoping that my commitment will be of some service to the Congregation and the Church.

Why stay? For a variety of reasons, none of them profoundly theological. I feel at home in the Congregation, and remain enthusiastic about its gift for proclamation. I feel at home in the mad mixture that we are: the saintly and the dedicated, the crooked and the cracked, the prophets and the wise men, the desperate and the frightened. We are a fragile people, and I feel accepted as part of that fragility, part of a group that has enormous gifts of charity and apostolic purpose within it. I feel useful because my talents, such as they are, are being employed to some pastoral purpose, one that has its focus in the extraordinary proclamation of the Word. When I fail, when I feel useless, I still have a sense of belonging.

I don't believe for a moment that the Congregation is a place for perfect people or a preserve for men of steel. It is not an arena for gladiators, but home to a crowd of sinners. It also serves as a refugee camp, a hospital, and for a few, a prison. Sin is part of our story, as redemption is. Sometimes we get lucky, sometimes God's grace shines through our halting attempts to be good news to one another and the people we serve. More importantly, the Congregation is also an occasion for growth and renewal, a field of possibility where you can still breathe deeply. We may not have many great men among us, but we do have people who are deeply committed to the Lord; we do have a great message to share and stories to tell; we do have a charism for sharing the Gospel in our own way. That's reason enough for staying.

The future of the Church in the Western world looks like a story of chronic disaffection and loss. Staying on in the Congregation means living inside that larger experience of loss, without going to sleep on what is happening. It's not easy to stay not knowing what is going to happen. Sometimes I feel as if we are seated in the dark of a theater, waiting for a new play to begin, and the only thing we know for certain is that the program we have been given is for a different performance.

This throws us back to the basic questions. Do I believe in God? Do I believe that God's purposes are being worked out in the muddle of what is happening? Do I believe that the Congregation still has a word of life to offer? I can say "Yes" to these questions. I stay because I have not given up the habit of hoping.

3. The Context for Jesus' Beginning

It is interesting to recall how Jesus of Nazareth began. To understand the beginning of the story of the adult Jesus, the four gospels point us to someone else, the figure of John the Baptist. John the Baptist is the independent prophetic force that stands between the hidden life of Jesus and his public ministry. Jesus does not begin alone. None of us do. Jesus, like many other people, is attracted by the person and preaching of John the Baptist; like many of his contemporaries, he submits to John's baptism of repentance for the forgiveness of sins. After his association with John, Jesus' life takes a dramatic turn. He follows John in the prophetic vocation and reinterprets the message of his mentor.

The four gospels have their own way of limiting the embarrassing memory of Jesus becoming a convert of the Baptist. By the time the gospels are written, John is domesticated within the Christian story, and his role is defined simply as a forerunner of Jesus. But John's independent ministry among the people, the moral authority he exercised, and the respect he commanded all still linger in the gospel tradition. John's place is assured at the beginning of the gospel as the nomadic prophet who attracted Jesus from his settled life in Nazareth. Jesus' beginning was not a solitary event in a landscape empty of people. Like many others, Jesus was attracted by John's reputation and was moved to journey to see this fiery reformer, who spoke the word of God with authority. After he saw John, Jesus' life was to take a new direction.

A picture emerges of John as a charismatic leader whose great popularity among the people is exercised apart from Jesus. His ministry begins before Jesus, and when John dies he leaves behind him a religious following that exists independently of Christianity. John's ministry dominates the beginning of the gospel, and the fact that Jesus submits to John's baptism clearly indicates that Jesus accepted the Baptist's message calling Israel to repentance. As an independent prophet, John displays no discernible respect for religious hierarchy, and he appears alienated from institutional religion. His natural sanctuary is the wilderness, not the Temple; his ritual act centers around the waters of the river, not around the priestly altar of sacrifice. John's alienation from normal society is underscored by his ascetic lifestyle in an uninhabited place, his Bedouin dress of animal skin and his peasant diet of locusts and wild honey.

The composite picture of John and his ministry that emerges from the gospels seems to set a stage of conflict, one that Jesus will enter on the side of John.

Jerusalem and the Temple	against	the desert
Institutional	against	charismatic
Priestly	against	prophetic
Temporal power	against	religious criticism
Aristocracy	against	the poor
Stability	against	nomadic

This stage of conflict is already established before Jesus begins his ministry. When Jesus walks onto the stage, he chooses to stand beside the wild man of the wilderness, an option that will soon alienate him from institutional religion. That is why it is worth recalling what the gospels note: Jesus begins *after John*, and while Jesus will develop his own pastoral outreach to others, John's influence remains. It is probable that Jesus began as a disciple of John the Baptist.[1] When Jesus embarks on his own ministry, his pastoral style is so like that of the Baptist that the ordinary people and Herod presume that Jesus *is* John (Mark 6:14–16). Jesus will speak about John in the way that Christians will later speak about Jesus: "I tell you, among those born of women, no one is greater than John" (Luke 7:28). John the Baptist is the determinative influence that sets Jesus on the course of his ministry.

The earliest gospel notes that when Jesus returns to his relatives in Nazareth, they want to restrain him because they think he is out of his mind (Mark 3:21). Similarly, when Jesus preaches in the Nazareth synagogue, his hearers wonder, "Where did this man get all this?" They cling to the identity of the Jesus they know, rejecting his new identity as a prophetic preacher (Mark 6:1–6). Clearly, Jesus' own people preferred him before he came under the influence of the Baptist: local carpenters are easier to handle than new prophets. The voice from Nazareth comes from those who knew Jesus before he went south to see John the Baptist, people whose everyday familiarity with Jesus did not prepare them for believing there was anything exceptional about him. That voice from Nazareth indicates how much Jesus had changed in the eyes of those who knew him. To account for that change in Jesus' life, the gospels point to John the Baptist and his ministry.

It is the rugged person of John, not just a ritual of washing, that stands at the turning point of Jesus' life.

4. Jesus Begins in Nazareth

Like Mark, Luke highlights Jesus' change by telling the story of his return to his hometown of Nazareth (Luke 4:16–30). The whole account moves from quick admiration through sour disapproval to violent rejection. Everyone in this village in the hills of Galilee would have known Jesus. According to Bargil Pixner, the Benedictine archaeologist, "The excavations during recent decades have shown that the population of Nazareth at the time of Jesus could hardly have numbered more than 120-150 people."[2]

The local people who knew Jesus as the son of Joseph are being asked to accept a new Jesus, a changed Jesus, the one who now communicates with the power and authority of a prophet. Luke's scene in the Nazareth synagogue, which he transposes to the beginning of the ministry, serves as a summary of the entire ministry to follow: Jesus' preaching is summed up in an outline sermon, and the people's reaction is typically represented. It also prefigures the transition of the gospel from its original Jewish setting to a Gentile one.[3]

It is a story of fulfillment and a story of rejection. The story of fulfillment is that ancient prophecy comes alive in the person of Jesus who is "sent to bring the good news to the poor." The story of rejection, which commentators are slow to point out, is that the poor of Nazareth reject Jesus and his good news. This is a hard story, which goes against the tendency to romanticize Jesus' programmatic option for the poor. In Luke's Gospel, Jesus' first mission ends in unambiguous rejection: to survive another day, he escapes from the poor in Nazareth and moves to the lakeside town of Capernaum, where he is welcomed by strangers ignorant of his unexceptional past.

5. "Good News to the Poor"

The Nazareth sermon has at its heart a combined quotation from Isaiah 61:1–2 and 58:6, together with the claim that these words are fulfilled in Jesus' ministry. The original context of Third Isaiah (chapters 56–66) was the return of the Jewish exiles from Babylon to the desolate city of Jerusalem in 538 B.C. While the prophet struggles with his own disappointment and melancholy, he sings protest songs in the slums of a ruined Jerusalem. He tries to seduce an exhausted people into sharing his vision of radical renewal, so he becomes lyrical about a restored Jerusalem (60:1–22), in which good news is proclaimed to the poor (61:1–11), and the holy city is celebrated as God's delight (62:1–12). Behind Jesus' sermon in Nazareth is that moving memory of one man stubbornly believing that his vision is as real as the wreckage around him.

The introduction of Isaiah 58 into the Nazareth sermon brings a sharp critique of religious practices: the prophet tells the people that their ritual fasting is wasted energy because on the day of the fast they pursue their own business—their real devotions—while oppressing the workers and striking the poor man with their fist. The fast that pleases God is when the oppressed are liberated and the homeless poor are sheltered. When ritual is separated from regard for the poor, it becomes a theater of the absurd.

The composite quotation from Isaiah is headlined as good news to the poor. The "poor" (*ptochoi*) has the literal meaning of those who crouch, the people who cringe, the ones who are bent from the weight of need. The word belongs to the root *pte*, crouched together (see also: *ptesse*, be afraid, *ptosse*, lower one's head in fear; *ptox*, timid). In its figurative meaning, *ptochoi* are the beggarly poor, the economically destitute, those who are utterly dependent on the help of strangers. Isaiah uses the term in 61:1 to refer to the returned exiles. As C. Brown notes: "The misery of the exile led temporarily to the use of 'poor' and 'needy' as collective terms for the people. They are found in a number of hopeful eschatological promises about the future of the people, for example Isaiah 61:1–4."[4] In Luke's scene in the Nazareth synagogue, however, the poor does not refer to the whole people of Israel, but to those who are weighed down by burdens, those who cannot take life or survival for granted. These are among the main target audience for the good news that Jesus brings.

Luke goes on to demonstrate in his gospel how Jesus keeps faithful to his declared preference for the poor. In his sermon on the plain, Jesus names as "blessed" those who struggle with the concerns of daily life: poverty, hunger, grief, hatred, and rejection (6:20–22). Interestingly, the disciples of John the Baptist keep their master informed about the progress of Jesus (7:18). John wonders if Jesus is the one who is to come, the fiery reformer, *Elias redivivus*. Jesus has rejected the role of the fiery reformer in his pastoral ministry; instead, he invites the two messengers to tell John what they see and hear: "The blind regain their sight, the lame walk, lepers are cleansed, the deaf hear, the dead are raised, the poor have the good news proclaimed to them" (7:22). Jesus' ministry acts out the program of reform promised in Isaiah 61:1. You can hear an echo of the voice: *"This text is being fulfilled today, even as you listen."*

6. Fulfilling the Text

How successful was Jesus in fulfilling his chosen text from Isaiah? How effective was he in earthing that ancient dream? In terms of making any dramatic sociopolitical difference to the poor of his time, in terms of changing unjust structures, it has to be said that the achievement of Jesus was modest. The evidence from the New Testament itself suggests that his program of reform had little success, and he paid the full price for his preferences and values in his own death. In the end, the reformer from Nazareth was abandoned by his own, taken by force, led away, interrogated, sentenced, handed over, tied down, and dumped on the killing fields. Another dreamer dismissed to the graveyard by anxious clerics.

Jesus' Nazareth program still stands as an unfulfilled challenge to the Church. The majority of religious orders and congregations include it as a governing text in their constitutions. We have it enshrined in our first Constitution. In his exhortation *Christifideles Laici* ("The Vocation and the Mission of the Lay Faithful in the Church and in the World), Pope John Paul II writes: "Christians can repeat in an individual way the words of Jesus: 'The Spirit of the Lord is upon me, because he has anointed me to preach good news to the poor...' Thus with the outpouring of the Holy Spirit in Baptism and Confirmation, the baptized share in the same mission of Jesus as the Christ, the Savior-Messiah" (par. 13). In this understanding, the Nazareth program is the mission of every follower of Jesus. The Isaian dream thus becomes the Christian agenda.

We are all called, as Jesus was called, to bring good news to the poor. As J. Sobrino observes: "Common sense tells us that proclaiming good news *to the poor* of this world cannot be a matter of words alone, since they have had more than enough of these. Good realities are what the poor need and hope for. And this is what 'bringing good news' means in both Isaiah and Luke: It will only be *good* news to the extent that it brings about the liberation of the oppressed."[5] We are not short of people ready with rhetoric to play the prophet and denounce the evils of the day; but the poor are not dying from lack of prophets. They are dying from hunger and want and disease. They are dying before their time from the weariness of life and from being ignored as worthy of serious social attention. They are dying from too much theological sympathy and too little political support.

The Isaian dream is the source of our charism. Other writers in this volume will reflect on working out the charism in practice. I have tried to say something about the beginning of Jesus' ministry and how Isaiah's prophecy has given pride of place in helping us understand the pastoral priority of Jesus' endeavor. Isaiah's dream and Jesus' endeavor still await their own time.

Notes

1. For an excellent discussion on this question, see J. P. Meier, *A Marginal Jew: Rethinking the Historical Jesus* Vol. 2 (New York: Doubleday, 1994), pp. 19–176; J. Murphy-O'Connor, "John the Baptist and Jesus: History and Hypotheses" in *New Testament Studies* 36 (1990), pp. 359-374.
2. Bargil Pixner, *With Jesus Through Galilee According to the Fifth Gospel* (Rosh Pina: Corazin, 1992), p. 15.
3. For a study of this scene, see M. Prior, "Isaiah, Jesus and the Liberation of the Poor (Luke 4:16–30)" in *Scripture Bulletin* 24 (1994), pp. 36–46; also his book, *Jesus the Liberator: Liberation Theology in the Synagogue in Nazareth: Luke 4:16-30* (Sheffield Academic Press, 1995).
4. C. Brown, "Poor" in *Dictionary of New Testament Theology* Vol. 2 (Exeter: Paternoster Press, 1976), p. 823.
5. J. Sobrino, *Jesus the Liberator* (New York: Orbis Books, 1993), p. 86.

3

WITNESSES OF THE LOVE OF THE FATHER CROSTAROSA—SAINT ALPHONSUS

Sabatino Majorano, C.Ss.R.
Province of Naples
Translated by Kevin O'Neil, C.Ss.R.
Province of Baltimore

WHEN I WAS ASKED to begin this article with the story of my own personal experience as a Redemptorist I was both hesitant and surprised. The mountain culture in which I was raised makes me reluctant to speak of the more profound aspects of my life: they are lived, rather, and "conserved" in the heart (cf. Luke 2:51). For a moment I was tempted to decline the invitation. Upon reflection, however, it seemed clear to me that brotherhood implies sharing even at this level. My "yes" then is convinced, even if marked by the discomfort of a mountaineer.

1. To Be a Missionary

My Redemptorist vocation grew in a familial and ecclesial context marked profoundly by the presence of Saint Alphonsus and of his sons. The Redemptorist community ("*I Liguorini*") was skillful and loved as the center of religious vitality for my town (Morcone, in Sannio Beneventano)—in spite of the fact that the novitiate of the Capuchins was also there (the one which had received Padre Pio of Pietrelcina in January 1903). Even recently I heard it said by more than one of my fellow townspeople: "Since you Liguorini left, the religious vitality of Morcone hasn't been the same."

It was not a community closed in upon itself. Perhaps because it was not a parish, it was truly an *ongoing mission* with an intense and close relationship with the people. For my family, in a particular way, the "college" of the Liguorians was like a second home, certainly with respect to the needs of our faith life. Every afternoon, after finishing my home-work, I would run with the other boys to visit them until the "service" of the evening.

The religious climate breathed in our home was marked very deeply by Alphonsian perspectives. This was especially true of my mother, who possessed a profound piety and lived with such simplicity: every morning, even when the weather was particularly harsh, she was in the church of the Redemptorists for meditation and the eucharistic celebration; every evening, again she was in church for the "service" (Visit to the Blessed Sacrament, to Mary, and Benediction). She had learned by rote the meditations on the Eternal Truths (*Massime eterne*) of Saint Alphonsus, yet in her later years she asked me to get her a copy with large print so that she could read it better. In fact, my mother died some years ago, right in church, praying the rosary while she prepared for the evening eucharistic celebration.

This was the context in which my desire to become a missionary grew. At only eleven years of age, I was already in the minor seminary. I attended the novitiate at Ciorani, the studentate at Sant'Angelo a Cupolo, and then Colle S. Alfonso. The years of formation, especially in theology, were not easy for any of us. They were the years of the Council, the renewal of our Constitutions and structures, and of student demonstrations. Everything was sustained by the missionary tension, nourished and deepened by a wise balance between study and first pastoral experiences, according to the province's formation plan.

In 1968, because of the urgency of the mission in Madagascar, I asked the provincial to send me there to complete my theological formation and to let me immerse myself better in missionary work. His response was nega-tive with an invitation to intensify my cultural and social progress and, above all, to do the will of God. The following year, barely ordained, I was told that the province intended to offer my services to the Alphonsian Academy. I accepted, even if the assignment was not what I had dreamed of: a factor influencing my leaning toward Redemptorist life was that I would not run the risk of ending up as a professor, but would remain at the service of people!

My contact with the professors of the academy, especially with Fa-thers Bernard Häring and Domenico Capone, made me realize immedi-ately how necessary it was for the good of the Church to work toward a moral theology completely permeated by the mystery of "plentiful Redemption." Moral truth must always be faithful to the *kenosis* (emptying) of Christ: it must speak of God's merciful outreach to human persons, wounded and distorted by sin, in order to heal them, to liberate them, and to set them on the right road toward fullness. The relevance of the great intuitions of Saint Alphonsus became clearer and clearer to me. One must constantly propose them, actualize them, and develop them. Convinced that this service is essential for the evangelization of the poor, I am responding to my Redemptorist vocation precisely in this way. Since my years of formation, something that has been very important for me has been the encounter with Sister Maria Celeste Crostarosa. This began in a casual manner. In the latter half of the sixties, Father Domenico Capone asked us young students to help him renovate the monasteries of the Redemptoristines at Sant'Agata and at Scala. We accepted enthusiastically, transforming ourselves into painters, masons, and electricians. This is how we spent the greater part of our summer vacations in our last years in the studentate. Between jobs, Father Capone spoke to us of Crostarosa, of her vision of the Christian life, of her religious plan, of her presence to Redemptorist origins.

When it was time to choose the topic for my doctoral dissertation, it was easy for me to lean toward Crostarosa, toward her Christocentric vision. It is a study which continues today, ever enriched with new discoveries. I am convinced that one cannot ignore Crostarosa if you really want to understand our origins. She has very inspiring words to speak to us even today; it is impossible to separate the Redemptorists from the Redemptoristines.

So the teaching of moral theology and a deepening of Redemptorist spirituality have been woven together closely in my life. At first glance this could seem like a forced union. But it is not. Both try to penetrate more deeply and to actualize for our world, especially for the most abandoned, the "plentiful Redemption" of Christ.

2. Alphonsus: the Missionary Community

A deepening of the specific elements of one's charism must accompany the life of every religious. The more or less marked waning of diverse institutes ought to be considered an impoverishment of the wealth of gifts with which the Spirit constantly renews the Church. During the years in which I was called upon to serve as prefect of students in the Neapolitan Province (1972–1975), I was further convinced of this being urged on by the difficulties and questions of the young men.

The renewed Constitutions speak of this directly. I have strongly warned of the need for a deepening at the historical level, according to the recommendations of *"Perfectae Caritatis"*: "They will interpret and observe faithfully the spirit and end proper to their founder" (n. 2). Above all, I considered decisive this question: What are the elements that Alphonsus and the primitive community highlighted as characteristic of the original project.

In order to formulate a convincing response, I began to analyze the material in the archives about the process of redacting our primitive rule. My surprise was immediately great: the information was not yet clearly nor totally cataloged. Then as I turned the pages one by one, some of which contained only simple sketches written by Alphonsus and other members of the primitive community, the importance of all this documentation became clear to me; everything was fresh and direct in expression. I could actually touch with my own hands the awareness of the primitive community of its distinctiveness: to be an evangelizing missionary community among and for the most abandoned.[1]

Two texts in particular seemed critical to me. In May 1743, less that one month after the death of the "director," the first capitular assembly was held at Ciorani. The first Redemptorists synthesized their own identity in these words:

> That it is not to be a religious order, but a congregation of priests
> similar to the Fathers of the Mission and the Pious Workers Fathers,
> but with this difference that the fathers of our least Congregation must
> attend in a more particular way to helping country people; and that,
> therefore, they must always live outside the cities and in the center of
> the dioceses.[2]

After the long process of redacting the rules, this identity sounds like the 1747 text by Alphonsus:

> The purpose of the priests of the Most Holy Savior is to follow the
> example of our common Savior Jesus Christ by devoting itself, under
> obedience to the ordinaries of the places, principally to helping areas
> of the countryside most destitute of spiritual help. They are to be like
> the congregations of the Fathers of the Mission, the Pious Workers,
> and the Oratorians, but with the absolute difference of being always
> obliged to situate their churches and houses outside populated areas

and in the middle of dioceses, so that they can move about with greater ease in the surrounding areas with missions; and so that at the same time they can more easily, in this way, make it convenient for the poor people to come to hear the divine words and to receive the sacraments in their churches.[3]

This is much more than a *uniqueness* merely of ministry. As Redemptorists, we are called to make present in history the evangelizing Christ of the poor. For this reason we choose the same means that he adopted to make himself "Good News": he became flesh, sharing our sinful condition; he became the presence of the healing and liberating love of God; he preached, preferring the little ones and the poor. The Redemptorist community is a strong witness that continues yet today. With its constant "exodus" into the world of the forgotten, it proclaims that not only are they not forgotten by God, but that they constitute the starting point of his ongoing self-gift to humanity. In a word, the community is the "tent" of the risen One where one experiences how plentiful Redemption is.

The dynamics of acceptance and presence refer to and sustain each other reciprocally. The balance is in the ongoing search for the means that truly respond to the needs of the abandoned and the poor. We are not speaking so much of applying a rigid model, but of constructing methods wisely, beginning with an evangelical discernment of the historical situation.

And the focus of our preaching is on the merciful and infinite love of God for every human being, as shown in Christ. In the mind of Alphonsus, the dynamic of the mission was to have the people arrive at the contemplation of Christ crucified, that is, of the "love that he has shown us on the cross."[4] Thus on our missions, and especially on the last three days, we do not speak of anything but the Passion of the Redeemer in order to leave people bound to Jesus Christ."[5]

A passage from Tannoia confirms that all of this did not remain merely something on paper:

After the preaching of the Eternal Truths, there was a pious meditative exercise for three or four days, which he called the Devout Life. This consisted first in instructing the people about the method of mental prayer; he explained its necessity and clarified the utility of this pious practice. Then he had them meditate for half an hour on the sorrowful Passion of Jesus Christ. His [Alphonsus's] feelings about the Passion were so tender that one saw in the church rivers of tears; and where previously there were tears of sorrow, in the meditation there were tears of love.[6]

From this came the warm recommendation to all preachers: "One must be convinced that conversions made only out of fear of divine punishment are of short duration....If the holy love of God does not enter into the heart only with difficulty will one persevere." Hence "the principal task of the missionary preacher must be this: to ensure that in all his preaching his listeners are inflamed with holy love."[7]

"Plentiful Redemption" ought to inspire sacramental ministry as well by stressing mercy. Tannoia reports some statements of Alphonsus about the eucharistic practice of the rigorists.

> The poor Blood of Christ, trampled upon and mistreated....With a kiss of peace Judas betrayed Jesus Christ, and with a kiss of peace, these also betray Christ Jesus and his souls....I know that the angels are not worthy [of the Eucharist], but Jesus Christ has considered the human person worthy in order to raise him up from his misery. We have every good thing from this sacrament: without this help everything goes to ruin.[8]

Above all an attentive and welcoming love ought to be essential in the sacrament of reconciliation. Tannoia writes again: Alphonsus,

> even in his very old age, could not tolerate a certain disdain that this group of confessors [Rigorists] showed toward sinners. Alphonsus wished, and insisted, rather, that the greater the sinner, the more they needed to be embraced. Jesus' own behavior, he said, was like this. Don't scare them, he repeated, with delaying [absolution] for months and months as is the current practice. This doesn't help them but hurts them. When the penitent has known and detests his state, there is no point in leaving him with only his own strength in the fight against temptation. One must help him; and the greatest aid is found in the grace of the Sacraments.[9]

Only by making him experience the intensity of the mercy which God has for the human person, in order to heal and liberate him, is it possible to make everyone, even the most humble and poor, discover the call and the way to sanctity: "The religious as religious, layperson as layperson, priest as priest, spouse as spouse, merchant as merchant, soldier as soldier, and so one for every other state in life."[10]

The Alphonsian vision for moral theology belongs within this context of witnessing and preaching "plentiful Redemption," and it draws precisely from this perspective its most profound meaning. Basic is the conviction that it is not sufficient simply to formulate moral norms correctly; but we must do so in such a way that we touch the concrete story of a person that leads to salvation. Moral preaching demands the awareness and the competence of a physician. Moral truth is an indispensable medicine for the human person wounded and weak from sin. As such, it (moral truth) must, therefore, always be proposed as an option: it must actually be helpful to the person who, "called to live God's wise and loving design in a responsible manner,...knows, loves, and accomplishes moral good by stages of growth" in his own life.[11]

I limit myself to recall one page from the *Praxis Confessarii* which our present-day context, dominated as it is by the manipulative power of the mass media, renders even more meaningful. "The confessor is also obliged to instruct the penitent if he is *culpably* ignorant of any point of natural or positive law. If he is *inculpably* ignorant, it depends. If he is inculpably ignorant of something necessary for salvation, then the confessor is obliged to instruct him. If he is inculpably ignorant of some other matter (of which he can be ignorant)—even something of the divine law, the confessor should prudently decide whether the instruction will be profitable for the penitent. If it will not be profitable, he should not make the correction, but rather leave him in good faith." The reason for this is the fact that "the danger of formal sin is a much more serious thing than material sin. God punishes formal sin, for that alone is what offends Him."[12]

Once again we are speaking of being faithful to the "practice of the Redeemer," to his merciful and healing love, by being receptive of the one marked by sin, announcing to him the possibility of forgiveness and of liberation, raising him up, placing him on the road toward sanctity, and sustaining him so that he will not stop.

Confidence is found in the power of the truth which, as *Dignitatis Humanae* reminds us, "cannot impose itself except by virtue of its own truth, as it makes its entrance at once quietly and with power" (n. 1). This brings about a certain reciprocity between conscience and law, the clarification of which Alphonsus dedicated his life: "The norm of human acts is twofold: one is called 'remote,' the other 'proximate.' The *remote* norm, that is material, is divine law; the *proximate* norm, or formal, is conscience. Although conscience, in fact, must conform itself in everything to divine law, still, the goodness or evil of human actions is revealed to us according to conscience's grasp of divine law."[13]

3. Mother Celeste: the Remembering Community

The documentation in the archives concerning our primitive rule affirms clearly that the first steps along the difficult road of its redaction were made starting from the Crostarosan Rule for the Redemptoristines. It would be wrong to quickly ignore or underrate this fact.

The heart of the Crostarosan project is the community as remembrance of the love of the Father in Christ for all humanity. It is sufficient to read the preface to her *Regole*. The starting point is the plan of the Father: a plan of love, of life, of fullness:

> Greatly have I desired to give my Spirit to the world and to communicate it to my intelligent creatures, in order to live with them and in them until the end of the world. With infinite love I gave them my Only-Begotten Son, and through him, I gave them my divine Consoling Spirit, in order to make them like God in life, justice, and truth, and to embrace them all in my affection for the Word, Son of love. This is the reason for every outpouring of my grace, justice, and truth. And through him eternal life. The world was made through my Divine Word and by means of him all things live: in him is life and he is being and life of all things that were made; and by him all things are alive with love and affection in myself.[14]

The Father's plan of salvation is one of communion and participation. The Christ makes it a reality, by communicating the Spirit with us. We become, then, "deified" in the gift of "life, justice, and truth"; all of humanity is united in the "love" in which Christ himself lives as "son of love." To him, we are indebted for "every outpouring" of grace, of justice, and of truth, which he bestows in eternal life.

This is where the Redemptorist community sinks its roots: it does not wish to be anything else but a "remembrance" of the love that sustains and permeates this plan:

So, in order that my creatures might be mindful of the eternal charity with which I have loved them, I have been pleased to choose this Institute so that it might be a living memory, for all people of the world, of all which it pleased my Only-Begotten Son to do for their salvation in the span of the thirty-three years that he lived as a man in this world. And his works are alive before me and are of infinite worth."[15]

The heart of the Crostarosan religious vision is the community as witness of the love of Christ. Placed within its eighteenth-century context and in the light even of the Falcoian revisions to which it would shortly undergo, the entire significance and novelty of this can be seen.[16] Its fundamental perspectives are those of sign, of presence, and of witness: the key for interpretation and development is eucharistic. The theology of religious life today gives prominent place to these themes; as Redemptorists we can enrich these themes with a significant historical example.

Religious life ought to be a "living memorial" *(viva memoria)*. Hence the insistence on imitation, seen, however, as an expression of participation in the power of the Spirit. Sister Celeste continues:

> Stamp on your spirit the features of his life and the resemblance of him that comes from imitation. Be, on earth, living and inspired portraits of my beloved Son, and have Him only as your Head and your resource.
>
> And you will carry him about as the life of your heart and as the goal of your existence and as the Shepherd of your flock and as the Master of your spirit.
>
> Your life will be regulated by the truths taught by him in the Gospels. There are hidden all the treasures of the heavens, there is the fountainhead of life where the human person, while still on his/her earthly pilgrimage, partakes of the eternal riches of the dear Son of my love, in whom all have their existence and their life....Let your spirit, then, live in my divine love, while giving to my Only Begotten all the glory and the honour....
>
> It is He who will obtain for you, and breathe into you the Spirit, the Consoler who will enlighten you and fill you with his gifts and virtues.[17]

The reader, I am sure, will forgive the long citation. It is, however, a page to rediscover for its depth and inspirational power. It can be a helpful resource in that search for interior renewal and integrity of life which nowadays we consider crucial for the future of the Redemptorist community.

The relationship between "memory" and "imitation" is the key to the whole Crostarosan religious project. It is a circular dynamic: for the community to be a "memorial," all its members must be "living and inspired portraits," and vice verse. It rests fundamentally on the power of the Spirit of love; that is, participation, existence, and life.

Individualistic and dualistic approaches to the religious life are thus supplanted. "The 'memorial-imitation' of the Savior consists in making him present, realizing his works for the good of the church, indeed for all people. This is the preaching-witness of the Savior, formed by and upon the Gospel, which sheds light on the same Gospel and causes it to be 'reborn' within those who hear it."[18]

The love of the Father in Christ is a gift to be welcomed with watchful gratitude. Defining itself as a contemplative community, the Crostarosan community wants to testify not only to the priority of the gift but also to the brotherly and sisterly coresponsibility in receiving it, deepening it, and witnessing to it. "At the center of its life is Christ as the mystery of love, to be loved and deepened constantly. It cultivates, therefore, an atmosphere of deep recollection and of sincere brotherly and sisterly charity. None of this, however, implies withdrawal into oneself, closedness, and isolation. Rather, it is to live the 'unobtrusiveness' (cf. Matthew 6:16) that causes charity to become the visible presence of the love of the Father in Christ."[19]

The points of convergence and divergence between the Crostarosan and Alphonsian communities appear rather easily. Both are communities of presence of and witness to the God's merciful love in Christ. The Crostarosan underscores primarily the welcome-sign dimension; the Alphonsian the evangelical concern for the abandoned. We are talking, however, about two issues closely linked with each other. It strikes me that we can quite rightly speak of a complementarity in the witness-preaching of "Plentiful Redemption."

Another point of convergence between Alphonsus and Celeste is the undivided understanding of religious-community life and the spiritual life. The virtues, for Crostarosa, are the traits of the life of Christ, the pilgrim, which the Holy Spirit imprints upon us; they are born in loving contemplation of the Savior, through a deepening of Gospel truth; they transform us into "living portraits" of Christ in a community which is a "living memorial." For Alphonsus, the virtues are aspects of the "example" of the Redeemer, and consequently tend to render his "continued presence"; they grow out of a memory of the love of God in Christ that is renewed constantly in loving meditation of the crucified One; they aim to form us as a community in mission among and for the abandoned.

Once again, we find ourselves before complementary dimensions. "To continue" the Redeemer among and for the abandoned implies necessarily to be in his presence, in an ongoing deepening of the "truths" of the Gospel, allowing oneself to be enlightened by him, permitting the Spirit to transform us into him. Only then is missionary preaching truly "to follow the example of our common Savior Jesus Christ."

4. Conclusion

Everyone is aware today of our need to give greater depth and authenticity to our Redemptorist life. However, we do not always manage to discern the best ways to do this. Many times we lament the lack of clear common points of reference that would facilitate our journey together.

I am convinced that delving into our roots will sustain and inspire us. This does not mean passively repeating forms and structures from the past; but of arriving at an ever-clearer awareness of the original "intent" about which every Redemptorist must agree. Then we would be more able to actualize it and develop it together, responding to the expectations and the hopes of the abandoned today.

We must, however, return to our roots in their integrity. In the past we were not without presuppositions and forced interpretations in this regard, which certainly produced nothing positive. Today we are in a position to reach our roots in all their richness. It would be a grave mistake not to do so. It will become clear to us, then, that from Alphonsus and Celeste we can draw much to be effective witnesses of the merciful love of the Father in Christ, by producing communities that are unambiguous and evangelizing "memorials."

Notes

1. For the results of this study see *"Idea" dell'Istituto*, in D. Capone—S. Majorano, *I Redentoristi e le Redentoriste. Le radici, Materdomini, 1985, 347–424; Testi regolari anteriori al 1749*, in F. Chiovaro (editor), *Storia della Congregazione del Santissimo Redentore*, Vol. I/1 (Rome, 1993), 431–451.
2. See *I Redentoristi*, 349. Translation of this text is taken from "Decrees of the General Congregation of May 1743," in *Founding Texts of Redemptorists. Early Rules*

and Allied Documents, edited by Carl Hoegerl, C.Ss.R. (Rome: Collegio Sant'Alfonso, 1986), 328.

3. See *Spicilegium Historicum*, 16 (1968): 385. Translation of this text from the *Ristretto* is taken from *Founding Texts of Redemptorists. Early Rules and Allied Documents*, edited by Carl Hoegerl, C.Ss.R. (Rome: Collegio Sant'Alfonso, 1986), p. 230.

4. *Pratica di amare Gesu Cristo, Opere ascetiche*, Vol. 1 (Rome, 1933), 5.

5. *Foglietto in cui si tratta brevemente di cinque punti su de' quali nelle missioni deve il predicatore avvertire il popolo di piu cose necessarie al comun profitto, Opere*, Vol. III (Turin, 1847), 289.

6. *Della Vita ed Istituto del Venerabile Servo di Dio Alfonso M. a Liguori*, Vol. I (Naples, 1802), 311–312.

7. Foglietto, 288.

8. *Della Vita ed Istituto del Venerabile Servo di Dio Alfonso M. a Liguori*, Vol. III (Naples, 1802), 152–153.

9. Ibid., p. 153.

10. *Pratica di amare Gesu Cristo*, 79.

11. John Paul II, *Familiaris Consortio*, Encyclical Letter of November 22, 1981, n. 34.

12. *Pratica del confessore*, Cap. I, n. 8. Alphonsus adds:

   "The following cases are exceptions to leaving the penitent in good faith: (1) When the penitent's ignorance redounds to the harm of the common....Consequently he must always instruct rulers, confessors, prelates....(2) If the penitent asks about something, the confessor is then obliged to instruct him in the matter....(3) If the confessor realizes that the penitent will quickly accept the correction, even though he would fight it at first" (n. 9).

   The translation is taken from *Guide for Confessors from the Praxis Confessarii of St. Alphonsus Liguori*, translated by R. Schiblin et. al. (Esopus, New York: private publication by Redemptorists, 1978), 10–12.

13. *Theologica Moralis*, Lib. I, tract. I, cap. I, n. 1.

14. Cf. S. Majorano, *L'imitazione per la memoria del Salvatore. Il messaggio spirituale di Suor Maria Celeste Crostarosa (1696–1755)* (Rome, 1978), 150.

15. Ibid., p. 151.

16. Cf. Ibid., 219–229.

17. Cf. Ibid., 152–153. The translation for this section is taken from *Florilegium of Texts From Mother Maria Celeste Crostarosa*, edited by Sabatino Majorano, C.Ss.R., translated by Michael Baily, C.Ss.R., in *Readings in Redemptorist Spirituality*, Vol. 2 (Rome, 1988), 119–120.

18. Ibid., 123.

19. S. Majorano, *La Figura e l'opera di Maria Celeste Crostarosa*, in T. Sarnella, editor, *Atti del primo convegno di studi crostarosiani* (Foggia, 1991), 50.

4

THE "FOUNDATIONAL" CHARISM
OF ALPHONSUS DE LIGUORI

Théodule Rey-Mermet, C.Ss.R.
Province of Lyons
Translated by Emmett Collins, C.Ss.R.
Province of Denver

1. Why I Am a Redemptorist

For a child to give any thought to whether he could be a religious, a priest, or a missionary is not easy nor likely. Without a personal invitation from someone, the notion would never have occurred to me. Quite the contrary. I had an uncle who was a butcher, and his life as a butcher looked very attractive to me, so I had decided that would also be my profession.

But one summer—I was ten years old at the time—a missionary of Saint Francis de Sales accompanied our pastor to our home. He took me aside and asked a stunning question: "Wouldn't you like to be a missionary?" He went on to explain that glamorous word, *missionary*, for me. A bit reassured, I answered, "Me? You mean I could be a missionary?" "If you want to," he said. I answered, "Then with all my heart I want to."

He said nothing to me nor apparently to my parents about Saint Francis de Sales. He did, however, tell my parents of my desire to be a missionary. He made arrangements for me at the school, but paid no more attention to me until I turned eleven. In my heart, however, the missionary had driven out the butcher.

But in the spring, the Redemptorist Fathers, Armand Dorsaz and Romain Marie Bouvard preached a stirring mission in my parish. My brother, Jean Maurice, two years older than I, was an altar boy. Father Bouvard noticed him and wound up asking him the same question, "Wouldn't you like to be a missionary?" The same answer. Within the next month, without waiting for the beginning of the school year, we were on our way to the Pensionnat d'Uvrier in Switzerland, which was then the juvenate of the Redemptorists of the Gallo-Helvitic Province of Lyons. I was wholly unaware that I was leaving Francis de Sales for his disciple, Alphonsus Liguori.

At Uvrier, the superior, the professors, and the brothers were all attractive and joyful models for us. They formed a united community glowing with missionary spirit; this spirit also became a part of us. They let us share in the great missions given in the province by our voluntary work, our prayers, and our sacrifices. They interested us in the apostolate of our vice provinces of Chile and Peru. During the years of our secondary studies, we lived as young missionaries.

We considered ourselves Redemptorist missionaries. Our director, Father Stanislas Bedon (1867–1948), had a profound understanding of our saints—Alphonsus, Gerard, Clement Mary. He shared with us his understanding and his passion for them and for our great forefathers of the Congregation. So well did he succeed that in arriving at the novitiate, we had nothing more to learn about the Congregation and could not have loved it more. Aside from that, my only fear in the novitiate was that of not being admitted to vows.

Why have I remained a Redemptorist?

First of all, at that time a person did not put aside his first commitment, though it was canonically temporary. We, eleven novices, made our vows for three years. The four who are still alive are Redemptorists and happy to be such. The seven others died as Redemptorists, among them was my brother Jean Maurice, a missionary in Quetchua, and Huanta, Peru.

To be honest, where shall we find a founder more outstanding, elders more inviting, and a spiritual and apostolic purpose more likely to fill us with enthusiasm: to be the continuation of Jesus Christ bringing the Good News to the poor?

Our youngest brother, Ernest, and then our nephew Bernard joined us in the Congregation, and they are living there happily and radiant in their good fortune.

2. The Founding Charism of Alphonsus Liguori

From the age of fourteen he occupied a seat as a magistrate in the *Seggio de Portanova*, the neighborhood Council. He was the oldest of eight children, talented and at the same time hardworking. At the age of sixteen, he was a doctor of both Church and civil law. At eighteen he was a practicing lawyer.

It is at that age, in the year of 1714, that Alphonsus makes his first closed retreat with the Jesuits at Conocchia. The preacher, Nichola Maria Boviglione, makes such an impression on him that he leaves the exercises resolved to join the Theatines with his two cousins, Dominico and Emmanuele de Liguori, who are his neighbors in the Via Tribunali. Their zeal is already well known in the Church of San Paola Maggiore and at the cathedral.

While getting ready for this change of career, for which he had to prepare his irascible and ambitious father step by step, his legal dossiers and encounters with the guilty and innocent as a lawyer plunge himself into the life and misery and sin of the world. Even though he is winning all the cases he pleads in court, he is giving his heart and time largely to prayer, to the adoration of the Blessed Sacrament, and to the caring for the unfortunate patients at the hospital for the *Incurabili*.

He loves to hunt and gamble. He is intoxicated with the music of the opera at the theater of San Bartolomeo. He frequents the fashionable salons where his father drags him with the dream only of marrying a duchess with a rich dowry. His yearly retreat, however, with the Jesuits or the Vincentians sustains his fervor to a point where it well can be called mystical.

Up to about the year 1720, when Alphonsus grows bored with shallow friendships and whiffs the captious scent of the world that he fawns upon, there is enough to assure us that he is not a saint right out of the plaster mold.

Fortunately, his Easter retreat in 1722, wakes him from his slumber and stirs the burning flame of love in him that reduces his innocent pastimes to ashes: good-bye cards, guns, salons, theaters. From here on, the place he can be found—when not with his clients, of course—will be with the *Incurabili* and before the Blessed Sacrament. It is there that the founder of the Redemptorists is born.

To be with him

Alphonsus writes:

It is not a fact that holy souls have made their most generous resolutions at the foot of the altar? I should here bring to light, a certain fact from my experience: it was the persevering practice of visiting the Blessed Sacrament, despite the coldness and imperfection I brought to this pious exercise, that drew me out of the world where I had lived unhappily up to the age of twenty six.[1]

This personal disclosure of Alphonsus in the introduction to his *Visits* digs down to the deep wellspring of the Congregation. It is especially at the foot of those same altars, where he will linger several hours each day in the future, that he will bind himself in friendship with him who will be the first promise of his Institute, Giovanni Mazzini, and soon with a whole group of young worshipers, among whom will be the first foundation stones of his edifice: Vincenzo Mannarini, Michele de Alteriis—who will be ordained a priest with him on December 21, 1776—and Gennaro Sarnelli.

Let us be careful not to pass carelessly over the importance of this primordial fact; for it reveals and underlines the mystery of all apostolic charism, and especially that of Liguori.

"Jesus went up the mountains and summoned those whom he wanted and they came to him. He appointed twelve [whom he named apostles] that they might be with him and he might send them forth to preach and have the authority to drive out demons" (Mark 3:13–15).

It is not a question of physical hills, but of theological heights: nearness to God. It is there that Christ calls those whom he wants to be with him and whom he appoints from the beginning and perseveringly thereafter in an intimacy which alone allows him to be known, then afterward from that blessed experience to preach the Good News of Jesus.

Every evening in the course of three years, the group meets with Alphonsus for a long period of adoration in a Neapolitan church that is celebrating the Forty Hours. After that he goes on to another nearby church—Naples had more than five hundred—for a special visit to the Blessed Virgin. This change of place is meant to underline the importance of this childlike approach to the Mother of the Redeemer.

Holy Mary, Queen of Apostles

It is at the feet of Our Lady of Ransom, in the Church of Our Lady of Mercy in Naples, that the young lawyer of the house of Liguori comes to lay down his cavalier's sword on August 29, 1723, after the dire drama of breaking away from his profession, his father, and the world to give himself entirely to God. As a seminarian, he has himself admitted as soon as possible into the Congregation of Secular Clerics of the Apostolic Missions under the patronage of Mary Queen of Apostles.

Mary: She will be after Jesus the second pillar of his life and his foundation. Under the title of her Immaculate Conception, he will present her to his Congregation as its principal patroness. In his *Considerazione per Coloro che Son Chiamati Allo Stato Religioso (Considerations for Those Who Are Called to the Religious State)* written for his novices and published in 1750, he will write:

> How can anyone doubt that Mary uses all her power and mercy in favor of religious. This is particularly true for us, the members of this hallowed Congregation of the Most Holy Redeemer, that makes, as is known, a special profession to honor the Virgin Mary by its visits, the Saturday fast, the special penances during novenas, etc., and by promoting everywhere devotion to her by sermons and novenas in her honor....Also we owe God special thanks for having called us to the Congregation where the customs of its communities, and the example of the confreres makes us remember and almost constrains us to have recourse to Mary and constantly to honor this most loving mother, who is called and who is the joy, the hope, the life, the salvation of whoever invokes her and pays her homage.[2]

Our life, our joy, our hope, these are the three keywords of the "Salve Regina" with which Saint Alphonsus concludes a commentary he began to write at the time of the founding of the Congregation and which will be the greatest Marian bestseller in the history of the Church.

An ardent devotion to Mary is certainly the second apostolic pillar upon which Liguori will establish his institution. The third will be the preferential choice for the poor and the abandoned. "Inclined toward the poor and the little ones" is the way Tannoia describes the newly ordained priest Alphonsus de Liguori.[3]

Naples was teeming with ecclesiastics: upright and well-educated diocesan priests abounded along with some fervent and zealous religious communities. Let us, however, not mention the lazy vagabond clerics who drifted in from the outlying provinces. It would be better if they had not existed. But who was taking care of the *lazarelli* of the Mercato and the other slum areas of the city?

The brightest lawyer of the Kingdom of Naples did not renounce the bar and the highest magistracies to embrace a comfortable and eminent apostolate. He wanted the parish of his choice to be made up of the poor of whom no one took any account, and it was to them he brings his young companions. These will be the *Capelle Serotine*, where those excluded from the ongoing pastoral care will become, through him, base communities. From these will arise masters of prayer and teachers of faith.

After these communities have no need of him, his gaze turns to far-off China, and the pagans of the Cape of Good Hope. He is restless to proclaim Jesus Christ to those who still do not know him.

In the meantime, he travels through the Kingdom, taking part in the work of the Apostolic Missions in which he is an active member since his taking of the tonsure.

He discovers—how amazing!—that the missions are given only in populous centers, and that the country folks are as ignorant of the God of Jesus Christ as are the Chinese or the Zulus. China is the gates of Naples! And like that faraway China, there is not one to bring her salvation.

This discovery quickly becomes a torturing case of conscience for Alphonsus: he must dedicate himself to instruct and reconcile these poor people and eventually establish a special missionary band for them. Their souls and the glory of God is at stake.

This is the petition[4] he will address to Benedict XIV in 1748 to obtain the approbation of his young Institute:

> The priest, Alphonsus de Liguori, of Naples, with the other priests, his missionary companions, united into a society under the title of the Most Holy Savior, lays before Your Holiness, the following most humble request that follows:
>
> Having given himself for many years to the holy missions as a member of the Congregation of the Apostolic Missions erected in the Cathedral of Naples, the petitioner has learned the great abandonment there is of the poor people, especially, those of the rural areas in the vast regions of the kingdom. He, therefore, associated himself, in 1732 with the priests here mentioned, his companions, under the direction

of Monsignor Falcoia, Bishop of Castellamare, so that he might vow himself to the aid of the poor of the country by missions and other exercises. These country folks are the most destitute of spiritual help. Often, in fact, there is not one to administer the sacraments to them and to proclaim the Word of God to them. It has reached the point that many, for lack of apostolic workers die without knowing the basic mysteries of faith, because there are so few priests who give the time to the spiritual need of these poor peasants; they are fearful of the cost of dedicating themselves to this work and of the many hardship that must be endured in this ministry.

This is why ever since then the petitioners have gone to the aid of the poor people by means of the missions, covering the countryside and the most abandoned regions of the six provinces of the Kingdom. Everywhere it was grand success.

Their [four] houses have been centers from which the petitioners have continually gone out on missions, and also places to where the country people can come from their villages where they have had a mission to go to confession again and strengthen themselves with holy sermons. Besides, in these same houses, closed retreats are conducted several times a year for ordinands, pastors, and priests sent by their bishops, and also for lay persons. From this results a great profit for them and others.

The petitioner and his companions beg Your Holiness, for the love he bears to the glory of Jesus Christ and for the spiritual salvation of so many country folk who are the most abandoned children of the Church of God, to give his apostolic approbation to that which this company in question has erected and constituted as a Congregation of secular priests under the title of the Most Holy Savior...with this special note that they must always live far from populous places and in dioceses most in need, so as to be wholly at the service of the country people and to assure them the quickest assistance.[5]

Is that clear? It is for *the most abandoned children of the Church of God* that the Redemptorists exist. It is in the Mezzogiorno of the Eighteenth Century, that the especially poor of the country were to be found. This petition, begun in the plural with the missionaries of the Holy Savior, switches very quickly into the singular drawing upon the ten years of Alphonsus's lived experience of taking part in the work of the Apostolic Missions *in the vast regions of the kingdom* of Naples. His convalescent stay during May and June of 1730 at Santa Maria dei Monti, made him gradually acquainted with the goat herders on the heights of Scala. That was the drop that filled the vessel to overflowing. Stunned by their spiritual neglect, he came down from there in the middle of June with that new resolve to establish a congregation of missionaries wholly devoted to the ministry of the most abandoned country folk. He wanted to have a meeting with his director, the Oratorian, Tommaso Pagano. It is Father Casparo Caione who testifies to this. He adds: "I learned this from the very mouth of the Servant of God…and hardly out of his room, I put it in writing."[6]

A false start in 1732

Enlightened by his faith and soon by his experience, Alphonsus will not be assured of a foundation unless it be planted on Calvary like the Redemption itself. He is going to be the *servant* of his Congregation.

As soon as he returned from Scala, in June 1730, he consulted his director, Father T. Pagano, and his longtime advisers. Among the members of the Apostolic Missions, the project was considered scatterbrained. But in contrast, the Vincentian Vincenzo Cuttica, the Jesuit Domenico Manulio, the Dominican Ludivico Fiorillo, assured him that it was a call from God and urged him to lose no time. The following year, Monsignor Falcoia, the bishop of Castellamare, and Maria Celeste Crostarosa, a nun of Scala, will come to the rescue and settle upon making a start at Scala, the little episcopal village on the heights above Amalfi.

Alphonsus in the meantime felt as if he had fallen into a pit. Giovanni Mazzini comes upon him in tears, "Where to find companions?" Four are immediately suggested. He does not know any of them except Vincenzo Mannarini, who was headed for the missions of China. The official founding of the Fathers of the Holy Savior takes place humbly in the guest house of the nuns, on November 9, 1873, under the presidency of Monsignor Falcoia, who becomes the personal director of Alphonsus and will head the young foundation until his death in 1743.

Then under Falcoia's presidency, one week of torment follows when it becomes clear that of the five involved no one is in agreement about the rule, the habit, the Office in common, the practice of poverty, the authority that Falcoia wants put in place, or—and this is the most serious disagreement—the purpose of the new Institute. The missions, of course, but they will be established in population centers, and there will be schools to tend in those places.

Alphonsus falls from his lofty dream. He begs, he explains, he explains again, but in vain. Powerless to rally his companions to his project, he has nothing left but prayer, while he waits for the storm to break and the ship wreck to follow.

In fact, everything crumbles, except the decision of the founder. At the end of this frightful week, he writes on page sixty-six of his personal journal *(Coza di conscienza)*: "Even if I remain alone, God will help me. Today, November 15, 1732." Again two weeks later on page sixty-seven: "Today, November 28, 1732, I have vowed not to abandon the Institute." The Institute for him is the preferential choice *in favor of the most abandoned sons of the Church of God.*

It was not, however, the choice of his pledged companions of November 9. Four months later, they had left Scala one after the other, and had regrouped at Tramonti to establish an institute according to their notion. Alphonsus, having remained alone, will be hard-pressed to join them and give in to their plan.

In Easter week of 1733 on the second of April, Alphonsus in fact goes down to Naples. There he meets Mazzini, Sarnelli, Sportelli, de Alteriis, his loyal friends from the *Capelle Serotine.* Then at the beginning of May, he goes to Cajazzo and visits the church and the residence of Villa degli Schiavi, offered to him by Monsignor Vigilante. It is there that he will recruit Saverio Rossi, and there he will establish and build the first house of his Congregation in March 1734.

Scala, in fact, where there is only a *casa* on a provisional site, will not see an eventual foundation, because after six years of experience Alphonsus will judge it to be unsuited for Redemptorist ministry. He will write in 1742:

> Experience made us understand that the site [Scala], on steep and dangerous mountains, was inconvenient for the people who wanted to avail themselves of the ministry of the Fathers, and at the same time very prejudicial to the health of the confreres themselves because of the harshness of the cold that prevails there.[7]

To continue the example of the Savior of the poor

The absolute destitute among the poor gather around Alphonsus. He establishes himself at Villa degli Schiavi in March 1734, at Ciorani in September 1735, at Pagani in October 1742, and at Materdomini in November 1746.

In 1747, the prepares a *Ristretto*, a condensation of the Rules of his Institute. He defines the Institute in these words:

> The aim of the priests of the Most Holy Savior, so as to continue the example of our common Savior, is to engage themselves principally…in helping the rural areas most devoid of spiritual help…by placing their houses and churches in the midst of those poor people.[8]

The following year he presents his foundation to Pope Benedict XIV in these words:

> The sole purpose of this Congregation will be to continue the example of our Savior Jesus Christ by preaching to the poor the divine Word, according to that which he says of himself: "He has sent me to proclaim the Good News to the poor" (Luke 4:18). This is why its members engage themselves wholly in going to the aid of the people spread throughout the countryside and the rural villages, especially the most abandoned spiritually….They must therefore locate their house outside of cities so as to be always available to travel from village to village…and to welcome the poor folk of the country.[9]

Alphonsus prefers the word *seguitare* to the word *imitare* that Falcoia wished to impose: not *to imitate the examples and virtues of Jesus Christ*; not even *to follow the example of Jesus Christ*; but to *continue* today. Continue what? *the example*, in the singular. The example of whom? Of our Savior evangelizing the poor.

The next year, 1749, Rome approves the Institute under the name of the *Most Holy Redeemer*. The founder writes and has printed for his three novices short works about vocation. We must read and reread consideration number 13:

> The one who is called to the Congregation and the Most Holy Redeemer will never be a continuer of Jesus Christ and never will sanctify himself unless he fulfills the purpose of his vocation. Moreover, he will never have the spirit of the Institute, which is to save souls, and the souls of the most deprived of spiritual help, as are the poor country folk.

Let us note the phrase *as are,* which gives the local example, but which reveals the Alponsian aim toward all categories of the abandoned. He continues:

Such was already the purpose of the coming of the Redeemer, who declared: "The Spirit of the Lord is upon me; he has consecrated and sent me to preach the Good News to the poor" (Luke 4:18). He would not be able to say he was a true member of this Congregation who would not accept with all his heart this task that obedience assigns him but would prefer to retire within in himself in a life secluded and solitary.[10]

The years will pass. The charism of the founder will remain his fixed idea. Almost thirty years later, in October 1777, the old retired missionary bishop will write to the two communities established in the Papal States:

My dear fathers and brothers, help the people, but especially the poor, the uneducated, the most abandoned. Remember that God has sent us to evangelize the poor of this time. Keep this maximum well in mind, and seek God alone in the abandoned poor, if you wish to please Christ.[11]

Three years later, it was proposed to him to take the place in Rome of the Jesuits who had been suppressed by Clement XIV. On August 25, 1774, he responded to Father De Paola: "What will we do in Rome? Farewell to our principal purpose, farewell, to the Congregation! We would become courtiers."

That same day, he writes to Father Villani:

What will we do in Rome? That would be the end of our Institute; for once our missions are neglected and the Institute turned from its purpose, the Congregation ceases to exist....Our Congregation was made for the mountains and villages. From the moment we would mingle with prelates and courtiers, knights and ladies, goodbye to the missions, goodbye to the country, we would become couriers ourselves. I ask Christ that he preserve us from such an evil.[12]

But Rome is not just a court of prelates, it is also and above all the center of the universal Apostolic Church. Besides, the Congregation has to reach out to the whole world. The founder is always hearing the calls of the Chinese, the Zulus, and the neglected poor of all nations and of all classes. To Pietro Paolo Blasucci, who speaks to him again about Rome, he replies at the end of October 1776:

It does not seem to me to be expedient that we establish ourselves at Rome either at this time or at some distant future date. I pass over in silence the reason that make me believe this....But with time, the matter will become necessary....If God lets us know some day that he wants us in Rome, we shall obey him.[13]

Less than eight years later, Saint Clement Mary Hofbauer and Thaddeus Huebl will be ringing the bell at the gates of the Redemptorists of Saint Juliano in Rome.

Notes

1. S. Alfonso, *Opere Ascetiche*, IV, 296.
2. *Considerazione 15*. Avec ces *Considerazioni*, Alphonse écrivit, pour ses novices, deux autres petits traités: *Avisi spettanti alla vocazione religiosa* et *Conforto ai Novizi*. Ils forment ensemble ce qu'on a appelé *Le vrai Rédemptoriste*. Les Archives générales des Rédemptoristes, à Rome, en conservent deux exemplaire de l'édition originale, portant la date de 1750, l'année de l'approbation pontificale de sa Congrégation. En des rééditions pour les jeunes du grand public, Alphonse supprimera presque toutes les dénominations C.SS.R. pour les remplacer par "religione." Il oublie quelques fois, comme ici. Cf. *Opuscoli sulla vocazione*, Ed. Paoline, pp. 120–121.
3. A.M. Tannoia, *Della vita ed Instituto del V. Alfonso M. Liguori,* Napoli 1798, I, 43.
4. Ce *Libellus supplex* est la charte de la C.SS.R. Aussi figurait-elle en tête des *Constitutions et Statuts rédemproristes* provisoires établish par le Chapitre général de 1967 to 1969. Le Chapitre général XIX de 1979 l'a, hélas ! rejetée, la renvoyant, avec le *Ristretto* et d'autres decuments, à un volume-dossier... qu'on attend encore! Cf. *Acta integra Capituli generalis XIX*, 1979, p. 198, Prop. 4–6 et 8–9.
5. S. Alfonso, *Lettere*, I, 149–151.
6. Sacra Rituum Congregatio, *Positio super introductione causae*, Rome 1796, 30–31.
7. *Lettere*, I, 85.
8. *Spicilegium Historicum C.SS.R.* 16 (1968), 385.
9. *Ibidem*, 400.
10. *Opuscoli sulla vocazione*, 114–115.
11. Tannoia, IV, 44.
12. *Lettere*, II, 291–292.
13. *Lettere*, II, 386–387.

5

TO BE A
REDEMPTORIST TODAY

Josef Heinzmann, C.Ss.R.
Province of Switzerland
Translated by William Bernard, C.Ss.R.
Province of Edmonton

1. Why I Became a Redemptorist

November 1807 to November 1808 was a turning point for the Redemptorists outside of Italy. Their only stable foundation, St. Bruno's in Warsaw, was dissolved with great brutality. The confreres were forcibly expelled and scattered. Clement Mary Hofbauer, their vicar general, had to go in exile to Vienna. The rector, Joseph Passarat, fled through snowed-in mountain passes in Switzerland with a few confreres from Chur into Wallis. After a dramatic journey, they arrived in Visp, where they found refuge until 1813.

The mountaintown of Vispterminen stands just a few kilometers above Visp. There in 1925 I was born. In many ways I had a hard childhood. As a boy I always wanted to become a priest. But our family was not only small, it was poor, so I had to forget my wish for a time. I became first a goatherd, and later a factory worker in Visp; there was no chance for studies. But during the three-hour trek to and from the factory, I still often dreamt of becoming a missionary in some faraway land.

How and why, then, did I end up becoming a Redemptorist? In the end I can come up with only one answer: it was by grace. For the Redemptorists were completely unknown in my home village. True, from 1813 to 1818 three Redemptorists had been parish priests in Vispterminen. But who still remembered these three men, or even the Redemptorist Congregation, which was banned in Switzerland until 1973?

My first connection with the Redemptorists came through a picture. After the end of my primary schooling, I made my first retreat. On this retreat, I discovered a picture of Our Mother of Perpetual Help and this prayer: "You can help me, powerful Mother. You wish to help me, O good Mother. You must help me, faithful Mother." Suddenly, it all seemed clear to me: Mary, my Mother, would help me overcome everything that stood in the way of my becoming a priest. I resolved to say that prayer every day until my wish had been granted. My resolve and patience were put to the test, until one day they achieved their goal. One day I joined a group of people from Vispterminen on a pilgrimage to a shrine of Our Lady. At the small pilgrimage chapel, I gave free rein to my feelings and to my little faith. I ended my insistent prayer after this fashion: "Mary, if you don't listen to me today, I won't pray anymore. Because either you *can't* help me or you *won't*."

This bit of pious pressure succeeded. On my way back home after the retreat, my father came to meet me saying, "If you insist on becoming a priest, go talk with the pastor. Tell him to register you at a college where you can study as cheaply as possible. You know how little money we have." A few weeks later I was at the minor seminary of the Redemptorists at Bertigny, near Fribourg. I was more than a little surprised when I found that in every larger room (in fact, in practically every room of the house), the picture of Our Mother of Perpetual Help was hanging. One of the priests explained it to me: "This old icon is found in our mother house in Rome." I found this connection wonderful, since up until that time I had known little or nothing about the image or about its connection with the Redemptorists. I have always felt there was something miraculous in this roundabout way that led me to the Redemptorists.

The second link that eventually drew me ever closer to the Redemptorists was *the goal and the spirituality of this Congregation*. The poor and a handful of saints stood at the beginnings of our Congregation. It was the poor that moved Alphonsus to found a new congregation. "To evangelize the poor" is the Redemptorist motto. "With Him Is Rich Redemption" stands under our coat-of-arms. With these two phrases, Alphonsus reached into the heart of the Gospel. The first of our Constitutions captures the missionary concern of our founder in these words: "[The] purpose [of the Congregation of the Most Holy Redeemer] is to follow the example of

Jesus Christ, the Redeemer, by preaching the word of God to the poor, as he declared of himself, 'He sent me to preach the Good News to the poor'" (Luke 4:18).

Our Congregation, especially in the last thirty years, kindled my enthusiasm with this program of action. Our general chapters from 1969 on have sought both to adapt our work to today's conditions, and at the same time, to reflect seriously on the goals we set ourselves as missionaries and on our spirituality. These general chapters emphasized certain points:

Bringing the Good News to the poor. The poor get first place. I thank both God and the Congregation for making it possible for me to work among the poor who live in the midst of our society's plenty: for the last twenty years in ministry to the divorced and separated, for many years in the service of married couples in crisis in their marriage, and for some time as chaplain in two psychiatric clinics. As a Redemptorist, I feel at home in these settings!

The explicit proclamation of the word of God. I have had the occasion as a Redemptorist to preach hundreds of parish missions, faith renewal weeks, and retreats. I am grateful for being able to be a messenger of joy and hope in this explicit proclamation of God's word. It took me almost fifty years to realize that Saint Alphonsus was also a missionary with his many writings. Alphonsus looked on the apostolate of the press as another aspect of his preaching ministry. In the same spirit, I now try to use the "permanent pulpit" of the written word. I have written a series of books on questions of faith, morals, marriage, and the family. I see these as a help to people in today's society.

Being evangelized by the poor. The missionary can never afford to present himself as someone with all the answers nor as someone to dispense alms. Mission must always mean dialogue, a gift of self made from both sides of the interchange. Experience has taught me that those overlooked by society and those cheated by it often possess gospel values that we somehow have overlooked. Those called "the poor" have taught me a great deal. For this reason I made a strong stand at two general chapters, that our Congregation should incorporate "being evangelized by the poor" into its self-awareness to complement and complete its understanding of what it means to "evangelize the poor."

The saints of our Congregation. These saints are another reason for my pride in being a Redemptorist. In the forty-six years of my Redemptorist life, I have certainly had to struggle with some aspects of community living: misunderstandings, departures, lack of vocations, aging of our membership, fragmenting of our missionary efforts, and the like. Nonetheless, I love the Alphonsian family. In this family I have found over the years many good friends who have supported me and given me trust and true friendship. The "saints" still living in the Congregation are at least as important to me as those who have died. I cannot and will not live exactly as the saints did; but they are examples for me nonetheless. These men of faith inspire courage in me, so much so that I wrote extensive biographies of Alphonsus Liguori, Clement Hofbauer, and Kasper Stanggassinger, along with a short life of John Neumann.

When I think back on the two hundred fifty years of Redemptorist history, I can hardly find grounds for triumphalism. Our Congregation began in misery; and later, much that is human and all-too-human can be found in her: tensions, divisions, persecutions. Still, it is fascinating how God wrote straight with these crooked lines. God gave the Congregation a collection of unusual personalities of which we can be proud.

Why did I become a Redemptorist, and why do I remain one? As honestly as I could, I have explained some of the reasons. But in the end, it remains a *mystery of vocation*. In any case, the Congregation has become a second family to me. I owe it a great deal. There have been sun and cloud in my life as a Redemptorist, high points and low, satisfactions and disappointments. Doesn't the cross figure in the life of every Redemptorist? And yet, there is one thing I can say without equivocation: I was always happy to be a Redemptorist; and, thank God, I have never experienced what is called "a loss of Redemptorist identity."

2. Saint Clement Interprets the Charism of Saint Alphonsus

It is not easy to compare two saints. Alphonsus, the Neapolitan, and Clement, the Northerner, had very different life stories and personalities, different talents and forms of missionary activity. Yet the two of them were similar in many respects—as a son and a father resemble each other. As someone very knowledgeable of both men once justly remarked, Clement was "a true son of Liguori."

2.1. How Clement Hofbauer "knew" Saint Alphonsus

Clement was barely six years old when his father died. Later in his life, two important men became a father figure for him: Nikolaus Josef Albert von Diessbach (1732–1798) and Alphonsus M. de Liguori (1696–1787). Hofbauer often called Alphonsus his "revered father." Through thirty-six years, the two were contemporaries, yet they never met each other—in fact, they never even corresponded. Nonetheless Clement knew his father in the Congregation well—through Fathers Diessbach and Landi and through Alphonsus's writings.

Through Nikolaus J. A. von Diessbach: Hofbauer was about thirty years old when he went to Vienna to study theology. There he became acquainted with Baron Josef Penkler (1751–1830); and it was in Penkler's house that Hofbauer got to know Nikolaus von Diessbach. He was to become Clement's best friend and teacher. Von Diessbach was a well-known former Jesuit. He had known Alphonsus personally, and von Diessbach was full of admiration for this founder of the Redemptorists. He went so far as to call Alphonsus "the first scholar given by God to his Church in our time; the only one who had the courage to stand up to the currents of our time and to defend the moral teaching of the Gospel against the pride of the Jansenists."

This former Jesuit had founded a group called "Amicizia christiana" in Turin around 1779. This organization had two clear goals: first, to promote the ongoing education and the growth in holiness of its members; and second, to combat the atheistic spirit of the times, principally through the distribution of good books, especially the works of Bishop Alphonsus Liguori. Von Diessbach had probably founded a branch of this group in Vienna by 1782. Hofbauer and his friend Thaddeus Hübl became members of this "Amicizia christiana." In that group they came to know and appreciate Alphonus' writings. I have no doubt that it was Father Diessbach himself who advised the two young friends to go to Italy to enter the congregation Alphonsus had founded.

Through Father Landi, his novice master: Hofbauer and Hübl entered the Redemptorist Congregation in 1784. When the aged and illness-plagued Alphonsus heard of it, he was delighted. "I would write to them," he said, "but God does not want me to interfere." The Congregation was still split at that time.

Father Landi was their novice master, a man Alphonsus knew personally and much admired. From him Clement "certainly received the spirit of
the founder." It was just about this time that Father Landi had completed a
history of the early days of the Congregation and a biography of its founder.
Hofbauer, as a novice and student, had occasion to study the manuscript
closely. Through Landi, Hofbauer came to know and love his Congregation's
founder ever more deeply.

Through Alphonsus's writings: Everyone in love wants to gain some insight into the inner life of the one they love, learning as much as possible
about the one who has captured their heart. And it is in loving that one
person comes to understand another best. Clement's love for Alphonsus is
documented again and again. Those who studied under Clement would say,
"His devotion to our founder, Alphonsus, was great. I noticed that he loved
Alphonsus with an exceptional love—as a father." It was for this reason
that Clement always kept seeking out information about Alphonsus, his life
and his writings; first from Warsaw and later from Vienna. His thirst for
information on Alphonsus persisted until the end of his life. A few examples will illustrate this:

Clement would often ask his confreres in Italy to send him anything
worth knowing about Alphonsus (biographies and so on). Although Clement was poor, he sent money several times to further the canonization process. When news arrived that Alphonsus would be declared Blessed, he
celebrated with childlike enthusiasm. Clement ordered pictures of Alphonsus
and had them distributed among the people. He wrote a remarkable letter to
the pope on July 2, 1818, asking for a quick canonization of Alphonsus.
Several times he expressed the wish to make a pilgrimage to Pagani, to the
founder's grave.

But the clearest sign of the respect and amazement that Clement felt
for Alphonsus was the way Clement ordered his books, distributed them, and
had them translated into other languages; and, of course, he read them himself. Those who knew Clement well claimed that he had practically memorized various books by Alphonsus. To sum up, Saint Clement Mary Hofbauer
knew his "respected father" very well indeed, even though he never met
him in person. Clement was "filled with the spirit of his holy founder."

2.2 How Clement lived out the "Alphonsian spirituality"

Clement had a strong personality. It would have been against his grain to imitate another saint. But when we say that Clement was "filled with the spirit" of Saint Alphonsus, it is clear that he sought to live out the charism of the founder in his own way. This charism of our Congregation's founder expressed itself in our Constitutions and Statutes. So I will now use the Constitutions to show how Clement understood Alphonsus's charism, explained it, lived it, and interpreted it in the light of the pastoral situations in which he found himself.

Vita apostolica: The first of our Constitutions presents the *vita apostolica* as something fundamental to us Redemptorists: "The Redemptorist Congregation truly follows the example of Christ in the apostolic life, which comprises at one and the same time a life specially dedicated to God and a life of missionary work." I would go so far as to say that it was just this "apostolic life" as it is described here, that gave unity to the life of Saint Clement. A division between religious life and missionary service, or between personal holiness and apostolate, was foreign to his way of thinking. Through and through he was a missionary, cast in a single piece. It was this that caused many, even in his own lifetime, to call him the "*homo apostolicus*." Hofbauer himself expressed it this way in one of his letters: "We bring together the active and the contemplative life. We seek to pour fire and spirit into the active life. Without the oil of the Holy Spirit, the wheels of the apostolic worker squeal."

Alphonsian spirituality: Alphonsus's spirituality had two key elements: *love* and *redemption*. Our founder's devotional life centered principally on those mysteries in which God comes especially close to us: crib, cross, and altar. Alphonsus calls the Incarnation "the miracle beyond all miracles." He sees suffering and death of our Savior as the perfect demonstration of Christ's love for us. Finally, the Redeemer remains among us in the Eucharist. In front of the tabernacle, we can speak in confidence with the Redeemer as one friend speaks alone with another (cf. *Visits to the Blessed Sacrament*).

Like Alphonsus, Clement Hofbauer was a man of faith. In this respect, he was outstanding. He was so caught up with God, that faith seemed for him something simply taken for granted. We find repeated in Clement's life these same key elements of Alphonsus's spirituality, though naturally colored by Clement's own personality.

As a Redemptorist, Clement bore the name of the Redeemer. We can hardly be surprised that his life centered on the *person of the Redeemer*. The Incarnation of the Redeemer, his love, his suffering and death, were recurring themes of his preaching. As a representative for all the others, we quote here Pajalich, one of his faithful students: "But the Servant of God made special efforts to hold up the unmeasurable and incomprehensible love before the eyes of others—the love that the Son of God, made one of us, showed during his whole earthly life in all he did and suffered; and which he continues to show in the Sacrament of the Altar—that unending love which he showed and shows still for every individual in particular."

Clement also proved himself the true son and follower of Saint Alphonsus in his great love for the *Eucharist*. Like Alphonsus, Clement often prayed alone before the Redeemer in the tabernacle. When he could see no way out of his difficulties, he would come before the Blessed Sacrament or even knock trustingly on the tabernacle door, saying, "Help me! This is the time for it!"

We can find a parallel between Alphonsus and Clement on two other points. The founder had a great *devotion to Mary*. Hofbauer, too, kept up a tender devotion to the Lord's Mother. He often went on pilgrimage to Marian shrines. In one letter he wrote how he preferred to have people add the name, Mary, to his first name, Clement.

Alphonsus, the great person of prayer, is rightly considered the "Doctor of Prayer." Clement, too, was a *man of prayer*. His entire life appeared to be a "close walk with God." "Hofbauer always looked within." One of his closest acquaintances said, "Father Hofbauer led a very active life in Vienna. One room was all he had, and this stood open to everyone. But here he was able to create a desert within his own heart: a cell, a little chapel. He could withdraw himself into this inner solitude at will, at any time, no matter where he was. Even on a street full of people, he would recollect himself in this way."

2.3 How Hofbauer put Alphonsus's "missionary charism" into practice

What sets a missionary apart is, before all else, compassion. "I feel compassion for the people" (Matthew 15:32). A comparison of the two missionaries, Alphonsus and Clement, makes immediately clear, how markedly both possessed the quality our Constitutions call *"caritas apostolica."* By this we mean the discontented love that seeks to save—the missionary's ability to discover the most neglected and the pastoral situations of genuine need—the missionary's spirit and zeal that makes the missionary able to find an apostolic answer suited to the needs of the time. Both these men went about this in the light of the Redemptorist motto, *"Evangelizare Pauperibus"*—two small words, two gospel fundamentals: the poor and announcing the Good News.

The poor: The Redeemer had a special preference for the "poor"; that is, for the little ones, the lost, the sinners, those who came up short in society, those living on the margins. It was almost by instinct that our two saints grasped with the eyes of faith that the poor were the first whom the Gospel addressed in their situation. Both recognized the call of God in the pastoral needs of the time. This was what happened when Alphonsus looked on the *lazzaroni* in the city of Naples, or when he came in contact with the shepherds in the mountains around Scala or with the poor country people of the Kingdom of Naples. The same happened with Clement in Warsaw and in Vienna. Both wanted to bring the poor the Good News of hope. But the "poor" in each case had different names and faces.

The materially poor and the people living on society's margins: It is common knowledge, that even before he founded the Congregation, Alphonsus worked among the neglected and the street people of the Naples harbor district; that he visited prisoners in jails and personally begged for the poor. Everyone knows that later as bishop he sold his ring and pectoral cross to help the poor.

And Father Hofbauer? He didn't take on every work that needed doing: rather, he picked out those works that best spoke to the charism of the Redemptorists (with the Redemptorist motto in mind, *"Evangelizare Pauperibus"*) in the concrete situation in which he found himself. Hofbauer built an orphanage and a school for the poor at St. Benno's in Warsaw. The only entrance requirement it had was poverty. He often had to go out to beg for these children, and there is one well-known story about this. Clement entered a pub and asked for donations for his orphans. In a rage, one man spit in Clement's face. Clement stayed calm: he wiped away the spit and said simply, "That was what you have for me. Now do you have anything you could give for my orphans?" In Warsaw he organized series of sermons and reflection days for prostitutes. He did all in his power to bring women who had fallen into prostitution back into the mainstream of society.

Later, in Vienna, Hofbauer made his concern for people on the edge of society even more clear. He invited the poor into his house as guests, to the point of becoming a "beggars' monastery." "Continually, he had the deprived and the destitute as his guests at table." He also made special efforts to rekindle hope in the depressed and suicidal.

The sick and the dying: Even as a young man, Alphonsus visited the hospital of the *Incurabili* to serve the sick and the dying. He was also a member of the "Bianchi della Giustizia," and as such he accompanied the condemned on the way to their execution.

In this regard, too, Clement walked in the footsteps of the founder of his Congregation. In any weather, he made daily rounds visiting the sick and dying in Vienna. Through the twelve years he stayed in Vienna, he is reputed to have served at the death bed of more than two thousand people. He was very sensitive and showed the human touch with the sick, often taking along flowers or some other small gift to encourage the sick or the dying.

Sinners: There is good reason why Alphonsus was named patron of moral theologians and confessors. He was good to sinners. Alphonsus opposed the severe approach to confession popular in his time (Jansenism/Rigorism) by promoting the freeing message of the Good News: that God is all-merciful—that in God there is rich redemption. "The priest who hears confessions," he said, "must be full of love and as mild as honey."

Just as it was with the founder of the Redemptorists, so, too, sinners were especially close to Father Hofbauer's heart. He often sat for hours in the confessional, sometimes until he fainted. It was said of him, "He brings about most of his conversions through the confessions he hears." It is hard for us to understand how the nobility and the rich, the learned and artists, the bishops and university professors, the craftsmen and the very poor, all chose Clement as confessor and spiritual director. Even the police reports stated that since Hofbauer had come to Vienna, "fanatical piety had come back into style." "And the confessional is the most powerful weapon to make this fashion persist."

Evangelizare: preaching the Good News: During the Age of Enlightenment, Alphonsus de Liguori was one of the most well known, perhaps even the greatest, of the mission preachers in the Kingdom of Naples. He preached very frequently, almost daily. And he founded his Congregation as a preaching order. He set this high goal for his spiritual sons, the Redemptorists: "To be a missionary means to follow the example of the Savior, who said of himself, 'He sent me to bring the Good News to the poor.'"

The sermon: Alphonsus considered preaching the most effective way to renew faith, since "faith comes from hearing" (Romans 10:17). He preached from his own convictions, and he aroused people to conviction about their faith. He preached simply, but powerfully. His preaching followed new paths. It was the person of the Redeemer and his Good News that stood front and center in his preaching, the message of God's love and salvation. And he wanted everyone to understand what he said: so it was with great simplicity that he preached.

Father Hofbauer, "completely filled with his spirit," said: "The work of preaching and of giving instruction in Christian faith" are essential to the duties of the Redemptorist Congregation. No other aspect of Clement's life shows the influence of the founder as clearly as this. His sermons show that they are largely the fruit of his reflection on books by Alphonsus. Often he quoted texts from Alphonsus almost word for word. Dr. Emanuel Veith, a well-known student of Hofbauer's and preacher at the cathedral, reported: "Very often, in fact almost daily, I heard him say solemnly and emphatically: 'The Gospel must be preached in a new way!'" What he meant by that Clement himself summarized: "The preacher before all else must pay attention to speaking in a way near to the people, and to a genuine preaching of the Gospel." A genuine preaching of the Gospel, simplicity and nearness to the people! These qualities were two great concerns of Alphonsus Liguori. In these we find the golden key to understanding Hofbauer's reform of preaching, and to his success as a preacher.

Genuine preaching of the Gospel: At the time that Hofbauer came to Vienna, preaching concerned itself with almost everything except announcing the Gospel. (One can read, for example, the sermon series, published in book form, on Preventing Swine Fever or on the Usefulness of Smallpox Inoculation.) Then the Apostle of Vienna arrived on the scene. For him, polished rhetoric as it was then practiced was the last thing the preaching of the Gospel was about. "The book he studied with exceptional thoroughness was his crucified Savior and Lord." His "wide-ranging grasp of Scripture" astounded many. His preparations for preaching were very simple: early in the week Clement had the Gospel of the following Sunday read to him several times. After a few verses he would say: "Sufficit. That's enough." Through the rest of the week he immersed himself prayerfully in the scriptural word. Before the sermon he took a quarter hour to gather himself and to pray. Clement asked one of his students what the best preparation was for preaching. Without waiting for an answer, Clement slapped his knees with his hand, as if he wanted to say that the preacher needs to prepare for a sermon on his knees.

Simplicity and nearness to the people: Hofbauer himself testified that he wanted to walk in the footsteps of his Congregation's founder: "God's word must be preached in such a way that everyone understands it: the small and the great, the educated and the uneducated. And this is what our founder ordered." Simplicity and a style close to the people were important concerns of his. For this reason he often began his sermons by saying, "Today I want to speak so simply and clearly that every grandmother and every child understands."

And again, the unexplainable! The success of his sermons far outweighed the poverty of the rhetorical devices he used. Clement had no great rhetorical gifts. From a technical standpoint, his sermons show real weaknesses. It borders on the miraculous that his sermons made the impact they did. Even intellectuals and academics were impressed. "We have never heard such a preacher. A single word from his mouth satisfies me for an entire week." "I often think, as I hear him preach, that the apostles must have spoken this way." The famous writer Zacharias Werner summed it up this way: "Hofbauer is unique. No one outperforms him. The Holy Spirit speaks from his mouth."

And parish missions? Saint Alphonsus considered the parish mission a preferred way to preach the Good News. The Redemptorists achieved great success with this in Italy. Although Hofbauer was very flexible in his choice of apostolic methods, he did want to take this part of Redemptorist work seriously. Unfortunately, parish missions were forbidden in both Poland and Austria at this time. Clement regretted this. Only in 1801 could the Redemptorists preach a few parish missions in the neighborhood of Warsaw.

The so-called "permanent mission" was a form of preaching typical to Alphonsus's style. Morning meditation, Visits to the Blessed Sacrament, sermons, catechism classes, evening devotions, and liturgical festivities: wherever he founded a Redemptorist house, he set up such a "permanent mission." This was the case even in his first foundations: Scala, Villa, and Ciorani.

Parish-mission preaching was forbidden to Clement and his confreres in Poland. In their place, they made a rich missionary offering to the people at St. Benno's Church, which Clement himself called "a permanent mission." This went on from six in the morning until late evenings: morning and evening prayer, Masses, sermons in many languages, devotions, meditations on the Way of the Cross, Visits to the Blessed Sacrament. Here the St. Benno's community built on solid Alphonsian tradition.

Preaching through apostolic lay groups/cooperation with the laity: Alphonsus was an exceptionally gifted missionary with a special charism. One of his most original innovations was the "Work of the Chapels," the *Capelle Serotine*. This ingenious invention was a combination of prayer and discussion groups—small-group building after the manner of Catholic action and neighborhood apostolate. Fundamentally, it was a lay religious movement that struck deep root in the everyday world.

And Clement Hofbauer? He picked up on the concerns of his two teachers: Diessbach, who adopted the idea of the "Amicizia christiana," and from Alphonsus, the "Work of the Chapels." Clement very deliberately pursued formation of the laity, and he worked hand in hand with them. In Warsaw and everywhere the Redemptorists came (Poland, Germany, Austria, Switzerland), they introduced lay communities of Redemptorist Oblates.

During the last years of his life, Hofbauer became the Apostle of Vienna, essentially with the help of lay groups and individuals working with him. His Vienna Circle included men and women, people from the nobility and the middle class, the learned and the artists, civil servants and church officials, students and professors. He was so impressive that many people from all social levels—and leading personalities at that—flocked to this simple priest and adopted his spirit and spread it further. This exceptional group gathered around the Apostle of Vienna has received the name "The Hofbauer Circle," or "The Circle of the Romantics."

In the Vienna of that time, youth at the universities were neglected.

Here the gifted Redemptorist missionary succeeded in another amazing piece of work. His small living quarters became an open house, a meeting place for young people studying at the university. His small Redemptorist house became a missionary center, a place where pastoral initiatives spread out in all directions. All Vienna became his mission field because many people worked in his spirit. I would have to overstep the limits of this article to speak in fitting detail about the group of Oblates, "The Circle of the Romantics," and the discussion groups for young people.

3. Conclusion

In summary we have to say that Clement had a strong personality and stood on his own two feet. *He was no slavish copier of Saint Alphonsus.* Yet Hofbauer was filled with the *spirit* of Alphonsus. He took Alphonsus's charism seriously and sought to live it and to address the basic concerns of the founder of the Congregation. In doing that he remained astoundingly flexible in his choice of mission methods. He began with life as it was being lived, not with textbooks or hardened traditions. His missionary spirit was one that made him adapt to the situation in which he found himself. Sensitive to the needs of his time, he was able to discover effective responses. We could say, in fact, that he gave the Congregation a breadth of vision that it often later (sadly) lost.

From 1788 until his death in 1820, Clement was vicar general: the representative of the superior general for the Redemptorists outside of Italy. I find an element of sadness in the lives of Alphonsus and of Clement. Both had a difficult way of the cross to walk because of their love for the Congregation. As the aged bishop Liguori died in Pagani, his Congregation was divided. The unhappy affair of the *Regolamento* had practically excluded those members of Alphonsus's Congregation living in Naples from the Redemptorists. Put bluntly, the founder and superior general of the Congregation was no longer part of it! For Alphonsus, this must have been a sword piercing to the heart. It was not much better for Clement. The unfavorable atmosphere of his time forced the Redemptorists north of the Alps to split up. Circumstances forced him to live for many years in exile in Vienna; not a single confrere could be present at his death.

There is just cause for calling Clement the *second founder of the Congregation.* Alphonsus took on many sorrows and sufferings as Father and founder of the Redemptorists. On May 30, 1776, Alphonsus had written in a letter, "The Congregation will never be a true Congregation, unless it strikes root outside Naples." It was Hofbauer, the man of vision, who had the greatest part in making the Congregation worldwide in scope.

Clement's thirty-four years of religious life demonstrated clearly his love for the Redemptorist Congregation. Establishing this Congregation north of the Alps was his heart's desire and his life's work. For more than three decades, he worked with unparalleled persistence to make this dream come true. Under the most trying conditions he negotiated and traveled from country to country, searching for a permanent foothold for his Congregation. He failed at two dozen attempts. But he never gave up. On his knees, he placed his concerns into God's hands.

He gradually came to realize that the Congregation would be permitted to exist north of the Alps only after his death. And his prophecy to this effect came to pass with the punctuality characteristic of God's fidelity. Exactly five weeks after his death, the Austrian emperor announced the official approval of the Redemptorists in Austria. The Upper Passau Court in Vienna and the church next to it, Maria am Gestade, became the first Redemptorist house in Austria. And at almost the same time, a second foundation, Bischenberg in France, was established.

This northern branch of the Redemptorists spread out from here, directly or indirectly, into many countries. The seed that Clement sowed in tears, grew. His dream, frustrated during his lifetime, to send missionaries across the world, now became reality. Thus he became a kind of second founder of the Redemptorists; or at least, the pioneer of the Redemptorist outreach to the entire world.

6

MY CALL TO
FOLLOW THE SAINTS

Laurentino Miguélez, C.Ss.R.
Province of Mexico
Translated by Gerard Brinkmann, C.Ss.R.
Province of Baltimore

1. Biographical Sketch of Laurentino Miguélez

I was chosen to be a Redemptorist and, therefore, called to be a saint. So how did the call unfold?

To begin with I should mention something about my religious and Spanish upbringing. The town where I was born, Santibanez de la Isla, is a mere fifteen kilometers from the famous route trod by the pilgrims through the ages, on their journey to venerate the remains of Saint James the Apostle in Campostela of Galicia. The title of Our Lady, Our Lady of the Way, comes precisely from the patronage of the pilgrims on their way to Campostela. Her sanctuary looks down over the route of the pilgrims from León. My mother used to attend the novenas held in Our Lady's honor during her patronal feast in September.

Around the turn of the century, my maternal grandfather, Romualdo, was chosen by popular acclaim to teach in the newly constructed school in his town of Villarnera de la Vega. The school building was finished, but no teacher was sent. Naturally, the people wanted to see their children in school and being educated, so they chose my grandfather to teach, even though he had no academic degrees.

Let me say something about my uncles and aunts on my mother's side: Toribia, the eldest, was a religious in the Order of Our Lady of the

Most Abandoned. She was sent to Cuba after her profession in the year 1910. While traveling to Spain from Mexico in 1960, I stopped to see her at the convent in Havana. Within two months of my visit, I received the news of her death.

Eugenio taught school and eventually earned his master's degree in education. Maria Antonia also took her vows with the Order of Our Lady of the Most Abandoned, but was forced by ill health to return to her home. This proved to be a blessing for me because she became my private teacher. Thanks to Aunt Maria Antonia, I learned the Our Father by heart very early in life. When her health improved, she entered the Order of the Concepcionists, a cloistered order, where she died in Bajadoz and was buried in their cemetery. Rosalina, was made a Redemptorist oblate and died in January 1944. My uncle John's two brothers-in-law were Redemptorist missionaries, Father Jeronimo Martinez served for many years in Espino and Father Valentin Martinez worked in Central America and Cuba.

Manuel, my grandmother's brother, adopted a son, Santos Cavero, who became a Redemptorist coadjutor brother. Santos worked in China, where he died at a very early age. The historian Luis Fernandez de la Retana wrote a short biographical sketch about Brother Manuel titled, *Still There Are Saints*, which he published in Madrid in 1934. A cousin of the same maternal grandmother, Father Pedro Perez Fuertes, was one of the Redemptorist pioneers in Mexico in 1908.

I had the good fortune to know the Capuchin missionary from my hometown who worked in Venezuela, Fray Ambrosio de Santibanez. I wish I could say that I knew him well, but I only met him when he returned to Spain in 1934. During the Spanish Civil War, he was taken prisoner and killed in Santander simply because he was a priest. Over the main door of our parish church in Santibanez is a marble plaque hanging in his honor that reads, "God's Servant." We pray that one day he will be recognized as a martyr for the faith and be raised to honors of the altar.

Another priest from my hometown, a Redemptorist, Father Miguel Martinez Brasa, worked in Mexico since 1909. His death in 1927 was not directly that of a martyr, but the result of circumstances connected with the religious persecution of the times.

When the Spanish Civil War started in 1936, the Redemptorist juvenate in Espino had still not closed its doors. There were but a few candidates, and the vocation director let it be known there was still room for any youth who wished to enter. My uncle John presented my name to Father Eladio

Diaz Marin, and I was notified to come to the juvenate on November 2, 1936.

I was still a fledgling of ten years and five months when I entered the juvenate. I did not even have time to learn the prayers an altar boy must know in order to serve Mass. Very quickly Father Gabriel Sabino Diez prepared me for my first Communion on the feast of All Saints. That same evening, the vigil of All Souls' Day, the whole town went to the cemetery, as was their custom to pray for the dead. The scene of so many people carrying lighted candles in the cemetery praying for the dead left an indelible memory on my young mind.

On November 2, All Souls' Day, a group of young teenagers, led by Father Eladio Marin, boarded the train for the Redemptorist juvenate in Espino. Five of these youths deserve mention: Juan Francisco Sanchez Mayo, Rafael Canseco Combarros, his nephew Antonio Cavero Combarros, Angel Iglesias, and Antonio Gonzalez Peréz.

I was a minor seminarian from November 2, 1936, to July 1943. My teachers, so faithful to their religious vows, inspired me and confirmed me in my calling. I believe I was influenced by the dedication of each and every one of them. Father Manuel Peréz, the cousin of Antonio Gonzalez, was the director of the juvenate. Both of them were the nephews of Father Pedro Peréz Fuertes, the vice provincial in Mexico. The older students told us that the director, Father Manuel Peréz, had frequent apparitions of the Baby Jesus.

In the far corner of the large seminary garden was the cemetery. The students pointed and in hushed tones indicated the grave of Father Jose Chavatta (1841–1931), a Frenchman who had the reputation of being a saint. Father Patricio Gonzalez Amurrio wrote his edifying biography.

As our days in the juvenate progressed, so did the Spanish Civil War. We often huddled around our Father director to hear news of the Redemptorists who were killed—killed only because they looked like priests. We looked on them as martyrs.

On the last day of 1941, I received a letter from home telling me the sad news of my father's death. He died on Christmas Eve, at the age of forty-five.

From July 1943 to August 1944, I was a novice in Nova del Rey. Father Rafael Cavero (1874–1966) was my novice master. He constantly spoke of sanctity in his conferences, and his life gave brilliant testimony to it. His favorite phrase was, "Even saints have to grow in holiness." One day we received a visit from Father Saturnino Martin Lucas (1874–1955), who was on home leave at the time. The two priests and the novices made up a good-sized group. As we listened attentively to Father Lucas telling of his experiences, he glanced toward Father Cavero and with a motion of his head he said, "This novice master of yours is truly a saint." The surprising compliment was not wide of its mark. Father Cavero nodding his head gently said, "Not too holy. Not too holy."

From August 1944 to July 1950, I studied philosophy and theology in Astorga, one of the bigger cities on the pilgrim route to Campostela. The studentate always keeps a chronicle and that job fell to me for some time. As the chronicler, it was my job to write the cherished memories or account of the life of a deceased classmate, Paciano Sambad Guisamonde (1927–1949), who died before ordination. In writing his account, it was not necessary for me to use panegyric exaggeration. I knew the man and his heroic efforts to be holy, as our founder, Saint Alphonsus, had in mind when he write the Redemptorist Rule.

In those days there was a confrere in Astorga, Francisco Barrechegueren (1881–1957). In the chronicle, I described details of his life among us. Later on, Father Juan Perez Riesco took the initial steps to begin the process of canonization for both Francisco and for his daughter, Maria Concepcion (Conchita). Father Perez read my entry in the chronicles and used it as testimony in the process of canonization. For that reason I often remember that I lived with and brushed elbows with a saint.

Finally the day of my priestly ordination arrived. The date of my first solemn High Mass in Santibanez de la Isla was pushed back to June 16, the feast of the Sacred Heart of Jesus, so that Father Valentin Martinez could get here from Central America. He was to be my archpriest and homilist. He returned to Central America, and I was headed across the seas as well.

On October 13, 1950, I began my priestly assignment in the brand-new seminary of the vice province of Mexico in San Luis Potosí. My grandmother told me to give her regards to Father Pedro Peréz, who is my cousin. He was enjoying a prosperous old age in Puebla, Mexico. He could not travel, so I sent him a letter that he faithfully answered. We both looked forward to seeing each other soon. It was not to be. Peter died on March 20, 1953, before we could meet. Out of the great respect I had for him, I wrote his biography, *You Too Are Peter*, in which I detailed his wonderful work in the founding of the Redemptorist work in Mexico. A few years later in 1961 the biography was published.

While in the seminary in Potosí, I once again took on the office of house chronicler. I not only entered the latest daily happenings, but I also had the opportunity to page through the records of bye-gone days. Father Martinez Brasa and I gathered material for an article in the *Missionaries*, a magazine that the seminary published. The article, "Between Two Revolutions, Father Miguel Martinez Brasa," was twenty pages long including photographs (February 1956).

I read over and over the chronicler's entry on the sickness, death, funeral, burial, and reputation for sanctity of Father Lesmes Miguel Palacios (1883–1934), and I was convinced that he was an excellent candidate for canonization. I also read a short article on him published in *Analecta C.SS.R.* (1936, pp. 38–42). I did a follow-up on his life in other sources including the chronicles of Espino and letters of confreres who had known him. As a result I published his biography under the title, *The First in the Kingdom of God, How Father Lesmes Miguel Palacios Saw It* (1963).

Around the same time in San Luis Potosí, I uncovered two letters to which I devoted faithful and loving attention. The first one was a letter of Father Antonio Sotes (1903–1953), an accomplished musician and superior of the community. I was at his side when he slumped over and died instantly at the keyboard of the organ on Thursday, January 15, 1953. The second letter was about Father Francisco Javier Saez, known as "Santitos" (1875–1959), who had lived and suffered during the atrocities of the persecution of the Church in Mexico (1926–1929).

I was enthralled by the fact that in such writings I was able to get in contact with the personalities of many confreres. I was able to get an insight into their efforts to be faithful to their Redemptorist vocation, striving to do things well for the love of God, which is no more than living holiness. I learned this from Father Eduardo Perea, the vice provincial of Mexico, who was a longtime famous spiritual director. He lived to the ripe old age of eighty-nine (1896–1985). Having said this much I quote the words of Father Fernandez de Retana on the frontispiece of his book, *Saints Still Live* (1934). I add that I knew a few of them, and they were Redemptorists.

2. About Holiness and Getting to Be Holy

The word *holiness*, first and foremost, is applied to God as we read in the Old Testament. God must not be confused with his creation. He is separate and apart from all limited created things, from all evil, from all sin. God is the center of holiness. God is holy. Holiness takes its beginning in God.

This holiness goes out to things, places, and times and especially to people. The people of God can and must share in the holiness of God, and they will if they get freed from sin—which is the opposite of the holiness of God.

Holiness is a very old word, but it is still part of our contemporary vocabulary and is still found in the lexicon of the Church. Sanctity, sanctification, is a fundamental component of the Christian commitment and, therefore, of the religious life. Every day of the year has its saint or saints, and November 1 is dedicated to all of them.

What would it be like to live in a world of saints? Is it possible to imagine such a thing, a world without hate and rancor, complaining and jealousy, attacks on persons and thievery? Imagine no beggars, no poor people, a world where arms manufacture did not exist. Would such a world be possible?

In Saint Paul's time, the words *holy* and *Christian* had the same meaning. *Holy* and *Christian* were used interchangeably. As the years passed, the word *Christian* has been diluted and a gap has opened up that gradually has become a chasm between the two words. There are more Christians than there are saints. A saint tries to restore in his own life and in the lives of others the lost identity between the two words, trying to make them identical again.

It is possible to think of a perfect human being, the Blessed Virgin for example, or a holy man and even desire perfection and sanctity for one's self. If one cannot reach that level of perfection himself, he can see it in others and feel a kind of pride and satisfaction that he is the brother of a saint. It would not be wrong to consider sanctity as the deepest yearning of a human being. Sanctity is not something added, an afterthought tacked on to our human nature. It is something that man had lost and regained.

A saint does not stand out because of the odor of sanctity that he emits. He travels the road of heroism, but it is not always evident from the way he walks. Before being singled out, he was walking the same roads that we were walking.

We Christians turn to the saints in heaven to help us and to work miracles. Some of the saints even worked miracles while they were alive. We kind of feel that to work miracles, holiness is necessary. Is there any relation between holiness and miracles? Isn't it true that we seem to give preference to the holiness of a saint without considering the miracles that have been received through his intercessions?

The rest of the life of the saint is ordinary then. The extraordinary, simply because it is extraordinary, should not be confused with holiness. A saint is a disciple of Christ who does good things in a good way. Usually a saint draws more attention to himself when he is dead than when he is alive.

The Church reserves the right to recognize the holiness of a person in order to guarantee that the faithful are not mislead. A saint is an intermediary between God and the devotees of the saint. The devout faithful ask the favor of God through the saint.

Holiness does not destroy or weaken the human personality, but rather perfects it. There are not two identical saints because there are not two identical human beings. Even within the same school of spirituality, two saints are still different, even though one may imitate the spirituality of the other.

In the early Church, the martyr saints were the first to be venerated because they were the ones who gave their very lives to remain faithful to Christ. The nonmartyr saints, however, gave their lives in a different way, without the need of torture and suffering, throughout their whole lives.

3. Contributions of Saint Alphonsus to Ascetical Theology

In the fall of 1748, Saint Alphonsus wrote a letter to Pope Benedict XIV (1740–1758) entitled, "Petition presented by Alphonsus Liguori and his followers to the Holy Father Benedict XIV asking for the pontifical approval of the Congregation of the Most Holy Savior" (letters tome 1, 149–151).

One of the first pastoral experiences mentioned in the letter of the priesthood of Saint Alphonsus, as a member of the Congregation of the Apostolic Missions, helps to introduce his petition, citing the great abandonment of the poor, especially the ones in rural areas in the Kingdom of Naples. He emphasized the spiritual and Christian abandonment caused by the economic marginalization of the people. I will treat of this at greater length further on.

The biggest step forward was taken on November 9, 1732, when Alphonsus, without severing his ties with the Congregation of the Apostolic Missions, started with a few of his friends the Congregation of the Most Holy Savior in the small town of Scala in the mountains of Salerno. The project was not new. What was new was the idea of working exclusively in missions, instructions, and other spiritual exercises for the "poor of the rural areas who are in such need of spiritual help."

With very clear and forceful words, Liguori describes the reason. The poor are in need of the frequent administration of the sacraments and the preaching of the Word of God. Many of these poor abandoned people pass their whole life with no knowledge of the Faith. This is simply saying that they lack the knowledge and the help they need to follow Christ. He goes on to put his finger on the cause: there are so few priests who dedicate themselves to helping the poor peasants because of the hardships involved and the inconveniences.

In the years 1732 to 1738, Liguori and his followers traveled through six of the most abandoned provinces of the Kingdom of Naples. He mentions in particular the benefits received by the poor goatherds, work that the king had recognized. He also mentions the work in the slums adjacent to the archbishop's palace.

The approval of His Holiness was in favor of a work already going on. With the approval of the respective bishops and the king, almost forty members lived in community in houses and monasteries on the outskirts of towns. He does not give the names of these communities. He only writes the names of the dioceses: Salerno, Bovino, Nocera, Conza, and the names of places where the houses were: Scala, Deliceto, Pagani, and Caposele.

What were the almost forty missionaries doing in 1749? They were taking care of the places where they had preached missions, but also the people in the area of the established houses could come to the monasteries for the care of souls. These four houses were upgraded to retreat centers where the faithful could come for spiritual care and growth. This proved to be a spiritual windfall for the area.

There is a piece of information for which Liguori wanted to take advantage. Benedict XIV had sent the archbishop of Naples a letter asking him to send help to Alphonsus to assist him in the missions. Liguori reminded His Holiness of this letter with gratitude, and it was because of this that Alphonsus had sufficient missionaries.

All of these ministries helped Alphonsus gain approval for his Institute. Since the papal approval was not given to a specific diocese, we must understand that it applied to the whole Church. "Humbly prostrate before Your Holiness, Alphonsus and his companions, for the love that Your Holiness feels for the glory of Jesus Christ and for the spiritual health of so many poor rural folk who are abandoned sons of the Church, ask that you deign to grant your Apostolic approval."

It is to be noted that the apostolate of the new Congregation was to be exercised among the most abandoned children of the Church. At least in Naples in 1748 these most abandoned were the rural people.

While not mentioned specifically in the proposal to His Holiness, it was only by being holy that Liguori and his followers could be faithful to what they were setting out to do. They were not to live in Naples, Benevento, or Salerno, but rather in the rural areas where the poor shepherds lived, as well as the slums of Naples. Their means were so limited that they got to face hardships on the missions and at home. They could put up with this only if they were saints. History shows that they were saints, Sportelli, Sarnelli, Cafaro, Liguori, Majella. Father Villani was also a saint, the first novice master who traveled to Rome to supervise the work of the papal approval.

The papal brief, *Ad Pastoralis Dignitatis Fastigium*, was signed under the authority of Benedict XIV by Cardinal Passionei on February 25, 1749. This was the answer made to the formal appeal made by Saint Alphonsus. A very satisfactory answer, indeed! The name of the new Congregation was slightly changed to Congregation of the Most Holy Redeemer. The brief contains the Rules and Constitutions that Liguori had drawn up in an ascetical, theological style and which on papal insistence Father Villani rewrote according to more judicial times.

In the papal brief, Saint Alphonsus and his followers are presented as a Congregation so that they could more easily follow the evangelical counsels for their own salvation and for those for whom they worked.

The purpose of the Rules and Constitutions is to unite secular priests to live in community and to dedicate themselves more seriously to the imitation of the virtues and example of Jesus Christ and to dedicate themselves to the preaching and the Word of God to the poor. In the text they do not use the words *holiness* or *sanctification*. Rather what you find is the expression, "to the imitation of the virtues and example of Jesus Christ," another way of expressing the same that Saint Alphonsus agreed to.

Also it is to be noted that in the whole of the Rules and Constitutions, the word *holiness* does not appear, but it is certainly paraphrased in such expressions, such as the priests will serve and edify...to meditate on the life and virtues of Jesus Christ of which they will be a living example....The lives of the members of the Congregation are to be a constant recollection and to achieve this they must practice the presence of God....In imitation of the apostle they are to look for joy in suffering and to be despised and humiliated just like Jesus Christ....The novice will try under the supervision of the novice master to gain the salient virtues corresponding to his vocation.

Is there a holiness proper to Redemptorists? The charism of Redemptorist demands holiness and the exercise of the charism makes sanctification easier. For the sons of Saint Alphonsus holiness comes from the exercise of their charism. Holiness has been possible for all and effective for many. These are some of the structures that will aid in the sanctification of Redemptorists:

- The mission given them by the Church and its fulfillment
- The basic rule that he be an imitator of Jesus Christ
- Commune life and prayer with his brothers
- Imitation of the example of the saints and especially of Saint Alphonsus
- The vows of poverty, chastity, and obedience

The Redemptorist knows that the commune dangers and risks are not done away with, such as the worldly way of looking at things, superficiality, routine, and boredom.

Saint Alphonsus was impressed by the obstacles that the world presents. They are different in Italy or any other country or from one century to another. The obstacles are always there. The Redemptorist is consecrated to live in the world, but not to be of the world. Nothing in the world is foreign to him. He knows how to live his own charism in every place and every time.

The missionary work of the Redemptorist can be considered as a new evangelization for Christians who are not sufficiently mature. They are not involved in the things of new Christians, but of good Christians.

Saint Alphonsus thought that a Redemptorist should be both an apostle and a Carthusian, because holiness can be found not only in action but also in contemplation. You should not use action to put the damper on holiness nor holiness to slow down action. The greatest thing is to be Christian. To be a Redemptorist is a help to being a Christian. Blessed is the Redemptorist who learns to be a good Christian. Of course, holiness is not a monopoly of the Redemptorist, but there are many saints who are Redemptorists.

Do Redemptorist saints have their own characteristics? Is there a school of Redemptorist holiness? There is and we have proof from our own very first Redemptorist, Saint Alphonsus. We recommend his many writings, whose treasure we posses, and all the great examples of his sanctity to which his biographers give testimony.

These are some of Saint Alphonsus's personal ideas of holiness: He chose to work for and live among the poor. He evangelized the poor and was evangelized by them. When teaching about Jesus, he also taught about Mary and was one of her greatest devotees. Over and above all he preferred simplicity. His moral theology is a monument not only of knowledge but also about pastoral charity. He occupied no university seat, but still reigned in the confessional.

Saint Alphonsus was more interested in the holiness of all his followers than in the canonization of the few. He was also sensitive to the holiness of the few. Some of his followers were saints, and he wrote their biographies. In the same way that he had friends among the saints in heaven, so he had saints among his good friends on earth: Gennaro Sarnelli, Cesare Sportelli, Pablo Cafaro, Dominic Blasucci, and so on.

Saint Gerard Majella, the best known and most popular of the Redemptorist saints, was a contemporary of Saint Alphonsus and from the same area. He was a coadjutor brother acclaimed for his many miracles. He died in 1755 at the age of twenty-nine.

In the course of two and a half centuries and throughout the world, Redemptorist holiness has flourished. These are but a few noteworthy examples whose causes have been presented for beatification:

- The first ones outside of Italy in Central Europe: Saint Clement Mary Hofbauer (1751–1820), Joseph Passarat (1772–1834).
- In Italy in post-Alphonsian times: Vito DiNetta (1788–1894), Manuel Ribera (1811–1874), Joseph Mary Leone (1829–1902), Anthony Mary Losito (1838–1917), Alexander de Risio (1823–1901), Calogero Liotta (1811–1898), Nocolas de Santis (1818–1834).
- In the countries of Central Europe: from Germany, John Eichelsbacher (1820–1889) and Kasper Stanggassinger (1871–1899); from Austria, Juan Bautista and Francis Tendler (1820–1902); from Scotland, Edward Douglas (1819–1898); from France, Victor Humarque (1817–1896); from Belgium, Gil Vogels (1807–1877) and Louis Bronchain (1829–1892).
- In America: originally from Bohemia and later bishop of Philadelphia, Saint John Neumann (1811–1860); from Germany but worked in the States, Francis Seelos (1819–1867); from Canada, Alfred Pampalon (1867–1892); from Suriname but originally from Holland, Blessed Peter Donders (1809–1887); from Columbia, Argentina, and Uruguay but originally from Italy, Victor Loyodice (1834–1916).

I will close this partial and provisional list with the name of Francisco Barrecheguren, whom I mentioned earlier and whose cause was just opened in October 1993 by the archbishop of Granada, Spain. In the lives of the saints, Father Barrecheguren's cause will be rather unique. He was married, the father of a family, widower, and religious priest. His daughter Maria Concepcion (Conchita) has had her cause introduced as servant of God. Can we expect a beatification and canonization together?

The names that we have mentioned can also be grouped according to the accustomed titles:

First the martyrs, none of the above falls into this category, but even though their causes have not been advanced, I will make mention of the priests and brothers killed from July to November in 1936 in Spain because they were religious:

- Teachers or authors of spiritual books: Sarnelli, Vogels, Bronchain, Loyodice
- Bishops: Saint John Neumann, Alexander de Risio
- Confessors of the Faith: Sportelli, Cafaro, Saint Clement Hofbauer, Seelos, Blessed Peter Donders, Passarat, DiNetta, Ribera
- Coadjutor Brothers: Saint Gerard Majella, Calogero Liotta, Stoeger, Di Santis
- Youths: Blasucci, De Santis, Blessed Kasper Stanggassinger, Pampalon

The canonization of these few can justly be considered as a witness to the holiness of many. The saints are far more numerous than the canonized. Right behind the very holy come the holy.

7

BAPTISMAL CONSECRATION
AND RELIGIOUS PROFESSION

Vincent Van Vossel, C.Ss.R.
Province of North Belgium

1. To Be a Redemptorist in the Middle East

I was born in Belgium sixty years ago, on July 11, 1935. I believe I became a Redemptorist for the same reasons that motivated many of my generation. The Belgian Redemptorists were missionaries in many parts of the world and this enkindled our enthusiasm, leading us to dedicate ourselves to God and to others. At the age of twenty, I professed my vows, then passed to the major seminary at Louvaine. We were a good-sized group of philosophers and theologians. During this time, the Belgian Province was divided (1957). I was ordained in 1960.

In 1965 I arrived in Baghdad. Our mission then was to collaborate with the Chaldean patriarchate, with a special view to the intellectual formation of its seminarians. I began immediately to teach eastern petrology and church history. The classes were given in Arabic, but a working knowledge of Chaldean and Syrian was necessary for pastoral purposes. When the opportunity presented itself, I preached retreats and offered conferences on theology and spirituality. At that time we were only two confreres in the community; a third companion had died shortly before, at the age of only sixty-two. We belonged to the same region as did the Belgian Redemptorists in Lebanon, but communication with them was practically impossible.[1]

The major religion in Baghdad is Islam, in either its Sunni or Shiite confessions. Christians are barely three percent of the population and belong to many different denominations and rites. I now come to the question posed by the editor of this collection of essays: what does it mean to live the Redemptorist charism in the context of the Middle East? If I were to attempt an explication, it would demand many pages and probably would be confusing at the end. It would be similar to asking other Redemptorists to describe their experience of living under a communist regime. While they could speak of their lives in general terms, how could they really capture the day-to-day feeling of living in the silence and fear of the catacombs? Our life here has its own sort of silence and hiding, not only on the political level but also with regard to religion. It goes without saying that we are not permitted to speak about religion with Moslems or in any way to attract them. But, even within the Christian communities, we are allowed to do only what we are asked. We always remain "foreigners," and the word has at least the same force as when Europeans speak about Arab immigrants. One has to live with this status. To accept it as it is, one needs some sort of charism.

Another aspect of living the charism has to do with teaching. We were called here as professors of theology at the Chaldean seminary and, although we are engaged in many other forms of pastoral work, education remains as our principal task. We try to carry out this mission in an evangelical sense that connects us with the Redemptorist charism: our task is to teach-preach the Good News to the poor and to do so while respecting the venerable traditions of the Eastern Churches. Generally speaking, the Catholic theological formation afforded to seminarians in the Middle East over the last centuries has been strongly influenced by the sort of western postmedieval mentality prevalent in certain Roman seminaries where many of the professors received their training. A result has been that the poor, having lost contact long ago with their rich spiritual traditions, have had to be content with a sort of surrogate religiosity that was transplanted from Europe. Consequently, our work has much to do with what Gustavo Gutierrez describes as "drinking from one's own well." The wells of the desert contain the finest water, but one is obliged to cross some arid wasteland to find them. In the same way, while it demands a great deal of patience to study languages and learn ancient traditions, unless one makes that effort, he can never hope to lead others to drink from their own wells.

This article might be viewed as an effort to listen to ancient and forgotten words, to carefully and reverently filter from them the dust of time so as to preserve their original freshness, all the while protecting them from a rudely western superficiality and pretension.

2. The Sacraments of Initiation and Religious Profession

This essay opens with two considerations, that of the sacraments of initiation, then religious consecration. A reflection on the nature of the Redemptorist vocation will follow, enriched with some insights of Saint Alphonsus, then some conclusions.

2.1 Baptism and the "vows"

Baptismal consecration

There is a clear relationship between the sacraments of initiation (here grouped under "baptism") and religious consecration, insofar as the latter cannot be considered to be anything less than a full elaboration in a very radical manner of the former. Religious consecration (here indicated as "vows") is not extraneous to the baptismal commitment, but rather an essential consequence of it, although we are often unconscious of such a fundamental relationship.

In the first chapter of a book published more than thirty years ago, Father Häring speaks about the sacramental basis of the Christian life. The author bases his meditation on sacred Scripture, as well as on Justin and Cyril of Jerusalem. For some spiritual reason, virginity has been intimately linked with the Eucharist.[2] Several decades earlier in *L'Initiation Chrétienne*, a book which never grows old, Father Louis Vereecke offers a careful and detailed description of the rites of Christian initiation and their underlying theology as understood by the Fathers of the fourth century. Here can be found a valuable reference to a text that is crucial for the purposes of our essay.

Cyril of Jerusalem, in his *Mystagogical Catechesis*, explains the baptismal anointing by reference to the text of Isaiah 61:1. Some experts propose that it was Cyril who changed the place of this anointing from its original location before water-baptism to become a postbaptismal chrismation (the so-called confirmation). The motive behind the change was the parallel Cyril draws between the baptism of a Christian and that of Jesus: just as Jesus received the Holy Spirit as he came out of the water of the Jordan, so, too, the new Christian is anointed with the same Spirit after passing through the baptismal immersion.

Hence, speaking of holy chrism with reference to 1 John 2:20–28,

Cyril teaches:

> Now you were made Christ's by receiving the emblem [antitypos] of
> the Holy Ghost, and all things were in a figure [symbolically] wrought
> in you, because you are figures [icons] of Christ. He also bathed him-
> self in the river Jordan, and having imparted of the fragrance of his
> Godhead to the waters, he came up from them, and the Holy Ghost in
> substance lighted upon him, like resting upon like. In the same man-
> ner to you also, after you had come up from the pool of the sacred
> streams, was given the Unction, the emblem of that wherewith Christ
> was anointed, and this is the Holy Ghost, of whom also the blessed
> Isaiah, in his prophecy respecting him, says in the person of the Lord:
> the Spirit of the Lord is upon me, because he has anointed me, to
> preach glad tidings to the poor (61:1).[3]

In the same catechesis (III,7) Cyril also cites a passage from Isaiah
25:6 (LXX): "And on this mountain [=the Church], shall the Lord make
unto all people a feast, they shall drink wine, they shall drink gladness, they
shall be anointed with anointment." Cyril also applies a passage from the
Song of Songs to explain the meaning of the baptismal unction: "The soul
who had been a slave, now can call the Lord her bridegroom, and he, seeing
her sincerity, cries out 'you are beautiful, my beloved!'"

The following considerations flow from the catechesis of Cyril:

1. The baptism of Christ was itself a special consecration to a mission, that of preaching the good news to the poor (Isaiah 61). Such
   a broad statement should be modified with other factors: that his
   fundamental consecration had already occurred at the moment of
   the Incarnation as well as, in the thinking of Mark, the three greatest events in the life of Jesus—his baptism, transfiguration, and
   crucifixion—should be viewed as united as a single consecration
   in salvific action. On the other hand, Peter's speech in Acts leads
   us to consider this moment of anointing with the Spirit as the Father bestowing upon the Son his particular mission.
2. The baptism of Christians is a consecration along the same lines as
   the baptism of Christ. Theodore of Mopsuestia, for example, considers baptism as the moment when a Christian is consecrated to
   the life of Christ in the specific sense of Isaiah 61, that is, a dedication to a life of service. Thus the foundation and the heart of

Christian baptism is the baptism of Christ, reenacted and represented in the baptism of each believer.

3. At a third level we can speak of the vows as a completion of the baptismal consecration, again along the lines of Isaiah 61. That is, the vows of religious life are themselves a dedication of the whole person, all his being and will, to the service of Christ and his gospel.

Although this logic is quite clear and straightforward, there remain in fact many questions. From the standpoint of history, was there any connection in the first centuries of Christianity between baptism and some sort of "religious consecration"? Why had the connection between the consecration of baptism and that of religious life disappeared for centuries, to be reestablished only in the last decades through a "return to the sources" regarding the sacraments of initiation (Daniélou) and religious life (von Balthasar)?

Baptism as consecration (III-V centuries)

Faith and community: From the very beginning, the baptismal vows were seen as an expression of one's own belief, but never restricted to a personal relationship with God, but rather formulated as a commitment toward a community. The communal nature of the baptismal vows was a concern of the primitive Church, but has needed a continual emphasis in the history of asceticism. The Fathers of the fourth century insisted on the communitarian aspect of baptism and considered the enrollment of the catechumens to be in fact the beginning of the celebration of the sacrament. This inscription, which took place at the beginning of Lent, was the moment when the names of the candidates were solemnly enrolled in the book of life, making them citizens of heaven. The whole community was involved in the preparation of the candidates, particularly in their instruction and in their struggle against the treachery of the devil. Both the renunciation of Satan and the declaration for Christ are really an engagement of the candidate with the community, which itself communicates the God's consecration of the new Christian through water and oil, bread and wine. The communal nature of the baptismal vows should never be overlooked. The candidate entrusts to the community his faith and the community commits itself to care for this treasure, holding him to its bosom as a loving mother.

Death and resurrection: Here is another profound dimension of the baptismal mystery. The exegetes of the Antiochene School, especially Cyril of Jerusalem, refer to the famous text of Romans 6 to explain the redeeming dimension of baptism as a sharing in the death and resurrection of Christ. In later texts, such as Maximus the Confessor, this theme undergoes a further development, connecting the participation in the death of Christ with the remission of sins and the sharing in his resurrection, with new life as sons of God. These ideas received masterful treatment by Father F. X. Durrwell's *In the Redeeming Christ,* where he also connects the Christian vows of obedience and virginity as coherent with the redeeming action of Christ in baptism. It is a grand theological vision of Christian existence:

> Christ consecrated himself to God in immolation. He vowed himself to God by total renunciation of himself. He dedicated himself to God, in his death to himself and in the life-giving holiness of the Father. Christians, at baptism, unite themselves to Christ, and become one body with him (Galatians 3:27) and participate in his death and resurrection (Colossians 2:12) (p. 12). When the Church sanctifies herself in her individual members, she is, in her turn, cooperating in the redemption of the world....She becomes Christ's body, and the death and resurrection in which she dies and rises are his. Redemption is accepting in total submission, God's saving justice, submitting our will to His. In Christ we have been baptized, in him we are placed forever, transformed into him in participation in his death and resurrection....It is in his death of obedience that we are baptized and that we live (Galatians 2:19). The resurrection consecrates his obedience: it is God's total possession of this man who has handed himself over in order that God's glory may reign within him. Obedience is the supreme law of Christian life, the life of the Spirit. Baptism also calls to virginity. Man is wholly baptized, body and soul; in principle he is wholly dead with Christ. There are Christians who determine to live according to that principle, they renounce the flesh and its laws. Because they are baptized, they wish to be virgins. They attach themselves to the reality revealed in the risen Christ.[4]

In the Spirit: Many books have been written on the theology of baptism. The author just cited has also described the role of the Holy Spirit in the life of Christ and that of Christians. It would be helpful here to recall Isaiah 61:1 as the fundamental text that connects the baptismal vows with both the consecration of Christ and the prophetic vocation described in the Old Testament.

A vow is not a static promise, made once and good forever. As we see in the life of Jeremiah, a vow is a continuous call, to be answered day by day—a divine mission, even when, humanly speaking, it is unpleasant and difficult.

Already in the third century, Ireneus of Lyon calls attention to the role of the Holy Spirit at work at the very dawn of salvation history, then in the life of Christ himself. Because of the fullness of his own consecration, Christ can communicate this same gift to his Church by means of baptism, when the Spirit begins the restoration of human beings, to be completed in the Parousia. Theodore of Mopsuestia considers the Holy Spirit as the hidden power and strength of the sacraments, at once linking them with the past and preparing them for their future plenitude. The Spirit is the fundament of the renewal of the divine image in man, as well as the pledge of its completion in the resurrection. It is the Spirit who makes the baptismal vows blossom and flourish.

The understanding of the baptismal commitment in Mesopotamia

Baptism and the Bridegroom: By the testimony of their very lives, the martyrs of the first centuries are the witnesses par excellence of the baptismal commitment. The *Acts of the Mesopotamian Martyrs* is a unique declaration of this sense. However, there are other texts from the third century, such as *The Acts of Thomas, The Acts of John, The Odes of Solomon*, that develop the special character of the baptism pledge. Here we find a parallel drawn between baptism and the vow of chastity, the former consecrating the believer in a special way to the Bridegroom, Jesus. The is a scholarly dispute regarding the origin of particular asceticism of the Old Syrian Church with Judaism, Manicheism, or Gnosticism proposed as possible sources. This theme is present throughout *The Acts of Thomas*. The life of the apostle Thomas, his preaching and teaching in India, demonstrate the virginal life is a direct consequence of the baptismal commitment. The long consecratory epiklesis over the oil, water, bread, and wine illustrates that baptism touches the believer, who receives Jesus as the "Lover of the Soul" and who continues to be attracted by him, so that the soul is elevated to a unique status which enables the beloved to enter into a spousal relationship with its Bridegroom and accompany him into the nuptial chamber, the kingdom of God. This spousal relationship seems to be at the very heart of the preaching of Thomas and in his doctrine, the final aim of baptism.

In five different examples *The Acts of Thomas* offers a detailed explanation of baptism that also includes the postbaptismal renunciation of all sexual activity by the new Christian in favor of an exclusive love for Christ, the Bridegroom, including the example of the just-married prince who opts for celibacy in the wake of his baptism. Here Christianity appears essentially as a loving relationship with Jesus, one so demanding that the baptismal vows not only include the renunciation of Satan but also invite the Christian to go further by giving up all natural, carnal relations in favor of an exclusive love for the Bridegroom, who alone is capable of fulfilling his deepest yearning. Although this form of ancient Syrian Christianity has evolved and been assimilated into the mainline Church, its values remain in the most fundamental expression of this Semitic Christian community.

Before touching on other areas, one could refer to the beautiful book of Saint Alphonsus, *The Spouse of Christ*. In the first chapter, he understands the whole of religious life as a loving engagement and spousal relationship with Christ. Only a reference to baptism is lacking. However, in the *Baptismal Catecheses* of the Fathers of the fourth century, one finds numerous references to *The Song of Songs* as a admirable type of the mystery of baptism. In line with this thinking, it may be said the original conception of baptism as a loving relationship with Christ would later influence and inspire the monastic movement toward a similar self-understanding as a spousal consecration. Traces of such a connection between baptism and monasticism can be found in the writings of the Syrian mystics of the fifth century.

Virgins and the local Church: In the writings of two Fathers of the fourth century, Aphrahat the Persian Sage and Ephrem of Nisibis (as well as in other sources dating from the third through the eighth centuries), there is made frequent mention of a special class of Christians. These are the "sons and daughters of the Covenant" or the "covenanters," laypeople living and working in society at large, but who dedicate a significant portion of their time to service in the local Church, especially in liturgical roles. What immediately identifies them is their vow of virginity. Ephrem, for one, always refers to them as the "Virgins," men and women, either single ("dedicated to the Only-One") or even married, but living celibately ("consecrated to the Holy One"). The precise nature of this group is unclear and could have changed over the course of time. But these exist as an identifiable group in the "church-orders," distinct from the monk and from the ordinary laity, as well as from the sacred orders (bishops, priests, and deacons), although some of them seem to be drawn from the ranks of the "covenanters." Their name and origins are still matters of discussion, but it seems to me that the original Syrian enthusiasm around baptism, envisioning a consecration to Jesus of the total person—body and soul—was kept alive in this group, of whom Ephrem speaks with the greatest respect, considering them to be Christians par excellence.

An example from Aphrahat the Persian Sage might further clarify the preceding thoughts. I refer to his *Tracts*, or *Exhortations*, addressed to the "covenanters" around the year 340. Drawing on examples from the Old Testament, Deuteronomy 20:1–9 and the Gideon story, Judges 7:4–8, both militant appeals and the latter, the account of a dramatic use of water to select warriors, the candidates are queried about their willingness to consecrate themselves in a most radical way to the Bridegroom and to spiritual warfare for the sake of his kingdom, including strict virginity. Here is a portion of this ancient Syrian formula:

> Therefore it is right that the trumpeters, the heralds of the Church [i.e., the priest] should call and exhort the whole Covenant of God [the Church] before baptism, those who have offered themselves for virginity and consecration [continence in marriage], young men and virgins and consecrated ones. The heralds are to exhort them and say:
>
> Whoever has set his heart on the project of *marriage*, let him marry before baptism, lest he fall in the contest and be killed.
>
> And whoever fears this choice of battle, let him turn back, lest he break the spirit of his brethren with his own.
>
> And whosoever loves *possessions*, let him turn back from war service, lest when battle overpowers him he remember his possessions and turn back to them.
>
> Whoever turns back from the contest is disgraced.
>
> Whoever did not offer himself or put on arms is not reproached if he turns back; but whoever did *offer himself* and put on arms, if he turns back from the contest, is disgraced.
>
> For the battle a man must strip himself, so as to remember nothing of what is behind him and return to it.

It is not possible here to make a more detailed analysis of the passage. Let us turn instead to Ephrem of Nisbis, writing some twenty years later. In his *Hymns* he also connects the baptismal commitment with the vow of virginity. Like Aphrahat, Ephrem calls these virgins by a particular name:

the "single-ones" (*monachoi* in Greek), covenanters who have dedicated themselves in marriage to the Only-One, the Unique (only) Son. Here are some passages from the *Hymns on Epiphany*:

> By his wine, the betrothed became married (John 2:1)
> By his [baptismal] oil, the married became holy [living in
>   continence]
> At his wine, the marriage
> Through his oil, the chastity [abstinence] (3:22).

> Look, our priest is like a fisherman,
> Although he stands at a small water,
> he gets out of it a great catch, of all kinds and sizes.
> He gets a catch, which is offered to the heavenly King.
> Simon caught the fishes which were brought on land (John 21)
> to be presented to Our Lord.
> Our priests catch from the water [of baptism]
> —through the imposition [of hands] from Simon—
> Virgins and Chaste, who are offered to the Lord of the Feast
>   on the Feast (7:26–27).

> See, Our Lord's sword is in the waters,
>   which divides sons and fathers;
> for it is a living sword which makes division
>   of the living among the dead.
> See, [men] being baptized and becoming Virgins
>   and consecrated ones,
> having gone down, been baptized and
>   put on that single "Only-One" (8:16).

> For whoever is baptized and puts on the Only-One,
>   the Lord of the many
> occupies the place of the many,
>   for Christ becomes his great treasure (8:7).

> In the garden was the Bridal-Chamber prepared,
> but the Serpent destroyed it.
> Instead, baptism is given to the children of the Light
> in order that the fair ones find consolation (12:4).

[You] baptized, who have found the Kingdom
    in the womb of baptism,
Come down, put on the Only-One,
    who is the Lord of the Kingdom.
Blessed are you who are crowned (13:14).

Clearly, such radical demands could not be asked of all believers in the Church of the fourth century, but in the Syrian atmosphere, at least, the spiritual ideal was for a time embodied in a temporal commitment. Even in the *Testatum Domini* of the late fifth century it is said: "If anyone wishes to make a promise of virginity, first let him be baptized by the bishop." Regarding such bridal consecration of the individual to his Beloved, it might also be observed that this attitude carries certain spiritual dangers, if it is exaggerated or unconnected to an ecclesial understanding of the whole Church as being espoused to the same unique Bridegroom. This history of the Syrian Churches has betrayed this weakness several times.

Baptism in the Spirit: Through the pen of Aphrahat, the ancient Syrian tradition speaks in a unique way about the Holy Spirit, as if this Spirit of God, received at baptism, comes to dwell in a material or sensible way in man as in a temple, and who departs from the baptized who sin gravely. He also has a particular role as the one who would intercede before God on behalf of the resurrection of the body, since he was intermingled with its soul. Continuing this line of thought, Ephrem makes references to the Gospels (Luke 3:16) and closely connects "fire" and "spirit":

You [John the Baptist] have baptized the Baptizer,
he who baptizes the nations,
with a flood of fire and the Holy Spirit.

In fire is the symbol of the Spirit,
    it is a type of the Holy Spirit
who is mixed in the baptismal water,
    so that it may be for absolution,
and in the bread, that it may be an offering.

In your bread there is hidden the Spirit who is not consumed,
in your wine there dwells the Fire that is not drunk;
the Spirit is in your bread, the Fire is in your wine,
manifest wonder, which our lips have received.

When the Lord came down to earth to mortal men,
he created them again in a new creation, like angels,
so that in a hidden manner they might be of Fire and Spirit.

See: Fire and Spirit are in the womb of her who bore you.
See: Fire and Spirit in the river where you were baptized.
See: Fire and Spirit in our own baptism.
In the bread and the cup, Fire and Holy Spirit.

The consecration of the oil, water, bread, and wine is understood literally as a sort of incarnation by the "Fire and the Holy Spirit," in order that they might communicate to the believer in an almost material sense this same material reality. Hence, mortal man becomes filled, or in Ephrem's terminology, "mixed" with this fiery Spirit. This Spirit inspires the baptized and converting him into a spiritual being, "like the angels." The Spirit clothes him with the same garments of glory that were shed by Adam, in order to prepare him for the Bridegroom. The Spirit is the fire of love present at the nuptial feast that is baptism.

Let us list in summary fashion the most important ideas indicated so far:

1. Baptism signifies and actually contains a commitment that is brought about by the *consecration* of the Christian to his crucified and risen Lord (*adhesion Christi*). But in the Old Syrian communities there existed a direct relationship between baptism and virginity, the latter being a condition for receiving the former. Virginity is understood not only in a negative sense, as total abstinence, but rather (and above all) as absolute and total dedication and consecration of the believer, body and soul, his goods and his will, to his heavenly Bridegroom. In this positive sense, virginity is a loving commitment which involves the whole person, as a condition and consequence of baptism, and is possible because of the action of the Holy Spirit, who becomes "mixed" with the human at baptism.

2. For both the Greek and Latin Fathers of the Church, the baptismal commitment is an ecclesial event, the insertion of the believer into a community with mutual rights and responsibilities. Without this loving community as its ground and atmosphere, a personal decision would remain futile.

3. The inspiration and energy that empowers the personal commitment and constitutes the community as fertile ground in which to live such a decision, is the Fire and the Spirit, who first mixed with Jesus at his incarnation and baptism. He is able thus to communicate the Spirit to the Church through the mysteries of the cross, resurrection, ascension, and Pentecost. Now the Spirit mixes with the matter of the sacraments and, by means of them, with the hearts of the members. Thus the Spirit of God's love consecrates the believers to preach the Good News of redemption to the poor (Isaiah 61).

2.2 Vows and baptism

The bishops and the monastic movement

The monastic life gradually assumed a variety of forms: from the hermetic and cenobitic life in Egypt and Syria to the charismatic lay movements in Cappadocia and Mesopotamia. It would be interesting to examine the relationship of these movements to the local Church, since there were always "lay-monks" who were integrated into the indigenous ecclesial communities. Monasticism as such is mainly a question of discipleship, the following of Christ in a unique, evangelical manner. The emphasis in the fifth century was placed squarely on the community; for an explicitly juridical understanding of the vows one must wait until the tenth or even the thirteenth centuries.

As is the case in the previous treatment of baptism, it is impossible here to enter into a detailed study of the history and theology of the monastic movement. We will be content with touching upon a few and perhaps often overlooked elements in connection with our subject.

After his baptism, Basil, like Augustine, began to live the more radical demands of the Christian life in the company of a group of his friends. After becoming the bishop of Caesarea, he incorporated these "monks" into the service of that local Church toward the sick, poor, and needy. Like Augustine, he also composed a *Rule* for these laymen who desired to dedicate themselves in a special way to Christ and his flock. This *Rule* had a singular impact upon the monastic movement and religious life in general throughout history until the present day. It is worth remembering that the first enthusiastic movements of laity, like the one led by Eustathius of

Sebaste, were later integrated by Basil of Caesarea into the context of the local Church. In fact, the major portion of his *Rule* speaks to the questions posed by believers regarding the Gospel and how to live it in response to their baptism.

The original description of the life of the primitive Church in Acts of the Apostles 2–5 was accepted by Augustine, himself a man who could not live without friends. He bases community life on the same essential elements: the teaching and witness of the apostles, the union of heart and mind, the sharing of material goods, prayer and the breaking of bread, and healing. Taken together, these elements show us the face of Jesus himself: the prophet-teacher, the healer-redeemer, the revelation of the Father's love for the suffering and poor (the sharing of goods), praying and combating evil. The community is the actual continuation of the same Jesus in the world. His Spirit makes this possible and baptism is the seal of a corporate commitment. To become a disciple of Christ is to be integrated into the community which continues his mission and, as such, to reveal the Master. In the first chapter of his *Rule*, Augustine insists on the centrality of love, the most basic requirement for community life. Like Basil, Augustine started a community after his baptism at Milan and later sought to integrate his communities into the local Church of Hippo.

The second baptism

The spiritual writings of the Syrian and Greek monks occasionally mentions a second baptism. In his *Hymns on the Nativity* Ephrem of Nisibis, for example, following the line of Jesus' words to Nicodemus, has Our Lady singing about her relationship with her Son. Mary sings that the One who was born from her, also gave her birth. Her birth from Jesus was brought about by a sort of baptism from him. Here Ephrem might be referring to the Holy Spirit, who came to Mary at the Annunciation, but in the context of his other hymns, it is more likely that he is referring to the Christian life of Mary, who, by following and imitating Jesus to such an extent that she underwent a second birth to real discipleship, became herself a living image of Jesus.

John of Apamea, a Syrian spiritual writer of the fifth century, mentions that the visible baptism is not enough for the monks, who need to undergo an invisible baptism which enables them to reach the vision of God. By this "second baptism" he is referring to the monastic life of abnegation and union. In time, and especially in the movement of the Messiahlians, this second spiritual baptism becomes all-important, achieving its prominence at the expense of the sacrament. The latter was considered as less important and less necessary than the baptism of the Spirit which opened the monk to the freedom of the itinerant ascetical life.

Bishop Philoxenus of Mabbug (+523) wrote a series of *Homilies* or *Discourses* for the hermits and monks, including the laity in the audience, in which he traces the foundations for the truly Christian life. In the ninth Homily he avers:

> You have two baptisms: one of grace, which takes place in the baptismal water, the other of your own will, when you are baptized out of the world into the love of God.
>
> It appears that the man of God experiences three births: the first from the womb into creation, the second, from slavery into freedom, from being a man to becoming a son of God, something that takes place by grace at baptism, while the third birth is when a person is reborn of his own will from a corporal way of life to a spiritual one, and he himself becomes a womb which gives birth to complete self-emptying.
>
> The person of the Spirit cannot come to full perfection, to the full stature of humanity, as long as that person remains in the world, as in a womb. One must be born again, leaving the world as completely as the fetus leaves the womb. Then, the newborn receives a fresh growth which will bring him to spiritual perfection.

Similar expressions can be found in many spiritual authors, who describe the religious life as a particular ascent to union with God. In a large way, this line of thinking can be traced to Evagrius, who in turn adopted the portrait of the Christian life in the writings of Origen to the specific vocation of religious life. For our purposes, it is sufficient to indicate the important link between Origen, who wrote for Christians in general, and the adaptation made by Evagrius for monks in particular. It may be true that Origen made a distinction between a literal and a spiritual understanding of Scripture and recognized several different grades in the Christian life, but without completely separating the spirit from the letter. So the same spiritual principles that were later applied to monks, effectively setting them apart from the faithful in general, were, in their most primitive form, connected with Christian baptism.

The present doctrine of the Church

Official documents: In the wake of *Lumen Gentium* and *Perfectae Caritatis*, both the popes and the Sacred Congregation for the Religious and Secular Institutes have published several other letters, developing the basic teaching of the Council (1966–1971) and adapting them to the changed circumstances of the modern world (1978–1980). In the encyclical *Redemptionis Donum* (n. 7), there is an important declaration regarding the nature of religious consecration. Here his consecration is considered as a covenant of love between God and man, a surrender to the Father in Christ by the power of the Spirit. In other words, religious consecration is a further development of the attachment to Christ which began in baptism. It is God who initiates the covenant, inviting a person or a group into a mutual relationship in which the person accepts the special demands of the covenant and the mission enclosed within it. The covenant is God consecrating a person to himself; the response of the one consecrated is always secondary to the divine initiative.

Jesus himself is consecrated to the Father through his incarnation, baptism, passion, and resurrection. He consecrates to his Father his body, the believing community. Because of his baptism, each Christian shares in this consecration. Within the general consecration or vocation enjoyed by all believers, there are particular forms of the Christian life for the service of the Church which we call the religious life.

These documents attempt to avoid dividing the Christian community into two separate groups, insisting that the "deeper" consecration of religious is nothing else than an ecclesial service that is rooted in the original consecration of baptism and thus in the same dynamism of the Christian life. "Because they put their whole life at his serve, this forms a special consecration, which is rooted deeply in the baptism consecration, and brings it to fuller development" (*Perfectae Caritatis*, n. 5). God calls a person and consecrates him to the service to his kingdom. The baptized who accepts this invitation, dedicates (consecrates) himself in a strikingly new way, giving himself to the service of the Church by means of the total and public gift of self in the three vows offered within a specific institute, itself committed to a life that is marked by prayer, the common life, and mission.

It seems that the official documents of the Church generally struggle to avoid the traditional division between "ordinary" Christians and religious because of the special consecration of the latter. However, there remains in some texts a certain ambiguity, as if religious consecration was qualitatively distinct from that of baptism.

Theological investigation: Ever since the Reformation, the vows have been criticized and attacked. Today, both the shrinking of many institutes as well as advances in exegetical, anthropological, and historical studies have led to an attempt to view the vows in a different light than the tradition of the last centuries. One could cite several different theologians as representative of this scholarly trend, among whom is a professor of New Testament theology, Teodoro Matura, OFM, the author of several books treating evangelical radicalism and religious. The radical demands of religious life must be understood in the wider context of the salvific message of the Gospel, which proposes Christian perfection at its very core. The fundamental requirements of discipleship call for the following after and imitation of Jesus: "Whoever wishes to save his life will lose it, but whoever loses his life for my sake and that of the Gospel will save it" (Mark 8:35). Accepting these radical demands presumes a personal relationship with the Lord and is expressed in a tender and patient love toward one's neighbor, even love for one's enemies. It leads toward the common life, the sharing of one's possessions with the poor, freely chosen celibacy—all without any trace of pretension. Some of the demands are in fact interior attitudes; other concerns embrace the material world. The radical demands of the Gospel are open and unlimited, inviting everyone to conversion that would have one forget oneself and follow Jesus.

Most of the founders of religious institutes found their inspiration in these radical demands of the Gospel. They considered religious life as the unqualified acceptance of the requirements of the Gospel and as the full realization of the Christian life. Their followers try to live without compromise to the whole Gospel, the ideal of all Christians, by listening to the Word of God in union with Christ, by prayer and celebration, and by constructing a community that has its own mission and particular form of witness. Whatever its concrete form, religious life always presumes four elements: an obedient listening to the Word of God and the central place of the Gospel as a message of salvation, the imitation of Christ that is based on a personal relationship with him, integration into a community that is ruled by unity and service where goods are shared in common and celibacy is an element for the building up of the community, and finally, the particular witness of the vowed community. Thus consecrated religious are believers who try to live the consecration of their baptism by accepting the demands of the Gospel in all their radicalism and vigor.

3. Conclusion

This essay has attempted to present religious life as a response to God's call, based in the demands of the Gospel and first accepted in the baptismal commitment. Three perspectives of this position should be highlighted: the baptismal consecration, the community, and the Holy Spirit, three realities that are often forgotten in our Congregation.

Consecration: From what has been said, it should be clear that the baptismal consecration is fundament, not only for the Christian life in general, but for the religious vocation in particular. This basic fact is not usually part of everyday life, so a baptized child grows up unaware of this reality and only by religious formation will become conscious of his vocation and choose to be a committed disciple. Are religious in fact any better off?

First and foremost, the baptismal consecration signifies redemption. The fullness of God touches the believer through Jesus Christ in the power of the Spirit. Henceforward a relationship of love—a covenant—exists between God and the believer. When we are addressed here as "Redemptorists," we become uneasy and would prefer a slightly different pronunciation of our name which conveys the sense of "redeemed," a much more acceptable concept in an Arabic environment. How can one be a Redemptorist without being redeemed himself? Humanly speaking, being consecrated means entering the freedom of the Gospel, surrendering to God's love with the totality of one's being. This relationship of love is always radical and the fundamental demands of the Gospel can never be forgotten. Here, too, the Redemptorist hears the word of the Catechesis of Saint Cyril: "I anointed [consecrated] you with the Spirit to announce the good news to the poor," words that are intimately connected with the baptismal consecration itself. To be a Redemptorist is to fully live this reality.

Furthermore, it may be suggested that the future of Redemptorists will not be found in repeated adaptation of the Rule and philosophy of the Institute, but rather in a completely new understanding of both. The Redemptorist of the future should be first a lay-Redemptorist, a believer who strives to live his baptismal consecration according to the fundamental criteria of redemption itself. Together with his teachers, such a Redemptorist is challenged to discover what redemption means, as he preserves and deepens his consecration in the context of our Institute where, hopefully, the vows and rules help this consecration to flourish fully.

Our mission preaching remained as a great work as long as it expressed this consecration. It was undoubtedly this spirit that moved Saint Alphonsus toward the poor and inspired his evangelization of them. But when his disciples became known as preachers of hellfire and damnation, the message became one of hard words, memorized and delivered by rote, rooted in pretension and personal ambition rather than in the heart of the preacher. The absence of a personal experience of baptismal consecration and redemption rendered the content empty and the mission void.

Community: As indicated above, the baptismal commitment is intimately linked with a community. Just as the commitment is put into the care of the community and at the service of it, so, too, the totality consecration itself can only be understood with reference to a community. The consecration of Redemptorists should follow the same pattern. One could distinguish two levels of community. Redemptorists are first committed to the Church, here understood as the local Church with all that implies. The second level of commitment is to the specific Redemptorist community. This raises many questions. To highlight only one, we must ask what is the relationship between the diocesan and religious clergy, between a religious community and a local church?

It is clear that the Redemptorists are challenged to rethink their relationship with local churches. But let us consider the Redemptorist community as such. Can it be considered to be a truly evangelical community? How does it measure against the criteria found in the Acts of the Apostles? Is community life truly a priority for the confreres and are they in fact prepared to live it? Like so many other founders, Saint Alphonsus was made to suffer by both his particular group as well as by the larger community of the Church. When he states in his Rule that his Congregation is a community of priests dedicated to the salvation of the poor, it may be that, like so many foundations of his century, he gives too much importance to the "mission." As a matter of fact, the attention of his followers was directed toward and absorbed by the "work," sometimes understood as the particular projects of individuals. Although the community was completely at the service of the "work," the community was made up of individual workers, not a living Christian community which witnessed to the world the love and mutual respect. So, once the "mission," that is, the "work," lost its importance, the communities crumbled and disappeared as well.

A final observation about the challenge of the community to be truly evangelical: it should be characterized by "one heart," by its concern for the weaker members, by an absence of suffocating regulations or tyranni-cal, aged superiors. Those who would be great must be at the service of the rest. One of our respected and honored seminary professors, on the occa-sion of his sixtieth year as a Redemptorist, produced a card with his picture and the inscription: *Sixty Years Outside the Convent*. Perhaps like many others, he felt that the truly evangelical life was absent, even impossible to live, in some of our communities.

The Holy Spirit: Isaiah 61 remains as the basic text that describes the con-secration of Redemptorists. The Spirit, first received at baptism, conse-crates us in a particular way for the evangelical mission. But mission here is an expression and consequence of the fullness of the Spirit's presence, the Spirit of the Pentecost community—the Church born from the pierced heart of its crucified Lord—which draws the same water of mercy from each believer (John 7:35). Without the Spirit, there is no life for the mission and no love for the community. Together with Saint Ephrem, we could af-firm: the same Fire and Spirit which burns in the water of baptism and which consecrates the bread of the Eucharist, that same Spirit throbs in the community. There can be no Redemptorist mission or community, if this redeeming Spirit is absent from its inner life.

In concluding this brief essay on the sacraments of initiation and reli-gious consecration, it would be helpful to remember that consecration con-notes an alliance of love, a community with the Father, the Son, and the Holy Spirit. Like the invitation of Roublov's icon, the consecration of reli-gious life beckons us to share in a continuing celebration of our redemption through prayer and building a community that will accomplish its evan-gelical mission. It is nothing less than the radical baptismal consecration finding natural expression in the vows and bringing fullness of life: *Copiosa apud eum Redemptio.*

Notes

1. In recent years there have been aspirants to the Congregation in both Iraq and Lebanon, but because of a lack of formative structures, these have gone on to other religious communities (Dominicans and Carmelites). At the end of 1995, two young priests, an Iraqui and a Lebanese, are making their novitiate. [Editor's note.]
2. B. Häring, *A Sacramental Spirituality* (New York: 1965), pp. 165–181.
3. Cyril de Jérusalem, *Catéchèses mystagogiques*, (Sources chrétiennes 126), III, 1.
4. F. X. Durrwell, *In the Redeeming Christ: Towards a Theology of Spirituality* (New York: 1963), pp. 4,12,13,27,162,171.

8

THE CONSTITUTIONS:
A BOOK OF LIFE

Santino Raponi, C.Ss.R.
Province of Rome
Translated by William Bueche, C.Ss.R.
Province of Denver

I HAVE BEEN ASKED to present some reflections on our Constitutions as a book of life. The theme seems a rather arduous one. To tie together life with books, spirit with letter, is an extremely delicate task, but I'll try to do my best. I was also asked to give a brief profile of my vocation as a Redemptorist. The two requests go practically hand in hand. I'll begin with the latter.

1. Why I Am a Redemptorist

I would like to retrace the steps that brought me knocking on the door of the Fathers in Scifelli; that is, to return in search of the first footprints, or might one say, the prehistory of my vocation. I must say right away, and not without some embarrassment, that this is the first time I have faced this question, at least posed in such a direct and explicit way. In reality, I found myself in the "boarding school" at Scifelli without ever having questioned myself specifically why or how. In this regard, a poem comes to mind—a poem by Enrico Panzacchi, which I learned by memory some years later while still at Scifelli. *(Come nasce una strada, How a Street is Born:* Panzacchi 1840–1904). In this poem, Panzacchi describes the almost imperceptible way in which a path finds its beginning: from the first faint trails and elusive tracks, to the outline and contours, ever more marked and distinct which, little by little, transform themselves into a real honest-to-goodness road. I have never again read that poem, nor do I remember even one verse by heart. Yet, over the years, that title has come to mind many times—so much so, that it has almost become a key to my life. When faced with the task of writing this autobiographical sketch, I returned to the library of my youth in search of the anthology that contained the poem, but I never found it.

Why did I become a Redemptorist? It's difficult to recapture the first steps along that road. The "how" of my vocation seems rather vague to me. It's true, in my earliest years I could listen to "the preachers of Scifelli" (as they were called in those parts). They came for the village feast days (Chiamari did not yet have a parish, but only a chapel) and were greatly appreciated. A picture remains clearly in my mind of a priest gesturing and preaching with great animation. Later, I came to know that priest—Father Mezzanotte—who had been a lieutenant in the First World War and a prisoner of war. He became a Redemptorist through Father Francesco Pitocchi, was an author of memoirs and novels, and my future professor of Italian literature in the seminary at Cortona. Was this a first step?

On October 25, 1931, a cousin of mine, Father Peppino, was ordained a Redemptorist priest at Cortona. I remember, even if only vaguely, Uncle Enrico and Aunt Colomba preparing to attend the ordination. I remember that event even more because my father, Angelo, accompanied his brother and sister-in-law. When they returned to Zampone (as my district was called), they were filled with stories to tell. Another step?

At the end of June 1932, I finished fifth grade elementary school with good grades. Alfred Schimperna, my teacher throughout those five years, told my father to let me continue to study. In those days, practically speaking only the children of nobility could continue their studies, even if they were less gifted than the children of peasant farmers. (I remember the son of Count Lucernari, who was my age. He had his own separate little table, all to himself. So we called him "the little lord." Talk about privilege!) Barred from the school for the elite (mandatory middle school would arrive only thirty years later), parents in those days aimed toward the schools of the religious orders where the burden, while still heavy for the pockets of the poor farmers, was less costly than that which the nobility provided for themselves. Continue studying? But…where? But…how? Meanwhile, Padre Peppino was transferred from Cortona and assigned to lecture in the boarding school in Scifelli. By chance he also showed up in Zampone. Another step?

The fact is that one day I said to my father that I wanted "to go to

Scifelli." At that time the expression itself said it all: to go to study and to become a priest. From all outward appearances, my father was not against it. The advice of my teacher, Schimperna, must have been of some help. But my mother, Grazia, was unhappy—not because she was against my continuing my studies, but because she couldn't accept my becoming a priest. My mother (may she be blessed) was very fond of me. I was the first of six children (two more would be added after my departure for a total of eight). Naturally, I had also begun to be an economic help to the family. However, the real reason for my mother's pain was in losing me. At times, during those months of research and preparation (between August and November), I came upon her unexpectedly and found her crying. I understood why. But I was determined to "go to Scifelli." I arrived there on December 8, 1932, already late for the school year which had begun October 1. For some time I did make-up classes with Father Peppino, until I was back on track with the other students.

One episode somewhere between serious and facetious, Cataldo ("Catalleglie Moro") brought me to Scifelli in a little carriage pulled by a mare somewhat advanced in age. A few days after returning home, the old mare died. A portent difficult to interpret! Cataldo always reminds me of it—happy anyway to have "brought Santino to Scifelli to become a priest."

I went back home only after five years, and then only for a few hours—just long enough to greet my family before departing for the novitiate at Ciorani. Zampone is only about ten kilometers from Scifelli, yet for five years I was not allowed to return to my family. However, they came to visit me once in a while. That's how the world was in those days!

Receiving the habit (September 19, 1937) and first profession (September 29, 1938) etched the contours of the "road" still more distinctly. My seven years at Cortona (1938–1945: high school, philosophy, and theology), together with experiencing the war years, brought a deeper understanding of my vocation and a definitive choice of my "road." Taken as a whole, the years in Cortona were very good ones, and even exhilarating at times. Certainly poverty of the war left its mark on me. Nonetheless, in regard to my physical health, I came though it fine, and spiritually, they were years of great fervor. Among the spiritual books recommended by Luigi Vori, an ascetic of the first order, were Desurmont and Colin—which says everything. During that whole period from novitiate to ordination (March 17, 1945), I don't remember having second thoughts, at least none of any consequence.

Judging me capable of further study and with a view to eventually teaching in the studendate, my superiors sent me to the Collegio Maggiore in Rome. After obtaining a license in theology at the Angelicum (1948), I went on to the Biblical Institute for three years (1948–1951). A crowning point was the trip I took during the summer of 1951, spending over two months in the countries of the Bible—Egypt, Lebanon, Syria, Jordan, Israel, Cyprus and Greece—lodging in the houses of the Franciscans of the Holy Land together with other companions from the Biblicum, all Cappuchins (two Spaniards, a Brasilian, an Argentine: a very enjoyable crowd!).

In October 1951, I began fifteen years of teaching Scripture (and similar material) in the studendate at Cortona to satisfied students. In the 1960s, named prefect of students and assisted in the teaching of Scripture by Father Giacomo Spagnolo (fresh out of the Biblical Institute), I took on the teaching of patrology, a subject very dear to me. In 1965, I sought a diploma in liturgy in order to qualify for teaching this subject newly raised, according to the prescription of the Council, to the level of those materials fundamental to priestly formation.

I was occupied with teaching patristic moral theology in the Accademia Alfonsiana (1971–1995), and patristic anthropology in the Teresianum (1981–1995). In 1995, I reached the age of mandatory retirement and ended my teaching in both institutes.

Let's go back a bit. Named a "vocal" in the special Chapter of 1967, I was elected consultor general. Later, I was nominated, by the new government of Father Amaral, as president of the Commission for the Redaction of the new legislative texts mandated by the Chapter. Thus we arrive at the Constitutions, precisely upon which I have been asked to reflect as a "book of life." I will try to develop the subject in stages.

2. The Constitutions as a Book of Life

2.1 To the origins of the text

Often it's heard from the mouths of the confreres that it was Father Raponi who "did the Constitutions." I believe it opportune to begin with a clarification, and if such is the case, a correction. I have partly done so in my *Comment on the Constitutions* (p. VI–VII), but it's worth repeating.

The present Constitutions are based upon the contribution of Fathers

Hitz and Durrwell, two theologians already well-renowned at the time of the preparation of the Chapter (cf. the meetings of Delémont). The influence of Father Durrwell unfolded principally in the draft of the Ends (Goals). The traces of his work are barely perceptible in the definitive version of the text. The line pursued by Durrwell was replaced by that of Hitz, because it seemed to the capitulars to be more dynamic and missionary. Clearly, it was not a divergence of the two lines of thought, but rather diverse emphases. The Hitz plan, based on the "mission of Christ," is very visible in the first three chapters of the Constitutions as they now stand.

While asserting that Hitz's line of thinking runs like a central thread throughout the new legislation, one should not dismiss the relevant contributions of other capitulars, much less that of the Chapter itself. It is worth noting that my specific biblical formation, as well as liturgical and patristic studies, led me already in the prechapter meetings to embrace almost by instinct Hitz's approach: the approach actually taken in the *"Textus Italicus"* (TI) which I drafted on behalf of the "Italian group" at the start of the first working sessions.

I should also specify that in the succeeding reactions of the texts, my contribution was not limited to transcribing the thoughts of others, even though I was in full agreement, but consisted in the actual editing, that is, drafting and proofing, as well as eventually giving added depth to the themes—above all, for references to biblical fonts or texts regarding our beginnings. In my *Comment*, I justify, step by step these integrated elements.

2.2 Law and Gospel

In speaking of my formation years at Cortona above, I recalled Father Colin, a name connected with rather famous titles: *Culto della regola, Culto dei voti*, and similar works. For nearly three decades these books were bestsellers in the ambient of religious institutes, male and female, in both the active and contemplative life. They were characterized by the prevalently ascetic-voluntaristic model as a function of "regular observance" and the detailed examination of conscience. They entered into crisis with the progressive appearance of a more biblical, liturgical, and sacramental spirituality favored by and then carried forward by Vatican II. It was intended that our Constitutions be inserted into this new theological-spiritual (and milder) climate in which the law manifested itself as a "light burden" when intimately joined to the Gospel. With this basic conviction as our point of departure, the question became: What does a legislative code represent for those who embrace it? The answer can be given on three levels: objective, subjective, and cognitive.

2.2.1 On the objective level

The Constitutions can be defined as a more acute awareness of the Gospel, or as a rereading of the Gospel in light of the present-day reality of an institute—a code, therefore, which is able to bring about a renewal of life. In other words, the Constitutions should spur the members of an institute to a more marked "following of Christ" with respect to the "following" which is already inherent in baptism. Just as baptism implies a fundamental option, so also religious profession as reflected in the Constitutions implies a continual conversion (cf. Constitution 41,1). It implies a process directed toward the interiorization of the Gospel according to the perspectives of the founders, who point the way for their followers. It is on this foundation that the Special Chapter applied itself to a new redaction of the legislative text: it should constitute a *vade-mecum*, a guide, a stimulus to actualizing the one Gospel according to the variety of charisms that the Spirit distributes to the Church. For that very reason, the Constitutions objectively constitute the "Magna Carta" of the spirituality of an institute. For the Redemptorists, it is a spirituality eminently "missionary," according to the biblical-theological dimensions that the Constitutions identify as the "Mission." Therefore—a book of life (cf. the term *Vangelo* [Gospel] in the index of themes in my *Commento*).

2.2.2 On the subjective level

It can happen, unfortunately, that a document offered in view of life can become an occasion of death, or a "dead letter." This happens when the ring of the "letter" does not resonate in the "spirit." It has to do with a general law of hermeneutics, from which even the greatest of books—the Holy Scripture—is not exempt. The Word of God itself can remain an inert document if the riches buried in the text are not unearthed through the capacity to listen, that is, by means of the interior dispositions and the openness of faith in the one who comes upon them. This is even more true of a constitutional text, or even more basic to the charism of the Institute. The

Constitutions can be rewritten in the best way possible, they can be approved by the Church, yet they remain substantially human writings that must be internalized. We could apply to the text of the Constitutions the celebrated words that Gregory the Great said of the Bible: "*Eloquia divina crescunt cum legente.*" Between the written word and the reader there must exist a synergy. Any Constitutions, ours included, remain in some ways unrealized without the loving embrace of the one who puts them into practice, thereby releasing the potential embedded therein. Thus the importance of their progressive translation into the lives of individuals and groups. Turning once again to a comparison with the Gospel, I would like to refer to the title of a book—the master-work of Marco Pomilio: *The Fifth Gospel*— a book that was very successful as a result of its challenging message. The "fifth gospel" is not a gospel added to the well-known four. Rather, it is that gospel which each one of us writes every day—as a way of putting into action the fourfold Gospel, or better, the one Gospel. It is a transcription entrusted to an ever-attentive and inventive love. Every member of the Congregation writes his own "fifth gospel" by transcribing into daily life our charism, which otherwise remains confined to the pages of the Constitutions.

2.2.3 On the cognitive level

Closely linked to the subjective level, the cognitive level deserves more careful reflection precisely because of the synergy that must flow between the constitutional dictate and the person or group to whom it is addressed. In this particular perspective we can question the extent that the Constitutions have penetrated the life of our communities—at a distance of twenty-five years from their promulgation. The question isn't a new one. It recurs with regularity. I recall, among other things, that the General Chapter of 1973 postponed the approbation of the text by the Holy See precisely in order to permit the development of a more intense conscious awareness of it on the part of the Congregation. The pontifical approval (1982) was not meant to signal a respite. Quite the contrary—the appeals of the Chapters of 1985 and 1991 push in the same direction: toward an ever-greater consciousness of the text of the Constitutions. It would be interesting to be able to turn to objective statistics to verify the precise degree to which the texts have penetrated the consciousness of individuals and communities. While such an undertaking seems to me quite unfeasible, or at the very least, strenuous on the level of both method and actual willingness, such an instrument could be the Visitations at the various levels: general and provincial. But—do these Visitations actually make room in their methodology for an adequate examination of this area?

Again, we can presume that every member is in possession of a copy of the Constitutions. But is the reading of it actually practiced? I have formed a sort of conviction—fruit, it is true, of impressions more than actual analysis—that leads me to identify some missing elements in that regard, behind which might hide apathy and lack of interest. Elements lacking would deal not simply (or at least not so very much) with the single sections of the Constitutions or the particular articles therein but, rather, more often with the global sense of the categories implicit in the texts. To be more specific, for example, the members seem to be sufficiently aware of the meaning of "apostolic life." But one might wonder whether basic categories like "evangelization" and "mission" are understood in all their theological-biblical and historical-salvific breadth. As a matter of fact, one need only notice how the term *mission* can sometimes come to be understood in a minimalist sense, that is, reduced to meaning "the giving of missions," or "apostolic works," as used in our tradition. If this occurs, the key categories that support the whole constitutional edifice would be emptied of the richness of content that the writers wished to introduce in the new redaction of the texts. Putting it another way, it would deprive the ship of its mast.

2.3 What to do?

By now the reader will have gathered that *something has not worked and is not succeeding even now* in regard to the communication of, and reception given to, the Constitutions. It would seem to me that this phenomenon can be ascribed not so much to voluntary ignorance as to something missing in the structures or to inadequate modes of transmission. How to remedy it? The General Government needs to acknowledge the forces that have arisen in recent years which lead in this direction. In my *Commento,* I list various initiatives instituted by the General Secretariate for Formation. It's hardly necessary to add that the various *Communicanda* issued in the meantime, being intent as they are in turning us back to the Constitutions, are a stimulus to absorb them. But we come round to the same question: To what extent do documents such as these, and therefore the Constitutions referred to in them as well, penetrate the soul and the conscience of the very ones for whom they are intended?

In the past it has been suggested to the General Government that a plan is necessary (yet to be invented!) of *programmed and integrated (organic) consciousness-raising* which would go beyond sporadic and piecemeal—even *if* well-meaning—attempts. Such structures functioned in the old rule: Saturday reading of the text and suchlike. Listening to the text over and over at fixed times led, almost without being aware of it, to memorization. In the present circumstances of community life, the superiors should tailor opportune times in which, at definite intervals, the members could read the text and exchange reflections in community. It's difficult to find time, you say? What if we were to simply reduce, for example, the time spent in front of the TV channel-surfing?

2.4 Starting points for reflection on certain aspects relevant today

2.4.1 Community life

Even the most inattentive reader will not fail to recognize that Chapter II of the Constitutions, in the structure of the text taken as a whole, is a hinge element linking apostolic activity (Chapter 1) and the consecrated life (Chapter 3). Formation (Chapter 4) and government (Chapter 5) are tightly bound to the first three chapters. At the very least, it could be said that if Chapter 2 falls out, everything crumbles. The subject deserves to be addressed articulately and, at times, pointedly. The General Government has taken note of the crisis that is spreading in the body of the Congregation in regard to authentic community life, threatened by a sometimes excessive individualism, which is lethal to the survival of the Institute. One of the symptoms of this dissociation is the dichotomy that places pastoral activity in opposition to community life. It is not the place here to describe the diverse phenomena connected with this slow deterioration. But facing such a dramatic picture, we are thrown back on the same question: The Constitutions as a book of life? It might be agreed, however, that the identity crisis of which the abovementioned documents speak, if it *is* a real crisis we are dealing with, is not due to inadequate legislation, but rather to a one-sided reading of it (if one can actually speak of reading). It is urgent that we recover the whole message of the Constitutions concerning the fundamental importance of community for Redemptorists. It is a life-and-death issue. A code destined to be a book of life—if not known, and above all, not applied—risks (however unintentionally) failing in its objective and being transformed instead into an instrument of death.

2.4.2 Poverty and the poor

I would like to call attention to an area of community life whose identity I feel is threatened—the topic of poverty. That we are witnessing a certain "ungluing" of the constitutive text and the practice of some or more confreres seems to me a phenomenon visible to the naked eye. In this area individualism raises its head in various ways: the availability of money, sought in a variety of ways and often hidden from the community and superiors; superfluous trips—sometimes transformed into long-term sightseeing; clothing constantly being replaced, and so on. And this is not to say that such phenomena are limited to the rich provinces. Quite the contrary!

It is not superfluous to recall that in the history of the Institute, the chapter on poverty always constituted an infallible warning light of any relaxation in community discipline. Not everyone is aware of the extreme rigor that surrounded the exercise of the vow of poverty in defense of "perfect community life." In the new legislation this rigor is partly mitigated in practice, but the principles regulating the use of material goods remain ever the same: the *Decrees on Poverty* are of a constitutional character. For that reason, they are always valid, and gravely valid, even if at times (or maybe often?) the legislation is somehow eluded or circumvented. It would not be out of place for a future general chapter to take up the issue in connection with the evangelization of the poor with which the Chapters of 1985 and 1991 were occupied. Not rarely, the prospects of the poor—of whom many speak, perhaps at times too much—remain a good deal distant from the concrete, real-life prospects of many confreres.

I don't consider it moralizing on my part to call attention to the urgency of recovering that sense of simplicity and austerity that has always been one of the characteristics of the Redemptorist missionary. He must, even within the plurality of situations and cultural adaptations, witness to "apostolic detachment" and total availability for the Kingdom. The theological-pastoral motivations that stand at the root of a simple, evangelical life seem to me to be very well expressed in Constitutions 63 to 67, and in Statutes 044 to 045. It seems more opportune than ever to reflect on these texts and their challenge to renewal.

2.4.3 The cultural level

This is not a side issue. It seems to me that culture can be a factor in repairing certain distortions of our charism. By the term *culture*, I mean a commitment to study—above all, on a theological-pastoral level. Such a commitment is necessary for a missionary institute such as ours. Redemptorists must get back to the books. Without strict and arduous study, the missionary betrays his vocation. It's extremely worthwhile to run through some texts from the old constitutions:

> [The members] must dedicate themselves to proficiency in the human and divine sciences; so that they can become truly learned and wise in every way, especially in sacred literature, in order to serve Holy Church in all her needs: while the uneducated worker, even if prayerful, is like a soldier without arms (*Codex Regularum*, pp. 31–32, n. 7).

Again:

> They will study diligently and pore over the books, in order to make themselves fully competent in those sciences in which our own Redeemer and Master was steeped (*Codex Regularum*, p. 41, n. 29).

Getting down to aspects more pertinent to the formation and the spirituality of the members, I would like to call attention to the history of the Institute, especially in its origins. It is necessary to nourish a "consciousness of Congregation" among the new generations, with a view to preserving that unity and those characteristics of the charism that otherwise "run the risk of becoming obscure or perhaps even of being irretrievably lost" (*Communicanda* 2 [1994], n. 36). The *History of the C.Ss.R.* is a valuable instrument. More particularly in regard to Redemptorist spirituality, very respectable aids have been produced in recent times: I would point out *Readings in Redemptorist Spirituality* and *Espiritualidad redentorista*—both current series; and for the exegesis of the Constitutions, might I be permitted to recommend my Commentary, *Il carisma dei redentoristi nella chiesa* (Rome, 1993).

2.4.4 The superior-animator

I am convinced that the "active and responsible obedience" of which the Constitutions, in line with Vatican II, speak represents for everyone—

superiors and subjects—a difficult challenge. Put more simply, the traditional obedience, primarily receptive in nature, seemed—all things considered—easier and psychologically more gratifying. "Active and responsible" obedience presupposes "venturing out of one's own territory," coming out of one's shell, leaving behind one's own security, venturing out into the open where it is necessary to confront, discuss, research. And this, often enough, with little satisfaction, precisely because the new methodology of obedience implies at times the renunciation of one's own point of view, and in the end, the risk of psychological frustration.

This new type of obedience, while difficult for everyone, is probably more difficult for the superiors, or directors in general, since they are called to demonstrate a spirit of initiative, of dynamism, of reading the signs of the times, and of human sensitivity; not to mention, the capacity for synthesis. On a deeper level, the superiors are called to lend "spiritual support" in community relations, to be guides—both spiritual and in some sense charismatic—for the community. The Constitutions foresee a model of superior-animator at various levels: general (Constitution 115,b), provincial (Constitution 126), and local (Constitution 139). Superiors, that is, must be inspiration for the community, "fathers," and promoters of harmonious growth.

The Constitutions are aware that the new understanding together with the exercise of authority do not form an easy assignment. Therefore they provide for sessions for deepening the understanding and sharing experiences of the task (cf. Constitution 103).

In that way, they will not be simply "walking discipline whips" (a graphic image used by the founder), but rather living persons who, instead of simply following the gang or letting themselves be manipulated, push ahead and lead. Superiors, in summary, will be able to give wing to the community only if they themselves, first and foremost, take off in flight. The choice of superiors, then, seems like one of the decisive factors in combatting that individualism and that "care for oneself" that appear to corrode the roots of community. The Constitutions become a "book of life" also (and perhaps above all?) through the efforts of the superiors, who by authorized exegesis call forth from the "letter of the law" the breath of the "spirit."

3. Why I Remain a Redemptorist

Coming to the conclusion, I would like to return to the autobiographical sketch that formed the starting point of these reflections, in order to answer the following question: Why am I still a Redemptorist? I will do so in small steps.

First of all, I must call upon my faith-conviction, which is impossible to demonstrate by concrete links or factual evidence. If my vocation as a Redemptorist missionary, at first uncertain and little by little more conscious, has become the road my life has taken, all this is first and foremost a gift and a grace from our Lord. I will pass over my slowness and (why not?) pass over my infidelities—more or less recognized. I know not how or why the Lord has saved me and brought me thus far: His ways escape me.

At the age of seventy-five, and with fifty years of priesthood, I thank the Lord, bless him, and praise him. But I also admit to him my sorrow for my wounds to his fatherly heart and renew my resolution of conversion. Looking back on the road I have traveled, I long to think, almost to cry out, that the presence of the Lord in the span of my life has been truly "plentious redemption" and, I am certain, will be until death.

Second, I must admit that, among the gifts of the Lord should be listed the contribution I made to the Constitutions. Between the two sessions of the Special Chapter, and particularly during the work of the Redaction Commission, I experienced moments of great satisfaction and intense joy. The Constitutions represent the results of a choral endeavor that has brought the Congregation to an intense recovery of its missionary vocation. This recovery was both the fruit and the cause of a deeper consciousness of the charism and spirituality of the Institute. The traditional spirituality placed the accent on regular observance and individual asceticism, unwittingly fostering a certain dichotomy between observance and missionary fervor. In that regard, I mentioned the books of Father Colin, symbols of the whole era. The new texts have created room for a spirituality which is more unified, more ecclesial, more open to a missionary spirit. Evidently, this new climate has expanded my joy in belonging to a Congregation propelled to the very frontier in announcing and witnessing to Christ the Redeemer.

Such joy is also multiplied by the impact of the new legislation on the consciousness of the members. Beyond any partial resistance, the impact has provoked a more conscious rootedness of the consciousness of mission above all among the younger generations. A new shiver has passed through the missionary soul of the Congregation.

In the preceding pages, I referred to a certain identity crisis which seems to be rocking the unity and charism of the Institute. But I still believe that the crisis, if it *is* a crisis we are dealing with, will be reabsorbed by the living organism which is the Congregation. To sustain this fundamentally optimistic vision, there stands the presence of the founder. That presence was palpable in the Special Chapter (which had to respond to another identity crisis that rocked the Institute). The capitular fathers recognized the almost miraculous character of this spontaneous and communal turning to the founder, alive and well among his own. The presence of the founder remains a confirmation even today of the mission of the Congregation in the Church and in the world. It is a great comfort to me to remember what many Redemptorists think of as the prophecy of Saint Alphonsus: that the Congregation will continue throughout history, right until the end.

In reality, there is no rupture or break in continuity between the Constitutions and the original inspiration of Saint Alphonsus. Constitution 2 has included the "Cossali text" precisely to reinforce the missionary spirit of the Congregation in the evangelization of the poor. Therefore there exists a continuity between the "Intent" of the founder and the new possibilities opened to the Congregation by the new legislation. It is a continuity which, on the one hand, rests on fidelity to God and the word of the founder, and on the other hand, depends on us—each one of us. A continuity, therefore, that grows in our hands and which constitutes the highest adventure in the personal history of every Redemptorist. Also for Father Sante Raponi the Redemptorist, who all things considered, is happy to have lived, and to live still within the common house of the Congregation—proud to hand over the torch to those who will brandish it on high.

THE DIMENSIONS
OF THE CHARISM

9

FOLLOWING JESUS CHRIST
AS A REDEMPTORIST

Márcio Fabri dos Anjos, C.Ss.R.
Province of São Paulo
Translated by Norman Muckerman, C.Ss.R.
Province of Denver

1. Discovering My Vocation

The history of my Redemptorist vocation begins with a family legacy. In a small Brazilian village called Monte Belo, in the state of Minas Gerais, my parents raised a family of eleven children, four daughters and seven sons. I was the sixth child. In seeking employment to provide for his large family, my father became first a merchant, then later a tax collector for the state. We were always very poor. As a tax collector my father spent more time trying to teach the people how to manage their own monetary resources. As a result he lost a lot of his own salary because it was based on a percentage of the taxes he took in. My mother worked miracles in managing the economy of our own household. She provided food and clothing for her children, and her door was always open to those who needed help.

My legacy was not of a monetary nature. What we received was a deep spirit of faith, accompanied by a strong sense of generosity and solidarity. Even though they were poor, our parents taught us to have compassion and to be concerned for those less fortunate than ourselves. One of my clearest childhood memories is going with my mother to bring food and clothing to the lepers, who lived isolated from society in general, but who were recipients of my mother's charity.

All the boys in the family became altar servers. Five of us went to the seminary; two became Redemptorists. Today it would be impossible for us not to appreciate the solid foundation in the faith and the resolute determination to serve the most abandoned which we inherited from our parents.

Deepening spiritual roots

A second important phase of my Redemptorist vocation was my contact with Redemptorists, first in the seminary and later, even until the present, in community life. I entered the seminary quite young, when I was only ten years old. Entering this young was not unusual, especially since there was no school in our hometown. An older brother had gone to the seminary six years earlier, and this proved to be a decisive factor in my becoming a Redemptorist and not a Franciscan. As a young boy, I had been an altar server for our Franciscan pastor, who treated me quite well and insisted that I go to the Franciscan seminary. But as I told him with childlike logic: "I am going to the Redemptorist seminary because if I get into a fight there with another seminarian, my big brother will defend me."

The most important feature of the seminary for me was the testimony of the Redemptorists themselves, who communicated to us their missionary enthusiasm. They talked about their missionary activities, and they demonstrated remarkable apostolic zeal and ardor. Thus they helped me to formulate and create in my own mind a sense of achieving holiness along these same pursuits. I remember two phrases in particular. The first was *Dies impendere pro redemptis*, which I translated as "Give your life for God's poor." The other was "Save the most abandoned souls." Later I discovered little by little that this did not mean "souls" in the strict sense.

These axioms became an agenda for life, which appealed to me as the way to follow Christ the Redeemer and to be the kind of holy Redemptorist missionary that our seminary directors urged us to become. During my formation years, Saint Alphonsus and Saint Clement appeared to me to be very austere. Saint Gerard Majella, humble and more of an ordinary person, seemed to be ascetical and more human. However, in these first Redemptoristic experiences what stood out, above all else, was the image of giving up my life for the most abandoned and searching for a deep spirituality, namely "to be a saint." As a young apprentice, this compensated in my mind for the semblance of rigidity and even intransigence, which to my sorrow I sometimes saw in my spiritual heroes.

Another consolation for me was the person of Mary. In the seminary

I developed the devotion to Our Lady, which I had basically learned from my mother. Two principal factors contributed in the development of my Marian spirituality. The first was the legacy left by Saint Alphonsus that was taught to us in the seminary. The second was a devotion to Our Lady of Aparecida, which I had since childhood and which gave a Brazilian cast to my veneration of Mary. Besides this, my first seven years in the seminary were spent in the shadow of the famous sanctuary of Our Lady of Aparecida, where the Redemptorists provide pastoral care. The dark and popular image of Our Lady of Aparecida, mother and protector of the poor and needy, and the object of veneration of some six million pilgrims annually, became for me a powerful pledge of God's protection in life. At the same time, Our Lady of Aparecida became a great missionary symbol. The sight of so many unfortunate people who had recourse to her, and who in turn were being spiritually cared for by my confreres before my very eyes, became for me a clear call to be a missionary and to evangelize the poor.

The Redemptorist ideal shared

I am quite certain that I was—and even today continue to be—spiritually sustained by the numerous confreres who share in the same Alphonsian ideal. Besides those canonized saints in our Congregation, there were also other important personages whose heroic witness I came to appreciate. These were the German Redemptorists, who some one hundred years ago founded our São Paulo Province. From my seminary days on, I was impressed by their zeal and enthusiasm, as well as by their creativity in pastoral initiatives. Also important for me was the image of the Redemptorist lay brothers. Their kind of life showed me, even more clearly than that of the priests, that to be a Redemptorist means, above all else, the call to follow Jesus, to be "people of God." Today, after more than thirty years of living as a Redemptorist, I recognize how much I owe these older confreres, as well as my present ones, for sharing their enthusiasm for the Redemptorist way of life.

I cannot appreciate my Redemptorist vocation without thinking of the people to whom I see myself sent. They are as the explicit voice of God, which calls me to places for specific tasks of evangelization. In this sense I also see my vocation increase and even change. Here I wish to cite two insights that were fundamental. The first is the discovery that the "most abandoned souls" also have real, tangible faces, and their spiritual poverty means material and daily want. For some time I came to be troubled over the meaning of "to be a missionary." How was I to look into the face of these poor people and tell them that the salvation of God was at hand?

A second insight followed upon the first. From the point of view of someone who operates, confers, and distributes God's gifts, I came to discover that I had much to learn and to receive from these poor people to whom I had been sent. Out of their needs, I assessed and examined my own preaching methods and the contents of my evangelizing message. Besides this, in their own simple faith and their way of life, and particularly after I made contact with poor Christian communities, I began to discover an incredible spiritual affluence, especially a loving and exciting solidarity, a dynamic sense of hope, and the capacity to reinvent a Christian community in the midst of the changes and necessities of life.

In other words, I discovered in practice what in theory was cryptic: that the Holy Spirit precedes our apostolic works and goes far beyond our small circle of action. Spiritually, I came to see myself more as an apprentice and disciple of Jesus along with the people. And I was happy when we, the Congregation, began to describe our missionary work as "to evangelize the poor and to be evangelized by them."

For about thirty years now, I have been a professor of moral theology, but at the same time, I continue to minister to some of the local communities, poor people of the area where other confreres are also working. Despite the limitations caused by my role as a professor of moral theology, these communities broaden my own studies and help me to keep my feet on the ground in my little theoretical world. Also they ensure in some way that my scholastic inquiries, studies, and academic initiatives will go in the direction of service to the most abandoned.

My experience shows me that the vocation to which God calls us strongly involves people who shared and still share our lives—the people who gave us life, the people with whom we live in the various stages of our life, the people who motivate us, the people who call out quietly for help and assistance during our life. Thus I see that God calls us and, at the same time, places in our path real people, specific people. With them, we learn to hear the call of God and to become better disposed to follow his mission.

2. To Follow Jesus as a Redemptorist

Now let us face a simple and direct question: how are we Redemptorists to follow Jesus? Our response should not be a theological/spiritual treatise on discipleship. Rather, we will in the manner of giving testimony reveal our own experience and understanding of the subject, for the purpose of offering some considerations that the confreres may wish to reflect upon personally.

Followed and hounded by Jesus

When I think of following Jesus as a Redemptorist, I see primarily his roots in our human condition. The invitation to follow Jesus is strictly connected with the challenge of our own salvation. In other words, just as all people in the world, we face an existential question: how to negotiate our way through this life here on earth and still arrive at a full and eternal life at the end?

This is a question which all religions commonly try to answer. On this point we are indeed one with a searching humanity. Through our faith, we assume that the way of Jesus will lead us through this life to a Life that is full and guaranteed. Thus to follow Jesus is, before all else, to believe in him and to believe that his way leads to salvation. Summing it up, we say to Jesus as did Peter in the Gospel: "Master, to whom shall we go? You have the words of eternal life" (John 6:68).

This simple and basic relationship between discipleship and salvation places before us something very profound: Jesus is our Savior. But if Jesus is our Savior then even before we follow him, it is he who seeks us out, it is he who accompanies us, even follows in our errant way. The gospels clearly point out this eager and attentive love of a God who comes to meet us and seeks us out as lost sheep; he becomes our companion as we go our confused way, much in the manner of the disciples on their way to Emmaus.

Thus it is that when speaking of following Jesus, it is necessary to have clearly in mind and in heart that we ourselves are already being followed and persecuted by the infinite love of Jesus. Saint Alphonsus knew very well how to transmit this idea to us. The problem of salvation is our own problem, as well as the problem of those to whom we announce the Good News. It is absolutely fundamental that we accept the Good News, that we are evangelized, that we comprehend how much we are loved by God. From here discipleship starts. As Redemptorist preachers we might be tempted to reduce this following of Jesus to working as a missionary. But we cannot avoid this basic experience and understanding that we are loved, sought after, and saved by God in Jesus.

"Who do they say that I am?"

Sometimes following Jesus is reduced to a doctrine, so that disciple-ship would become something intellectual and abstract. The gospels show that in no way should this be so. Jesus invites us to follow him in the way he acted, in the path he followed throughout his own life. There was a time when people thought that to follow Jesus meant to imitate his way of acting, and even in dress. Today we understand that in following Jesus, it is much more important to have the same convictions and conclusions, the same basic actions and attitudes, as Jesus. Here is found "the way" of Jesus. For this reason we can say that our way of following Jesus in our own life will be revealed in our convictions, our choices, our actions, and our attitudes.

Jesus lived in a different time and culture than ours. This makes it necessary for us to reinterpret the way he lived and the path he followed. Our task is to respond to these questions: How would Jesus act? What paths would he take today, in our time, in our culture, and in our circumstances? In other words, the following of Jesus demands a "translation" (interpreta-tion) for actual times.

Generally speaking, this effort of interpretation has been done con-stantly, for good or evil. It comes to us now through at least four avenues, all interrelated, which we can call tradition. The first consists of different emphases that the universal Church, during the course of history, has given in the matter of following Jesus. The second lies in the interpretations and recommendations that individual churches, from their different cultures and regional conditions, offer as the "way" of Jesus as they understand it. The third lies, in my opinion, in Christian family traditions that strongly define our interpretation of Jesus through feelings and emotion. And the fourth consists precisely in the Redemptoristic tradition, which we received from Saint Alphonsus and the Congregation—to know, love, and follow Jesus.

This is the same as saying that our following of Jesus depends on our image of Jesus. This image, which is transmitted to us and which we trans-mit to others, changes according to our life experiences. It changes for the better, in the measure that we get closer to the Master and better contem-plate his face. Or it changes for worse in the measure that we distance ourselves from him as we go our own way.

From this some important conclusions occur. When we speak of fol-lowing Jesus, we are trying to remember the common characteristics and basic overtones of his image, according to our Redemptoristic spiritual perception. Our "Redemptoristic" image of Jesus cannot be the same through-out the various eras and the regional differences of the Congregation. The image changes according to the faithfulness of our discipleship, or perhaps according to personal or community conversion; it also changes with the adaptations that we make as we confront new times and new circumstances on our way.

This opens an interesting subject that we can only mention at this time: how the personal and common images that we have of Jesus have evolved in our history of following him. We can understand, for example, how in the history of the Church we had periods in which to follow Jesus meant to flee the world, or how the predominant image of Jesus was of Someone who expiates the sins of mankind.

It would be interesting to examine the different images of Jesus within different cultural contexts, even within the Congregation or to let the reader himself analyze how in his own personal history—from infancy, adolescence, and even until today—a particular image of Jesus has developed in his own heart. Or even more to observe how the image of Jesus was interpreted in the history of the Congregation, beginning with our holy father, Alphonsus, and continuing through the different Rules and Constitutions, the novitiates and community life, and how, for example, it was important for Vatican II to relocate Jesus in our lives and in our Constitutions.

The history of our own lives and that of our communities offers different nuances in the image of Jesus and designates different ways in which to follow him. They mirror in great part the different backgrounds that we have experienced, as well as different points of spiritual discernment in our encounter with Jesus.

"And you, who do you say that I am?"
Redemptorist emphases on the image of Jesus

The question before us today is this: what are the principal traits or features of the Jesus we follow? Although we call ourselves "Redemptorists," the most evident characteristic of our following Jesus is, at first glance, to be missionaries. We are proclaimers of the Word of God, and we follow closely the evangelizing Jesus, Evangelizer of the poor and all those most in need of spiritual help. One might conclude from this that it would be more logical to call ourselves "evangelists."

Evidently this is a little disconcerting. But it permits us to recognize better the deeper foundations on which we build our following of Jesus. In our spiritual heritage we see that the missionary role undertaken by Jesus runs throughout his mission of being the Revealer of God's mercy and love. For this reason Jesus, for us, is not a simple teller of good news. He bears in his historic life all the marks of this mission. In our Redemptorist tradition we see then the face of Jesus the Evangelizer in the light of his incarnation, his passion, as well as in his eucharistic presence. "Crib, Cross, Sacrament" …in the expression of Saint Alphonsus, Jesus is "a fool for love," who being God is born as a child and gives his life and does everything for us. To sum it up, the evangelizing mission of Jesus consists not simply of words spoken, but of deeds done to demonstrate a complete offering of his own life.

This will also be our way. Under this light we can better understand the person of Jesus whom we follow. It is a question of following Someone who loves us profoundly, who inflames us with love, and who draws us also to be proclaimers of mercy in the world, by our action and by our words. At the same time, our Redemptoristic way of following Jesus is nourished and maintained by the experience of being ourselves loved, and by the call to love by witnessing and preaching the Gospel.

"Lord, where do you stay?"
Ways of following

In which direction does this spiritual motif move us to follow Jesus? It offers us, first of all, some important attitudes to have when we take up this kind of following. We might even dare to lump together these attitudes into an explicit contemplation of the trilogy: crib, cross, and sacrament. Thus I see that we ought to follow Jesus:

- *in the incarnation*, by cultivating a feeling of love for the poor and abandoned, as well as a feeling of mercy for the weak and the fallen; also by inserting ourselves into the lives of these people in order to help them
- *in the cross and resurrection*, by a pledge to defend life in its totality; by giving up honors and amenities; by self-denial and discipline, even to the point of sacrifice; and by having an attitude of hope that presumes things will always turn out better

- *in the sacrament*, by having the attitude of someone who wishes to share his life with the most abandoned; by being a support and spiritual food for them; by being the proclaimer of the Word who makes all things new

The path on which we follow Jesus points unequivocally in the direction of the poor and abandoned. It brings us to those who are in need of salvation. This is a huge concept, but in our traditions there are abundant signs of preference for persons who are the most humble and the most excluded or eliminated from the Church and from society. These are the people who determine in great part our missionary methods, and can even silence us, allowing us to give testimony without words, while waiting for a more appropriate moment when we can proclaim the Word in explicit terms (Constitution 9).

"What did you discuss along the way?" *Uncertainties and mysteries*

Following Jesus in the Congregation is not something peaceful and secure. This happens primarily because we ourselves are always in need of conversion. Both as individuals and as entire communities, we can faint along the way and distance ourselves from our Lord and Master. What can more easily happen is that we lose that alertness with which the Lord listens to the marginalized on the side of the road (see, for example, Mark 10:46–52). And then we remain fixed in our own self-assurance, discussing opinions and practices. The "most abandoned" become nothing more than a simple theory and a remote interest. We lose our courage and our creativity. It is necessary to ask some profound questions with total frankness to see if our discussions are no more than some kind of attempt to find motives for avoiding the poor and the needy in our apostolic options and methods.

On the other hand, there can occur rapid change in situations and circumstances, leaving us confused about goals and methods. The discernment of goals and methods demand prayer, conversion, and a critical sense for discerning and interpreting the signs of the times in our own days. Vatican II was a focal point in the Church; it shook us out of our lethargy and put us into new times and situations where we were to discover the signs which the Lord was displaying. Our General Chapters were precious forces that took up the same themes.

The present times have brought before us questions that imminently refer to some characteristics that are central to our following Jesus as Redemptorists. Today the attitudes of authority and power, which the disciples in the Gospel talked about along the way, are repeated facilely in the stances we take and which we refuse to give up. Instead of offering service to the most abandoned, there are the positions we take and the conditions that we impose upon the poor who approach us. Our stance is an expression of power. This is something totally different from the appearance of Jesus made man. The persistent demands made in the General Chapter of 1991 for our own inculturation and insertion into the life of the poor seem to me to be very important for correcting the temptation (to power).

We cannot simplify this question by saying that the present moment through which we are passing is complicated. Study, logic, and prudence are necessary for us to perceive how to confront the challenges to salvation; in other words, to discover how today the lives of the poor and needy are threatened, and what we can do to proclaim and promote salvation intelligently. Besides this, it is also necessary to consider our own personal fears that make us unprotected, even in the security of our already guaranteed positions. Thus we might find ourselves compromising ourselves in the goals, methods, and the whole framework of life.

"He reunited them and sent them forth."

The Redemptoristic following of Jesus would be difficult if not impossible if it were not rooted in community life. We follow Jesus as members of a community, that is, we are people who share the same ideals, and embrace apostolic ministries in common. We cannot do without a personal experience of God, but by our commitment to live a common religious life we accept the fact that we will help one another in following Jesus. Thus to follow the Lord, we, in a way, act as did Saint Gerard when he left his home to associate himself with the followers of Jesus.

I envision three important areas, naturally interrelated, of our sharing in ministry. The first is in the many ways we have of bolstering the ideals that stimulate our religious life: common prayer, discernment, witnessing to one another, cultivating the remembrance of Saint Alphonsus as well as that of our other saints and the many confreres who have led edifying lives. In the measure in which the spiritual life grows in our communities, we gain strength in following Jesus.

The second area would include our apostolic endeavors and the enthusiasm with which we dedicate ourselves to them, which intensifies significantly our giving of self. Thus we build up enthusiasm in following Jesus. To do this it is necessary to emphasize the importance of getting along together, of having a friendly and fraternal atmosphere in our common life. Then we will be able to share the burdens of the journey and along the way enjoy the benefit of happiness.

The third area of helping one another in the following of Jesus as Redemptorists seems to me to be equally fundamental, although it might eventually become for us less perceived. We are talking here of our engagement with the poor and most abandoned. In all truth, to follow Jesus in his evangelizing mission demands that we discover the tangible face of the poor and abandoned, and ask, as Jesus himself did, "What do you want me to do?"

The response to this question gives rise to action and also to changes in what is being done. It is not as an isolated missionary that we Redemptorists seek to evangelize the most abandoned. It is in community and as a missionary team. Therefore, the needs of the poor bind us together, call out to us as a community, and provide new ways for us to follow Jesus as a community. This is one of the ways in which the poor evangelize us. The living, breathing needy people for whom we are giving our life are in a certain manner the thermometer of our discipleship. In going to them, in adapting ourselves to their needs, we are following Jesus who evangelized the poor; if we are successful in communicating to them joy and life, we can be certain that we are proclaiming the kingdom of God as Jesus did (Luke 7:22).

I see our following of Jesus as Redemptorists uncompromisingly linked to the question of salvation. Our own personal salvation, and the salvation of God's loved ones, beginning with the poor and most abandoned. In this we ourselves are pursued and followed by Jesus all our life. The development and growth of our following of Jesus fix deep roots in our lives through our individual and communal interiorization of the person of Jesus, as well as of the attitudes and choices that dominated his life and which led him to real and solid actions in behalf of humankind, especially people in need of salvation. It is an interiorizaton that demands constant conversion.

After that we can try to follow Jesus in his "idiocies of love" for us. Proclaiming and witnessing to the Good News to the poor and most abandoned is a strong emphasis that we have learned from Saint Alphonsus and from the experience of the Congregation in this form of discipleship. Today, social and cultural changes offer us many challenges in our attempts to discover concrete ways to express our discipleship. But the voice and the face of the poor and abandoned are the great indication of how the trail of following Jesus leads to where they themselves are.

As a community, let us move in that direction, encouraging one another, helping one another, as we uncover and overcome our uncertainties. And let us also gather the fruits of joy and peace, through the good things that we share.

Finally, not withstanding our perplexities and our sins, let us be glad that we are able, as was the beloved disciple himself, to recognize amid our many duties the person of Jesus whom we are following and say: "It is the Lord!" (John 21:7).

10

MESSENGERS OF
PLENTIFUL REDEMPTION

François Noboru Yoshiyama, C.Ss.R.
Vice Province of Tokyo

1. The Grace of Conversion, a Witness

The Christian faith and the vocation as Redemptorist have been the foundation of my life since 1948 when I was baptized a Catholic at the age of twenty-one. Now at sixty-nine years of age, I am very conscious and full of gratitude for the grace of my conversion just as much as for my life itself. During the first ten years after becoming a Catholic, my life seemed somewhat strange and inconsistent. I had a fear that I might lose my identity as a true Japanese. It took many years to overcome this feeling; I had to pray, to study, and to work at following my vocation. Consequently, today I can analyze theologically my conversion as an experience of life.

My parents and relatives are completely closed to Western culture. As for many ordinally Japanese, the Shintoist, Buddhist, and Confucian way of life has been deeply ingrained in them. What had greatly influenced me regarding the decision to abandon these traditional facets of Japanese culture for my future life was the defeat of the militarists in Japan and also the war crimes. I began to seriously doubt as to whether or not there existed true spiritual values in our traditional culture. The crisis was real for me at that time. Why I was to question this—not being a Nihilist like many other young people of those days—I don't know the answer even now. Thanks to a lovely God, I was simply looking for a kind of real, spiritual liberty that our traditional religions were not giving me.

More than Redemptorist vocation, my conversion to Catholicism is still a mystery of grace that I cannot fully comprehend. I have never been inclined to publicly comment on my conversion, because, even if my being baptized into the Catholic Church seemed to be understandable as it happened, to me it was a supernatural event. I cannot really interpret this happy event in myself even now.

According to my way of thinking, one of the essential elements of my vocation as Redemptorist is an ever-ongoing contemplation of this loving, salvific work of God. During my theological studies and in my apostolic works, I found that I was something like a contemplative, meditating how I have lost all unessential ambitions through my conversion and also desiring to be a better witness to this grace from God as sincerely as possible. Since my baptism in my youth, I have never ceased seeking God, so the conversion has been a continual drawing toward him, whose voice I have heard calling me. I am sure that the turning to Catholicism was a beckoning of a merciful Creator. Why I decided to become a Redemptorist priest not long after my baptism was for me no other reason then to know better and better the God who was summoning me. This intention has not changed, not even up to the present day. In my younger days I suffered a spiritual dryness being a convert, isolated to some degree from the ordinary Japanese. During thirty-five years as a Redemptorist missionary, because of this separation, I have been studying and meditating on how to speak about the God who is always calling me and how to explain that to my compatriots living in a quite different religious atmosphere compared to the Western peoples.

On the occasion of the tricentenary of the death of our holy founder, Saint Alphonsus, I wish to express in my own simple words about the God who has called me to accept his unconditional love. All this helps me greatly to realize what my vocation as a Redemptorist really means. I am not exposing a theology of conversion, but I am just telling my experience with a theological language.

Who is this God who is calling me?

When an ordinary Japanese thinks about God, it is in many cases just one of many gods in nature or some transcendent existence in a philosophical sense. Certainly, I myself keep trace of a religious feeling of Shintoism representative of the animistic religion of Japan that is sustained by our national mentality. However, after my journey to the Roman Catholic Church in the twenties of my life, I had never consciously thought about God with an animistic outlook. I had been an atheist, like many other Japanese in the traditional religious way of thinking. I appreciate our religious culture as having many really human values, especially regarding aesthetic values. However, the God who had called me was so different that I could not imagine just through my religious knowledge of the traditional religion.

So I decided not to go into a deep study of the Japanese traditional religion. I preferred to stay completely aloof from our traditional beliefs. This attitude has not changed fundamentally even today. However, it was rather difficult for me to approach God, even if he knew me, because I was not sure how to know him. Western Christians have quite practical answers for that, that is, reading the Bible and praying to God. For me, the Bible as word of God is accepted in a different way. Why does God find it necessary to speak, since his presence can be felt in silence itself and also his words felt likewise? It took quite some time to get accustomed to reading the Bible and meditating on God through his spoken message. However, I don't think my conversion was a conversion to the God of the philosophers. Prayer also had difficulties because, for the Japanese, it was considered as superstitions or at most a simple respectful expectation for the grace of gods.

As Saint John says in the preface of his gospel, "The word became man"; God not only speaks in words but also through human realities. I have readily believed this truth. Among the traditional religions in Japan, Buddhism and Confucianism are the religions or morality that respect the Scriptures very much. We Japanese have accepted these religions from both India and China. However, the Japanese retain as its nationalistic religion that of Shintoism, which is a religion of nature and without any Scriptures. They have no confidence concerning "words of God." The Japanese, for the most part, are inclined to venerate their deity in silence as the authentic Ultimate Reality. When contemporary Japanese individuals are asked what kind of religion they belong to, the common answer is atheist. They don't recognize a personal deity as described by the words of Scriptures. The anthropomorphic gods are just venerated like the ancestors, not believed with a personal commitment by words of any single god. Therefore, in Japan a religion involved in prophecy is not popular such as in the Old Testament.

Who is Jesus?

How I could believe that Jesus was one with God cannot be explained by means of a simple conversion story. It is a mysterious grace to be able to believe in Jesus Christ. Without knowing the Gospel, we cannot believe in Jesus Christ. On the other hand, it is also true that without the witness of the Church, we cannot believe in him either. If the Japanese don't believe the religions using the Scriptures, the existence of the witness community is primordially important compared to the Bible. For those peoples who cannot believe the Scriptures, the Catholic community looks like a very fascinating existence. This was one of the fundamental reasons why I entered the Catholic Church, and thus began to study the Bible. I had never read the Bible up to that time.

Strictly speaking, the mystery of Christianity is not solely the mystery of God, but also the mystery of man. God is mysterious in all religions, whereas in Christianity, man himself became ultimately mysterious by the mystery of the Incarnation and the Redemption. This is the unimaginable message of the Gospel! Like many Eastern religious peoples, including the Japanese, the profound seemingly ambiguity of human nature is an unsolvable problem of life. Man looks like he is living an evil existence, and sometimes a divine existence. Man could be looked upon as an illusory being. In order to overcome these false illusions, the wisdom of the East has enlightened its peoples on the problems of the nothingness of man like in the Buddhist teachings. If a Japanese understands Christianity as simply a doctrine of God, he will continue to remain as an atheist or enlightened person, as do all Buddhists, and to stay as a believer of the scientific enlightenment in the modern times. Such as in my case, if he had had a contact with the Christian faith community, he would have found a new type of humanity in the Christian way of life.

It took time for me to adjust living as a Christian and more so as a religious in a Redemptorist community. It required a lot of patience to find the real source of this new humanity in the Gospel of Jesus Christ. After I had studied Christianity, then I followed the doctrines of the Holy Trinity, and so on. My ordination to the priesthood took place in 1960. Ever since then I have been working as a Redemptorist missionary among my compatriots. I realize now that I had been following the Christ of the Gospel, the one who is really part of the mystery of God and man. Recently, there has been a spate of books telling us about the historical Jesus, but I have only an intellectual interest in them; rather, I am more interested in the mystery of Jesus Christ.

The pascal mystery

The Resurrection of Christ has really happened, and the Father, the Son, and the Holy Spirit reign over the world and all that is in it. This is not a reality that can only be proved by the Scriptures, just as we judge worldly events. So it is that I am not always soley satisfied with the exegetical methods of the contemporary study of the Scriptures. The decisions of the Second Vatican Council are still having a big influence on me and for my apostolate as a Redemptorist. It seemed to me that my becoming a Catholic is confirmed by the teachings of the Council. For me, the central meaning of the renewals of the Council is based on the restoration of the pascal mystery, and it strengthened our faith. Thanks to the guidance of the Holy Spirit, Vatican II has revealed to us the living presence of God in the contemporary Church and the world. I am very happy to have lived the years prior to and also after the Council, because these years have been a special period of grace bestowed by God on mankind. I look upon the pascal mystery as an answer from God to all religions of Asia concerning the fundamental problem of life and death.

The Japanese, like many other Asian peoples, are inclined to believe consciously or perhaps unconsciously in the doctrine of reincarnation, because it is a matrix of our cultures. If the celebration of Easter were to be correctly announced and accepted by the Asian people, it would become an earth-shaking matrix of the new cultures in Asia. No human efforts can change deep spiritual foundations of Asian cultures. I discovered the celebration of Easter to be the real core of the Redemptorist mission. I believe that the grace of plentiful Redemption by Jesus has the potential for the conversion of Asian peoples from the belief in reincarnation to the belief in the Resurrection of Christ. If we consider the very sophisticated and difficult theories concerning the belief in reincarnation in our Asian religions, we hope that the grace of conversion will work in our mission accompanied by the witness of the renewed life of the faith in regard to the mystery of Easter.

I remember my first visit to a Catholic church when I was only ten years of age. My first impression was the cheerful brightness, in comparison with that of the Buddhist temple which was mysteriously dark. Because I could not forget that first impression, I decided to seek for the light to dispel the darkness of my spiritual life after World War II. Ever since then, what I have been looking for has always been the same.

Saint Alphonsus's "conversion":

What interests me the most in reading the life of Saint Alphonsus de Liguori is his so-called "conversion." To me, it seems that his biographers do not pay sufficient attention to his change of careers. I would like to understand the "conversion" of Saint Alphonsus from a theological point of view rather than from a purely historical perspective. Even the recent biographers, such as Father Rey-Mermet or Father Jones, just follow the traditional edifying "conversion" story without any theological interpretation. The historical events of the career transition of Saint Alphonsus are told just for dramatic effect for him and his family, and commended because of his voluntary reaction to a crisis in his life. After all, the conversion of Saint Alphonsus is told with a moralistic interpretation common to his days, considering the transition only as an abandoning of the world. For my part, the changeover must have a symbolic meaning of the whole life of a real convert. Consequently, the meaning of the "conversion" of Saint Alphonsus should be interpreted theologically how it affected his whole life. I believe that the "conversion" of Saint Alphonsus was, in his deep insight, an authentic conversion in its evangelical meaning. It was a special time of grace for him and for his days, seen in the lights of the Enlightenment period from which modern atheistic Western culture has begun. He could hear the calling of the Lord for the evangelization of the world by founding a preaching community of the genuine Gospel, especially for the poor in spirit in his days, when the whole Western society needed a real conversion.

The conversion of Saint Alphonsus was ultimately the grace of the God of love. So an authentic convert wished to respond to the love of God with a life of preaching the Gospel, just like Paul the Apostle or Francis of Assisi. Among the poor in spirit of his days, Saint Alphonsus had found the love of God as an infinite redeeming love for the poor in the biblical meaning. I believe that our present generation is essentially in the same condition as in the days of Saint Alphonsus. That is, we are suffering the consequences of the modern enlightenment and the growing tide of atheism by scientific technological development. From a theological point of view, the life of Saint Alphonsus has a symbolic prophetic meaning for us, even in our days of a highly developed world.

We can find the abandoned poor living not only in a spiritual poverty but also in material poverty. When we analyze the political and economic situations of the highly developed countries, it can be very enriching for us to put Saint Alphonsus among us comparing historical differences of his days with ours. Regarding this point, the recent biographical studies of Saint Alphonsus give us good insights into his life and work.

Asian Redemptorist mission

If I authentically converted like Saint Alphonsus, I feel the responsibility, an overwhelming grand task among the people of Asia, as a Japanese Redemptorist. Quite differently, when we were initiated into the Redemptorist mission like in Japan by the Western missionaries immediately after World War II, now we, Japenese Redemptorists have come to realize a responsibility extends to all Asian countries because of the particular economic and political strength of Japan. We must be always mindful of the last war and of the colonization to the peoples of Asia. Also we must be more aware of the fear and ever-present danger of a so-called economic invasion in the underdeveloped countries of Asia.

Besides all this, we Japanese must never forget that our nation was the first country in the world to experience the real destructive power of an atomic bomb. If we meditate with true seriousness on this event, the mission of Redemptorists in Japan should, I think, be oriented fundamentally toward peace before all else. I truly believe that Hiroshima and all that it symbolizes could influence the whole Redemptorist Congregation regarding its overall mission goals, simply because Saint Alphonsus was not living "Hiroshima."

Besides, the spirit of world peace should be a basic characteristic of the Redemptorist Asian mission, because peace is certainly a fundamental aspiration of the different Asian religions, such as Hinduism, Buddhism, Confucianism, Shintoism, and so on. Over the past centuries, missionaries sent by the triumphant Church had difficulty in identifying this vital essence of the authentic religious feelings of the Asian peoples. Their primary goal was simply to convert them from so-called paganism. Vatican II fortunately opened the way for showing respect and tolerance toward all religions in the world. It was from this time that we were encouraged to dialogue with Asian religions so everyone could speak in the peace of Christ according to their own lights. I believe it is not a problem of missionary strategy, but rather it is the mission itself.

If we really believe in our Redemptorist mission as being the mission of the plentiful redemption, then Hiroshima and all that it signifies can open a new page in the world. It is possible that some contemporary Redemptorists may be able to feel the zeal of mission like our holy founder, thinking seriously about Ausswitz and Hiroshima. Today we have to hope and dream more than ever before for the plentiful Redemption.

The Asian Redemptorist mission can become a very important one since the people of Asia have begun to advance the last ten years on the economical front. The time has come, I believe, for all Redemptorists to respect more fully the various spiritual cultures and the authentic humanity and to help them preserve their precious human values among the turmoil and confusing economical development. As a Japanese, I realize more fully the tragedy of the possible dehumanization which can be caused by the never-ending struggle for economic existence.

Some important elements of contemporary mission

The mission methods in the days of Saint Alphonsus can be an interesting and valuable port of historical research, even in our days. Thanks to the writers of the biographies of Saint Alphonsus, I now understand how he lived and labored in the complicated social, political, and ecclesiastical environment of his days during the century of the Enlightenment. I have begun to take a new interest to study the present social, economical, and religious situation of the world. We must do this before we decide to adopt the methods that were perhaps suitable for his era, but not necessarily fitting for our era.

Economic progress is truly remarkable in the countries of Asia where the Confusian ideals are still one of big elements supporting their national policies. This applies to their political, social, and military strategies as well. I would like to use Japan as one example to explain my opinion. After the military defeat of World War II, the American occupation army had put a lot of pressure upon Japan to adopt a liberal democratic policy accompanying an effective free-market economy in order to overcome the poverty caused by the military conflict. With the truly generous economic assistance and moral support of the American government and its allies, Japan regained its economic strength due to stabilizing effects of the democratic policy for about fifteen years after the war. It was then that Japan decided to continue its economic development with the basic intention to equal and to even surpass the United States of America. At that time, the Japanese politician and the new capitalists had consciously or unconsciously begun to revive the traditional Confucian concepts of morals and ethics and incorporate them into their national enterprises.

Regarding evangelization, thanks to Christian principles democratic civil morality made great strides. The Catholic population has grown almost double due to the preaching Gospel and the widespread charitable works in the postwar days by missionaries of many Christian groups. As it frequently happens in any country, when the Japanese economy made great strides, people sometimes forget the spiritual forces that help them. Many individuals began to show a different attitude toward a liberal democratic policy, and they started to revive the traditional culture influenced of the neglected Japanese religions. If the missionaries had accepted this significant regression and showed a deeper respect for the Japanese cultures and traditions at the deeper level, perhaps evangelizers could have accommodated themselves to the reality of the situation.

I have already mentioned that Confucianism was and still is a very important element to be considered in understanding the Asian people, for instance, Japan, Korea, Taiwan, Singapore, Vietnam, China, and the immigrants all over the Asia-Oceania region. It is our responsibility and duty to study the Confucianism with all its subtle and not so subtle influence as a very dynamic system of thought or as a religion, especially concerning morality in order to realize the political, economical, and spiritual influence on the Eastern nations. We cannot afford to announce the message of the plentiful problems of the Asian people of today. This fact of reality should be a central theme in the inculturation plan of our Redemptorist mission.

Unconditional love is then sine qua non message

A turning to Christianity is essentially motivated by a love for God. This is quite different from the conversion that comes about by Englightenment contained in Buddhist teachings or in Confucianism. Simply speaking, the people of Asia cultivate Buddhist compassion and Confucian courtesy without knowing anything about the love of God, which allows us to be free to love one another in a more perfect way like God loves all mankind. However, the revelation of the love of God, as shown in the death of Jesus on the cross and his Resurrection, is very difficult to accept by human beings because of the existence of evil and sin. It took many centuries in the Western world as church history shows us. And much of the Western people succeeded in this solely through the grace of God. If we think about the differences between the Hebrew biblical cultures and the Greek Roman cultures, it seems simply miraculous. I fervently hope for the same miracle for the conversion of the Asian neighbors with the fraternal assistance and cooperation of the Western Christian peoples. Asia could be the central field for evangelization in the near future. May God bestow on us the charism of Redemptorist mission. Up until the present, when the Redemptorist missionaries were sent from Western countries, they still possessed many nationalistic ways of thinking concerning the triumphant Church that existed before the Vatican Council II. They were not convinced that a coherent unity of the foreign missionaries could give the East a very precious witness of the Gospel.

Many religions in Asia also possess a message of love. But how to efficiently announce the love of God revealed by the mystery of the death and resurrection of Jesus Christ is our very important problem. The Christian doctrines could be explained by using the methods of inculturation spoken in those days. However, the mystery of the death and resurrection of Jesus Christ is not a religious ideology and social activities. It is only the divine grace that gives us a real life transcending the laws of life and death, which we consider as part of our natural human destiny. The religions of the East show how to overcome death in order to attain a happy eternal life. It is the doctrine of helping them to realize the eternal instead of the happy life they aspire after the life on earth. We can say that probably all religious doctrines teach such a spiritual vitalistic principle or the immortality of the soul. Whereas the mystery of death and resurrection of Jesus affords us an absolutely different insight concerning life and death. The eternal life is to know a personal life of God and Jesus Christ (John 17:3). In the Gospel of John, Jesus revealed the eternal life by the symbol of the nuptial love of God with human beings, for example, in the story of the miracle at the wedding of Cana. The New Convenant promised human beings eternal life, not just by purification or by the spiritualization of life we know. This is the revelation of love of God, not just any kind of "enlightenment" of the human spirit as exists in Asian religious teachings. Saint Alphonsus was in this way an authentic convert, an ardent missionary of the Gospel. He was primarily a saint concerning the love of God. He summed up his spiritual life in his book *The Practice of the Love of Jesus Christ*. His characteristic humanity known in his days could be possibly revived among the Asian people of today just like everywhere else in the world where his spiritual sons and others like him have realized it so far.

The moral theology of Saint Alphonsus and Confuciansim

As a moral theologian, I believe that the humanity of Alphonsus is revealed particularly in his *Moral Theology* and could possibly be a basic element for a democratic policy for Asian countries. I am convinced that the Confucian humanists could acquire a genuine Christian humanity from the moral teachings of our founder. I remember even now as I visited a Catholic church for the first time to study Christianity, I wished to know about a kind of universal morality. Unconsciously as one with a Confutian background, I believed that any authentic religion should be able to teach universal moral principles like natural law. For someone who had never read the Bible up to that time, I had to find first of all a real code of human morality. Really, I needed an absolutely sure morality after the defeat of militaristic Japan. Certainly, Christianity is not by itself morality, but the Confucian intuition led me to seek for a universal human morality in any particular religion, especially when the religion looked as mysterious as Christianity.

After the Second Vatican Council, I studied the "resourced" moral theology, especially with Father Bernard Häring in Alfonsiana. The Catholic moral theology had liberated me from the moralistic tradition of Confucianism. Since 1980, I have instructed a course on moral theology in the Jesuis University of Tokyo. Meantime, what I have studied personally was to find the essence of Confucianism that could correspond to the Christian message of salvation of human beings. What actually interests me most is the difference between the patriarchy and household codes in the Mediterranean culture and the traditional Confucian culture. This theme is very important for the future ecclesiology and for the adaptation of the moral theology in Japan.

We have to realize that it is strange to teach only Western tradition of moral theology to Asian Catholic. I now have the impression that the authoritative centralization of Roman church teaching does not show a practical catholicity of the divine truth, for which I have been seeking since the time of my conversion. Recently, I have read an interesting report on the actual influence of Confucianism among the representatives, politicians, and influential capitalists in Japan. I have found almost all of them con-

vinced of their task to put new order in the future world. They are not traditional Confucianists, but very flexible, respecting Christian social morality. Anyway, their basic conviction is Confucianistic. Probably, they succeed to overcome the premodern Confusian conservatism, which is actually present in the underdeveloped countries of Asia. Consequently, it is an
important task to keep sincere dialogue with them and also to communicate
the authentic universal morale value of Christianity. They are not too close
to the essential Catholic truth. This is why our Redemptorist mission has an
actual importance for them, and if we are really open-minded we will be
respectfully accepted by them.

2. Evangelization of Asia

When I visited India for the first time several years ago, I experienced an intimate feeling for the Indian people. I recalled hearing about
Buddha and his teachings in India. On the other hand, very few of its people
are Buddhist today. Even being a convert to the Catholic faith, I realized
that my heart has some profound sympathy to the Buddhism. Regarding
Buddhism, contemporary India is quite different from Japan, but it is not
simply another foreign country as far as I am concerned. Japan is a small
island country when we consider the large eye of Asia as a whole. However,
thanks to the common traditions of religion, I feel that Japan and Indian
continent at the other extremity of Asia both have some profound elements
in common.

In 1993, I had a visitor from Vietnam and was very much impressed
with his polite behavior, since many citizens of Japan have almost lost such
a delicate regard for politeness in our westernized social way of life today.
These experiences have helped me rediscover a profound identity as someone belonging to some common cultures in Asia. This seems to me to be a
deeper dimension of my life than the fact of ethnic identity. I more fully
understand now how important it is, that there be an evangelization of whole
Asia in its cultural existence, to complete my personal conversion. I feel
there has to be a sharing with others of my conversion. That is why perhaps
one French foreign missionary in Japan told me that he was always hoping
for the evangelization of Asia—even while staying in Japan only for the
conversion of the Japanese people.

Thus the evangelization should be essentially a universal idea. That is
why the Lord wanted to send his disciples to the farthest ends of the earth.

So, in the twenty-first century, the evangelization of Asia will be a very important project. It is not only for the people in Asia but also for all other nations and tribes. The Redemptorist missionaries should be particularly conscious at all times of this fact.

New understanding of Asia

This is not a missiological study. As in the first part of my article, I continue to enlarge my personal reflection on the experiences of my life. When I tried to understand Asia as I did intellectually in Europe or in the U.S.A., I was not able to have a convergent idea about Asia. Asia seemed to me so complex to compare with Europe or North America. However, nowadays I have made changes in the method to understand more fully Asia by itself.

Reflecting on my life experiences, I have rediscovered Asia in myself. For me, Asia is no more an object just of the sciences, but a concrete existence with which I am totally immersed. I understand that the different cultures are the expressions of this existence. As I study Asia and its people, I am sharing in those religious cultures in a very profound level of human life. Because the various Asian religious have their long histories, the people are morally supported by them in their deep conscience, even up to the present times. In many cases, they cannot explain their positions due to education, but their convictions are in their very bones.

The various religious cultures could be understood in several dimensions, for example, ideology, philosophy, spirituality. Consequently, there are big gaps in agreement among the different cultures, but there is still an unexplainable unity, concerning mankind and the meaning of his existence. Why there is syncretism of religions? Japan itself can be a real example. My answer is this. Asian people consider the religious cultures as the expression of a most fundamental dimension of human existence, which is nowhere like the intellectual dimension of the cultures. I believe that it is due to the wisdom of these civilizations which have never tried to convince themselves of having the ultimate answer to the meaning of life, compared to the Judeo-Christian revelation according to our way of thinking. In any case, if we try to understand Asia as individual nations and tribe then, we discover more and more the diversity and differences. Instead, if we study Asia from deeper cultural dimensions, specially regarding religion, we will be able to find a form of unity like a common soul for the life of the Asian people. I have experienced this with a study of Confucianism.

Christianity and cultures

Analyzing in retrospect my own personal conversion, I have come to a conclusion concerning one tendency of foreign missionaries when they teach Christian religion in Asia. They are perhaps, it seems to me, not always to be conscious of the complete Christian religious doctrine formulated in the history of church in the West. In other words, some but not all missionaries seem to understand that the Gospel message is a pure, intellectual affair of the mind which could be communicated universally as truth transcending human cultures. Sometimes many seem to be, but not all, teaching a Christian culture of the West alone with the Gospel message. This is why, maybe, Asian people consider Christianity as a Western religion.

For instance, the word itself of the Gospel is a strange term for us explaining the essence of Christianity, because we Asian people do not always understand cultural context of the origin of the Christianity. How many missionaries have assisted us in overcoming this cultural shock so far? Since the apostolic exhortation *Evangelii Nuntiandi* was published, the Church has begun to take into consideration the cultural value necessary for evangelization. However, as far as some missionaries may not study as well as they should foreign cultures, the term *evangelization of the cultures*, or *inculturation*, can be quite misleading and the cause of some intellectual and emotional confusion.

The study of cultures is an enormous undertaking that theologians should accept before all else. The urgent necessity for the study of the cultures should be requested of the moralists today, because they are inclined to study only the normative morality without studying the cultures of the people. I feel that if the Redemptorist moral theologians follow their holy founder, they would study the cultural background of the people before imposing the normative morality. Saint Alphonsus was certainly more human than speculative when he proposed his moral theory of "equiprobablism" in his days.

As for the methods of study of different cultures, anthropology, and the comparative study of religion are accepted as normal. However, for a deeper Christian study of the cultures, the theological reflections are necessary, that is, reflection on how God may appreciate human cultures or reflection on how to appreciate cultural values and cultural differences. We Asian respect and appreciate the so-called Judeo-Christian cultures of the

West. However, it is our fervent hope and prayer that the authentic Gospel message would help us to re-create in Asia improved human cultures for our salvation in Asia. So the messenger of the Gospel is expected to be open-minded and understanding.

Eschatology in Asia

Foreign missionaries from the Western world sometimes study only the language of the country where they are assigned. They are so busy teaching Christianity and announcing the Good News that the study of the cultures of the people are considered only as a free option, or a hobby perhaps. Then they unwittingly impose Christian doctrine formulated in Christian cultures from their own hometowns and after the conversion of the people, they also wish to Christianize (practically westernize) the cultures of the people too. This is the ordinary method of evangelization in many instances. Sometimes the missionaries profit from the intellectual and spiritual ignorance of the people for the success of their evangelizing. We don't doubt their goodwill, kindness, and generosity, but goodwill is just not enough. Certainly, we need their material and moral support, for example, when Japan was in its dire poverty after World War II. We were thankful for the generosity of material supplied by various Western countries. However, at the time we experienced a deep dissatisfaction, since no one could even imagine our sincere longing for spiritual consolation beyond the purely material assistance.

The people of Asia are living with deep eschatological expection. We also have apocalyptic imaginations, which are quite different from Judeo-Christian teaching. In any case, we are living with the eschatological problems through the eyes and minds of different universal religions different from Christianity in Asia, Hinduism, Buddhism, Taoism, and Confucianism. The eschatological expectations are not just philosophical questions. There are authentic problems of life. The conversion as an amazing grace of God must be the answer. Then, a new life in the eschatological meaning should be lived in the culture of the people which they were born into by the providence of God, who wills all people to be saved.

One of the most important problems for the evangelization of Asia, as I see from here, is how to live a new Christian life in our individual and separate religious cultures as far as authentic human cultures. If we understand the term *inculturation* in this meaning, it will be a very heavy assign-

ment to carry out over the next millennium. Are the Redemptorist missionaries ready to accept this task for the evangelization of Asia?

3. Conclusion

Why is Asia so materially poor and destroying much of its natural
resources and environment? This is the first and fundamental question when
we try to look at the actual situation of Asia. What is the cause of this
extraordinary poverty of the majority of the people? I think that one of the
causes of poverty could be clarified by historical conditions rather than
geographical ones.

It is important that we all do some reflections on how Asia has lived
in the modern times since the seventeenth century (approximately the lifetime of Saint Alphonsus), especially how Asia has interpreted the movements of Western enlightenment and the civilization. I believe that Asia has
had its own cultural problems to accept the Western civilizations. Even
today Asian peoples who love their own original cultures have difficulty in
accepting Western civilization in its entirety. When Japan had to open its
doors to Western civilization at the end of the eighteenth century, the Japanese wished stubbornly to preserve their own spiritual values. They wished
to learn about only technological advance of the West.

Under various forms of colonialism by the Western countries, Asia
has had a long cultural struggle to preserve its national identity. Consequently, the people of Asia preferred to be poor materially in order to keep
intact their cultures. Today they have to face a new cultural struggle against
Western democracy and free-market economy, even if they are not ready
for it, which is widely accepted by many nations. A future world economy
has put Asia in the spotlight as a most important economic market. Asia is
now faced with this Western type of economy and trying to retain their
spiritual values. It is the time for the Western countries to reflect profoundly
on the benefits and defects of the free democracy.

Western thinkers are nowadays speaking about postmodern culture
or civilization and human values they wish to spread. We can find the social teaching of recent popes containing critical reflections on the Western
democratic cultures, especially free-market economies, for example, in
"Centesimus Annus."

The people of Asia must continue to seek for an ideal human culture
today as a world problem, because it is especially an ethical problem to be

resolved together with the West. There are special concerns regarding the environmental ethics, bioethics, ethics of human dignity, and so on. The evangelization of Asia should be planned in a global context with common welfare of all mankind kept in mind.

Thanks be to our loving God, holy Redeemer, and thanks to our holy founder of the Congregation, Saint Alphonsus. I hope I can continue my spiritual journey as a poor convert in order to realize a real vocation as Redemptorist and to give thanks for the immense grace of conversion.

Copiosa apud eum Redemptio.

11

THE PROPHETIC VOCATION OF THE RE-DEMPTORISTS WITHIN THE CHURCH

Antonio Hortelano, C.Ss.R.
Province of Madrid
Translated by Damián Wall
Province of Puerto Rico

ON FEBRUARY 2, 1945, I decided to be a Redemptorist for the rest of my life.

The Congregation of the Most Holy Redeemer was founded in Naples in 1732, the result of a series of fantastic and providential happenings. Mother Maria Celeste Crostarosa developed a Christocentric mysticism at a time when the "Illuminated" were content to talk about God as the universal Architect totally disinterested in human trivia from the rooftops down. Saint Alphonsus Mary Liguori, however, insisted on the Redemptorists' missionary vocation in favor of the most abandoned, who lived under those rooftops, and the necessity of the study of moral theology as the foundation of a serious commitment with life in all its realities. The Austrian Saint Clement Mary Hofbauer, patron of Vienna, added to this Redemptorist commitment the notes of universality and openness to the whole world, along with the formation of committed laypeople within their own earthy realities.

At the moment there are about six thousand Redemptorists spread throughout the world.

1. Why Did I Become a Redemptorist?

My mother was left a widow in 1931. She was an extraordinary woman, fair-skinned, blue-eyed and with exceptional social graces. Although very young when my father died and somewhat pressured by various suitors, she had no intention of remarrying; rather, she dedicated herself completely to raising her three children and to a sundry of social activities. She actively participated in the founding of the "Accion Catolica," a center to right political party (La CEDA), and in starting a semi-clandestine group of Christian women leaders supported by various bishops, who among themselves were known as "the confraternity." Father José Machiniena, the Redemptorist provincial, belonged to this group.

We lived on Nicasio Gallego street, near the sanctuary of Perpetual Help, the provincial residence of the Spanish Redemptorists. It was there that Father Ibarrola organized a youth group of the "Accion Catolica," at that time perhaps the best group in Madrid. I belonged to this group and through it I came to know the Redemptorists.

During the Spanish Civil War, the "Reds" closed all the churches in the Republican Zone and shot thirteen bishops, some five thousand priests, and about five hundred religious sisters. In collaboration with some Redemptorists, my mother organized in our home some clandestine house Masses. Four Redemptorists that celebrated in our home were shot as well as my uncle. My mother was sentenced to death by a military court. They accused her of having participated in the "CEDA" and "Accion Catolica"; she defended herself as best she could against the political charges, but as to the accusation about the "Accion Catolica" she told the military: "I am a Catholic one hundred percent. If for this you want to shoot me, then do it." The head soldier answered her: "You have spoken very well, comrade. You are free to go." Of course, she continued with the home Masses celebrated by Father Ibarrola with the help of Brother Telesforo.

One day during the celebration of one such Mass, just after the consecration, the military broke in on them. The Mass was being celebrated at the dining-room table. Father Ibarrola, fearing lest one of the soldiers were to grab the glass with the consecrated wine, casually took hold of it himself, raised it, and with the greatest serenity said: "To your health, comrades." Perhaps the theology of the Eucharist has never been better expressed!

After the Civil War, Father Ibarrola was assigned to the Redemptorist community at the sanctuary of Perpetual Help, which had been converted into a warehouse by the "Reds." With the help of a youth group, he cleaned it up, rang the bells, and celebrated Mass. He had to distribute communion for almost forty-eight hours straight. The people were simply hungry for God.

It was then that I decided to be a Redemptorist. My sister had just begun her studies in pharmacology, and I had been interested in architecture. But I thought that it would be more interesting to help God build men rather than houses. The house Masses organized by my mother during the religious persecution and the people's hunger of God at the end of the Civil War were for me the finishing touches on my vocational process.

2. How Did I Become a Redemptorist?

I had decided to become a priest and a Redemptorist. But I wanted to be a Redemptorist and a priest in a new style. It was something that I had very clear from the beginning. I wanted to be a prophet of new times, but to be a prophet is like being a stone in the soup—one can crack a few teeth denouncing unjust and anachronistic structures and announcing dreams and utopias. Many years later I discovered my ideas voiced by my good friend and Swiss confrere Paul Hitz when he said that the Redemptorists should be prophets "in the central nave of the church rather than in the side chapels."

I began forming myself in this new style of priest and Redemptorist in our theologate in Astorga (Spain). The first point I considered was to make myself as strong as steel. I knew that to be a prophet in the twentieth century, it would be absolutely necessary to be tough. To be, as Saint Paul puts it, willing to suffer hunger and deprivation, heat and cold, live in other countries, be praised and criticized—in a word, to have "hippopotamus skin." To help me, I had an incredible superior, Father Zabalza, a man of steel, who took it upon himself to toughen me up. When I finished my theological studies and took leave of him, he embraced me with tears. He asked my forgiveness for having been so rough with me. He said he really did trust in me, although we were of such different mentalities.

Another important point that I had clear was the role of poetry in the formation of creative and integral persons, thanks to Father Rada, philosopher and poet. We got very involved in what we called "chemically pure poetry." We identified with the generation of '98 and of '27; we enjoyed the visit and encouragement of the extraordinary poet Gerardo Diego; we tried our hand at every possible poetic form. "Chemically pure poetry" is that which is left after translating a poem into another language and defies translation. It is beyond logic, but with the use of metaphors as dazzling as flashes one can get insights to indescribable horizons unaccessible to logical concepts. Today more than ever, we know that to be an investigator, philosopher, executive, communicator, and mystic, part of our being needs a good dose of poetry.

A third point was that I realized the importance of philosophy, especially metaphysics, to find the ultimate foundation of being. We questioned everything and anxiously searched for the ultimate "why" of things and happenings. We accepted nothing simply "because." It's not that we felt insecure. We believed in Aristotelian logic and was fascinated by the history of philosophy and identified with the School of Madrid: Ortega, Unamuno, Morente, Marias, Zubiri. I devoured the complete works of Ortega; he was my preferred philosopher. I enjoyed the clarity of his ideas, his brilliant metaphors and their connection with the concrete realities of the world we lived in. My pedagogy and style of preaching has been inspired by this Ortegian stance to which I would add the brevity and incisiveness of Azorin. These two authors have helped me to reinterpret the Alphonsian style of announcing the great truths to the public in such a way that even the most simple can understand them.

Philosophy, however, was never for me just a lengthy exercise closed in on itself but rather, as Professor Rada told us repeatedly with the words of José Antonio, the true philosopher is the one who is willing to give his existence for his essence and not the opposite.

Ascending beyond the limits of transcendence, I encountered Christ. Grateful for the influence of the venerable Crostarosa, Saint Alphonsus put Christ as the focal point in our lives and our need to follow and imitate him. In an epoch such as the "Illumination" of the seventeenth century, with its insistence on a Supreme Being disinterested in our little lives, to speak brazenly of the baby Jesus and to praise him with Christmas carols ("*Tu scendi dalle stelle,*" the national Italian carol composed by Saint Alphonsus), to paint pictures of Jesus, graphically crucified, and to put Christ in the very center of life was a veritable scandal. I was delighted with this Christocentric dimension of Redemptorist spirituality. But sad to say, the theology taught in our times in the seminary was not very palatable. It lacked a biblical base, did not consider the real person nor the real world in which he lived, and used an abstract language that had no grasp on reality. To fill these voids, I read everything we had in the library—books and magazines— that dealt with the French and German "New Theology." I thoroughly enjoyed its use of sources and its orientation toward life.

For me, theology was not just a purely academic pursuit that one did seated at a desk. Rather, as Urs von Balthasar so well put it, theology is an activity of the knees (before speaking of God, we should talk with him first) and an activity of the feet (theology is the base for the mission and preaching). I was deeply struck on learning that Saint Alphonsus, after having preached so many popular missions, shut himself in his room for many years to write his *Moral Theology* for the purpose of forming his missionaries.

Several of us as students, organized the Saint Alphonsus Missionary Academy. We read, gave conferences and congresses, and made ourselves known throughout Spain for our creativity and commitment. Thanks to Father Sagredo, a Redemptorist missionary in China, we were vibrant with the missionary ideal to the point that many of us volunteered to go to China, one of the poorest regions in the world—with temperatures that dropped to forty degrees below zero. I wasn't accepted. My superiors told me that they didn't want volunteers and assigned me to other works.

I had to go to Rome to obtain a doctorate in theology, but I carried very deep in my heart the missionary virus. It has always oriented my theological studies and teaching career toward life. This was precisely the subject of my doctoral thesis. Any theological presentation of the salvific "Good News" of Jesus that "does not complicate our life" is an alienation from his Word. At the end of any theological course, one has to "pass something" and, if one doesn't pass, then the theology isn't what it should be, that is, a deepening of the salvific message of Christ. "Faith without works is dead," says James.

Another very important aspect of the Redemptorist vocation for me was the openness of the Congregation to the laity. With several other confreres, we wanted to form a kind of "shock troop" composed of young laypersons. Saint Clement Mary Hofbauer, the second founder of the Redemptorists and the one responsible for establishing it throughout the world, helped us with this concept. We rediscovered his ideas and made them stylish among the younger Redemptorists.

In the middle of the crisis caused by laicism and secularization, Saint Clement organized a group of laypersons, men and women, committed to the Gospel and social issues who were willing to live the Word of God to its ultimate consequences in the world that surrounded them. They had such influence in the fields of earthly realities—arts, science, education, and politics—that they became a concern for the police of various countries of central Europe. It seemed to me then, and still seems so now, that "given the lack of priestly vocations and the incongruity of having priests actively involved in politics and other similar temporal affairs," the Church should be able to count on well-formed and truly committed laypersons. Why, then, do not we Redemptorists of the twentieth and twenty-first centuries do something similar to that which Saint Clement did during the eighteenth and nineteenth centuries? Since I was a theological student I have always wanted to work in this area and was able to achieve this goal when we began the "Committed Christian Communities (EAS)" in Paris in 1959, which are now established in several different nations.

Saint Clement also taught us to be citizens of the world. His father was German and his mother was a Slav. He traveled throughout Europe and dreamed of extending his field of action to the Americas and Asia. Today as we become more conscious of the world as a great global village, I thank Saint Clement for his influence in having formed me in this universal spirit. I have spent a good time of my life going hither and yon on three continents; this has made me more open and flexible and at the same time it has enriched me extraordinarily.

Universality helped us to discover the importance and reality of ecumenism. Saint Clement, as Saint Paul, attempted to be all things to all people. For him, it didn't matter if he was working for Catholics, Protestants, or Jews. He was open to all persons. Such was the case that some of his Redemptorist confreres remarked that where he lived it seemed to be more a madhouse than a rectory.

The Redemptorists are perhaps the group from the West that have the most communities of Oriental Rite confreres in Russia, the Ukraine, Byelorussia, Syria, Iraq, Canada, and the United States of America. Thanks to Father Santiago Morillo, we had, as students, the opportunity of participating in the eucharistic celebrations of the Byzantine Rite, which helped us live more vividly the possibilities of ecumenism. Much later, because of my relations with Taiz, the Anglican Church, and certain Jewish communities, I have been able to appreciate that ecumenical openness we enjoyed as students.

The pinnacle of my formative years was moral theology. I finished my doctorate in theology at the Gregorian University in Rome. A gold medal that I received on the occasion was to orient my life in unsuspected ways.

During the term of office of the Dutch Redemptorist superior general and moral theologian, Father Leonard Buyjs, the Redemptorists wanted to open in Rome an Alphonsian Academy of Moral Theology, mindful of the fact that Saint Alphonsus, Doctor of the Church, was also the patron of confessors and moral theologians. I was informed that I was to be a professor at the projected Alphonsian Academy and as theology was a bit too abstract, I was sent to Louvain (Belgium) to obtain a master's degree in psychology and another in economics. I was there for three years and then another year in Paris to study depth psychology. In 1959, I began to teach moral theology in Rome.

While in Paris we organized, along the lines that Saint Clement had drawn in times past, the Committed Christian Communities (EAS), which is composed of married couples, young single men and women, and some religious and diocesan priests. Today the EAS has extended to various countries throughout the world and constitutes a private society of faithful that have committed themselves to share their lives in community. Some live in their own homes and meet periodically; others live in geographic communities in independent housing in the same area with some communal areas (chapel and meeting rooms); and others have geographic communities that share work and resources. The EAS communities are a way of life and a commitment to social progress and evangelization based on earthly realities. Thanks to the EAS, I have been able to evangelize and do moral theology with my feet firmly planted in the realities of this life.

3. If I Had to Do It Over Again,
Would I As a Redemptorist?

I am celebrating fifty years of priesthood. If I were the age that I was when I was ordained a priest and with the accumulated experience of all these years, would I do it over again as a Redemptorist? I would like to answer that very indiscrete question with absolute sincerity. I do not deny that the Redemptorists have had problems with me and I with them. It is certainly true that celibacy costs in certain moments of life. It is true that sometimes the structures of the Church are burdensome. It is true this, it is true that... But despite all of this, all of them, and myself, today I can say with absolute sincerity that I would do it over again as a priest, a Redemptorist, a moral theologian, and as a member of EAS.

I like being single so I can be an itinerant, with suitcase in hand and little baggage to worry about. I like the Redemptorist prophetic vocation of being in the middle of the Church and not in a side chapel. I like the equilibrium of Saint Alphonsus in his defense of the essential and his relativization of the accidental. I like his openness to the most needy whom we should never deny absolution. I like the simplicity of the Redemptorists and their closeness with the people. I like the mission announcement of the

Good News to the abandoned. I like the way Redemptorists talk to the people in a simple, dignified way so all can understand the message. I like Alphonsian moral theology and the way it serves as a swing between the utopic and the realistic for men and women in a real world. I like ecumenism as a fraternal opening to our older brothers in the faith—the Jewish people, and to our separated brothers—the Orthodox, Anglicans, and Evangelicals— all followers of the same Christ who recapitulates in himself all things and all persons. I like the respectful courage of Saint Alphonsus and his sons when, with great respect for Holy Mother the Church, we manifest our sadness over ecclesiastic limitations: for example, when Saint Alphonsus insisted that Pope Clement XIV not unjustly suppress the Jesuits; or as now, when some Redemptorist moral specialists valiantly express, with great respect, their viewpoints concerning such conflictive areas as bioethics, responsible parenthood, and the pastoring of divorced and remarried Catholics.

For all these reasons, certain regrets notwithstanding, if I were twenty-five years old again, I would become a Redemptorist. From this vantage point, I encourage our youth who feel called to be Redemptorists to fearlessly take that step, confident in the knowledge that they will receive the help they need from Christ and the community, to announce with clarion call, as is were, freedom for the poor of the world. Ah, and one more thing: that they don't forget that in order to do something great for the kingdom of God, they will have to decide to swing on the high trapeze without a safety net below!

12

A Charism to Be
Lived in Community

Samuel J. Boland, C.Ss.R.
Province of Canberra

1. Curriculum Vitae

My first contact with the Redemptorists was on the occasion of a mission in my home parish of Kangaroo Point. I must have been very young when my older sisters and brother took me to hear Father Jack Walsh, who for his fame as a children's missioner was being called "the Australian Father Furniss." He certainly held me spellbound along with the other children who filled the church. Years afterward, as a novice, I tried to enliven the common room with an edifying anecdote. The master rather spoiled the effect by interjecting, "That's just something you heard from Jack Walsh." It is true that the children did not easily forget what they heard from Father Walsh. When I met him in Ireland after the lapse of thirty years or so, we were able to exchange many happy memories of Kangaroo Point and of so many other places where he had worked his magic to captivate the hearts of the children.

From that first meeting I was strongly drawn by the dream of one day being like Father Walsh. In the years that followed, the attraction was strengthened. It was a good time for missions before World War II. Every three years the Redemptorists came back to the parish, and they never failed to create an atmosphere of intense excitement. Their life attracted me more and more. Looking back now, I must confess that I was not impressed by the good they seemed to be doing for the people as much as by the fact that they seemed to be quite special priests, different from the ones we saw Sunday after Sunday. In any case, in spite of motivation no doubt less than ideal, I met with nothing but encouragement from my family and from the curate of the parish, so the way was made easy for my going to the juvenate. That for me was the decisive step. Those that followed were a matter of course, even though they affected me at the time, novitiate and studies, even profession and ordination.

After ordination my dream of being a great missioner like Father Walsh quickly evaporated. World War II had not long ended, and it had become necessary to replace almost the entire staff of our studendate. I was asked to fill in for those who were being prepared to replace those men who had become incapacitated by age or ill health. For half a dozen years I taught, or perhaps I ought to say I stood in front of classes, sacred scripture and philosophy. Then the provincial approached me, apologetically it seemed, with the suggestion that I fill the one remaining post, that of church history. That was to remain my mission, not one I had chosen, but one to which I was sent. After all, that is what a mission means. It was to remain so until my last classes—in the nineties.

As it happened, there was no time for regrets over the vanished missionary career. My work absorbed my attention. It has continued like that to the present. It is not as exciting as the missions, but it has been by no means unrewarding. I know very well that my life has been enriched by the study of material I had to prepare for the students; and it has been warmed more than once by those who have expressed appreciation of my efforts. Most of all, perhaps, I have found reason to be thankful that it has been possible to give more time to Saint Alphonsus, his life and his writings. That is an immense blessing. At the start of my teaching, I was fortunate in having a rector who was sympathetic and encouraging. He is only one among the many whose companionship will always be a treasured memory. There have been times when I needed help. It is the same, surely, for everyone. In my own case, which is not at all special, I have never had to look far. There has always been someone only too ready to offer the little word that was needed—and often enough, it was not even necessary to ask. It has also been most gratifying to find in Redemptorist communities a ready sense of humor. Is there a special Redemptorist style of humor? I know I have found in other parts of the world the same sorts of anecdotes that have brightened my life since my days in the juvenate; and that is more years ago than I care to remember.

A precious benefit of Redemptorist life is competent spiritual direction. It is so close at hand. For myself, it has always been a source of encouragement, at times sorely needed, to find just a few doors down the corridor the very man to answer my queries. I cannot even imagine that my experience in this respect has been unique. It is not the sort of thing one talks about, of course; but without the need to ask, one can be sure that many others besides myself have reason to thank God for the experienced and understanding confessor always ready to answer a call for help.

Companionship in the Congregation has always been for me a happy memory. I shall always be most grateful for the close friendships I have found among my fellow Redemptorists. Some of those who were closest to me are already dead, and for me their memory is a constant incentive to remain a Redemptorist like them. I hope to join them one day. If that should seem an unworthily human motivation, let me add that as a Redemptorist I have come to know God's redeeming love in ways that would otherwise have been closed to me. He will always remain my principal reason for being faithful.

2. The Redemptorist Community

Redemptorists are gregarious creatures. They work together and they live together. They share a common purpose, which is, as their Constitutions say, "to follow the example of Jesus Christ, the Redeemer, by preaching the Word of God to the poor." It is their manner of sharing in the mission of Christ, which is their distinctive characteristic, and the bond that unites them, as their Constitutions go on to declare,

> In carrying out its mission in the Church, the Congregation unites members who live together and form one missionary body. These dedicate themselves to God by profession, and so devote themselves to their mission as a living unit, each contributing through his ministry what belongs to him.

That is the way it was from the beginning. The Congregation of the Most Holy Savior, which was inaugurated in Scala in November 1732, was different from the other types of congregation that existed at the time. There were, in fact, several associations of priests engaged in the preaching apostolate, but their members generally lived apart, busying themselves with other pastoral duties and coming together for their missionary campaigns or for common study. What was different about the new Institute was that its members were devoted solely to their common apostolate. That was a risky thing to do in the suspicious atmosphere of regalist Naples.

Gennaro Sarnelli, one of the first and most enthusiastic of the pioneers, wrote from the city that rumor was busy about a new religious institute that was being established in Scala.

A Congregation was not a name likely to alarm the sensitive ears in the royal court. The name covered a wide variety of pious associations. The way the new band was living, however, was decidedly hazardous, under a superior and according to a regular order of the day. After an initial uncertainty the first members were enthusiastic and dedicated, even venturesome. From Scala, a new foundation was made at Villa degli Schiavi, and others were contemplated. It was not long before the missions proved themselves to the extent that the king's ministers gave their blessing to further expansion, generous with promises even while they withheld the all-important royal approbation of the Institute itself. At an early stage the character of the missionaries of the Most Holy Savior, soon to be known as Redemptorists, had become established. They worked for the people in teams, and in their houses they formed the team spirit that was to give power to their preaching.

3. Beginnings

The small group that assembled in Scala in November 1732 was not yet clear as to their identity. Clarifying that identity occasioned much heartbreak. For the moment, though, the would-be pioneers were content with the leadership of Alphonsus, whose innovative mission preaching was already being acclaimed. Early in 1733, Alphonsus set out with three companions—Mannerini, Donato, and Romano—to evangelize Tramonti, the rugged hill country above Scala. It was a new experience for the preachers, accustomed to the large crowds and spectacular ceremonies in the fashionable churches of Naples. The four men went to tiny hamlets of a couple hundred or so inhabitants, nestling in the folds of the hills, spending ten days or more with each. For the simple villagers, so isolated in their poverty, it was a rare spiritual treat to be offered so much instruction and exhortation and spiritual guidance. A campaign like that for the marginalized people of society was new, and highly successful too. It demonstrated the distinctive contribution the Congregation of the Most Holy Savior was to make to the Church's mission of continuing redemption.

Unhappily, the Tramonti campaign and the ceremony on the ninth of November turned out to have been premature. Disagreement about the direction the Congregation should take led to a division that left Alphonsus and Brother Vito alone with the amiable Canon Pietro Romano ready to lend a hand as required. It was not long, however, before others came to replace Mannerini, Donato, and the insufferably self-important Tosquez. Men of the stamp of Sarnelli, Mazzini, Sportelli, and Rossi offered better promise of permanence. The new beginning was slow and painful through Falcoia's insistence on "seeing to everything," as he put it. But this time the foundation was thoroughly laid, as can be seen from the correspondence between Alphonsus and Falcoia. By the time of the latter's death in 1743, the charism of the Congregation had been sufficiently identified and needed just the clarification Alphonsus could easily provide with his unerring pastoral sense and acute understanding of the regalists of the court.

Scarcely a month after the "schism," the bishop of Castellammare wrote to Alphonsus about the *Regola* on which he had been working. Ever since Maria Celeste Crostarosa had spoken in October 1731 of the new institute seen in a vision, Falcoia had embraced the project with possibly more enthusiasm than sound judgment, referring to it in his correspondence as l'Opera. On this occasion he spoke of having reached agreement with Don Giulio Torni, who had been consulted by Alphonsus about the rules. Concerning poverty, wrote Falcoia, he and Torni were in accord in looking for a way to keep the subjects free of distracting preoccupations. That expressed very well a basic principle of the Institute, one that was to become especially underlined in the formulation by Alphonsus. The members were to preach the Gospel to the poor after the example of Christ, the Redeemer, and nothing was to be allowed to obscure that dedication.

During the years that followed, as the Congregation found its way toward its definitive shape, the direction of its members to their apostolate remained unchanged. What is most likely the very first formal description of the new Institute came in the submission made in 1736 to the chief minister, the Marchese de Monteallegre, in the hope of gaining royal approbation. The text seems to have been composed by Falcoia; but his correspondence shows that he had consulted Alphonsus after he had heard that the Marchese might be favorably disposed.

The document introduces the priests living together in the houses of Scala, Villa, and Ciorani, and then goes on to tell of their life and work. "In the abovementioned houses they live a perfect community life, under their own superiors, giving of themselves for the people." The members of the Congregation lived together for the sake of their ministry. That is how

Alphonsus formulated the end of the Institute in the text of the Rules he submitted to the Holy See in 1748.

> The purpose of this institute is to form a Congregation of secular priests living a community life under the title of the Most Holy Savior....The sole purpose of this Congregation is to follow the example of our Savior, Jesus Christ, in preaching the divine Word to the poor.

Dedication to preaching the Gospel was most emphatically the bond that united the first Redemptorists. When the work seemed to be threatened by a certain instability of membership, they bound themselves by a vow, to which was added later an oath, of perseverance. This obligation, added to the religious vows, emphasizes their consecration to their apostolate. The same is to be said of the vow, taken from 1743, to renounce all offices, even ecclesiastical, that might conflict with the vocation of the Institute itself.

The companions of Saint Alphonsus took seriously their dedication to preaching. They wrote into their rules the obligation to weekly gatherings for common study of mission practice, of theology, sacred scripture, and the spiritual life. Many, no doubt, still remember the "academies." They were a common feature of eighteenth-century Naples, and Alphonsus had known them when he was a member of the Propaganda. They remained too long, perhaps, after their enthusiasm had unhappily cooled. They were diligent students in those early days, as is still plainly evidenced by the libraries that have survived, for example, in Pagani and Scifelli. They were an invaluable resource for the apostolic workers provided by a major superior, who was the Most Zealous Doctor.

Under the leadership of Alphonsus, the inspiration was entirely apostolic. In his circulars he asked what the people would think if the missioners did not live poorly, and how could the preaching have effect if one was not prepared to pull one's weight in the team. Even the houses in which they lived, he assured the pope, were to be in country places so as to be handy to the people to whom they were especially sent. They were authentically apostolic communities.

4. Beyond the Alps

The community Saint Clement established in Warsaw was apostolic, dynamically so. From the beginning in 1787, the numbers quickly grew through the compelling attraction of the superior's restless zeal. In 1802, a report to the nuncio, Severoli, in Vienna described an almost unbroken daily sequence of Masses, sermons, and devotions in the church, together with a demanding ministry in the confessional. The activity in St. Benno's was aptly described by Clement's biographer, Father Hofer, as a "perpetual mission," which entailed, in fact, "a multiplicity of divine services, such as can hardly be crowded into the space of an ordinary mission nowadays." This was in addition to the schools for the long neglected children of Warsaw and the orphans whose numbers had so sadly multiplied as Poland was divided by rapacious neighbors.

Those who lived in St. Benno's in those days included novices and students, as well as those so busily occupied in the church. Fathers Joseph Passerat and Jacques Vannelet had scruples about so much activity, which they saw as incompatible with the prayer life of the community. Their complaint to the rector major, Father Blasucci, resulted in an exchange of letters between Warsaw and Pagani, the outcome of which was that St. Benno's and its apostolate were left undisturbed. There had, however, emerged different attitudes toward the Redemptorist community. How divergent these views were would soon become apparent.

Shortly after Saint Clement's death in March 1820, the emperor formally admitted the Congregation into the empire, granting it the church of Maria am Gestade with an adjacent residence. At the end of May, Father Passerat was named vicar general by the rector major, Father Mansione. When Passerat arrived in Vienna in October, he found a dozen novices with more waiting to join them. One of the novices said that practically all of them "owed the beginning of their vocation, as well as their fervor, to their association with the Apostle of Vienna." Following a personality as charismatic as Clement Hofbauer could never be easy. In the case of Father Passerat, it became clear that he was still the man who had been so much troubled by the incessant activity he had experienced in Warsaw.

It soon became evident that all was not well in the community at Maria am Gestade. Some of those who had come to the Congregation so eagerly began to ask for dispensation from their vows, and cases of the brilliant preacher, Father Johann Emmanuel Veith, set rumors flying. It was a disturbing time for the new Redemptorists, and it occasioned some correspondence with the rector major, some letters complaining of a situation calling for remedial action, and others defending the vicar general. Of the latter, the one that commands most respect was from the learned and saintly disciple of Saint Clement, Father Johann Madlener, who wrote: "Our good vicar wishes that we sanctify ourselves first and then others; many of us, on the other hand, wish to sanctify others first, or ourselves and others together." With the writer's own underlining highlights the basic cause of tension. It was a question of a view of community life different from the one that had been known in St. Benno's and different, too, from what many of the admirers of Clement Hofbauer had expected.

It would not be incorrect to say that under Father Passerat the community had become introspective. It would serve no useful purpose to detail the complaints made to Pagani. There was a difference in perspective, marking a new direction for the Congregation outside Italy. Historians speak of the nineteenth century as the Age of Revolution. Some of them speak of the Churches generally as being bewildered by the changing times and tending stubbornly to resist progress. It was a time when religious leaders clung, almost desperately, to the past—to what was tried and proven. It was in this spirit of anxious nostalgia that Father Passerat went to so much trouble to acquire a copy of the Constitutions of the Chapter of 1764, which had been considerably modified among the Redemptorists of southern Italy.

That further source of tension led, inevitably one has to say, to the unfortunate division imposed by the Holy See in 1853, setting up the "Congregation of the Most Holy Redeemer in the Kingdom of the Two Sicilies." It was the other and larger part of the original Institute that celebrated the General Chapter of 1855, in which the capitulars "canonized" the Constitutions of 1764 and the Passerat regime. When the Neapolitans in 1869, exhausted by their sufferings at the hands of the Garibaldians, asked for reunion, that regime extended to the whole Congregation.

The pattern of Redemptorist life confirmed in 1855 proved remarkably durable, as did the nostalgic conservatism of the nineteenth-century Churches. It is a way of life that many still remember and not necessarily with regret. Naturally, with the long survival of the legislation of 1764 much of the very earliest observances remained.

The Redemptorists kept their emphasis on the preaching vocation, with particular importance given to the missions. The missions were not merely their principal works, but in many places their only pastoral activity. That, of course, gave a strong sense of unity to the Congregation. There was, at least in theory, a heavy stress on study for the continuing preparation of the preachers. The academies were held each week, as in the days of Saint Alphonsus. But things had changed very much since eighteenth-century Naples; and one might fairly question whether these meetings, regularly checked by provincials, were kept for their formative value or just because they were in the Constitutions. One frequently heard it said that "we spend our lives among books." Certainly, the Rule insisted on care for maintaining and using the domestic libraries to promote study by the missionaries. It must be said, too, that the importance attached to the order of the day, especially the times of prayer, created an atmosphere in which it was easy to find God and prepare for his service.

Although there was a lot of good in the life of Redemptorist communities, it must be admitted that they did not escape the formalism that was the besetting defect of Church communities in the nineteenth century. There was, for example, what one is justified in calling a heavy-handed exercise of authority. Few, if any, would fail to disagree with Father Passerat's exhortation that Redemptorists remain novices all their lives. A complaint that recurred in letters to the rector major was his insistence on a blind obedience that can only be called extreme, expecting his opinions to be accepted, even in matters of theology and history. Father Mauron, elected in 1855, also showed a markedly authoritarian manner. His decisions were made with little reference to his consultors and announced boldly as the will of God. Generally speaking, the spirit of Redemptorist community life was most typically represented in the person of Father Achille Desurmont, that long-serving French provincial. Long after his lifetime his Harmony of the Rule was seen as expressing the ideal of Redemptorist life.

It would not be right to leave an impression of unrelieved gloom in those generations that have passed. There was much that was excellent in Redemptorist communities which lived by the strict order of the day. They were of necessity thrown so much together that there was inevitably an interaction that was in many respects healthy and often really enjoyable. Time of recreation, when the entire community was in the one room, provided much amusement in the relaxed conversation, anecdotes, and even card games. It was a force for unity that unquestionably welded missionaries into a team when they preached to the people. And it must not be forgotten that this kind of life produced Saint John Neumann, Blessed Peter Donders and Kasper Stanggassinger, and even the Venerable Joseph Passerat.

With the real benefits achieved in the Redemptorist family, it must still be regretted that values no less real had been lost. Most of all, it had become harder to find the link between the community and its apostolate. A community that had become introspective had lost that admirably clear vision that Saint Clement had expressed in his own typically rustic fashion: "We join the contemplative to the active life, because without the anointing of the Holy Spirit the workmen's carts creak." Before him, Saint Alphonsus had made the same point in more elegant and lapidary style: "If we look after the work, the work will look after us." It would be hard to find a better description of a community of apostolic life; and one would have to admit that the cautious nineteenth-century mentality had reversed the priorities of Alphonsus.

5. The Redemptorist Community Today

Under the legislation "canonized" in 1855, Redemptorists were quite remarkably uniform, and they remained so until World War II. The global upheaval acted as a catalyst on the Redemptorists as on society at large. The most immediately observable effect was in their pastoral activities. A catalog published in 1955 showed that, with the exception of no more than half a dozen, the provinces generally had undertaken care of parishes. In less than a decade, the safeguards of the parish missions scrupulously erected by superiors general had collapsed. In addition, the postwar years revealed almost innumerable ways in which mankind had become afflicted; and the Redemptorists responded with exemplary promptitude to the needs of so many whose plight would certainly have touched the apostolic heart of Saint Clement. The General Chapter, which revised legislation in 1967 to 1969, identified a large number of new and praiseworthy activities in most provinces. A consequence of this sudden increase of commitments emerged and occasioned anxious questioning in the subsequent Chapter of 1973. It was found that a disturbingly large number of Redemptorists were living apart from the community, *soli viventes*. They had to be taken into account in the community—but how far was unclear.

Redemptorist life as the century comes to a close is much less structured than it was in the two hundred years after 1732. Redemptorists do not come together as often as they used to. Those weekly academies that served the companions of Saint Alphonsus have disappeared: they had, after all, survived mainly as a matter of form. In their place are community meetings, which are held with varying regularity—if at all. If one were to ask how effective they were proving, it would be right to answer that in the present time of transition, it is hardly yet possible to judge. Very much the same must be said of the disappearance of the set times of prayer and the monthly recollection and annual retreat. Such matters, which all must recognize as the greatest importance, are left to personal responsibility. And now, naturally enough, those who had been accustomed to being summoned by bells are somewhat at a loss. It could well be that time is yet needed for the necessary responsibility to mature. The older times of recreation, when all were expected to take part, have not found replacements. It might well be questioned whether they should; but it could not be questioned that the camaraderie of those who have to work together is too precious to be set at risk.

6. Permanent Community Values

It would, of course, serve no purpose to waste time lamenting the things that have changed. There have, however, emerged in the two centuries of Redemptorist life certain values that deserve to be treasured. It is satisfying, for example, that Redemptorists have still an identifiable spirit, in spite of a wide variety of occupation as well as nationality. It is not very difficult for them to find common ground when they meet. Very likely that is due in large measure to the common heritage, spiritual and pastoral, they share. That is surely a sound foundation for an authentic community of life. To that end capitulars in 1967 to 1969 and later have devoted much thought, commencing a lengthy treatment with the declaration, "To perform their mission in the Church, Redemptorists perform their missionary work as a community."

New structures of community life have scarcely had time to become sufficiently assimilated to be as familiar as is desirable. It is still necessary to be alert to possible mistakes. The Cambridge historian, Owen Chadwick, has pointed out one he found as he looked at religious life in the Catholic Church after Vatican II. Some religious, he said, have tried to establish a "fraternal" lifestyle in small groups with a consequent diminution of authority. This tendency he sees as leading to what he calls another form of "inward looking." It would be a pity if an old form of introspection were to be replaced by another, distracting just as much from care of those in need. Another damaging effect of what Chadwick calls "inward looking" he finds in the separation of these small groups from such important resources for pastoral activity as a good library, liturgical celebrations, and adequate personnel. Rather typically, he emphasizes a decline of serious study as an inevitable result. For Redemptorists, there are other considerations that call for emphasis.

In every community, whether large or small, there must be provision made for personal prayer. In stressing this point, Alphonsus spoke in his authentically apostolic fashion in a circular of July 1779.

In order to bring light to others, the apostolic worker must himself be enlightened, and in order to enkindle in others' hearts the fire of Divine love, he must himself be on fire. This comes from meditation.

With a similar emphasis the Constitutions from 21 to 76 present a Redemptorist "Charter of Charity." Everything is admirably directed to the following of Christ, the Redeemer, as he proclaims the good news to the poor. He is discovered in prayer and in the liturgy, and the mission given him by the Father inspires the dedication of his followers. Without tracing the details of the program, it is sufficient to recall the terms in which Alphonsus, genuine disciple as he was, exhorted to poverty and obedience as affecting those to whom his confreres were sent. That has been very much the spirit in which the chapter of revision performed its task. It requires patience to allow the renewed inspiration to have effect.

It is never easy to make a transition from settled ways to others which, however good and authentic, seem revolutionary. With Redemptorists, it has meant a return to the conflict in the days of Father Passerat, so well and sympathetically described by Father Madlener. It is a matter of no longer putting one's own spiritual advantage in the first place, but of looking directly to those in need, with all that entails for one's own spiritual development. That earlier introspective mentality seemed to find support in the dichotomy introduced by the Pontifical Rule of 1749, declaring that the end of the Institute was to imitate the virtues and examples of Jesus Christ, the Redeemer, especially by preaching the Word of God to the poor.

The capitulars who revised the legislation made a happy choice of phrase, "the apostolic life of the Redemptorists," returning to the unity of life expressed in the text submitted by Alphonsus to the Holy See in 1748. The members are now said to "follow the example of Jesus Christ, the Redeemer, by preaching the word of God to the poor."

That formula provides the ideal of the Redemptorist community. It is very much as it was described by Falcoia and Alphonsus right at the beginning in their approach to the Marchese de Montealegro. The members of the Institute "live a perfect community life...giving of themselves to the people." That vision which called the Congregation into being enables one to appreciate the profound wisdom Saint Alphonsus expressed so concisely. "If we look after the work, the work will look after us."

13

THE POOR
ALSO EVANGELIZE

Francisco Moreno Rejón, C.Ss.R.
Vice Province of Peru-Sur
Translated by Joseph Tobin, C.Ss.R.
Province of Denver

1. Why Am I a Redemptorist?

The only way for me to overcome the gripping shyness that comes from composing one's own biographical sketch is to attempt to do it in the form of an imaginary letter.

The single most important influence in my life was being born into a family of migrant farm workers who liked to read. I cannot forget the venerable figure of my grandfather who, after returning from his daily work in the fields, would gather us in front of the fireplace to read from a bulky almanac that was pegged to the wall. This was a real encyclopedia for the family, with advice about the best time to plant, weather forecasts, ditties, anecdotes, amusements, and Bible stories. An elderly rustic schoolteacher, bereft of sophisticated materials, used *Don Quixote* to teach us to read. That particular tome has been my personal guidebook ever since. The moving figure of a weather-beaten Redemptorist missionary suggests the possibility of understanding life as a combination of intellectual preparation and intimate service of people. In his own way, the man from La Mancha helps us grasp the Alphonsian ideal of "one-part monk, one-part apostle."

I now understand more clearly my long fascination with the idea of melding study with ordinary life. There were simple events that charted this path for me. My novitiate year, spent in an hoary edifice on the Spanish plain, was decisive. At Nava del Rey the novices worked shifts in the garden, the chicken coop, and the barn. I had the additional responsibility of being the house librarian. It was a memorable experience to try to wed the care of chickens to the study of the documents of Vatican II. The year was marked by the birth of lasting friendships and by thousands of hours dedicated to devouring books. At the same time, we began to discover the contradictions inherent in the Church and the Congregation. It is impossible not to smile benevolently as I recall the list of forbidden books then in vogue. It still is astonishing to remember that our esteemed Father Pedro Sanabria joined Emmanuel Kant on the list of proscribed materials. Thus the double pleasure—a privilege of librarians of that time—to secretly rescue the authors from their particular "Hell," the section of the library reserved for the banned tomes, and then to avidly read collections of taboo sermons or *The Critique of Pure Reason* with a pleasure made even sweeter by the fact of their prohibition.

My years in the major seminary at Salamanca coincided with the presence of an extraordinary group of professors in the faculty of theology. It was a time of serious formation and demanding academic requirements. At the same time, there was a pact among the Redemptorist students to do our part to offset the unavoidable costs of education by offering mimeographed copies of our notes to our classmates. The rich interaction with the students from the diverse faculties allowed us to develop different, but complimentary aspects of our formation. There was forged a taste for literature and drama (with a company called "The Chariot of Thespis"), for folk music as well as rock (with the group "Barandal"), for chess and film (with the Hispano-American Film Club). For us Spaniards, this was our first contact with Latin America and, as we came to know many friends from the respective countries, we savored one another's music, even as we passionately argued the social and political reality. Nor was the role of the Church and of Christians absent from the discussions. We were greatly affected by the Council, but even more my Medellin and liberation theology, which then was making its first appearance. In this context, the choice to specialize in moral theology was very natural. It was an attempt to be faithful both to the Redemptorist charism and to the challenge posed by a world in flux.

Pastoral ministry and theological reflection in Latin America

At the conclusion of our studies, we were three Redemptorists who were ordained priests. All three volunteered for the mission in Peru. After my arrival in 1978, I united pastoral ministry with theological reflection. I began my priestly work in Vitarte, a working-class neighborhood of Lima, dividing my time between service in the poor parish of Santa Anita while collaborating in an itinerant mission team that labored in the Andes. I also worked in a research center directed by the Peruvian theologian, Gustavo Gutierrez, authoring a number of articles and publishing some books.

The commitment to bring together intellectual effort and pastoral work ultimately became both painful and gratifying. It was painful, because it generated a permanent tension born from the impossibility to respond in a satisfying way to the demands of both areas. But there was also the joy of living an intellectual commitment that was challenged and verified by pastoral work, with a mutual enrichment as a consequence. Pastoral ministry gained enlightenment and clarity, while reflection became rooted in daily life. The attempt to be both apostle and monk continues as a passionate motivation.

2. A *Pauperibus Evangelizari*

From the moment our Congregation adopted as its sexennial theme *evangelizare pauperibus et a pauperibus evangelizari*, there arose among some Redemptorists a polemic and irony around the formula. More precisely, the controversy centered on the second part of the theme, insinuating that it was more demagogic than theological in its basis.

Such reactions do not evade the suspicion that their authors, settled down in a comfortable lifestyle that is contradictory to the Constitutions, hope to discredit those called to conversion. Yet the theme did not startle us in Latin America, since many of us have experienced in our own lives the fact of being evangelized by the poor. Already in 1979 the document of Puebla spoke of the "evangelizing potential of the poor" (n. 1147) and the document of Santo Domingo recalled the same concept by affirming that "the poor evangelize" (nn. 95 and 178).

To tell the truth, I first heard this formulation in May 1978 in a basic community of Vitarte (Lima) during a discussion of the preparatory document for the Third General Conference of Latin American Bishops. The text eventually began part of the contribution of the Peruvian hierarchy at Puebla. Paragraphs 435 to 441 of the final document amply develop the theme that "the poor in Latin America are both recipients and protagonists of evangelization." It takes note of the fact that "announcing the Good News to the poor brings about the experience of being evangelized by them…thus is discovered evangelizing charism of the poor."

Since it is neither just nor healthy to succumb to exaggeration or a reductionism that would be out of place, the title of this essay affirms that *the poor also evangelize*. The title hopes to capture a double concept: first, among the other protagonists of evangelization, a place must be given to the poor; second, besides their other contributions, the poor in fact evangelize. Now I would like to offer some ideas regarding how we are evangelized by the poor.

Our stance in the face of the poor and poverty

The poor exist: they are right over there. The statement is obvious, but not superfluous, since many would attempt to live and conduct the world as if the poor did not exist. However, their presence becomes irksome because, whether we like it or not, their proximity turns into an outcry that is at times silent, at others, threatening and impetuous.

In the face of the poor, just as before Jesus, a decision must be taken: we are either for them or against them. It would be impossible to fashion a typology of the different stances toward the poor, for these are as many as there are personalities and historical situations. But it may be helpful to attempt a description of the different postures adopted most frequently.

Flight: There are those who act like the prophet Jonah: they know where the poor are, but they look the other way and take the opposite path. Nineveh frightens them and they are at odds with God. The poor alarm them, and they look for some means to escape: a refuge far from the poor and far from the God who loves them. Many set out on the same road as did Jonah. But to run away is impossible: sooner or later these end up facing those they had hoped to forget.

Naiveté: This is the position of those who live without taking into consideration the real situation of people and believe only that all are citizens with the same rights and obligations. God loves everyone, whatever their station in life. All are equal in the Church. The most important matter, it is said, is to feel God in one's heart and trust in his divine providence. If this is the way of the world, God knows why, since he made it. What interests God are souls and every soul has the same worth in his sight. Everything else belongs to the kingdom of this world and ultimately is not important.

Accommodation: This is the attitude of those who idealize the poor. Its adherents one day will discover, even meet them. From then on, their outlook will change. The poor are good, simple, and welcoming. Whatever the poor do is right and their words are all oracles. Nothing can be told them that they do not already know. To think otherwise would be to disrespect their culture or customs. The most that can be done is to listen to the poor, venerating them all the while. This is the exact position of individuals who are full of good will, but without any sort of realism. What is important is an imaginary ideal, not people of flesh and blood.

Disqualification: Such is the perspective of those who rebuff the poor for moralistic reasons. These know the behavior of the poor and can attest that they have many faults: chauvinists, womanizers, violent, thieves, irresponsible, drunkards, self-centered, egotistic, insolent, liars, panhandlers, insulting, predatory, etc., etc. If the truth be told, the lives of poor people are not exactly paragons of virtue. And these should evangelize others? As a first step, it may be said that the moral life of the poor is neither better nor worse than that of the average human being. But the truth is not to be found along those lines. In this context, let us recall the opinion of Jesus regarding prostitutes: they will enter the kingdom before us (Matthew 21:21).

Conversion: There are those who are willing to make the effort to view the poor through the eyes of God. Those who would either appease or disqualify them, in the final analysis, do so on the basis of human criteria, be it from sociology or a false sense of religion. What is really needed is to come to the poor and love them, not because they are good or pious or because to do so is politically correct. They must be loved for God and as God loves them: love of the poor is literally "for God's sake." Such a posture presumes the need of a radical conversion in our criteria and our judgment. Our motives must be purified and given a theological basis. To love this way is first and foremost a deeply spiritual experience. In this way we are immersed in a process of evangelization. God reveals himself here and now in the mutilated face of the poor. The presence of the poor poses the question about God.

What do the poor reveal to us?

There are people, especially those who themselves are open but who skillfully attempt to juggle the claim the poor place on us, asking, "Who are the poor?" As a reflex, there comes to mind the question put to Jesus by the master of the law: "And who is my neighbor?" Today, just as then, it must be admitted that the question is poorly asked, that the masters of the law occasionally were mistaken in their questions and, consequently, in their answers as well. In the same sense, one must begin by making what could be termed a "Samaritan investment" and ask oneself who in fact acts as a neighbor. It is not by deciphering the economic, political, historical, cultural, etc., factors that one in fact commits oneself to the poor. To the contrary, it is done by shouldering the evangelical charge of service to the poor that enkindles the dynamism of love, even as one begins to understand the urgency and complexity of the issue.

Human misery: When one approaches the world of the poor and poverty, the first message received is scandalous. That is, the brutal contrast in the living conditions of rich and poor is an authentic disgrace. This shame is even greater when it happens among Christians, since they are all members of the same body. What is more, we realize that the reprobation of Paul against the community of Corinth is still very relevant (1 Corinthians 11:20–22). But the scandal does not end here. It happens that the lifestyle of the poor, their customs, and their being are also scandalous. In this sense, just as in the case of King David, the episodes that are least edifying are revelatory, uncovering for us human misery and the depths of its roots. The shadowy, least favorable side of humanity is exposed. The genuinely human need for redemption is clearly shown. The miserable life of the poor declares something to us, that is to say, it evangelizes us—for scandalously does God love them with a preferential love. And this is Good News (Gospel) for the whole human race.

Its effect on us: The world of the poor, insofar as it constitutes a permanent challenge to our own lives, acts as a powerful ingredient of self-understanding: it wakes us up to who we are, that is, it places us before our own truth. It reveals to us what we are, as well as what we are capable of. This happens, above all, if encountering the poor is not limited solely to the level of confrontation, but rather progresses gradually to an experience of immersion or insertion.

Even as we discover that poverty is an injustice, a sin for which we are not totally guiltless, there echoes in us an incessant call to conversion and change in the way we live. Little by little, the manner in which we see the world changes, thus refashioning our way of being so that our encounter with the world of the poor becomes an experience of spiritual infancy.

The love of God: But above all, it is in revealing how God is that the poor evangelize us. They offer irrefutable testimony of the gratuitous love of God, who chooses to love first. But there is more: that God chooses as the favored beneficiaries of his preferential love those who are the least and most despised in this world. And we know well that there is no love that has a greater claim on us than that which is offered with full largess.

If God loves them just as they are, how can we argue over doing the same? If God favors the poor in a way that we could term "brazen," if he always aligns himself on their side, what reasons can we offer to ignore them or leave them behind? How could we dislodge them from the first place, if the God of the kingdom has promised it to them?

The poor evangelize us in no greater way than in revealing to us the true nature of the God of Jesus Christ and how that God loves. To share the lot of the poor is an experience of grace that purifies our faith and our love.

The mystery of Christ

It is already commonplace in theology to affirm that the face of the poor reveals to us the suffering face of Christ the Lord. One discovers in the poor the reality of a God made manifest in weakness, so that the historical anguish of the poor presupposes for the theological task, the same scandalous stumbling block of the cross of Christ.

We must learn to recognize in the disfigured bodies of the poor the newness of the paschal mystery of Christ that will transform our mortal bodies in glory like his own (1 Corinthians 15:24). It is impossible to follow Christ and serve anywhere else except where he wants to be followed and served: in identification with the poor, so that in the weakness of Christ will be shown the power of God (2 Corinthians 13:4). The poor evangelize us because they are a living reminder of Christ. So John Chrysostom spoke of the "divine agape" that obliges us to unite in an indissoluble way the "altar of the Eucharist" and the "altar of the poor," since the same Christ is immolated in both.

The poor evangelize us because their eruption into the world and into the Church hinders us from falling into the temptation to disregard the flesh and the historical reality of the mystery of Christ.

Vocation of the Church: A sweeping examination of the history of the Church is enough to demonstrate that the periods of its greatest vitality and renewal coincided with epochs which evidenced a return to the poor: Francis of Assisi and the mendicant orders; Bartolomé de las Casas and the evangelization of the Americas; the flourishing religious congregations of the eighteenth and nineteenth centuries; most recently, Vatican II and the Medellin conference are some milestones in this process.

In the last decades, above all in Latin America and other countries of the Third World, religious life has contributed powerfully to the credibility of the Catholic Church. The reason is none other than religious taking seriously the preferential option for the poor and doing so in significant actions, not just in words. The poor also evangelize us because they remind the Church of its vocation. In the words of John XXIII: the Church is called to be and wants to be the Church of the poor.

The **raison d'être** *of the Congregation:* In fulfilling their mission of evangelization (to proclaim the Good News to the poor), we Redemptorists are ourselves evangelized. The reality of confronting the life of the poor leads us again and again to the question of our foundational charism, that which is the reason for our service in the Church. The existence of the poor examines religious life at its very roots, as well as its value as a prophetic sign for the world. It is a frontal challenge to our sense of poverty and our style of life.

The magnitude of the problems, calamities, and needs of the poor is such that it oppresses us. But this experience, which initially is felt as a frustrating impotence, gives way to another, more profound dimension. We eventually discover that it is not a question of just "doing" things to remedy the destitution of the poor. What is called for is a new way of "being": communities where the poor feel welcomed as persons and not simply as those in need, communities which are truly signs of the mystery of the risen

Christ and the newness of the kingdom. The poor evangelize us because, as we serve them, we can discover the paschal joy that is at the beginning of the proclamation of Jesus: the Gospel only is Good News for the poor.

14

CHARISM AND
FREEDOM OF SPIRIT

Bernard Häring, C.Ss.R.
Province of Munich
Translated by Martin McKeever
Province of Dublin

1. Introduction

I was born in Böttingen, a town in the southwestern corner of Germany, on the tenth day of the eleventh month of the twelfth year—November 10, 1912. I remain very grateful for my parents. If they had followed a modern calculus, I would not have been born, since I was the eleventh of twelve children. The seven sisters and five brothers grew up listening to our parents pray.

The vocation of a religious missionary always fascinated me. But my real decision first took flesh in the spring of 1933, when I entered the Redemptorist novitiate at Gars am Inn (Bavaria). There I took my first vows in 1933 and was ordained on May 7, 1939. After my ordination, when I was able to go home for the first time in many years, my mother greeted me with a smile and asked, "May I still give you my blessing?" I replied, "Certainly, from now on your blessing will be the bedrock of mine."

The war soon began and I was involved as a member of a medical corps, ending up as a prisoner of the Russians. After the war I thought I would be sent as a missionary to Brazil, but my superiors destined me for specialized studies in theology. I obtained a doctorate in theology at the University of Tübingen in 1947, where, under the tutelage of Professor Theodore Steinbüchel, I presented a thesis treating the relationship between ethics and religion. For the next ten years, I was a professor of moral theology at the Redemptorist major seminary at Gars am Inn, although I did offer some courses in Rome from 1950 to 1953. I was named to the faculty of the Alphonsian Academy when it was formally opened in 1957, teaching there until 1988. I served as a visiting professor at various universities in the United States: Brown, Yale, Union Theological Seminary (New York), the Kennedy Institute for Bioethics (Georgetown), Catholic University, University of San Francisco, and Fordham. After retiring from teaching in 1988, I returned to the community at Gars am Inn to enjoy the beauty of my religious life as a Redemptorist.

During my academic career, I have published more than eighty books, including some three hundred translations and more than a thousand articles. I also have had the opportunity to preach many retreats and some parish missions. While still a young priest, it was precisely the experience of the parish missions that planted in me a compelling desire to prepare a new manual in moral theology. This hunger bore fruit in 1954, with the publication of the first edition of *The Law of Christ*. While the work had its opponents, it also enjoyed the support of many personalities of the time, including Angelo Roncalli and Giovanni Battista Montini, later John XXIII and Paul VI respectively. I served as an adviser to the preparatory commission of the Second Vatican Council and later as a theological expert during the Council itself, especially regarding the themes of *Gaudium et Spes*. In 1963, Pope Paul VI invited me to preach the Lenten retreat in the Vatican.

There is no doubt, however, that I consider teaching and directing students in the Alphonsian Academy as the most important work of my life. It is my joy to witness how the Academy continues to prosper after my retirement. Now, as I find myself in the sunset of life, I see that beloved institution resplendent with the light of divine mercy. I love the Church as it is, just as Christ loves me, with all my imperfections and shadows. I have experienced the Church in a singular way in my Congregation, which continues to be my household of faith and a model of the pilgrim Church. Sixty years after my first profession in this religious family, I still dare to describe myself as a "happy Redemptorist." Thanks be to God, in all those years I have never had a true crisis in my vocation.

2. Charism and Freedom of Spirit

In this paper I will first of all examine how charism and freedom of spirit are understood in sacred Scripture. I will then consider the significance of this charism in the life of our founder and of our Congregation. Finally, I will give a brief account of my personal experience in this matter.

The very word *charisma* indicates that freedom of spirit is something which is given to us. It is not private property. A charisma can only bear fruit and unfold insofar as we are grateful for it and intend to give God glory in all things. Charisma derives from *charis*, that is goodness and grace given by God. Charisms are found in many forms (Romans 12:6). Each receives a particular charism from God (1 Corinthians 12:7). For all their variety, these gifts of grace have the same origin in the one Spirit (1 Corinthians 12:4). By their very nature they are given in the service of all (1 Corinthians 12:6). They can only be understood by the whole faith community and are in the service of this whole community. "As each one has received a gift, use it to serve one another as good stewards of God's varied grace" (1 Peter 4:10).

The spirit of *freedom* of God's children, and in particular their courageous freedom of Spirit, must be understood in the light of the giver: that is, as a gift of the Holy Spirit *(pneuma)*. So there is no question of boasting or self-preoccupation. The Spirit leads the disciple into the truth. "He will teach you the truth" (John 16:13). Anyone who is grasped in this way by the spirit of truth glows with the truth of salvation. He dedicates himself entirely to his divine Lord, who has revealed to us the Father and his will to save us.

Before Paul calls Timothy to declare his faith openly, he reminds him: "For God did not give us a spirit of cowardice but rather of power and love and self-control" (2 Timothy 1:7). Only insofar as we entrust ourselves to "the law of the spirit of life in Christ Jesus" (Romans 8:2), do we group in our understanding of the liberating and saving truth. So we are concerned here with being free and being liberated: free from selfishness, free from sinking into the cycles of destruction, free in Christ and free to pursue his cause.

The liberating power of faith is given particular emphasis in John's Gospel and in the Letters of Paul. "When the Son makes you free, you will be free indeed" (John 8:36). "Where the Spirit of the Lord is, there is freedom" (2 Corinthians 3:17). The spirit of freedom is considerate toward the

conscience of others, particularly of the weak (1 Corinthians 10:23ff). However, regarding those who "spy on our freedom that we have in Christ Jesus,
that they might enslave us" (Galatians 2:4), Paul says decisively: "…to them
we did not submit even for a moment, so that the truth of the gospel might
remain intact for you" (Galatians 2,5). The basic conviction that it is "for
freedom Christ set us free" (Galatians 5:1) causes the Christian to be careful about every form of permissiveness and any kind of personal or collective selfishness (Galatians 5:13). Paul offers clear directives in this respect.

In the New Testament freedom of spirit is often called *parresia*. It
means the courage to trust in God and to give open testimony. It is often
explicitly said of Jesus that he spoke "openly," that is, with *parresia* (Mark
8:32; John 7:26: 10:25). Equally, in both the Acts of the Apostles and in the
Letters of Paul, *parresia* is noted as a key characteristic of apostolic ministry and living faith. Through it the apostles emulate Jesus who spoke openly
in front of everyone (John 18:20).

Saint Alphonsus and the charism of freedom of spirit

From the extraordinary abundance of relevant material I have selected
just two questions: (1) How did Saint Alphonsus come to his extraordinary
freedom of spirit? (2) In what particular ways did this freedom of spirit find
expression?

The connection between exodus and liberation: In my opinion the fundamental biblical experience of the connection between exodus and liberation is clearly exemplified in the life of Alphonsus de Liguori, Doctor of
Church and founder of Redemptorist Congregation. "Leave the world and
give yourself to me!" This is the underlying experience of liberation and of
conversion which, more than anything else, shows us how Alphonsus underwent a profound exodus and thereby was able to receive the gracious
gift of freedom and openness. Considering the view of the world adopted
by the Second Vatican Council (above all in *Gaudium et Spes*), it will be
useful to investigate what Alphonsus understood here by "world"—the world
he had to leave in order to give himself entirely to the Redeemer and to the
work of the Redemption.

It would be wrong to think of this "world" from which the Church
and every Christian must be liberated as simply a "pagan" world. On the
contrary, it is a "religious" world, in the sense of John's Gospel. It is, above

all, the world of the Sadducees and of many Pharisees. It is a view of the world and an enslavement to the world shared by many disciples of Jesus, including Peter. It involved the expectation of a powerful Messiah, who would raise the people of Israel and the followers of Jesus to a position of power. This explains their anger at Jesus' declaration of himself as the suffering servant of God. The faith of the first community was a radical exodus from the worldly understanding of the Messiah, rooted in collective selfishness, toward the crucified and risen One. On occasion one hears the criticism that the Second Vatican Council fell into a naive view of the world. This is quite incorrect. As a Council of reform, it saw clearly the danger of an excessive worldliness and strove toward a total conversion to the humble, suffering servant of God who was glorified by the Father.

The world to which the Second Vatican Council wished to turn was described as follows: "The joy and hope, the grief and anguish of the men of our time, especially of those who are poor or afflicted in any way, are the joy and hope, the grief and anguish of the followers of Christ as well" (*GS*, 1). We would do well to remember that Alphonsus was a religious individual, even before his "conversion." In the course of this conversion, however, he recognized the sinister dangers of using religion itself as a means of gaining higher status and social privilege. After his conversion and total dedication to Christ and the work of the Redemption, Alphonsus still had to cast off a heavy burden. This was the dark image of God that had formed in him because of his dominant, ambitious father and the alien image of God which resulted from the rigorism of those who had taught him moral theology. We can think of the process by which he freed himself of these burdens as a personal exodus.

He gave up his ambitious career, but not, as his father had hoped, in order to pursue a yet more spectacular ecclesiastical career. Above all, he set out to serve the rejected, the *Lazzaroni*, the poorest of the poor, without looking down on them from an aristocratic height. Rather, he followed the path of exodus in that he became "one of them." He offered them unconditional trust and made them into co-apostles through the famous "Evening Chapels."

To some extent I can identify with this out of my own life experience. In the years after the Second World War (at the time my three-volume work *The Law of Christ* appeared), I used to spend about ten weeks each year in the protestant diaspora as an itinerant missioner among those who had been driven out of their homes. How was I to "preach" to them the casuistic

morality which we had learned? Before our preaching we used to visit and
stay with the families who were living in unbelievable poverty. There was
not link between this world and the world of a moral theology centered on
rules and sins. But there was another call: "Comfort my people!" What
mattered here was to return to the simplicity of the Gospel and learn anew
from Jesus how he preached the good news to the poor.

The exodus of Saint Alphonsus was much more radical and original.
It included eventually the decision to leave the social sophistication of the
city of Naples in order to live and work in the poorer rural areas. His exodus
could be characterized as follows: coming down from the pedestal of the
nobility and utterly dedicating himself to the service of the underprivileged
in the Church. And all of this simply to be of service, without any thought
of personal glorification. These two dimensions are inseparable in the exodus experience of Alphonsus. They are a reflection of the humility of God
in Christ Jesus. They find expression in his preaching and in all his meditations on the incarnation (the crib), the cross, and the Blessed Sacrament.

It would be unpardonable to omit here a reference to the fact that
Saint Alphonsus dedicated himself to those with nervous troubles. In his
book *Saint Alphonsus on the Pastoral Treatment of Neurotic Disorders*
(Heidelberg/Kerle, 1947) our confrere, Father Bernhard Ziermann, has published and studied moving letters written by Alphonsus to people suffering
from nervous illness. In a review of this work, one protestant pastor has
written that by reading it he gained a completely new picture of Alphonsus
as a pastor.

The exodus of Saint Alphonsus was his turning to the poor. As he
turned in loving and healing care toward the poor, his own freedom of spirit
grew as a charism, as did his energetic struggle against the moral rigorism
and fear-centered religion of jansenistic elitism. He had found the way to
the promised land of *"copiosa redemptio."* He had heard his call to preach
the liberating message to the poor. It was a participation in the self-dona-
tion of the Son of God and a share in the joyful love flowing between Jesus
Christ and the Father. It was this exodus which led Alphonsus to the gift of
freedom of spirit in the service of the good news.

Some examples of the freedom of spirit of Saint Alphonsus

I was first made fully aware of the spiritual character and the particular charism of Saint Alphonsus when I read his *apology,* written in Italian/

Neapolitan. It is fascinating to note the frankness with which he expressed himself against his ecclesiastical critics and those who defamed him. He always preserves a correct tone. He does not respond in kind to the base tone used in the denunciations of some of those opposed to his moderate moral and pastoral theology. In this way his basic principle appears all the more clearly: God has made human beings not for the law but for love, and the freedom which love brings. The law only serves to ensure that this freedom is rightly understood. On this basis he states quite sharply: it is a great evil to burden people with questionable obligations in the name of God. This is the ultimate grounding of his equiprobabilism: as long as the arguments are not clearly in favor of the binding nature of the law, human freedom before the law—obviously meaning here the freedom to do good—remains in possession. The good is not by any means exhausted through the fulfilling of the demands of the law. It is rather a matter of learning to love Jesus and to love others in Jesus.

His courage to reinterpret the ban on interest: Alphonsus was the target of much hostile criticism, particularly because of the position he adopted on the ecclesiastical ban on taking interest. His opponents had little difficulty producing many church documents that banned all forms of monetary interest. Alphonsus had the courage to reinterpret this ban in the light of the totality of changes that had taken place in the economy and society at his time. He emphasized that the interest should be moderate and was not slow to offer clear directives in this respect. What moved him to persevere stubbornly with this interpretation, despite all abusive criticism, was his firm belief that all are called to salvation and to sanctity. A narrow interpretation of the ban meant that many businesspeople could not be given absolution unless they promised to accept no further interest. In the end, Alphonsus was fortunate in that he received the support of Benedict XIV on this question, although officially the traditional ban was not definitively lifted, or reinterpreted, until some one hundred years later.

His resistance to Augustinian sexual rigorism: The deep conviction of Alphonsus concerning "bountiful Redemption" and the fact that all are called to salvation and to sanctity forced him to probe deeply into Saint Augustine's teaching on marriage. Augustine and his school taught that the marriage act was only made into a moral act by the explicit intention to procreate. They considered it a venial sin to engage in the marriage act simply as a means of calming sexual desire, without the intention of procreation. Alphonsus was happy to discover another tradition of thought going back to Chrysostum, Gregory of Nyssa, and Dionysius the Carthusian. He wrote quite openly that he had decided to follow this tradition. So he taught in his *Theologia Moralis* that only two ends of marriage were inherently and absolutely necessary for marriage itself and for the marriage act, namely mutual devotion and the conservation of the indissoluble bond. Procreation and *remedium concupiscentiae*, on the other hand, were in his view, essential to marriage but only accidentally so. Against Augustine and indeed Thomas Aquinas, Alphonsus held that the marriage act as an expression of mutual devotion and the indissoluble bond was of itself worthy and good.

And he added by way of emphasis *"Et hoc est de fide"*—"this is a matter of faith" (*Theologica Moralis* lib VI tr. VI, cap.II, n. 900, cf. n. 882 and 927). This opinion also earned Alphonsus severe criticism and bitter rejection. In the end, however, he managed to defuse the problem of "interrupted intercourse" and most confessors did not feel the need to ask questions in this matter. This was the case until the encyclical *Casti Connubii*, in which the Augustinian position alone comes to the fore. As in many other instances, the once successful barrister became the advocate of conscience, and a prophetic voice warning against any attempt to limit the freedom of conscience through unsubstantiated legal burdens and hurdles.

Alphonsus was grateful to pious and learned Jesuits who were often his confessors and informants. Even when the Jesuit Order was caught in the cross fire and was eventually banned by the pope, Alphonsus made no secret of his ongoing approval of them. He was indeed deeply hurt by the ban on the Jesuits.

Freedom of spirit in the saints of the Congregation

Our Congregation has been the heir to the freedom of spirit of our founder. It will remain so for as long as it remains true to the option for the poor and oppressed. We must hold to the exodus spirituality of the founder in order to remain open to receiving the gift of spiritual freedom. From this point of view, it would be worthwhile to produce a comprehensive biography of the saints (and those declared Blessed or Venerable) of our congregation.

Saint Clement had the courage, even in the face of storms, to set out for new shores. But he also had the charism of freedom of spirit so that he could preach the Gospel anew in different cultural contexts. He continually and sharply reminded those in Rome that the German protestant christians were also genuinely spiritual in their faith. It is true that Clement was wrong in his condemnation of Johann Michael Sailer, who himself embodied freedom of spirit in considerable measure. But we all make some mistakes in life! We are always dependant on the judgments and prejudices of the world in which we live. Clement succeeded in gathering around him men of freedom of spirit and in filling them with enthusiasm. He was a great pioneer.

We can only wonder at the freedom of spirit of the humble Saint Gerard Majella. It is enough to recall how he constantly supported Sister Celeste Crostarosa, whose freedom of spirit he admired. Another courageous pioneer was Saint John Neumann, who is a marvelous example of a minister of the Gospel in a multicultural society. He broke down many barriers by giving religious Sisters a key role in the major Catholic educational system, which he founded. Blessed Peter Donders is not alone a fine model in that he served and healed the lepers, but also because he stood up with prophetic courage for the freeing of the slaves in Suriname. In the Blessed Kasper Stanggassinger we are impressed not only by his particular sensitivity and awareness of the Holy Spirit but also his courage to distance himself from the narrower educational methods of his older confreres. He did not threaten, grumble, or punish, but knew how to lead as one who is filled with the Holy Spirit.

3. Conclusion

My personal experience of freedom of spirit in the Congregation

I entered our Congregation when Germany was under the Hitler regime. I was impressed by the resolute rejection of this irresponsible regime on the part of the confreres. The large community in Gars was able to offer asylum first to Professor Theodore Steinbüchel and then, for a certain period, also to Bishop Sproll. The whole community could be trusted not to reveal this information.

As students, we could see that our teachers were well informed and that they were genuinely open to seeking new light in those changing times.

The provincial had it in mind to send me to Brazil and encouraged me to prepare myself for this eventuality by the study of Portuguese and the

Brazilian culture. It came as a total shock to me when, just after my ordination, the provincial told me that the professors had decided that I should do
further studies in moral theology. When I asked if people were not aware
that I was quite critical of the moral theology which we had learned, I was
assured that the point of the exercise was that I might hopefully be able to
contribute to the necessary renewal of moral theology. For this reason I was
not to be sent to Rome but to Munich or Tübingen. This was a major sign of
trust and confidence.

I was even more amazed when, just after completing my doctoral
studies, the superior general Leonard Buys invited me to a long discussion.
He explained his plan of founding an Alphonsian Academy as a faculty for
educating future moral and pastoral theologians, and asked me to work in
this faculty from the beginning. In all my years of work in the Alphonsian
Academy, from its foundation until 1988, I have a marvelous experience of
freedom of spirit. Father General enthusiastically agreed that I should give
a course in ecumenism ("What can Catholic moral theology learn from
Orthodox and Lutheran Theology?") in the first year of the new institute.
This was a clear step away from polemical theology toward ecumenical
dialogue.

Following Paul, I sought in my moral theology to emphasize the need
for sensitivity to the reality of the contemporary world. At this time the
Vatican had on more than one occasion expressed its rejection of every
form of "situation ethics." Unfortunately, and I believe incorrectly, many
understood my moral theology as another form of "situation ethics." Letters of complaint flowed to our superior general Father Gaudreau. Among
these complaints was the insinuation that I had abandoned the contribution
of Alphonsus to moral theology. The Polish General Consultor Schrant was
quick to warn me that under such circumstances he would not consider
himself bound to confidentiality if he judged it necessary to act so as to
avoid damage to the reputation of the Congregation. Shortly after this I
gave a copy of all my works which treated of Saint Alphonsus to the superior general. He was impressed by these and at the same time horrified at
the "slanderers." Looking back on this I can only wonder at the trust placed
in me by this superior, who was himself formed in the older theology.

When, after the Council, I was invited to be guest professor by prominent protestant/ecumenical faculties, I was enthusiastically encouraged by
the superiors of our Congregation to accept these invitations. I simply cannot imagine how my work in the renewal of Catholic moral theology would

have been possible without the constant trust and support of the Congregation and its superiors.

No doubt I made mistakes and not all of my statements were as balanced as they might have been. But my superiors and colleagues had the freedom of spirit to look at the overall body of my work and the principles upon which it was founded. I kept my superiors fully informed of the many invitations I received, which included giving lectures in Orthodox, Anglican, and Protestant faculties; retreats for teachers and ministers of other churches; and my numerous activities in Africa, Asia, and Latin America. I found it very helpful when my provincial superior decided that I should not accept any form of payment or costs for my work in the Third World. This fact allowed me an increased freedom of spirit.

Out of a sense of gratitude for the degree of freedom of spirit and all the positive encouragement that I have received, I have always been self-critical in my statements and writings. I have asked myself if I can justify them in the context of our Congregation and its institutions. Freedom of spirit and freedom of expression must always be understood in a spirit of collegiality and coresponsibility. The most important thing always is the service of the Gospel and the proclamation of the Good News of "bountiful redemption."

15

ALWAYS READY TO UNDERTAKE WHAT IS MOST DEMANDING (CONSTITUTION 20)

Dalton Barros de Almeida, C.Ss.R.
Province of Rio de Janeiro
Translated by Joseph Dorcey
Province of Denver

1. Introduction

Father Noel Londoño's invitation to write this article ended up taking me into some rather unexpected territory. It became for me a puzzle with almost no solution.

I began writing about Redemptorist self-denial and availability for missionary service as a result of the work of redemption, but I tore it up. I then wrote a few pages about the relationship between availability for, and actually doing, the most demanding and difficult missionary works, dealing primarily with mature communities dedicated to a humanizing and liberating ministry. I decided, however, to abandon that approach. I then considered the final part of Constitution 20 as an essential element of a missionary anthropology and spirituality, involving detachment and renunciations (*distacco*), like the grain of wheat that falls to the ground and dies in order to produce new life. Though I had nearly finished, I set those pages aside because it just wasn't what I wanted to say, something was missing. I also discussed the subject with my fellow provincials of the Union of Redemptorists in Brazil (URB). They gave me some very good ideas, which I have been pondering ever since.

After all these attempts, there was a prolonged, unproductive period. I finally tried to bring together some new material on this subject as it relates to the initial formation process of young Redemptorists today, who come to us already influenced by certain modern values and attitudes that can be contrary to the Gospel. Even this attempt, though well thought out, ended up in the wastebasket. I was stymied once again. I felt as if I was debating with myself in an empty auditorium. It was altogether too abstract and academic, and I wasn't pleased at all. I was frustrated with the whole project and ashamed of my inability to get the job done.

The next day I took a fourteen-hour bus trip into the mountains to join our team of missionaries (three priests and one brother) who were involved with the more "immersed" type of popular mission. It was already evening when we left. As we devoured the kilometers, sleepiness enveloped me. Suddenly, a myriad of scenes began to pass before me. They followed one another in rapid succession, like video images. I was finally able to perceive the interrelatedness of the scenes. They were images of experiences, both recent and from the distant past. They were images that had lain dormant in the depths of my heart for a long time. As my memory became more animated, the images grew sharper and more vivid. The memories were good and powerful. I made a mental note of them. I decided that perhaps in these memories was everything worth saying about those radical qualities of the Redemptorist as portrayed in Constitution 20. They were images of plentiful Redemption. With my heart at peace, I gazed upon the deeply blue, starry skies. Thank you, Lord! And I fell asleep.

It is here in the mountains of Espírito Santo, spending Holy Week of 1995 with the mission team, that I am finally able to write during the breaks between other activities. Yesterday I spent the whole day with seventy young people from twenty-six rural communities who are potential leaders for youth ministry.

I sit at a small table made of rough boards, with a roof over my head but no walls around me. Surrounded by trees and foliage, I listen to the gentle flowing of the waters down the mountainside and the singing of the birds. It is enough to raise my eyes to the horizon to see the spider flowers and senna trees coloring the lush, green meadows with their purple and yellow hues. Three toucans and a campanero bird insistently compose a counter melody to the other songs of nature. It is a setting that contrasts sharply with the stories now to be told. But such is life!

As I was saying, it is here that I write. Write? No, it is more than that, I relive my memories. I relive my memories today with perceptions and perspectives that have been dearly won through the years. This is the only kind of testament that I can possibly give: a witness to and a grateful recognition of all that has been and is given to me to live. Perhaps in this way, I will come closer to the original intent of this collection which is to be published. Who knows, Father Londoño might well agree that a simple reflection on lived-experience would be best? However, in his invitation he also said, somewhat mischievously I believe, that if possible it should also be wise, intelligent, and sensible!

Staying in touch with reality

At the age of seven, I already knew well what was expected of me. In our large family each of us had our assigned duties. Each one's contribution was considered important and necessary. We learned to do our part with responsibility and love for a job well done. If something were not done well, it would have to be done over.

Some tasks were unusually difficult, like shaking a glass container with a half liter of milk every morning and afternoon in order to separate the cream. I had to do this for my one-year-old sister because she couldn't drink whole milk. It was an important task, yet wearisome, because I would much rather have been out playing, especially at those times of the day.

My maternal grandfather was an important person in our lives, a steady role model and guide. We looked for any and every opportunity to visit him. During school holidays and our many other trips to the farm, his earthy, folksy wisdom always entertained us. He also gave us many difficult chores to do. Well before sunrise he would have us go out to the pastures to bring in the horses and mules, walking through the tall grasses that soaked our pants with the night's dew. Before nightfall we would have to herd the flock of sheep to the corral. He also had us beat bean stalks with a stick to separate the beans from the pods. We would often guard the drying rice, scaring off the greedy flocks of birds. And we carried baskets of corncobs and straw to the pigsty. No matter what the task, the same lesson repeated itself: "Hey, young man, if you want to know what the weather is going to do, look to the sky. Out here that's how we know how we should dress." "Now get going, boy, be a man and put on those boots." "Don't come into my house with muddy boots. Take 'em off and clean 'em first."

So I grew up looking to the sky in order to know what the weather was going to do and learning to clean the mud from my boots before I went into the house. I learned early on that I am a spiritual being in a physical world, existing somewhere between material reality and the dream of a better future.

The days of the missions

As a child in a Catholic family, I lived the month of October in a fever of competitive activity. I could never accept being on a losing team. So my friends and I would buckle down and work really hard to win. It was mission month! In those days, missions meant Saint Thèrésa, the Little Flower, patroness of the missions and missionaries. Missions implied going to pagan lands where God had not yet arrived, to people who would only be happy when God did arrive through the missionaries. From these attitudes flowed all our sacrifices for the missions, duly noted in a spiritual bouquet of the Eucharistic Crusade. Mission stories were told both in school and during catechism lessons at home. A list was made of all the donations to be collected for the missions. For a week, people would set up little concession stands. Every night the folks from the Eucharistic Crusade would sell their chocolates and other sweets, bringing in a respectable sum. The competition between the different teams increased as each tried to outdo the other in the collection of money for the missions. What zeal and sweet innocence! Such a mysterious thing, those missions.

The Redemptorist missions

Then one day, not in October but in the month of May, a "Redemptorist Mission" was announced throughout the little city of Mercês, in the state of Minas Gerais. What could this mission possibly be about, I wondered! My life became a whirlwind of excitement. The chance to know such missionaries as these! I met them for the first time in 1947 and was deeply touched by all that happened.

Two of the missionaries were tall and spoke with a strange accent, yet the people understood everything they said. I discovered what Dutchmen were by constantly observing them during the fifteen-day mission. One spoke focusing to the men and the other to the women. The third missionary, of medium height and a little more rounded than the other two, looking a bit like the baker down the street, visited the sick in their homes and preached to the young men and women, separately of course. He really liked the crackling and cornmeal served at my house. They constantly showed us the illuminated picture of Our Mother of Perpetual Help. I had never heard of her before. But after the candlelight procession, I exchanged Our Lady of Mercies, patroness of our city, for our Mother of Perpetual Help, once and for all with no turning back. But she needn't have been jealous, for I continue to value very much the mercies of Mary, which her perpetual help brings to us.

The fourth missionary, the short one, the size of a grown boy, riveted my attention to the word *Re-demp-tor-ist*, the most beautiful sounding word of the mission. His name was Father José Brandão de Castro. He would gather a thousand children in the city's main church, pray with us, tell stories, and teach us about Jesus. He held everyone's rapt attention. He was a real communicator. We would then leave the church and go in procession through the streets. It was a festive occasion. The center of the city would turn into a fascinating and charming wonderland. In the bandstand of central park, we had a poetry contest, told stories, and read original works on the themes of faith and life. There were prizes and awards for all the best. The mission was truly magical; different from, yet better than the circus or a parade of Gypsies on their majestic horses. But the missionary who spoke every day to the boys about the mystery of the Redemptorist vocation and the seminary was much more magical.

The missionary who became a bishop

That missionary who gathered the children in church went on to be ordained a bishop on September 21, 1960. He then turned his gentleness, his communication skills, and his many other gifts in favor of the dispossessed and marginalized people in the heart of Brazil's poorest region, the Northeast. He was the first bishop of Propriá, in the state of Sergipe. He did everything in his power to open avenues for liberation. His Redemptorist heart soon led him into the isolated and abandoned rural areas, going from village to village, visiting the most impoverished and abandoned people. Bishop José Brandão de Castro deeply touched the hearts of the rural folk in Sergipe. He raised their hopes and initiated a struggle for justice and freedom. (The sixties in Brazil saw the beginning of an increasingly repressive military dictatorship with a strong anticommunist ideology and its absurd National Security Laws.) He made his own the cry of the poor. He committed himself vigorously to all the struggles in favor of indigenous people, Afro-Brazilians and landless peasants. Such attitudes won him persecutions, and he paid a high price for his convictions. Despite this, he made himself heard in a variety of distant forums: in both national and international universities, parliaments and the pulpits of different ecclesial communities and traditions. He joined with all people of good will. He lived an ecumenism in favor of the world's lowly and oppressed.

This genuine disciple of Saint Alphonsus ordained that young boy who, in the same year as the Mission in Mercês—1947, had gone off to the minor seminary in Congonhas, also in state of Minas Gerais. He ordained the boy to the priesthood when he was yet to complete his twenty-fourth birthday (July 16, 1961).

Youthful energy, faith, and loyalty

In minor seminary days certain virile attitudes were demanded of us seminarians. Each one needed to know how to take care of himself and to acquire the courage to stand on his own two feet. A certain "rugged individualism" was fostered. Seminarians were considered morally weak when their approach to life included such things as self-pity, adulation, or always making oneself a defenseless victim. The Latin expression, *"mens sana in corpore sano,"* was implemented through the constant and healthy practices of playing sports, taking long hikes, climbing mountains, and taking cold showers. And how we worked too! Physical vigor, the Fathers always said, was a necessary condition for being able to endure the rigors of missionary life.

The major educational principles, constantly reinforced, were loyalty, camaraderie, and trustworthiness. A beautiful and well-celebrated liturgy served to captivate the young men, grinding the roughness from those precious gems, few of whom had any previous polish. The stones rolled on through the educational waters, year after year, mixing culture and faith. Many, however, remained behind on the banks of the formation river. Only a small minority became well-rounded enough to be fitted as living stones into that building which was the Province of Rio de Janeiro. How we all prided ourselves on having survived this very demanding, yet unquestionably good system of initial Redemptorist formation.

Missionary fervor was part of the air we breathed, and we always had the figure of Clement Hofbauer before us as a holy and inspiring mentor. We dreamed of a missionary future (quite idealized to be sure), marked by creativity, courage, and faith…and, of course, all in the welcoming arms of

God's people. Was it just for the applause? Some of it may have been, but we did truly desire to live a life dedicated to educating people in the faith and combating Protestantism, all with the confident pleasure of knowing we were part of the one, true church of Jesus Christ.

In the seminary, there was a variety of Redemptorist role models. But in general, the Dutch style tended to give more emphasis to individual autonomy. All the Fathers, who were also our professors, showed us one common and very attractive trait: dedication. Their competence as teachers, however, varied from one to the other. In the eyes of the students, the rector and his two subdirectors inspired integrity. And they demanded the same from the students. A certain harmony pervaded all our activities, such as choir, band, theater, and public speaking. It was necessary to rehearse often so that we wouldn't make mistakes, the show would be appreciated and our efforts would receive the seal of quality and good taste.

As in the arts, so also in life, we trained to live well together and to desire the best for one another. We were led to believe that, with this training, the people would one day come to see us missionaries as a community of men who shared life, walked in God's ways, and offered ourselves together for preaching the Gospel.

Learning to be alone and integrating one's personality

The time for learning to be alone came in 1955. In novitiate we sought to acquire the ability to be still and to wait, unmoved by external stimuli. It was a time for each of us to know himself more deeply, a time of internal purification through the exercise of classical ascetical practices. At least that's how I understood it.

It was a difficult year of many trials. We were tried in the crucible to see whether our vocational motivation came from within ourselves or not and if, from that internal font, there would come forth a water good enough to be consecrated to the Lord through religious profession. It was a time of solitude in which the interior life was developed, and the solidity of the missionary dream of those who desired to be Redemptorists was strengthened. Novitiate gave us, perhaps at times by somewhat primitive means, a consciousness of the sacrifices that would be necessary for continual growth in our vocational commitment. It provoked, even though artificially, a variety of "prunings" that made it clear that a Redemptorist life presupposed the capacity for sacrifice and giving generously of one's self. I tell myself today: it was a time for learning to live the dyings and risings of a paschal life.

Each of us came to know, in his own way, the multidimensional man, founder and saint, Alphonsus Liguori. We read Tannoia, Telleria, and Berthe. We meditated upon *The Practice of the Love of Jesus Christ, Glories of Mary, Preparation for Death,* and *Meditations for Each Day of the Year* (a collection of meditations from the works of Saint Alphonsus in Portuguese). We prayed the *Visits to the Most Blessed Sacrament* and used faithfully that famous compendium in Portuguese, *The Most Beautiful Prayers*. But what was really important for our novice master was the Deuteronomic-type cult of the Rule: "Keep the Rule, and Rule will keep you."

Otherness, reciprocity, and a pluralistic world

In the major seminary at Floresta, Minas Gerais, we had the very real experience of coming face to face with the one who is different and with some of the various idiosyncrasies of human nature. We were several generations and three different nationalities mixed together—Brazilians, Dutchmen, and Peruvians—all with the same ideal, but with three distinct ways of being and learning. The same high standards that we knew in the minor seminary were maintained with regard to our studies.

We enjoyed a highly qualified group of Redemptorist professors. Their intellectual ability was highly respected throughout the region. At this level, in 1956, the idea of evangelization, or apostolic work as it was called then, was being introduced as an essential element of initial formation. A new demand was beginning to circulate among the fraters (clerical students). Beyond catechetics, which was already pretty well accepted, pastoral action or ministry was claimed as the new place for real missionary formation. This demand, partially attended, became like a new leaven in the dough of formation. Along with this demand came the desire for more contact with the world.

In the major seminary we strived for mutual acceptance of and respect for differences so that in our nest we would all be birds of a feather. This same equality, however, did not occur with regard to certain privileges. There was criticism and, whenever possible, condemnation of privileges for professors and perpetually professed students, concessions for foreign students, and protectionism of native students. Another source of discomfort was the discrimination against the lay brothers practiced by some of the veteran clerics in the Congregation. Undoubtedly, this "nest" was formed by a network of several powerful and very different strands. This itself foreshadowed a very diversified and pluralistic world beyond the walls of the seminary. Even the charism of the Congregation seemed to become more diversified. There certainly was no lack of lively expression of thought or emotion with regard to Redemptorist identity—who are we? We often wondered how we could be missionaries in and for a world that, by means of a few cracks in the walls, we could already see moving in a very different direction.

In our formation process, it became clearer to us that a young Redemptorist would only earn recognition and distinction to the extent that he was able to be responsible and do well the work entrusted to him. "Work together," we would always say, so as not to diminish the effects of our apostolic work or divide the spirit of the group. Yet not everything we did back then made perfect sense!

In the voice of obedience

Around Christmas of 1961 the time arrived for each of the eight newly ordained priests to receive a first appointment. They were simply announced, without previous dialogue or prior consent. It seemed, however, to express a general perception and feeling of the time that wherever the winds of life might blow…there we would go.

As I got in step with the province's dance and was initiated into its apostolic life through formation work, I began to see more clearly how ministries and relationships were organized and structured, based more on duties and responsibilities than on any interpersonal qualities. Each ministerial group had its own niche. From time to time there were altercations and arguments between the various groups; for example, between popular mission preachers and seminary professors. Each group had its own identity and proven experiences, including the vicissitudes of life which were never camouflaged. But beyond all differences, the soul of the province made itself heard: "Don't worry about a thing, there's nothing we can't handle."

The confreres, whom we were getting to know better, seemed ready for all challenges: *"ad actus arduos et difficiliares disponibilitate."* Their readiness was clearly with respect to the people and so was directed toward new apostolic endeavors. Each one could easily repeat: *"non recuso laborem."* Along with all this, I began to become aware of something else I hadn't noticed up until then: the Brazilian confreres were beginning to assume leadership in prominent positions in the province. We were told that it was up to us to keep the province alive numerically and also maintain its demanding style of competence and gospel simplicity.

We were a province crisscrossed by pluralistic undercurrents, sometimes diametrically opposed. Yet up to this point, no major eruption had occurred. Some statistics will perhaps help to illustrate the expansion of the Congregation. In 1967 there were 220 members (150 priests, 40 lay brothers, and 30 professed students), 180 seminarians, 14 communities, 9 parishes, 1 retreat house, 1 juniorate, 7 popular mission preaching teams, 3 radio stations, 1 newspaper, 2 publishing facilities, and 2 parish schools. There was an abundance of health and energy. As a group, the idea that we might possibly be doing anything wrong never occurred to us.

Around 1963 the question of evangelization in the larger cities began to be debated by those engaged in itinerant popular mission preaching. The rural way of life and world-view of the people who were emigrating to urban areas was questioned. Though respected, there was felt a need for greater openness and adaptation to all the new things that were emerging in modern urban societies. There were also eight confreres helping in the province of Peru from 1955 to 1962. Even while the Second Vatican Council was still in session, there was a renewal of triduums, novenas, and associations in the parishes. There was intense preaching and a variety of courses offered for strengthening and clarifying the knowledge of the faith, helping the faithful come to a better understanding of the Council's teachings. In the area of formation, there was a serious search for answers, intensified even more as our team struggled with conciliar documents like *Gaudium et Spes* and *Optatam Totius* (1965). Meanwhile, the number of seminarians steadily increased.

In general, the confreres were eager to take advantage of all the courses for renewal and updating promoted by the Brazilian Conference for Religious and the National Conference of Catholic Bishops. At the same time, a hidden, yet well-orchestrated struggle for power was taking place between some of the Dutch and a small portion of the Brazilians. This struggle took place not so much at the grassroots level but more in the upper echelons.

Tribulations in turbulent waters

We were not well prepared for the waves of renewal, generated in the inner depths of Vatican II, which suddenly washed over us. Yet there were many courageous seafarers and bold navigators among us, ready to sail any sea in search of new ports and new ways to navigate. Violent winds began to toss us. A maelstrom was forming. A confusing time of anguish and distress, 1967 to 1977, was beating down upon us.

The army that had been trained for front-line combat duty simply crumbled in retreat and desertion. For those who remained at their posts, nothing more was desired than to communicate intensely the new possibilities of plentiful Redemption. With this desire the province boldly set sail for those distant and dangerous seas where insurrections, reforms, and innovations intermingle. These statistics speak for themselves: 42 confreres left the Congregation, 43 died, and 24 either returned to the Netherlands or were transferred to the northeast of Brazil.

What soldiers of Gideon, the handful of us who did not relax in the calm headwaters, but rather drank from the fresh, running waters (God only knows how or why), using the cup of our own hand. And we moved on, always seeking the right direction.

Humbled and learning anew

Years of desolation came upon us. We who persevered were humbled, here and there even despised, both admired for our tenacity and accused of stubbornness. Shaking off our dizziness, we walked forward hesitantly. Patiently removing the scales from our eyes, we recovered a partial vision of the correct way to proceed. We began to meet together more frequently in order to deliberate and strengthen our faltering steps. I remember a consoling phrase from those times, so often whispered in our ears: "God will not allow us to be taken for granted."

The daily dying that accompanied the departures or deaths of so many confreres, the limitations that were imposed upon us by a repressive government, and the experience of helplessness all served to frustrate any new effort to evangelize. How wearisome it was to live in that constant state of conflict. There were conflicts on all sides, and not all were relevant. There were conflicts with dissidents, with those who did not believe in us, with militant church groups struggling at the far end of the political spectrum, and with the vigilantes of the military regime who were constantly seeking to restrict our preaching. Undeniably, there were also conflicts among ourselves. We all failed miserably in so many ways. There existed among us a kind of excessive joy in questioning everything, revealing contradictions and inconsistencies, and using those passionate tones of voice that go hand in hand with denunciations.

At that time it was difficult to wash one another's feet, to eat our bread together peacefully, to forgive and ask forgiveness, and to savor even a morsel of apostolic fraternity. We became an inhospitable environment for new vocations. There was a pervasive atmosphere of uncertainty about the future and everyone was quite vociferous about all they thought and felt.

However, the province community did not drag its feet in going on with its mission. There were three elements that could still generate energy and the missionary mystique: the patience to keep believing, the courage to wager on the success of the innovations taking place in the Church and Congregation, and the deep desire to persevere in making things work out for the best. But even so, we still spent our energies too foolishly. It really was burdensome to deal with so many complications, both one's own and those of others. Meanwhile it was necessary to carry on, living and working together and giving generously of ourselves, without ignoring or disregarding the anxieties, queries, and insecurities. In all this we often wondered: "Where are the wonders of the Lord of which our elders spoke?"

Challenged by our common sufferings, we went on to organize a daily life based on participation

There were several diverse melodies within the province that weren't always sung in perfect rhythm and harmony. The "immersed" type of popular mission that began in 1970 and continues uninterrupted to this day became an integral part of an explicit and comprehensive provincial pastoral plan. Around 1967, we opened small formation communities (high school and philosophy), even before the old minor seminary, novitiate, and major seminary came to be closed. The promotion of vocations had ceased completely. The seedbed had become infertile. A generation gap developed. Gradually, however, we affirmed our commitment to a theology and preaching that inspired liberation. The feeling that a Redemptorist was not totally useless gained affective consistency, even if without the former brilliance of so many great men and great works.

Gaining perspective

I was absent from the province from August 1971 until December 1976. After ten years of service in the Redemptorist apostolate, I felt myself drying up within, needing to return to and drink from the inner springs. I asked for and was given an unparalleled opportunity. I went to study at Louvain. I experienced culture shock, which provoked a process of inculturation that relativized my homeland, people, and culture and universalized my faith and sense of belonging to the Congregation. I lived with exiled Latin Americans and other young confreres in specialized courses (Belgians, Argentineans, Chileans, and Brazilians). All around me the Congregation was suffering the loss of its younger members. I accompanied the vocational evolution of five of these young men. I presided at the weddings of three and saw the other two start a family without any legal ties. All told, eleven reoriented their vocational choice. I, for my part, buried myself in the studies, conscious of the need to rebuild myself from within. I questioned and was severely questioned. There are, however, some beautiful memories from this time: those occasional conversations with the French-speaking provincial, Father Noël Charlier, a simple, yet radiant presence; the friendship and affection of Broeder Julius on Brabanconnestraat 97; Father Marcel Praats' discreet way of showing interest in the students; and the visits I received from Father Ambrose Wynen, from Wittem, where I too had often gone to see him and the others who, in days past, had lived and worked with us in the Rio de Janeiro Province.

The academic result of this time was two masters' degrees. It was so gratifying to finally be able to make some sense of all that was happening in the Church, in the world, and in the Congregation. God took very good care of me. My guardian angel saw me safely around some of life's more dangerous curves, making it clear where things should be going. *Quid retribuam Domino?*

The return

My superiors had kept me informed about all that was happening in the province. I myself maintained a fairly steady correspondence with some of the confreres. When I returned to the province, I spent the first three months mostly observing and gradually getting involved again. I noted two things that were clearly the result of lived-experience:

1) The basic experience of the province was not exactly avant-garde, responding to all the newest urgencies of the times or occupying the most relevant or risky positions in the postconciliar renewal. At the time, perhaps the toughest challenge and most difficult task was to simply hang on with courage and deep faith, to persevere in giving continuity to Redemptorist apostolic life. And to do this from the humble position of those few who remained. We did, in fact, feel thrown into a situation that we had neither imagined possible nor ever expected, and was certainly not of our making. Nevertheless, we accepted it and assumed responsibility for it. And through it all, a silent, hidden, or perhaps unrecognized power of Redemptorist spirituality quietly and secretly nourished the confreres. It was the dynamism of constant conversion and the grace of perseverance.

2) The province had discovered that the dynamics of living the Redemptorist apostolic life are actually an integral part of evangelization. Similarly, the ways of facing crises and conflicts are also a part of the mystery of redemption. To build together a life-giving community, to evangelize in a way that generates a culture of life and freedom, to make a commitment of solidarity among ourselves and with the rest of God's people, always with a preference for the most abandoned, are all elements of the one thing we call "plentiful Redemption." We had come to know all too well the raw and sour taste of the disunity caused by excessive individualism.

The bishop's silence and his prophetic vision

I returned and was reintegrated into the province. However, pain was still pain. And how painful it was! There was little sunshine in all that was happening to us. However, it is consoling to note that, while reduced in number and overcautious, we were not paralyzed by fear, overwhelmed, or cowardly but, despite everything, faithful (Revelations 7:13).

The retired bishop, João Batista Muniz, the first Brazilian, Redemptorist bishop, came to live in our house in Belo Horizonte, Minas Gerais, in 1967. He was a pastoral giant. For twenty-four years, since 1942, he had been at the head of the geographically immense and economically impoverished diocese of Barra, in the state of Bahia. He dedicated himself untiringly to an evangelization at the service of life. He made countless pastoral visits, preached popular missions, gave weeklong missions among the rural people, developed courses for learning handicrafts and other types of professions, and promoted health campaigns. He was instrumental in the eradication of malaria and glaucoma in that region. He was even honored by the Brazilian government. At the same time, however, Muniz challenged the civil authorities and created public opinion in favor of his causes. He was a pioneering pastor. Feeling blessed, he would always say, "God is so good to me!" He would not get personally involved in our crises. Yet he deeply and tenderly loved the province. He commented very little on the sufferings we were experiencing or the harsh attitudes that he perceived in our midst.

I remember we met once in the community refectory for a midafternoon snack. Being two good mountainmen from Minas Gerais (*mineiros*), there was no lack of conversation. One subject lead to another until he abruptly concluded by saying, "We have managed to save what is essential. The members of the province are still able to live in community. I see the confreres who pass through here, and I know very well how things are going. Everything that can be done in favor of the people is being done." I interjected, "It's really good to hear you say that, Dom Muniz. How beautiful!" And he reiterated, "You are still together in the work and in your hearts. What is essential has been saved. I will continue to pray very much for the province. It is all I can do now."

Bishop Muniz's observations were very much on target. Writing now, at some distance from those painful times, I am surprised to perceive that the baptism of fire and water in which we were baptized has served to make us just a little more eucharistic. The province has reorganized itself in its financial, relational, and communal aspects, with a more day-to-day type of personal participation and mutual responsibility. The gift of Redemptorist apostolic life and our lives given as a gift have become like a new branch sprouting from the old, wounded, and dying trunk, with healing sap for our whole being. Our common life has become less fragmented and individualistic. We are more united in our struggles and sacrifices, in our common search, in our deliberations and in the sharing of our works. The unifying principle continues to be the growing awareness that we are a single apostolic body. The wounds are healing and we are slowly recreating the visible face of our common identity.

2. The Development of the New Constitutions of the Congregation of the Most Holy Redeemer 1969 to 1982

In writing this story, there is a coincidence that only now has grabbed my attention and gives an unexpected coloring to this reflection. The road we have traveled in the Rio de Janeiro Province is contemporaneous with the development of the new Constitutions. Reading them again now, especially Constitution 20, we can affirm that their content had already been present for a long time, at the core of Redemptorists' lived experiences.

Certainly the most enlightening aspect of this pearl of wisdom about the apostolic identity of a Redemptorist (Constitution 20) is its description of the lived-experiences of confreres from around the world. It lists traits already incarnated in Redemptorists' lives well before they were ever written. It is a faithful portrait. It is a definitive reference point for the historical continuity of the authentic Redemptorist. It is a Constitution to be learned by heart and to have permanently inscribed on the heart.

Here in the province of Rio de Janeiro, when we reread Constitution 20, which is such a fine profession of faith in all we are called to be, we discover that certain reservations, fears, and restrictions still exist among us. We can't quite take off and fly with it. There are still those little strings attached that hold us down…and they are of the purest silk! But we know we cannot turn back and go down a road already traveled.

A grateful gaze

We can't quite take off and fly with all that Constitution 20 calls us to be. However, our eyes light up and our hearts are full of gratitude when we see and feel, in the Brazilian units of the Congregation, how gospel simplicity of life and language, self-denial, and generous availability are chiseling to perfection the features of a genuine Redemptorist identity in this country.

We see the vice province of Manaus in a permanent state of self-denial and struggling with the demanding task of evangelizing the poor riparian populations along the Solimões River and its myriad channels, tributaries, lakes, and creeks in the immense Amazonian rain forest. Ah, those North Americans…and those in the province of Campo Grande too! And with them, the handful of Brazilians who inspire hope of renewed missionary vitality.

The young province of Goiás is bravely investing in social communication, above all in a chain of radio stations scattered throughout the midwestern part of the country. And there is the centenarian, yet vibrant province of São Paulo, now also zealously caring for the vice province of Recife that has begun to flourish.

The vice province of Bahia grows stronger and more vigorous in its inculturation and in the contagious enthusiasm of our Polish confreres. There is the province of Campo Grande, leaving some parishes and even helping the Congregation to get started in Korea.

The vice province of Fortaleza (and this name for us is practically synonymous with "Irish"!) is cast deep into the northeast of Brazil, increasing in native vocations and actively living out its commitment of solidarity with the poorest of the poor and giving special priority to young people. The province of Porto Alegre, from the extreme south of Brazil, extends its missionary activity to the far off north and northeast of Brazil.

And then there is the resilient heroism of Father Léon Grégoire and his confrere, Etienne, working in the great pockets of poverty in the state of Sergipe, guaranteeing the Redemptorist presence as a form of love and service.

Looking at all these units of the Congregation, with their silent sacrifices, sweat, fatigue, anxieties, and stumblings, it is safe to assert that the Redemptorists, scattered throughout the different regions of Brazil, are learning to be generous, renewing themselves in listening to Jesus: "Come. Offer yourselves with me. And go!" We are learning about personal relationships, listening to the people and responding to the challenges of our modern world. We are discovering new ways to live more simply. We already know a little about reading God's Word (the Bible and the Constitutions), with our actual lives as the true starting point, including the reality of the vast majority of poor among our people. This is what brings us ever closer to the people excluded from the blessings of life.

We are also beginning to realize that the geographical borders that delineate province territories are not fences that protect inherited properties or limits and obstacles to an organic and global Redemptorist project that is adequate for the various regions of the country. It is not so much theories that challenge us, but rather real lives that cry out for a more consistent presence and united action on our part. The poor cry out for plentiful Redemption. We perceive our Redemptorist vocation as more human and rooted in the sociocultural conditions of our people. We are moving forward. *Deo gratias!* Reality constantly alerts us to the fact that the joy of liberating service to the Word, prayer and perseverance are the distinctive marks of one who would, like Alphonsus, want to announce the Gospel to the poor.

"Always ready to undertake what is most difficult"
What does this really mean?

In this personal testimonial, for that's really what it is, we started with real events. The profile of a Redemptorist was highlighted in the lived-experience of a Province. We can now return to the dictum in Constitution 20.

What do these words really mean? They are a beautiful codification of real historical and personal events and precious experiences from all parts of the Redemptorist world. We arrived at these experiences by various means, some of which were quite unsuspected. But it was always God the Redeemer passing through a small part of his vineyard, protecting it from complete decimation and restoring its fidelity to the mission.

Yes, it is always the Lord who passes by and saves us. Equally, it is a group of Redemptorists that passes by and is saved. It is a mystery both old and new, from Abraham to Jesus, from Alphonsus and Clement, to us to-day. We live the Easter passage in our own flesh. It is in the very real, often painful, experiences of life that God awaits us. Yet we never imagined the possibility of entering through such a narrow gate. For this reason, the most difficult, challenging, and demanding situations will continue to be those in which we are thrown beyond where we could possibly have chosen to go. Should we all receive the gift of valuing the difficult, demanding, and challenging situations in order to reconsecrate ourselves and grow stronger in perseverance!

Above all, our work here and now, on the cutting edge, is to plant seeds of hope. What is most difficult, once again, is to defeat the demon of despair who wants to collar us with a sense of uselessness and powerlessness. For whoever plows, must plow with hope (1 Corinthians 9:10).

So, consequently here in Rio, 63 confreres (44 priests, 9 lay brothers, and 10 students of theology) plus 2 novices, 4 postulants, 12 students of philosophy, 11 minor seminarians, and 2 aspiring to be lay brothers have lost neither the dream nor the *cantus firmus*. We all zealously care for the flower of hope growing in the immense field of God. Our scars are slowly disappearing.

There remains but one thing here at the end that I need to repeat in all honesty with my poet friend: "How I envy those who live patiently, accepting the small portion that is there lot!" We must once again make our lives magnetic and thus captivate cultural environments with the beauty and mystery of the Redemptorist vocation. When will this day come, Lord?

16

IN THE SPIRITUAL SCHOOL OF MARY

Alois Kraxner, C.Ss.R.
Province of Vienna
Translated by John Ruef, C.Ss.R.
Province of Baltimore

1. Biographical Data

I was born October 5, 1933, in St. Marien, near Gratz, Austria. I attended the diocesan grammar school in Gratz from 1947 to 1954, then entered the Congregation of the Most Holy Redeemer in 1954. My theological studies were at Mautern (Steiernark, Austria) in the Redemptorist seminary, my ordination to the priesthood was in 1960, and I earned a licentiate in theology at the University of Innsbruck, Austria, from 1961 to 1962.

At the time of Vatican II, I studied at the Institute for Moral Theology, the Alphonsian Academy, in Rome, working on my dissertation under Bernard Häring. I served as university chaplain at the Montanische Hochschule in Leoben, Austria (1966–1969), provincial of the Vienna Province of the Redemptorists and its Vice Province of Copenhagen (1969–1981).

I participated in the apostolate of missions and retreats from 1976 to 1985, served as spiritual counselor for Catholic Action of Austria and spiritual advisor for the Katholikentag and the papal visit in 1983.

I was spiritual counselor for Catholic Action in the Archdiocese of Vienna (1981–1990), spiritual counselor for the Society of Catholic Academicians of the Archdiocese of Vienna (1985–1992), reelected provincial of the Vienna Province of the Redemptorists and its Vice Province of Copenhagen (1990).

When I entered the Congregation forty years ago, every evening we prayed: "I thank you for having called me to the Congregation." Later on it was not easy for me to express the same sentiments of thanks. The contradiction between what I sought and what I found in the Congregation struck me as being too great. This held true for the apostolate as well as for community life.

I saw the contradiction between the program that our Constitutions set forth and the reality of what we are and do. It is still true today. Despite this, I can pray with conviction: "I thank you that you called me to the Congregation." As I look back and review the different phases of my life, I must confess: It was good that I chose this way of life, even though it was quite different from what I had imagined. Now I am not interested in making a public confession. However, I would like to point out a few experiences that were important and that might also be of some importance for my confreres.

The first of these experiences was that of my vocation. This, of course, is different for each of us. It consists of various details of our lives that put us on the way to becoming a Redemptorist.

The certainty that I should go on to become a priest and also a Redemptorist was for me a singular experience. It was a sudden conviction that was not the result of a process of reflection and decision. My vocation was a simple yes. The knowledge that one has been called can be a significant factor in helping face problems later on. I cannot conceive life as a religious without this singular experience which goes by the name of vocation.

The second experience is this. A person needs encouragement and correction from without—be it from confreres, from those looked upon as models as a way of life, or simply from those who are different. Even the faults of such persons can help. Also the effect of illness can cut across one's life and plans with devastating effect. Then there are the consequences of success and failure.

We need to have experiences that mobilize us and change us. They are worth more than a thousand good intentions. I do not put much faith in plans that a person cobbles together as a program for life. For myself, I have translated the expression: "Pursuit of holiness" into "Pay careful attention as you go along." Instead of working out short- or long-range plans, a person should look to the possibilities and opportunities that God offers. We should consider how the present situation relates to the coming of the kingdom of God for oneself and for others and what challenges different events present. If we do this, we will keep our feet on the ground.

As I look back, I can see that a person can also miss many opportunities. This is not only through passivity or listlessness, the basic temptation of all religious, but also through accommodation to the ways of the world and through a misguided consideration for the confreres. A religious house, with its set structures and customs, can become a formidable obstacle to the attainment of the purpose for which it was established. At the same time, I must ask: What would I have been able to do if I had not become a religious? Our proverb holds true: He who carries the Church is also carried by the Church.

These forty years of my religious life were a time of upheaval and change. In 1961 the seminarians were asked to write a paper entitled: "Reflections on the Purpose of the Congregation." It was an expression of what we sought.

In 1974 to 1975 I conducted retreats in the German-speaking provinces. The theme was "Change in the Spirituality of Our Congregation." There were questions from the floor at the end of every conference. The superior general, Father Josef Pfab, had these interventions translated and distributed throughout the Congregation. Many of the remarks offered then are still open questions today.

For me these past forty years were a time of inquiry and search. The inquiry concerned not only the Congregation but also the meaning of being a Christian and a member of the Church in our time.

On this journey I have avoided two extremes: that of a liberalism that leads to a kind of disintegration, and that of a conservatism that makes a person righteous, narrow, and hardhearted. Noncommittal liberalism goes against my disposition. I had already encountered hardhearted, indeed even spiteful and regressive tendencies, when I was writing my dissertation. This experience made me cautious.

These forty years were not only an experience like wandering about in a desert but also coming across oases. There was the experience of grace, which showed that results could go well beyond the human effort expended. The Lord accomplishes great things not as a result of our efforts, but despite our mistakes and sins. And there were many persons who accepted me and what I stood for.

But did I live for the poor? Did I help our Congregation bring about the concern with "the abandoned" and to bring them the Good News? One of the motives that induced me to enter the Congregation was the dedicated work for the abandoned. But in this regard I was led along paths other than those I had planned for myself.

There are sayings that accompany one through life. I came across one of these some thirty years ago during the time of illness. Divine Providence forced me to reflect on these words during these difficult months. The words are from Psalm 31:15. "But my trust is in you, O LORD; I say, 'You are my God.' In your hands is my destiny...." These words can help a person regain a sense of balance and not give up. Perhaps they also helped me to keep a sense of humor.

2. Mary Our Guide

Saint Alphonsus ranks among the greatest of those who venerated Our Blessed Lady. Sufficient proof of this are his *Glories of Mary* and *Visits to the Blessed Sacrament and the Blessed Virgin Mary.* Practically all his prayers and writings conclude with a prayer to Mary.

It is not my purpose to present and praise Saint Alphonsus's devotion to Mary. I do not feel called nor able to do so. My assigned theme was the spiritual school of Mary. The word *school* reminds me of an Eastern representation of the Mother of God: Maria-Hodegetria, Mary-the-Guide. Mary is the guide to a spirit-filled life. She is not only guide but also companion. Both ideas find expression in the icon of Our Mother of Perpetual Help. This picture belongs to the category of Hodegetria-Icons. At the same time, it expresses the belief that as Perpetual Help, Mary accompanies Christians on their way.

Mary leads us to Jesus

In the representations of Mary as Hodegetria, the artist highlights the hand which she points to Jesus. This directs the attention of the viewer away from Mary to Jesus, whom she carries on her left arm. The child raises his right arm as in giving a blessing and in his left hand holds a parchment, symbolizing wisdom. Thus she begins her work of guiding those who enroll in the spiritual school of Mary. She points to Jesus.

Directing others in this manner corresponds to the life and faith experience of Mary herself. Mary owes her prominence in the history of the human race and in salvation history to having been chosen to be the Mother of God. This is also evident in the sacred Scriptures. Whenever she is mentioned, it is in her relationship to Jesus.

The better our understanding of Jesus, the more important is the figure of Mary. It is a long way from the praise of the woman whose "womb that bore you and the breasts that nursed you" (Luke 11:27) to the declaration of the Council of Ephesus solemnly proclaiming Mary, who gave birth to Christ, as Mother of God.

Thus it is understandable that Mary—as guide—points first of all to Jesus. She invites us to go to the school of Jesus. He is the master and teacher. He is the way, the truth, and the life. He will bless us and lead us on the way of salvation and life.

Mary gives the same advice at the marriage feast of Cana: "Do whatever he tells you" (John 2:5). In the Scriptures, these are the only words Mary addresses to fellow human beings. Mary stays in the background. She points to Jesus. He is the one who will lead us.

Mary: Our guide through her life and example

We know very little about Mary. In the Bible we find only a rough sketch of her. Under these circumstances can she be a guide through her life and example?

Is there not the danger that every age or every spiritual trend will picture Mary according to its own ideals? That has often happened in the past and happens also at present. The picture we have of Mary is conditioned by contemporary circumstances. We see this clearly in Alphonsus's *Glories of Mary*, especially in the chapter on her virtues. Mary is seen according to the popular ideals of the time. The same thing is happening today. The person of Mary, as seen in many Marian movements, is quite different from the Mary presented by feminist theologians. That the image of Mary should be conditioned by time and place is unavoidable. It can help or deter us from finding in Mary a model and guide.

These diverse representations of Mary must always be judged according to their conformity to the image of her that is found in the Bible. Only then can they be true to the original. Despite the scarcity of references, still there is enough in the Scriptures to give us the image of Mary as model and guide.

"Blessed is she who has believed"

Mary is for us a guide and model: There are two defining moments in Mary's life. Here her faith clearly stands out: her response to the angel agreeing to bring Christ into the world and her presence at the foot of the cross. Elizabeth's joyful greeting highlights the first of these experiences: "Blest is she who trusted that the Lord's words to her would be fulfilled" (Luke 1:45). Her yes to the angel manifests and proves her faith. She trusts the word of God even though what is promised seems impossible.

In terms rich with symbolism, Saint John tells us about Mary's faith: "Near the cross of Jesus there stood his mother, and his mother's sister, Mary the wife of Clopas, and Mary Magdalene" (19:25). Mary stands at the foot of the cross. Jesus entrusts to his mother the disciple whom he loved; and to him he entrusts his mother. This is not a passive scene. It is full of life. Mary does not collapse. She stands there. Through faith, she survives the experience of Calvary.

Inspired by the faith of Mary under the cross, countless individuals in time of need and suffering have found comfort and trust in God through the mystery of faith. Mary could accept these defining moments through faith because she was a believing person.

Her faith was rooted in the word of God. The accolade uttered by Jesus has special reference to her: "Blest are they who hear the word of God and keep it" (Luke 11:28). Her whole life rested on the foundation of hearing the word of God and keeping it, which is established through many references in the Bible.

Thus Mary is a guide who leads us to faith through her life and example. In the spiritual school of Mary, we can learn to believe. She is the sister of everyone who believes.

"Full of grace": The angel greets Mary with the words: "Rejoice , O highly favored daughter! The Lord is with you." As she is frightened at the sound of this greeting, he reassures her: "Do not fear, Mary. You have found favor with God." And to the question: "How can this be since I do not know man?" the angel answers: "The Holy Spirit will come upon you, and the power of the Most High will overshadow you" (Luke 1:28,30,34,35).

Mary stands before us as the highly favored one. God turns to her. He calls her by name and the Spirit of God overshadows her. It is through God's great favor that Mary has become what she is. She gives expression to this in the *Magnificat*: "He has looked upon his servant in her lowliness. ...God who is mighty has done great things for me, holy is his name" (Luke 1:48,49).

Mary has a singular position in salvation history. At the same time, her life shows the primary importance of God's grace and favor in the lives of all human beings. God brings them into existence, bestows his favor on them, calls them by name, showers his love upon them and empowers them through the Holy Spirit.

Mary—the guide—is represented against a background of gold. Gold is the color that symbolizes God. With her entire being, Mary shows her reliance on the living God who empowers her in her own life and in the life of the human race.

Whoever enters the spiritual school of Mary must learn to appreciate the love and favor of God. He must have faith in this and remain open to the graces bestowed by God. Only those who are humble, who realize that in the presence of God they are indeed poor, can accomplish this.

"Behold the handmaid of the Lord": Mary says yes to the angel. She accepts her mission from the Almighty for the good of mankind. This affirmative response at the beginning of her call has a dramatic history.

Mary will renew this yes again and again

- at the birth of Jesus in the stable
- at the flight into Egypt
- during the hidden life in Nazareth
- during the twelve-day loss in the Temple
- during the public ministry of Jesus
- at the time of Jesus' death on the cross
- as a member of the early Church

Mary stays true to her initial yes and to every situation, pleasant or painful. She joins the rank of the great personages of the Old Testament: Abraham, Moses, and the prophets—who responded to God's call in like manner and persevered during often dramatic events.

This yes is always associated with a no, in reference to all that stands in its way: with the no to disbelief; with the no to deviation from the true way; with the no to defiance and despair.

Mary has become a guide for all through this exemplary yes to her vocation and mission in highly diverse life experiences. She has become the guide for all who choose to follow Jesus and who accept the challenge he offers. We can learn from Mary how to remain true to our yes. Through her example we can also learn that such a yes does not handicap an individual, but lets one mature. This yes can bear fruit in the community so as to bring forth new life and vigor.

"How shall this come about?": Mary is one of us. She represents no unattainable ideal that from the start is beyond our reach. In the Bible she is more often the sister of those who are perplexed and in need rather than the Mother of Good Counsel or of Perpetual Help.

- Mary is perplexed: How shall this come about, since I know not man?
- Joseph is perplexed, since it was evident that Mary was expecting a child.
- Mary and Joseph are perplexed, since they do not know where to provide shelter for the newborn child.
- Mary and Joseph are perplexed when, at the age of twelve, the child remains in the Temple and they do not understand the explanation he gives them.
- Mary is perplexed when relatives want to restrain Jesus by force because he appeared to be out of his mind.
- Mary is perplexed and full of questions when she notices that Jesus continues to meet ever greater opposition and everything points in the direction of his death on the cross.
- After the Ascension, Mary prays with the perplexed disciples for the coming of the Holy Spirit.

Mary can be our guide, because she herself experienced perplexity and helplessness. She stands with those who are perplexed and helpless. For this reason the perplexed and helpless have come to her. They knew she would understand and thus have special confidence in her.

We can expect to find a sympathetic teacher in the school of Mary. With her we will be able to find a way out of our confusion and need.

"Mary however kept all that had happened in her heart": This is stated two places in the Bible (Luke 2:19; 2:51). Mary becomes aware of all that

happens and ponders in her heart both what is understood and what is not. In this manner she encounters the realities that surround her and becomes aware of the ways of God. Thus her life gains substance and depth.

Mary is a meditative, contemplative person. In this respect through her being and example she can also serve as a model.

Through contemplation we can gain an all-encompassing grasp of the realities of life and faith. All that we receive superficially or only with our reason, and do not weigh and ponder in our heart, remains outside of us. It cannot form or leave its stamp on our lives.

Through contemplation—and this is always the case—that which touches our lives, that which we experience or hear, becomes part of us. Like Mary, through contemplation we begin to understand and marvel at the ways of divine Providence. Many persons are neither ready nor capable of this. Now and then painful experiences are the only way that will give us this capacity.

"But a sword shall pierce your soul": The old man Simeon says to Mary: "This child is destined to be the downfall and the rise of many in Israel, a sign that will be opposed—and you yourself shall be pierced with a sword—so that the thoughts of many hearts may be laid bare" (Luke 2:34–35).

Mary participates in the destiny of her son and in the mystery of the cross. This is certain even though the Scriptures hardly mention it. It is a truth that has become rooted in the consciousness of Christians and shows itself in many representations and prayers. Mary also participates in his resurrection, even though again the Bible does not mention it. She also rose and ascended into heaven.

To be crucified with Jesus and to rise with him, this is the basic pattern of the Christian life. It is certainly evident in the life of Mary. Many works of art show Mary at the foot of the cross and Mary assumed into heaven. Here she is also our guide. She encourages all Christians to follow the way she has taken.

"My soul proclaims the greatness of the Lord and my spirit rejoices in God my Savior": Enlightened by the Holy Spirit, Mary recognizes the presence of God among human beings. Conscious of what God has accomplished in her own life and in the history of her people, Israel, Mary proclaims the *Magnificat*, the song of praise that the Church for centuries has prayed day after day.

Mary is a person who can rejoice in the Lord. She thanks God and praises him. In this too she can serve as a model. Whoever enters the school of Mary should pray to the Holy Spirit that he or she may be enlightened. We need to understand the part played by God in our own lives, in the life of the Church, and in the destiny of all human beings. Whoever succeeds in understanding the saving grace of the loving God will find offering a prayer of thanks and praise not a heavy burden, but a spontaneous reaction.

Mary: Virgin and Mother: Mary, the handmaiden of the Lord, is no slave. She is both virgin and mother. She is a virgin who out of love surrenders her freedom. Virginity is a symbol of the "integrity of faith, hope, and love" (Augustine). The opposite of the virgin is not the married woman but the prostitute who is abused by men and allows this to happen.

However, virginity must not remain barren. Mary, virgin and mother, is the symbol of fertility. Thus Mary, the mother of Jesus, becomes the second Eve, becomes the mother of all reborn through water and the Holy Spirit.

Mary is our guide as virgin and mother. Christians should imitate her as virgin. They are not slaves, but free sons and daughters. They should fall in love with God and strive after integrity in faith, hope, and love. They should orient their lives according to the maternity of Mary. Their lives should not be sterile but fruitful.

3. Mary: Our Companion on the Way

Mary is not only a guide who leads us to Jesus. Through her life and example, she is also our companion on the way.

The references in the Scriptures in this respect are sparse and reserved. In the symbol-rich narrative of the wedding feast of Cana, Mary tells her Son: "They have no more wine" (John 2:3). At the foot of the cross the disciple whom Jesus loved is entrusted to her: "Woman, there is your son!" (John 19:26). After the Ascension of Jesus, Mary, together with the disciples and the other women, persevered in prayer for the coming of the Holy Spirit (see Acts of the Apostles 1:14). Despite these sparse references there grew in the consciousness of the Church the conviction that Mary did intercede on our behalf.

The Second Vatican Council sees this position of Mary as rooted in her participation in the work of the Redemption.

She conceived, brought forth, and nourished Christ. She presented Him to the Father in the temple, and was united with Him in suffering as He died on the cross. In an utterly singular way she cooperated by her obedience, faith, hope, and burning charity in the Savior's work of restoring supernatural life to souls. For this reason she is a mother in the order of grace.

This maternity of Mary in the order of grace began with the consent which she gave in faith at the Annunciation and which she sustained without wavering beneath the cross. This maternity will last without interruption until the eternal fulfillment of all the elect. For, taken up to heaven, she did not lay aside this saving role, but by her manifold acts of intercession continues to win for us gifts of eternal salvation....Therefore the Blessed Virgin is invoked by the Church under the titles of Advocate, Auxiliatrix, Adjutrix, and Mediatrix (*Dogmatic Constitution on the Church*, 61–62).

That Mary is our trusted guide finds expression in many forms of religious piety, in the countless places of pilgrimage dedicated to her, in the titles given her, and in paintings that depict her; for example:

- Mother of Good Counsel
- Help of Christians
- Mother of Perpetual Help
- Health of the Sick
- Comfort of the Afflicted
- Refuge of Sinners

In the most popular of the prayers to Mary, her devotees invoke her with the words: Holy Mary, Mother of God, pray for us sinners, now and at the hour of our death. Amen.

For Saint Alphonsus, it is self-evident that Mary should be revered as our guide. For him, Mary is a symbol of hope. She is a true sign, being the first to receive the full grace of redemption. She is a sign of hope. We can rely on her intercessory help since she cooperates in the work of redemption.

(Author's note: The words of Saint Alphonsus's hymn: *O bella mia speranza* could be used as a fitting summary and conclusion.)

17

FORMATION IN
OUR PROPER CHARISM

Ronald McAinsh, C.Ss.R.
and Michael Fish, C.Ss.R.
Region of Zimbabwe

Autobiography of Ronald McAinsh, C.Ss.R.

I joined the Congregation for all the wrong reasons. It was in the early 1960s when I made contact with the Redemptorists. At that time, the changes mandated by *Perfectae Caritatis* had not yet begun to come into effect.

I grew up in a small Protestant town in Scotland that had a Redemptorist "monastery." (It is the most northerly house in the entire Congregation.) This monastery had been built in 1868 and was the first religious house to be constructed in Scotland since the Reformation. However, the "monks" lived just outside the town and had virtually no contact with the local community. I was only vaguely aware of the "monastery," and the priests and brothers were mysterious characters who occasionally appeared in town dressed from head to foot in black, with closely cropped hair.

A chance encounter with the Redemptorists during a mission in 1962 touched me. I was struck both by the enthusiasm and the apparent holiness of both missioners. I had from my earliest years wanted to follow Christ, but had absolutely no attraction to the secular priesthood. Indeed, priesthood itself was not important for me. Rather, it was religious life that I sought, and my only two inquiries to date had been with the Carthusians and the Cistercians. Both had advised me to wait several years, but the rigorous, penitential life of both groups was rather daunting to me.

I was invited by one of the missioners to visit the monastery. Here he explained very simply the Redemptorist ideal. He described it as the following of Jesus through a life of itinerant preaching combined with several months of the year spent in the community in prayer, fraternity, and study. He used the then-famous phrase "Apostles abroad, Carthusians at home." That was enough for me. Instantly, I knew that this is what I had been longing for; it was like coming home. In discovering the Redemptorists, I knew I had arrived at my destination.

It was only years later that the "Apostles abroad, and Cathusians at home" phrase was demythologized and attributed to Tannoia rather than Saint Alphonsus. However, the truth is that this is what attracted me to the Congregation. That is why I say, perhaps I came for the wrong reasons. I was, in my early years looking for a controlled apostolic life, coupled with a semimonastic life at home.

Now, thirty years later, why I am here…far from my home and (more importantly) far from my early ideals. It would be easy to say that I have simply grown up. But that would be too facile an answer. I remain in the Congregation because I believe profoundly in the charism of the Congregation; and equally importantly because I believe with all my heart in my own call to follow Jesus in this Congregation.

I am far from my ideals. I live a life of frenetic activity. Of this I am somewhat ashamed. I participate in regular community prayer and fraternal life. But I confess that at present the spark has gone. I live in the hope of its rekindling. This is not to say that I am disillusioned or even unhappy. However, I feel that the zeal and enthusiasm that characterized the Congregation which I joined, has dimmed somewhat. In seeking the rekindling of my own fire, I hope to be part of the renewal of the life of the whole Congregation. I believe that this is possible. I find in the revised Constitutions the ideals I once sought, although couched in very different language. I discover each time I study them, or share them with those in formation, fresh insights and wonderful inspiration for a life of itinerant preaching and authentic community living. I see in them an invitation to silence, to conversion, to radical gospel living—both through being and through action. And that is why I stay.

Autobiography of Michael Fish, C.Ss.R.

When I walked into the monastery in Pretoria in 1970 I knew I was at home. Although only nineteen years old, I had always wanted to be a religious. Throughout high school, my army training, and medical technology studies, I had seriously investigated different congregations and their spirit. In fact, I had applied to the Oblates of Mary Immaculate because they were priests serving our parish, but during my military service withdrew my application.

I had narrowed down my search to looking for a community which gave preference to prayer, who lived together in community and in simplicity; I found this in the Redemptorist community in Pretoria. Stephen Naidoo, who was in the house at that time and later became my spiritual director, advised me to complete my studies and two years later I finally entered. Throughout this period, I continued to visit Stephen and the community.

I was older than the other novices and ready for the spiritual year. I joined a youth organization before entering the novitiate, where I had been taught meditation which carried me through the year, a year fraught with the disparity between a conservative novice master and the new Constitutions. I had begun the inner journey before entering the novitiate.

My difficulties with the Congregation began almost immediately. Vatican II took its time to reach South Africa and so it was in the early 1970s, while in initial formation, that I began to notice that the very reasons for entering the Redemptorists—prayer, community, and simplicity—began to disintegrate. As the Redemptorists struggled to adapt, moving from the old to the new, I felt that in the process of renewal they had lost sight of central issues.

I was, however, fortunate in having capable directors during these confusing years. I made friends with the Little Sisters of Jesus and found good role models in the community and among other religious. From these I grew in the conviction of the importance of meditation, the value of creating brotherhood, and the beauty that comes from simplicity. My first love was religious life, but even as a Redemptorist student, we began to teach catechism in a nearby poor parish. Because of the disability of the elderly secular priest, we almost took over the running of that parish. This involvement with the poor gave new impetus to my studies at the seminary, gave purpose to my spiritual life, and made me feel I was truly becoming a son of Alphonsus.

After ordination I was appointed directly to the parish mission team and traveled all over South Africa and Zimbabwe preaching. I did this for a few years before being appointed by Kevin Dowling (the vice provincial) as novice master: a position I have held for twelve years. It was during this time as novice master—preparing conferences for the young brothers on the Constitutions and Statutes (C&S), our spirituality and prayer—that I made important personal discoveries. The method of prayer that I had learned before entering was based on the prayer of Teresa of Avila. I was amazed to discover her influence on the person and prayer of Alphonsus and saw how, for both of them, the humanity and person of Jesus was central. I was forcibly struck by their teaching that the way to Christ was through the Gospels in silent prayer. The vision of the C&S enthralled me as I began to see our spirituality was a call far beyond "crib and cross" to one of becoming "the continuation of Jesus."

Almost ten years ago, I was asked by the province to be part of a team who would give a workshop on our charism. It was to be taken from the perspective of Alphonsus, Falcoia, and Celeste. I was asked to give a presentation on Crostarosa's influence on our Institute. As I read her writings, so much fell into place. Up to then I had only known her as that madwoman who wanted red, white, and blue habits and saw visions. However, her writings amazed me: her Intent of the Father, the Living Memory, the fixed gaze, becoming one with the person of Jesus, and her intuitive knowledge of the Divine. Suddenly, I began to see what Alphonsus had in mind for me and who he wanted us to be. Much more than missionaries or religious of the day, he had something new and fresh in mind: not monks, not missionaries, but "apostolic mystics." I realized that Celeste added a new dimension both to Alphonsus and the C&S and that together the three came alive and brought forth a balance and harmony not only in me but in the presentation of the charism to the young men in the novitiate.

About the same time I discovered the conference Father F. X. Durrwell gave the 1985 General Chapter members: *To follow the example of Jesus Christ the Redeemer*. For the first time since entering I realized that I had, unknown to myself, embarked on a spirituality that had as its aim to become the person of Jesus and that this was, in fact, the heart of our charism and the essence of the spirit of Alphonsus. I felt that I had arrived, I had found my place in a spirituality that was natural and personal to me and which also happened to be that of the Congregation I had joined. I started becoming a Redemptorist long before I entered and have continued becoming long after my profession.

I joined because of what I saw on the outside, I stay because of what I have found within. Alphonsus, Celeste, the C&S, and Father Durrwell's conference point toward a future that, I feel, has always been. The question facing me now is "Can it be lived?"

Forming young men for life as a Redemptorist is essentially a work of the heart. It means helping them to get in touch with their own deepest longings, as well as with the mind and heart of Christ and Saint Alphonsus. We are very aware that such a delicate task requires a high degree of professionalism. However, in the final analysis, the radical response to Christ the Redeemer, focuses on a profound but simple "yes" to the call of God.

In the Church of today, many documents on formation and many methodologies are offered. We are grateful for these. We are delighted to have the ratios for the various stages of formation. However, for this celebration of the birth of Saint Alphonsus, we situate our response to the topic, "Formation for our proper charism," to be—in the spirit of the founder—simple, direct, and from the heart. Accordingly, our present offering makes no attempt to deal with the scientific, psychological, or didactic areas of formation as such. It is, rather, an offering from two experienced formators, both now working in Africa, that attempts to deal with the world situation in which we, as Redemptorists, find ourselves. We have arranged our thoughts in the form of a dialogue, and we hope that the realism as well as the idealism contained in this exchange will reflect both our experience and our hope for the continuation of the charism of Saint Alphonsus into the next millennium.

The Dialogue

Ronnie: Michael, I welcome this opportunity to dialogue with you on the topic of formation for charism. However, before we talk about formation, I feel we need to talk about Redemptorist life. It might sound simplistic, but the primary premise of any formation input is that you must have a fairly clear idea of what you are forming people for.

Are we forming men for the idea proposed by Saint Alphonsus and contained in our present Constitutions and Statutes; or do we, perhaps in a fatalistic manner, prepare our young men for the cold (and at times harsh) reality which *Communicanda 3* suggests is prevalent in many parts of the Congregation? This *Communicanda* tentatively suggests that in many units, the Congregation is dying. In some places, the spirit of community life is only half alive, and in other places there are serious difficulties in the areas of prayer, shared reflection, and apostolate.

This tension—and it can be a healthy one—is at the basis of all formation. I really believe that there is a tension between faith and fatalism. By this, I mean that there is a tension between realizable ideals which we find in our various ratios, on the one hand, and utilitarian pragmatism which is ever-present in our world situation on the other. What I would like to do is to see if the ideals contained presented in our Constitutions and Statutes are truly attainable in this day and age and in the Congregation as it really exists.

Michael: I think that you are very perceptive about this area of formation today being ultimately one of faith or fatalism. I must confess that in the past I have been tempted to leave the Congregation. This temptation has come not from a problem with the charism of Saint Alphonsus, but because of a serious doubt as to whether it can be lived authentically today. The turning point in my Redemptorist life was the day in which I discovered a conference given by Father Durrwell to the members of the General Chapter of 1985. In this conference he spoke of our charism as a continuation of the presence of Jesus in the world. It's sad to say this, but it was only then, after almost twenty years in the Congregation, that I discovered through his words and writings, who I was called to be—and that is the living memory or the continuation of the person of Jesus in the world today. This is what keeps me in the Congregation now. It seems to me that we have to find ways of training our young people so they can become first of all the person of Jesus in themselves and in the community; and equally important, this has to be something fresh and something new.

Ronnie: One of the things that would perhaps send waves of anxiety though certain sections of the Congregation is this concept of *Viva Memoria;* this fear that we might be turning the confreres into male Redemptoristines. We are a Congregation founded to preach the Good News to the most abandoned and poor, while living as members of a community. So how do we initiate young men into this charism without making them quasi-monks, since we are obviously an apostolic community?

Michael: I have no doubt that we are apostolic. I do not suggest that we are monastic. However, in my mind we are called according to the tradition and the charism of Saint Alphonsus, to be contemplative. By this, I do not mean enclosed monks, but men who are deeply steeped in the person of Jesus. I could go right through our Constitutions and Statutes and the whole heritage of our writings, and I feel certain that I could verify that Alphonsus himself had a deep, intense spiritual life that made him burn with a passion for God. And it was this that he communicated in his preaching and his service of the people. I am not suggesting any form of monasticism, but I am asking that we rediscover in ourselves, in our communities, and in the Congregation the mystical and contemplative dimension of our vocation. Here I would like to quote a few lines from an article by Father Durrwell: "Father Pfab wrote one time that the Redemptorist missionary is one in whom Christ is transparent. This remark is one of rigorous theological exactitude. Christ and the mystery of salvation, emerge in the world by the grace of God through the apostle. Saint Alphonsus and our Constitutions speak of the saving Christ being continued in the world; according to the Venerable Maria Celeste, God was 'pleased to choose this Institute to be a *Viva Memoria* for all the earth; a living symbol of the presence of Christ the Savior.'"

Ronnie: So we are agreed on an ideal for formation. Now what about the young men coming to join the Congregation? How do we train them in our proper charism?

Michael: Let me turn that question back to you. You have had years of experience as a formator both in the London Province and here in Southern Africa. So what would you take as a priority in initial formation?

Ronnie: That's a challenging question, Michael, and before I get to the heart of the answer, I have to first of all ask the question, "What kind of people are we attracting to the Congregation?" This is very important. If we are attracting men who are rigid or emotionally insecure, it seems to me that they are never going to be able to live a life of itinerant missionary preaching; and equally important, they are never going to be able to live at home with themselves in community. I have a gut feeling that the way in which we Redemptorists are living in many places, frequently projects a wrong image; and so some people are joining us simply to work as priests in a parish, as teachers or as social workers. Perhaps the heart of our charism is actually being obscured by the crisis the Congregation appears to be going through at present in many parts of the world.

Michael: Ronnie, I could not agree with you more. We have to take an in-depth look at who we are attracting, and why. Perhaps we do, as a Congregation, have an identity problem at present. Recently in my reading, I have been looking at ways in which many business corporations feel the need to make a fundamental statement of identity. This is the basis for their selection of people into their group. What I think we need to do is to look at some basic words that we would use to describe ourselves. Perhaps we could do this in terms of our charism—for the sake of formation.

Ronnie: Fine. I would begin immediately with the word *passion*. I would want to see in the people who are joining us, men who are passionately in love with God and in love with life. To this I would add, men who are in love with the idea of empowering others, men who really want to bring the Good News to those who have not heard it and to those who live in the most difficult situations. And with all this, I would stress that we must be people who can live and work with others.

Michael: So something is emerging. I see us describing ourselves as a group of men in love with God, determined to spread this love to others, living in community, but being prepared to be mobile, even itinerant.

Ronnie: In saying this, you are talking about men of deep prayer. Alphonsus, as we know, was a man of intense, daily prayer. So we are seeking people who would at least be open enough to be introduced to such an experience. However, for me, the problem is crystallized as follows. I can see this ideal being realizable in an isolated novitiate setting where we often have a hand-picked community. However, as soon as these men go into the mainstream of ordinary Redemptorist life, much of what they gained in the novitiate appears to fall away. In fact, they often seem to get caught up in total activity. It seems to me that if we want to revitalize formation, the work of renewal starts not in the formation houses, but in the houses of the province.

Michael: You have raised two issues that I would like to address. The first concerns the people we are attracting. I'm happy with what you have said, but for me there is an even deeper question. Is the young man capable of entering what I call "the inner journey"? The second issue, is he a mature human being who is capable of authentic conversion?

Ronnie: I am pleased that you have spoken about the inner journey, Michael. This is very much part of our charism, not only in the early years but throughout life. Enabling people right from the beginning to look at Christ in a very focused way, with what is often referred to as "the fixed gaze," of being able to put him before everything else, is vital. Your second reference to human maturity is also highly significant. All the current documents on formation reminds us of the need to deal with the human characteristics of those who join us. Pastores Dabo Vobis has several excellent insights into helping the human personality to emerge. So, obviously, in the early stages, without getting into heavy psychology or analysis, we have to help the young men to be at home with themselves.

Michael: This I find as one of the most challenging, yet difficult areas of formation...helping people to be at home with themselves and with God. From your experience working both in spiritual direction and in psychology, how can we facilitate this?

Ronnie: Well, obviously in all parts of the world today people are coming from less stable backgrounds. You yourself in South Africa, working in postapartheid times, are bringing in young men who must be scarred by the terrible pressure that such gross discrimination brought. So there are bound to be feelings of anger. For me, it is essential that the first thing we do in the early stages of formation is to help these people get in touch with themselves. This is what the prepostulancy is all about. We don't even begin to speak about novitiate until there is some level of emotional balance in which the charism of the Congregation takes primacy, and not just healing of emotions or some form of therapy or counseling. We are not looking for emotional supermen; but we are looking for men who are sufficiently at home with themselves to be open to Jesus. We need men whose primary preoccupation is not their own emotional pain, but the gospel of Jesus and the needy of our world. To my mind, this has to be the starting point of our formation process. To be itinerant apostles of the poor, there has to be some inner freedom. To accept the loneliness that celibacy often brings, there has to be some liberty of spirit.

Michael: Talking about isolation, you mentioned earlier that you did not agree with a novitiate that was isolated from the world. However, in my experience of eleven years in initial formation, I am convinced that since we have only one year of novitiate, it must offer the opportunity for a young man to have a profound God experience, expressed in a deep personal relationship with Christ. Of course the prenoviciate is a time for our candidates to grow in self-knowledge and even personal healing. It is also a time for experiments in basic apostolic endeavors, such as Alphonsus undertook at the hospital for *Incurables*. But I honestly believe that unless there is this intense encounter with God in the novitiate, unless the novice understands the whole concept of becoming another Jesus, he will never be offered such an opportunity in the studendate or later on in his Redemptorist life.

Ronnie: Well, of course, in the Congregation today, many people enter the novitiate after some years in the student house. However, I also believe that the novitiate is an important time set apart for focusing in a very special way on the charism of the Congregation. But the charism of the Congregation always involves closeness to the people. There is no closeness to Jesus for the Redemptorist without closeness to the people; they are inextricably linked. While I am in full agreement that the novices have plenty of time for prayer and reflection, I cannot see it having much value in a Redemptorist formation program unless it at least touches the lives of the abandoned and the poor. You cannot form people in isolation.

Michael: I fully agree with what you say, and I have no difficulty with the concept of closeness to the people. However, I am afraid of the heresy of activity which seems to be so present in the Congregation. I fear this spirit entering this most sacred year of novitiate. My feeling is that the Congregation as a whole is suffering from activism at present. This emerges clearly in *Commnicanda 3* (Reading the Signs of the Times). If we study this refection of the General Council, it is clear that we are in danger of loosing our spiritual depth as a religious Congregation and of even "drying up" spiritually—to quote Father Pfab once again. He once suggested that we are on the verge of loosing so much of the spiritual heritage of Saint Alphonsus and the early confreres.

Ronnie: I am very struck by your use of the word *sacred* in the context of the novitiate year. I do think it is a holy year. However, formation is more than just twelve months. It is a lifelong process, as you know. So I would like to move on to other aspects of formation, since for many of our young confreres, this often means six or seven years spent in a student community. How can we help them sustain this inner journey, this love for the most abandoned and the poor, this deep commitment to the Redeemer? How can we assist them to prepare for something more than simply a life of feverish activity? What about the contemplative dimension in the studendate?

Michael: I think this is a very wise question because if we invest everything in the novitiate, then we will find, as has happened in my own province and perhaps yours, that later on the young men will leave. We have to have this experience even before the novitiate year in a non-intense way and continue it throughout the years of the studendate into the life of the province. I feel that now, talking with each other as two formators with some specialized knowledge of our history and charism, we need to take a closer look at the spiritual life of the Redemptorist, especially with an eye to helping these younger confreres.

Ronnie: I'm happy about that Michael, but I should remind you that some people will react to the phrase *spiritual life* as though it was in some way detached from the rest of our lives. What I think you are talking about is that part of our way of living makes us different from Franciscans, Jesuits, or Carmelites. In some ways, defining it is the very stuff of formation. However, it is important, especially in an age in which so many of our young people attend intercongregational seminaries and where often the emphasis is on studies, on achievement, and on academic excellence—almost to the detriment of the interior life. While I have no problem with good academic standards, I often see that study becomes an all-consuming end for some of our men, and they can end up living like secular students. On top of this, we have the added challenge of inculturation. We are an international Congregation with international standards, and yet we cannot ignore the cry of the Church and the General Chapters that we become more and more inculturated. Would you like to say something about this in terms of formation and our charism?

Michael: I would be very happy to do so. Then I want to move on and pick out what I consider some highly significant features of our charism. Inculturation can be a very painful process. It is a difficult process, but it is vital. It means, first of all, trying to listen to where the local people are in their lives. It means, to some extent, adopting some of the values of the land in which we find ourselves. And it means, at times, actually trying to embark on a lifestyle that is in keeping with those around us. This does not mean that we pretend or that we be untrue to our Christian or international roots. But it does involve a very serious attempt to live in a way that will not alienate us from the people to whom we minister. I think that this, in itself, will be something fresh. I really feel we need to offer something new and alive to the young confreres. It has to be radical, and yet it has to be steeped in our tradition.

Ronnie: I agree with everything you have said about inculturation. You added that you wanted to pick out certain important points in the area of our spirituality.

Michael: Yes, I want to speak, first of all, about our prayer life. It is my conviction that at the heart of the life of Alphonsus and the early confreres was prayer. We used to have meditation three times a day, and it seems to me that this has almost disappeared from the active life of the Congregation. The prayer life of Redemptorists is the well which feeds our preaching. I believe that since we are not monks, mental prayer is more important to us than the recitation of the Prayer of the Church. I also feel that some form of devotional life is necessary. Devotions that were so important to Alphonsus and Clement surely should have some place in our Redemptorist lives. Devotion to the Incarnation, the Passion, the Eucharist, and to Our Lady must be offered in a fresh way so that our men may be steeped in the Word of God in a manner that touches their hearts.

Ronnie: You have raised a delicate issue here Michael, and I have some kind of reaction to it. It sounds as though you are trying to revive the eighteenth century Crib/Cross/Passion/Mary devotional kind of life. I fully appreciate that the theological implications behind these devotions are important, but do devotions speak to our people of today? A renewal of prayer life is necessary. But how is this achieved? I recall *Communicanda 51* of a previous General Government in which the whole spiritual basis of our missionary existence was challenged. At that time, we were invited to integrate the contemplative dimension of our life with our activity. If devotions help this, then I go along with you. However, a strong theological and spiritual base is also necessary. I well remember as a student, reading a book by Karl Rahner in which he predicted the demise of many religious congregations. At this time (1966), the danger did not appear very real. However, he said that religious life will die unless the members of communities become people "of prayer and mystical contemplation." He added that we are not contemplatives, we are nothing at all. It does seem to me that in many parts of the Congregation, his prophecy has come to pass. We have become professional churchworkers rather than apostles of Jesus. Father Pfab says that the Redemptorist missionary is one in whom Christ should be transparent. This only comes about through deep union.

Michael: Ronnie, I see we are back again with the article by Father Durrwell. He reminds us that by prayer we are transformed into Christ and the mystery of redemption; and so we become a mediator of Christ to others. This is backed by something very profound that I read in a talk by Father Capone in which he says that the Redemptorist does not preach about Christ, but that Alphonsus and the early Redemptorists entered into the very mystery of Christ himself and experienced his redemption in themselves. This was the way they communicated his presence.

Ronnie: That is strong language, Michael, and I could see people being rather uneasy about it. However, we cannot escape the basic truth that we really are called through prayer to be transformed into apostles of the very mystery which we preach. So my next question to you would be, "How do we teach contemplative prayer to our young people, many of whom are simply waiting for the day when they can get out into the apostolate?"

Michael: This is something that is stated quite clearly in our Constitutions and Statutes. The problem is that these Constitutions are so challenging that some people are afraid of them. If we study them, we will see a very clear call to continue the mission of Jesus. Now in many ways, the word *mission* has pushed us into activity, which we feel very comfortable with as Redemptorists throughout the world. However, I notice in a good number of texts that we are also called to continue the mystery of Jesus. Here there is a subtle distinction, since the mystery is inviting us into the very person of Jesus, into a contemplative and mystical experience that actually becomes us.

Ronnie: There is no doubt that the Constitutions call us to be men of prayer, but I feel you are avoiding my question about the practicalities of prayer. How do we go about it?

Michael: Well first of all, there must be a thorough grounding in the Word of God and in the Eucharist. Second, there must be a support system for prayer in our communities. It seems to me that we have reduced the times for community prayer to the bare minimum because of the demands of the apostolate. For instance, there must be times for silent prayer together, which was part of our early modus vivendi, there must be sharing of Scripture so that as a group we can come to know and understand one another's God. There must be time when the confreres come together to fix their gaze on the person of Jesus through Scripture and Eucharist. What do you feel about this?

Ronnie: I think that formators often feel inadequate to this task. Coupled with this, they frequently feel that this is not the reality of the province, and so why train people for an observance that is no longer lived? I think we need new and innovative ways of praying, as well as our traditional silent mental prayer. To help us facilitate this, we need to invite non-Redemptorists to work with our young people in various areas. For example, they can look at the creative use of the Scriptures, different methodologies of prayer, and so on.

Michael: Okay! I think we have spoken enough on this area of prayer. We agree that prayer is essential to our life. What else do you see as necessary in our formation training?

Ronnie: One of the things that makes me slightly anxious about the Congregation today is a lack of simplicity. I think that the call to live an uncluttered life goes hand in hand with being a simple missionary presence in any particular place. I also think that there must be some challenge to our young people to get back to the radical values which Saint Alphonsus and so many of the early Redemptorists lived. When I joined the Congregation, we were told that the characteristic mark of the community was austerity and love of the cross. Now, somehow or other, this has to be translated into some form of community living and simple personal lifestyle. This implies avoiding the acquisitiveness of our age, and the need for more and more possessions, status, degrees, and so on.

Michael: What has helped me greatly in this area has been *Communicanda 11* in which we are invited to reappraise our lifestyle. Through it, we were urged to live out in a radical way the important attitude of Alphonsus, viz., simplicity—and this in all the areas of our lives: dress, houses, holidays, relationships. If we are really sincere about something fresh and revitalizing in the Congregation, this aspect of our tradition cannot be lost.

Ronnie: Now we are really touching on a central issue of our lives as Redemptorists and that is community.

Michael: I think that bringing together the concepts of simplicity and community is something that is very much in the mind of the General Chapter, that is, of being evangelized by the poor. I know that this presents all sorts of difficulties for people in the Congregation. However, it is true that the nearer we are to the poor, the more they challenge us and our lifestyle. Therefore, our formation houses and many of our communities should be close to the poor, since that in itself is an invitation to simplicity.

Ronnie: This raises the whole burning topic of insertion. I believe that insertion is important, but I also believe that there are several levels of insertion and we must be aware of the ramifications of this for a formation community. I know that where I worked for eleven years in formation, we lived among the poor. This was a wonderful experience and also a challenge to a simple lifestyle. I do think that the more we live in big buildings, cut off from the people, the less open we will be to the challenge from them.

Michael: I think that one of the questions we Redemptorists must ask ourselves in this area is "What is asked of us, in this situation?" The insertion lived by some of the communities in so-called Third World countries is a special vocation. I would see insertion in the ordinary sense of the word as living near to the people, a simple lifestyle that does not inhibit formation, but at the same time, challenges us to reevaluate all our needs and wishes.

Ronnie: Talking about insertion keeps us on the whole burning topic of this age, which is community. Community life seems to be disintegrating. So how do we form people so they see some value in spending time with one another? When they first arrive, young people are often full of enthusiasm for community. Then when they discover the frustration and difficulty it often brings, it seems that they often wish to escape into the apostolate. We do not seem to realize that community can be an apostolate in itself. As I've just said, I lived in a poor area of England with a few people in what was a formation community, and it was one of the happiest periods of my life. However, I've also lived in "ordinary" communities that have brought me much happiness. I think the unity there came from the fact that we were of one mind and one heart. There was a focus on the apostolate, but there was also a happy home life.

Michael: All right, Ronnie, let's see if we can bring together a few words that would sum up our idea of community for young people today. So, one was small, the other was among the poor. We also spoke about it being noninstitutional, and we made reference to the benefit of a unified apostolate.

Ronnie: On this question of a unified apostolate, we have to remember that the last *Communicanda* from the General Government spoke of the importance of accepting a certain level of pluralism. With this in mind, I would want to add to your list of words, time spent together as being a priority, I would also add regular meetings and also some degree of sharing both at the spiritual and emotional levels.

Michael: I have also had experience in a poor rural community and one of the things I have learned is the importance of everyone pulling his weight. If one person opts out, then the community limps. Community takes time and it takes energy, and we have to let our young people know this right from the start.

Ronnie: I go along with much of what you say, but I am constantly reminded of one Constitution which says that community is always at the service of the apostolate. It is not an end in itself, but an important part of our lives in which we minister to one another. It is also where we are challenged and called to be accountable. Sometimes it is this latter feature, the pain of community, that makes people run away from difficult challenges that are often the very stuff of spiritual and emotional growth. Can I remind you that Sigmund Freud, the great father of modern psychology, once said that real growth only takes place in conditions of extreme frustration. Now I am not suggesting that we set out to frustrate our young men, but I do believe that creativity does not come naturally to many people. It has to be worked at. This is where I see some form of structuring necessary. I don't think it is realistic to say to a young man "Find your own level." That could be quite dangerous. I think we have to take very seriously some form of direction for those in formation. I often find today that both superiors and communities are afraid of challenging. But let us return to the question of apostolate. How do you see our young people being introduced to this central facet of our life?

Michael: Ronnie, for me the essence of our charism in the Church is that of proclamation, of finding new ways to share with people our experience of God. I feel that this should be part of the criteria that decides whether a young man should join our Congregation or not. Has he the enthusiasm to share with others the God within him? Is he prepared to go out and share this in new, vibrant, passionate, and exacting ways. And is he prepared to do this as part of a team and not as a prima donna?

Ronnie: That was a wonderful way of putting it. I like the concept of going out, of being sent by the community. However, I would also like to stress the fact that we are missionaries not only when we are out, but at home. We are missionaries for one another, for the people who come to our houses. From the earliest days of the Congregation, we have had a great tradition of people coming to us for retreats, spiritual direction, and the sacrament of reconciliation. This is where I feel it is important that our young men are flexible enough so that they always welcome guests into our houses. The whole concept of community living means that we are open not only to the changing society but also to those who come to share their lives with us. That is why we have a chapter in our Constitution on a community of conversion, which is really an invitation to be open to God as he comes to us in a variety of ways.

Michael: I think we are both agreed that a gradual initiation into the apostolate is very important, and that this should start early on. And I would once more remind you of *Communicanda 11,* where it is stated so beautifully that our first and most basic proclamation is our life together as brothers. It is in our apostolic community that we first make Jesus present.

Ronnie: That is the most difficult thing to sell to the confreres. I know that might sound paternalistic. I would really like to encourage the various secretariates to continue organizing courses and workshops on this topic. Otherwise we will end up with well-formed young men being sent out into a life of feverish activity.

Michael: As we draw our dialogue to a close, I would like to pick up again on your very first question about faith versus fatalism. I think we have to face a very basic reality and admit (as does *Communicanda 3*) that there are confreres who have opted for a way of life that is not in accordance with our Constitutions. I, therefore, believe that we must empower formators and superiors so that they may allow others who are looking for a more intense community experience to experiment. My life as a superior and as a formator convince me that if we don't respect people where they are and force them into a community situation they are not prepared to live, then the whole concept of community is reduced to the lowest common denominator.

Ronnie: I can't argue with that. But I would like to turn it into something more hopeful. I think we have something wonderful to offer young people. Rather than condemning other confreres, I think we can be realistic with the young and remind them that they simply do not have to follow as sheep. Saint Alphonsus was an innovator, he was a man of risk, who responded to the needs of his time. We must say to our younger confreres that the harvest is there, the panorama for Redemptorists is limitless, the challenges are enormous. So we must invite them, even in these early years, to dream dreams and have visions.

Michael: Yes, that is right on. Alphonsus could have been a Jesuit or a Carmelite; but he started a new religious Congregation. We are first of all religious, and we manifest our commitment as men invited to share in the great apostolic work of the Redeemer. I believe that the charism of the Congregation is developing, and, in the meantime, we continue to welcome generous, enthusiastic, and zealous men to join us in the work of proclamation.

Ronnie: So let us leave it there—on a note of optimism and hope. We have not, of course, covered everything. But I hope we have conveyed some of our hopes and fears, both for the present and for what lies ahead. I really believe that a revival of the spirit of the Congregation is possible, and it is in this hope that we have both shared this dialogue. Thank you Michael.

Michael: Thank you, Ronnie. It has been a joy and a privilege.

18

THE MINISTRY OF LEADERSHIP IN THE CHARISM

Juan Manuel Lasso de la Vega, C.Ss.R.
Province of Madrid
Translated by Jorge R. Colón Leon, C.Ss.R.
Province of Puerto Rico

1. Why Did I Become a Redemptorist?

I was born on July 25, 1936, just a week after the beginning of the Spanish Civil War. Three months later, my father was killed by the communists. With three children to raise, my mother confronted the difficult state of war that would last three years. The difficulties raised by the postwar, lasted many more years. My family was sincerely religious; faith came naturally and spontaneously, having an influence on all the dimensions of ordinary life and expressed in daily prayer, which we all enjoyed. Daily Eucharist, the rosary, grace before meals, were explicit moments of family prayer. Besides, faith was the frame of reference for dealing with the difficult situation Spain was going through. Faith also helped us to deal with the violet death of my father and the deprivation it caused in the social and economic life of my family.

I studied in the Marist Brothers' school close to home. However, the spiritual life of the family took place in Perpetual Help Church, where the Redemptorists held splendid worship services. Little by little, I came to know some members of that community, among them, Brother Conrado, who served as porter for more than forty years. I enjoyed serving at Mass. I felt attracted by the personality of the missionaries, whom I considered tremendous preachers.

Brother Conrado used to meet me and bring me into the front parlor to chat for a while. The most frequent topic of conversation was the life of the missionaries, who would go preaching the Gospel from town to town in Spain or in foreign countries. Through him, I came to know a bit about the Congregation of Redemptorist missionaries, about their life and the apostolate of the community. It seems that the poor and the most abandoned got more attention then, perhaps because the postwar conditions made almost all Spaniards poor. I was most strongly attracted by the parish missions at that time of my life.

Little by little, the desire grew within me to become one of those missionaries. Men who would leave their family behind, putting their lives at risk, to make Christ known and loved. I was thirteen years old when I entered the seminary at El Espino. My mother helped me to take this step that, as expected, was very difficult. Once in El Espino, I always felt happy; this is where I really learned what it meant to be a Redemptorist. I lived in the seminary with an admirable Redemptorist community. We had Redemptorist professors who would take any chance to speak about the religious and missionary vocation. We had moving conferences from our director on the following of Christ, the history and life of the Congregation, Saint Alphonsus and many other Redemptorists who were heroic in their vocation. This helped me to deepened my first desire, which perhaps had been too childish and immature. My time in the novitiate and the studentate strengthened my decision to become a religious. I would dedicate my life to Christ, living in community. Living with other men who, like me, felt the call to mission just like the priests who would visit us and tell us stories about their life and adventures.

After finishing my theological studies in 1962, I went to Salamanca to study canon law. Once I finished my licentiate, I went to the major seminary as prefect of students. Afterward, I studied moral theology in Rome, finishing in 1970. Then I spent three years in the Madrid Province, one as superior of our house in Granada, and two as superior and pastor of our recently erected house of Félix Boix in Madrid. Then came the General Chapter of 1973, in which, against all protestations, I was elected consultor general.

I believe that my initial formation in the minor seminary, the novitiate, and the studentate was good and helped to lay down a solid foundation. We learned to love Saint Alphonsus and the Congregation as our own family; we could identify strongly with the ideals of our Institute.

My life as a Redemptorist has given me a chance to know the Congregation well: its strong points and its weaknesses, its charism and identity in today's world, its hopes and its impossible dreams. To me, being a Redemptorist is the greatest treasure I possess, and I want to keep it well.

2. The Community Superior: A Leader in the Charism

My experience as leader of a community was quite diversified. My first experience was with the young philosophy students in our Valladolid seminary. It lasted four years. In a way, they were four difficult years due to the cultural revolution of the times. Yet they were also years of intense exchange, of new interests, of apostolic experiences with the students. Perhaps these are the years of which I am most fond. I was local superior in our communities in Granada and Madrid, both of which were quite large, and had many theologians. During my time as consultor, I was also superior of the community in Rome for six years, a huge community with many nationalities and different cultures. I believe this community helped me to discern nonessentials. It helped me to understand the normal differences that exist in an international Congregation such as ours. I have spent almost ten years as superior general and have visited the whole Congregation several times. I have attended many meetings of vice provincial superiors and the last four General Chapters.

To make my reflections more concrete, I have chosen the theme of this sexennium (1991–1997). Especially, I chose number 11 of the *Final Document* of the General Chapter of 1991. It seems to me that it contains the most important dimensions of our life. I have also added an introduction. It tries to place our mission as leaders in the concrete context being lived nowadays by religious life in general and by our Congregation.

The present context of the Congregation

1. One of the most relevant elements of our life is the intense activity we accomplish, vis-à-vis our founder, the history of our Institute, our proper charism and spirituality. There exists in the Congregation a new awareness of our own charismatic specificity, of our own identify, both in being and in action. There is also a renewal of our life and our activities, as a mission that springs out of Saint Alphonsus and his prophetic charism. This has caused in us Redemptorists a greater sense of belonging to a group that has its own proper place in the Church.

2. Another positive value being accomplished is the rediscovery of the centrality of mission in our religious life. There is a renewed sense of the mission, and a growing apostolic endeavor, a lively quest for our own identity stemming from the mission. We feel the need to have the apostolic commitment and the witness of our community life rooted in our charism, and backed by a proper spirituality. We are coming to understand our communities often as communities-in-mission and for-the-mission, who evangelize by living and reaching the message of Christ in urgent and difficult conditions. This is a new focus of leadership that will necessarily be successful. It corresponds to a new theology of religious life and to the hopes and aspirations of many Redemptorists. It is also the new accent that the last General Chapter placed on the theme of the sexennium, as we will see later.

3. Along with these present values, it seems that there are some attitudes and facts that worry us and that, at times, can make us forget that our track record is important. I don't know if we are going through a period of disenchantment, after the enthusiasm of the first years of renewal. The past is gone, but the present has not yet appeared, at least not totally. We have new ideas, but there are many difficulties in trying to bring them about. In other words: there is a gap between doctrinal comprehension and concrete life experiences. The intuitions and aspirations of the new Constitutions and of the General Chapter documents have not always taken root. This is causing disappointment and frustration.

We must be aware of this fact. If we do not produce concrete actions, according to our chapter declarations and our community decisions, disillusionment can cause us trouble in the future, especially among our youngest confreres. I am sure that we all want to respond to those new challenges in our Redemptorist life. The problem is how to do it.

The continuing formation of communities

The starting point is in the continuous formation of our communities. It is the only way to renew our mission, as we read in Constitution 90: "Redemptorists will be more efficacious missionaries the more they can conveniently adapt day by day their own apostolic activity, and link it more closely with a continuing self-renewal in the spiritual, scientific and pastoral fields." Continuing formation refers to our own theological and pastoral formation, but it includes all the dimensions of our religious and community life. The world is changing a lot, and it also demands radical changes in our lives, to preserve the prophetism of our witness. Continuing formation must also be global. It seems that many negative reactions we find in accepting new proposals have their origin in a lack of good preparation; work consumes most of the energy in our life. For many confreres, it is hard to find sufficient time to keep up in a state of continuous formation.

Continuing formation is the fundamental task of the community, both at the provincial and local levels. The superior must know well the meaning of the word *shepherd*, as present in Constitutions 126 and 139. "God's flock is in your midst. Give it a shepherd's care. Watch over it willingly as God would have you do, not under constraint, and not for shameful profit either, but generously. Be examples to the flock, not lording it over those assigned to you" (1 Peter 5:2–3).

A fundamental question

We can ask ourselves: *What kind of inspiration must we bring to our vice provinces or communities, which are the concrete actions that we, as superiors and animators, should promote?*

It is important to frequently read number 11 of the *Final Document,* in which the theme for this sexennium is defined:

> We are happy with the growth achieved in our Congregation during the last sexennium, and observing the areas of concern of our present moment, we declare:
>
> The XXI General Chapter (1991) wants to continue the theme of the pastoral priorities chosen by the 1979 Chapter. We now wish to emphasize the explicit, prophetic and liberating announcement of the gospel to the poor, being challenged by them *(evangelizare pauperibus et a pauperibus evangelizari)*, according to the charism of our Congregation, as expressed in our Constitutions 1,3,4,5, and in our Statutes 09 and 021.
>
> We ask the Congregation to continue with this theme, while deepening our common apostolic life as a prophetic power that opens new paths to an incarnated mission; to achieve this, we feel the need to stress the correlation between our inculturated evangelization, our consecrated life and our spirituality.

We could say that the theme of the sexennium has two main ambitions. The first is continuity with what we have done in previous sexennia.

It is not something totally new; yet we have placed new stress on some aspects. The second is unity. We want to consider our life as an organic whole, avoiding dichotomy and incoherence.

Continuity with the General Chapters (of 1979 and 1985), and unity among the areas of our life are two facts upon which we must base the new service of leadership and animation. It seems that in analyzing the theme of the present sexennium, we find a goal and a means to achieve it. That is not to say that the means is less important than the end. The means is so important that without it we can never achieve the goal.

The goal is to define well our pastoral priorities. To stress the explicit, prophetic, and liberating announcement to the poor (in the context defined in the 1985 Chapter), to deepen our community life as a prophetic force that opens new paths toward an incarnate mission. The means is the relationship between our inculturated evangelization, our common life, and our spirituality.

3. Stress on the Pastoral Service of the Leader

Each word of the theme of the sexennium is very important to promote the continuity and unit in our decisions. Although the order of the themes can differ, I prefer this, which follows the proposal of number 11 in the *Final Document:*

1. The pastoral priorities
2. The option for the poor
3. The prophetic power of the community
4. New ways to an incarnate mission
5. The relationship between inculturated evangelization, community, and spirituality

Based on these points, I will try to present some reflections, and at times I will insist on some initiatives for the future.

3.1 The pastoral priorities

This theme is the most widely repeated one in all the General Chapters, and upon it all the dimensions presented in the following paragraphs should converge. We cannot have a good definition of our priorities without keeping in mind the whole formulation of the theme presented in number 11. The pastoral priorities are not only a list of tasks that would reduce our Redemptorist charism to a simple activity.

The provincial chapters have worked a lot on the choice of pastoral priorities, describing in detail the missionary task of the vice province. Often we have combined well both activity and life; other times we have limited ourselves to formulating a catalog of the main activities. A reason for this is that the themes of the General Chapters have been evolving by stages. Each chapter has added something new to the previous theme. It seems to me that now, for the first time, we have a unitary global theme.

In almost all the units of the Congregation, the main difficulty we are finding is summed up in these questions: What is the relationship between the Redemptorist and the world in which we live? In a secularized prosperous world, or in a world marked by growing poverty, how are we to live the charism of evangelizing the most abandoned and especially the poor? How can we manage to make our evangelization an explicit, prophetic, and liberating announcement of the Gospel for them? What is our mission and our identity in this modern or postmodern world? How can we incarnate in this world the charism of Saint Alphonsus, being conscious that we are not the owners of this charism, but only its continuators?

There are various attempts, which signify a response to all these questions. However, it can also be true that our relationships with the new societies are still vague: We are neither "worldly" nor do we represent an "alternative" to the worldly. At times we lack a clearer awareness of the drama being lived by the world: the radical separation between culture and the Gospel, between the way things are and the way God intended them to be.

The greatest challenge for our communities is to show that there is a great difference between the way people live and the way they ought to live. For this, we need careful discernment about the present signs of the times and about our style of evangelical response.

For some confreres, our openness to the world is too big and our prophetic testimony too weak. Openness without witness does not make our life the light of the world. How are we to exercise our prophetic mission if we ourselves are contaminated by materialism?

Our task as animators

1. This is a field that offers us ample possibilities for our service as animators. When we find this problem, our first task is to know the causes well. It could be that there are objective reasons that force us to accept our impossibility for change. It could be that because of natural passiveness we are not doing what we still can do. It could also be that we, as animators, need a clearer social analysis. We need a greater conviction about the kind of answer we ought to give as Redemptorists. Or we need a capacity and greater mystique to convince and to encourage the confreres to reincarnate our charism in our world. "To read the signs of the times" begins with a social analysis, but closes with a spiritual analysis. As religious, we should be capable of facing the social conditions of our time. On the other hand, our response to these situations should not be based on dreams; we should be realistic about what we can truly achieve.

2. The world today forces us to rethink our apostolic life and to develop a more critical attitude: even to have the courage to be different to the world, as witnesses of the experience of God, through an inculturated and believable lifestyle. It is a question of incarnating our religious life in our culture, in fidelity to the culture and to our mission.

3. Evidently, at times our institutional traditions differ from the new programs of pastoral priorities. It is here that we find most equivocal situations and ambiguities. We don't always find an easy solution.

4. If our pastoral priorities have not sufficiently kept in mind our being and our activity, we should promote a reworking of those priorities. It seems to me that to do this, provincial chapters are not enough. We must commit all the confreres to this process, by means of provincial assemblies, formation courses, retreats, and so on. Even if the last word remains the Chapter's.

5. It will depend on our ability as leaders that these processes do not tire out the province. There are rhythms and sensitivities we must bear in mind. On the other hand, a chapter or a provincial assembly that gets to no conclusion can be very tiring and produce apathy.

3.2 The option for the poor

The option for the poor, according to our history, our tradition, and our Constitutions is inserted into the wider context of the option for the most abandoned. The last General Chapter went over this theme again. It decided that this frame of reference was clearly expressed in the present formulation of the theme of the sexennium.

Religious life in general and our congregation in particular, have become closer to the poor. I think this expression "become closer" is the one that best describes the results we have obtained thus far. This means that we have done something, but that there is still a lot to do. We pay more attention to the poor, we are more in solidarity with them, and at times we live among the poor. We feel more the problems of the poor and we take part in them.

What seems evident to me is that there exists everywhere a desire to have greater closeness and solidarity with the people. It is a characteristic of our Congregation from the beginning (cf. *Final Document,* n. 29).

We have taken all these steps, and they manifest that the Congregation still has a capacity to adapt and to be inculturated. Our option for the poor means an effort to look at the world from the perspective of its victims; a conviction that true transformation will come from the grass roots.

Points of leadership

1. That our commitment to the poor and the problems of social justice be exercised not just at the level of declarations, but at the level of actions. In all the provincial chapters the option for the poor and the most abandoned is accepted. At times, the concrete situation of the vice province changes too little in proportion to its decisions.

2. This option for the poor must be clearly "spiritual," and not just "strategic." It is the same option of Jesus, who emptied himself (cf. Philippians 2:5–8), and the experience of Mary, who experienced in her lowliness that God had chosen her to confuse the powerful (cf. Luke 1:46–55). Our option for the poor must go hand in hand with an explicit option to be poor.

3. Let us not forget in the upcoming years that we must continue to come closer to the people, to the poor and the lowly. We must form Redemptorist communities with diverse and various forms according to the concrete situations in which we live, and accepting the concrete implications it presupposes. Both in the vice provinces of the First World and in those of the Third World, there are enough communities created with this goal, which are an inspiration to all the confreres. At times, this closeness should become a greater insertion among the impoverished, really sharing

with the people and participating in their struggles and in their legitimate realistic aspirations. It is important that this option be born out of the entire province, and not just out of a few confreres.

4. The option for the poor should not be an option against those who are not poor, but must become a challenge to the rich. In this context the mission of the provinces of the First World is very important. They live in a very different sociocultural context, in which materialism and abundance mix in with new social and religious problems. Racism and emigration are two of the problems that are affecting the social life of many countries.

5. As leaders, we must be aware that we are always going to find personal and institutional difficulties. As persons, we have lost evangelical liberty and the missionary spirit. Our highly institutionalized commitments, the advanced age level of many vice provinces, and the lack of vocations are keeping us from new initiatives. Initiatives that, in principle, we see as more urgent for the Church. A superior must concern himself with these realities and must know how to raise concern among the confreres.

6. At times I am afraid that this option for the poor has remained too implicit in the formulation of the present theme, and that we will spontaneously escape into other demands of the theme.

3.3 The prophetic power of the community

A strong point to face the future is the prophetic power of the community. This is an important fact for young people, it says a lot to people of our day and it is a sign of hope for the future.

Right now the "prophetism of the community" as witness is more emphasized than the "prophetic gestures" of some confreres. In our society, community life should be presented as a "contrasting society." Religious community is prophetic. Not only when it calls us to conversion but also when it manifests an alternate way of building up and experiencing the Church as a community nowadays. Who can give a better witness to the world of communion, fellowship, faith, and prayer than a religious community?...A community that proclaims to have taken on as its proper task to follow Jesus more freely and to imitate him more radically? Our religious consecration, our religious vows, and our common lifestyle should become a permanent prophecy in the Church. As a community, we bring to life the communitarian ministry of prophecy. This ministry must be continually taken up and purified.

In order for a community to the prophetic, it needs to keep alive the memory of the origin of the Institute. I believe that *memory* and *prophecy* are two key words for our service of leadership.

It seems to me that the prophetic ministry of the Congregation has been growing. Our community life is manifested better nowadays as a reality that shows forth the values of the kingdom. I have experienced this often, especially in meetings with young people.

Our task of leadership

1. The superior should be the first prophet. He should know how to discern the concrete inspiration of our Constitutions that foster better the prophetism of a community in mission. As superiors, we need much reflection and much prayer. Since the sociological contexts in which we live are so different, I believe there are not ready-made plans for concretely defining the prophetic power of my community. The only thing we know is that each community needs to be prophetic in its context, and that this prophetism is born of the concrete life of the community. The best inspiration for our prophetism is found in our Constitutions. They insistently invite us to be humble and courageous witnesses of Christ, who is the principle and model of a renewed humanity.

2. In many units there are meetings of local superiors from time to time. The role of the superior as prophetic animator of the community is important. Continuing formation activities for superiors are necessary in view of the steady animation of the community.

3. In some vice provinces, at the beginning of the triennium a "community project" is presented in which the community's mission, life, and work is defined. It is important that the community itself work out its "mission," within the context of the provincial pastoral priorities. A Redemptorist community, to be prophetic, is always a community in a state of mission.

4. We must avoid the fragmentation of our communities in very small houses. It is difficult to live community as a prophetic power when the number of confreres is too small.

5. An important moment for provincial superiors will always be the assignment of our younger confreres, both priests and brothers. Growth and perseverance of young people after their formation depends a lot on the community where they are sent. Sometimes we hear phrases such as this: We, the young confreres, are not merely called to fill the slots in communi-

ties. Really, when a slot is not relevant for the life of a young person, or when that slot is created in a community that has no dynamic prophetism, it becomes a real problem.

6. In this context I would like to take up the perseverance of our students. The percentage is too high, and we are all concerned about it. The General Council has been insisting for years to delay novitiate until the end of the philosophical studies, so that the novices will be more mature. In fact, most provinces have delayed it. Formation programs are frequently revised, adapting them to the needs that come up. Our young people face special problems, such as inconsistency, insufficient motivation, fear of insecurity, family ties, and so on. All these are root causes of deficient perseverance. But might it not be the case that there is something missing in our lives which is further complicating our perseverance rate? I think this theme deserves very special attention.

7. Communities should also be redesigned in attention to the laypeople called to participate in the mission and spirituality of the Institute. We must remain open to the possibility of new forms of the extended community. In this context we must make some decisions concerning the lay missionaries of the Most Holy Redeemer (cf. *Final Document,* nn. 57–60), and concerning communities that welcome young people (n. 56b). In the past sexennium the Congregation worked a lot on the ministry of youth. I believe that during this sexennium and in this direction, we must intensify our work regarding the collaboration of the laity based on an authentic association.

8. Spirituality is not something juxtaposed to the prophetic presence of a community. The origin of all prophetism is permanent union with God, who chooses us and sends us into the world.

3.4 New ways for an incarnate mission

I believe these expressions "the prophetic power of the community," "incarnate mission," "the relationship between new inculturated evangelization, community, and spirituality" express the same thing in different words. Only a community that possesses a prophetic power can open new ways for an "incarnate mission." A community has no prophetic power if it is not an incarnate mission. Our prophetic power and our incarnate mission depend on the relationship between evangelization, community life, and spirituality.

A question we can ask is this: What do our brothers understand by the word *mission*? Often, when we talk about mission, we think only of the challenges we find in today's world, in the more needy areas, the most emarginated groups, in conditions of pastoral urgency, and so on.

We hardly come to understand the mission as a dimension of our being. The mission is a way of being and a way of acting. It is not just an action of the Church, but its own being. Just as the Church, we are mission and we are missioning in world. This means that the mission must always be in intimate relation to the challenges the world presents. It is difficult to define mission without continually looking at the world today, with its joys and hopes, its grief and anguish. The ways of the mission in today's world are witness, proclamation, and conversion. In this world, our life should be lived as mission and in a state of mission.

It has been stressed nowadays that you can only give a good description of the identify of each institute from the perspective of its mission. Seeing how we live and how we work, we will define well what we are in the Church. Abstract definitions are not convincing. Young people want to know our life and our activities well before they make a vocational decision. To start with definitions of the charism is, at least implicitly, to start with presuppositions. On the other hand, we must develop our ways of life, of service, of community, and of apostolic structures to preserve and maintain the charism in a specific way.

Points for animation

1. The *Final Document* says that we must open "new ways for an incarnate mission." While respecting always the legitimate cultural pluralism, the General Chapter has thought that we need these new ways so our mission may be more incarnate. It seems to me that the Congregation, and ourselves as superiors, cannot stop our search for these new ways, which must emerge from our communitiarian prophetism.

2. Sometimes we are bound more by the desire to maintain our activities than by the mission. This can be explained because of the lack of personnel or the urgent needs of our pastoral ministry. Because of this, we have lost mobility, creativity, and fecundity. A comfortable lifestyle, at times even secularized, can blur our witness and commitment. Easy money is a counterwitness for the mission. Our religious life is the starting point for an "incarnate mission."

3. At times we find difficulties with the diocesan Church, which pre-

vents us from organizing ourselves as a religious community in mission having a proper charism. We should manifest clearly to bishops our responsibility and our obligation to live according to our identity and our legislation, which has been officially approved by the Church.

4. During the past few years, new communities with different missionary objectives have been emerging in many vice provinces. Communities that are more closely inserted among the poor, communities that are more open to young people, and so on. I believe it is important to continue creating this style of community, which has a specific incarnational mission, and that can become models with which other communities can identify. Because they are "new," these communities should be more directly animated by the provincial superior. The creation of these communities corresponds to number 27 of the *Final Document:*

> The option for the most abandoned, and especially the poor, demands of us an incarnation and inculturation in geographic areas, in social milieus, and in ecclesial locations related to the peculiar dynamism of our mission.

Experience shows that it is not good to begin a new community without a well-defined mission.

5. However, the "new communities" are not the only responses to the General Chapter's mandate. Every Redemptorist community "should be the first sign of our missionary activity. Not only is it the place out of which we are sent but also and, above all, it is an efficacious presence of the kingdom of God between men and women, our brothers. They simultaneously, reveal to us the face of God" (Cf. *Final Document,* n. 23).

6. Within this context, although it is not the only one, it is important to recall what the *Final Document* tells us about continuing formation (nn. 52–54). If we make no further efforts in this direction, we could maintain an outmoded community style. We could create more barriers between the young and the old, thus losing appeal for young people today. In many vice provinces there is an annual common retreat and a week on pastoral renewal. I believe this to be a good initiative, which helps us to put into action what we read in the *Final Document,* number 16:

> The General Chapter recommends to the various units of the congregation a special theological and cultural formation of the confreres,

especially those who are assigned to the explicit proclamation of the Gospel.

3.5 The relationship between inculturated evangelization, community, and spirituality

It is interesting that this theme, almost word for word, has been chosen by many religious congregations as their theme for the next few years. In many institutes the question posed has been the problem of the "unity and relationship between consecration and mission"; while others have stressed the "integration between consecration, community, and mission." All these dimensions are not juxtaposed, but make up an organic whole and are intrinsically linked.

Our *Final Document* insists on the coherence between inculturated evangelization, community, and spirituality. It stresses two dimensions, which are complementary: relationship and incarnation. For us, coherence means the linking relationship between the apostolate, community life, and spirituality. It also means the incarnation of these three dimensions of our Redemptorist life in historical forms that express the option of the Congregation for the most abandoned and the poorest.

The need for "coherence" appears often in the *Final Document*. Speaking about spirituality, number 39 states:

> According to Saint Alphonsus, Christian perfection and spirituality consist in the practice of charity. For a Redemptorist, this charity, to be salvific, should be incarnate in historical conditions and should commit itself to the cause of man. Thus, it is a committed charity.

This coherence gives us credibility in the world and assures us of a harmonious growth in our religious personality as a community.

Some brief reflections

1. The basis for our inculturation is born out of the very mission of the congregation in fidelity to the mission of Christ, in the historical course of our charism.

- Among religious congregations there is a greater awareness that, at times, the charisms have been "occidentalized" for a long time, and they should now be reinterpreted. It is difficult to distinguish well between the essential and the contingent elements. This distinction is not done easily nor rapidly; it must spring out of the praxis. On the other hand, inculturation also refers to occidental countries that are undergoing deep and rapid cultural changes. How do we get inculturated in a world and in a culture that is more technological, more secularized, and where lives are based more on images than on the word? As superiors we should learn how to conjugate fidelity to the tradition and openness....The need for a spirit of dialogue for all and with all and not just among ourselves. We should participate in this process with great enthusiasm.

- *Inculturation* refers to our life as such, in all its component dimensions. Our religious and community life must be subjected to a process of inculturation and incarnation. Our identity is not exhausted in good works and activities. There are external expressions of our charism, and thus, are necessarily contingent.

- Trying to present with our lives an evangelical alternative to society is not something negative, as long as the openness we proposed refers to the situation in which we live, and since it uses the same language and is not seen as alienating.

2. When we speak about spirituality, we refer to the entire man, because he is open to the action of God and his transcendence. To live in the Spirit presupposes a new freedom in which God is encountered more as presence than as definition, more as sense than abstraction.

The lack of personal and community spirituality could make up the greatest obstacle for us to walk better and more quickly. It could be that one of our present deprivations is the lack of a spiritual life, or the lack of connection between our spiritual life and our mission.

Religious life moves under the action of the Spirit, who calls us to mission. Obedience to the Spirit gives us mobility for apostolic responses to the needs of the world. At times, it seems that the Spirit is finished talking to us, or that we do not find a space in which to listen to him.

In the origin of all religious congregations, there are always two elements that are concomitant and affect each other: a new way of experiencing God and a perception of a reality as a pressing challenge. In Saint Alphonsus, these two elements are evident. To respond to God and to respond to the poor, he founds our Congregation. In the same experience, Saint Alphonsus feels touched by God (spiritual experience) and by the challenge of the mission. His experience of God would have been different without the striking encounter with the poor in Scala. His response to the poor would also have been different without a living experience of God. The mission is authentic when it is the expression of an incarnate experience of God. The charism is the original way of seeing the unit between these two elements: spirituality and mission. When there is a split between the spiritual life and the mission, one loses the charism and becomes incoherent.

Our task to animate

1. Some questions we can ask are these: How can we help our confreres to reinforce the spiritual dimension of our life? How to live a spirituality that is coherent with our mission and with the prophetic identity of our community?... A spirituality that stresses the significant and prophetic radicality of our Institute? What can we do to better discover the value of religious consecration, of our religious vows, and of our witness? Where do we start living the complementarity between action and contemplation? The *Final Document* insists that our commitment to man be born out of our union with God (n. 39).

2. To promote a revitalization of our spirituality by means of courses, workshops, publications, that will help us revise the style of our life and of our mission, unifying them. I think that in continuing formation programs, spirituality should be the binding force.

3. To develop a methodology for communitarian discernment that will lead us to grow in attitudes that seek the will of the Father.

4. In some countries we see that there is a greater desire for "spirituality" among the young people. A question we must ask ourselves is: Why aren't young people more attracted to our religious life?

Conclusion

It seems to me that it is worthwhile to assume this ministry of leadership with love, and to invest all our creativity and enthusiasm in this direction. There are plenty of opportunities to continue growing, adapting, and re-creating our charism in today's world. Our Congregation is making a significant effort, even in vice provinces that find more difficulties due to the ecclesial and social conditions. The condition of the Church itself does not always help religious life to find new ways. In spite of this, I do not think that we should renounce becoming "prophetic communities," and to find new ways for mission among the most abandoned and the poorest. Although the going may be slow, we should not stop walking.

One difficulty that the General Council finds which would be the same one faced by some provincials and local superiors is that our administrative work is too big and, at times, leaves us with very little time for an authentic animation and reflection. Sometimes we say: we work a lot and we reflect very little. The same thing can happen in local communities.

All the negative aspects we can find should never cause disillusionment or pessimism in us, who have accepted the ministry of animation. What it should produce in each of us is a great desire to share our task as animators with the provincial council. Also, with all the confreres who are called, as the *Final Document* states, to be "mutually evangelized by each other" (n. 24).

The ministry of animation is a pastoral service in which our true love of Christ is manifested. In this book on religious vocation, Saint Alphonsus has this to say:

> When He wanted to have clear proof of the love Peter professed toward Him, He asked him nothing more than to take on a pastoral ministry saying: "Simon, son of John, do you love me? Tend my sheep." That is why Saint John Chrysostom writes: "Christ did not say: give up riches, punish your body with fasting, sacrifice yourself in a thousand works and privations. He only told him: Tend my sheep" (*Religious Vocation*, n. 13).

May Saint Alphonsus, especially during these years close to the third centennial of his birth, fill us with hope and with commitment to the ideals he had in Scala when he founded us, which he maintained until the day of his death.

19

CHARISM AND THE REDEMPTORIST LAY VOCATION

Carlos Gaspar, C.Ss.R.
Vice Province of Cebu

1. Mindanao

This is an island, roughly the size of Ireland, which is located in the deep south of the Philippines. It is the part of the country that is adjacent to East Indonesia and East Malaysia.

Mention the name and the average person living in the central and northern part of the Philippines will think of it as a very dangerous place to live. This is an irony, because there was a time when this island was referred to in terms of a biblical image. It was called the Land of Promise.

A number of reasons have led to its being known as a hot spot in the country. During the martial law and dictatorial regime of the late Ferdinand Marcos, Mindanao witnessed wave after wave of evacuation as government military forces fought rebels of both the New People's Army (NPA)—the army of the Communist part of the Philippines (CCP)—and the Moro National Liberation Front (MNLF). As with other wars, the civilian population were caught in between. There were hundreds of internal refugees who left their homes and farms in the interior and sought the safety of the town centers.

Given the militarized state of the country, gross violation of the people's human rights was rampant. Hundreds of innocent civilians—suspected of sympathizing with the rebels—were arrested, tortured, and imprisoned, if not killed. One of the victims was Father Rudy Ramano, C.Ss.R., one of the Philippines' *despaparecidos*.

The perpetuators of these crimes were members of the military and paramilitary troops deployed in many areas of Mindanao. There were also instances when the rebels were guilty of violating the rights of civilians. Throughout this period, there was fear in the hearts of the people.

The downfall of the dictator and the ensuing restoration of democratic institutions that followed the people's revolt in Manila in February 1986 has not drastically changed Mindanao's situation. There is still militarization in many areas, although the regularity of military operations and human rights violations have decreased.

The rebels are still fighting a guerrilla war against government military troops, although it is reported that this warfare has been reduced. The present government of President Fidel Ramos has sought to hold peace talks with both the NPA-CCP and the MNLF. But the process has been very slow and peace continues to elude all the parties concerned.

The latest reason why the guns of war continue to rage across some parts of Mindanao has been the war between government military troops and an armed group of the Muslim fundamentalists who are part of the worldwide phenomenon of Islamic revivalism.

This dirty little war has led to the kidnapping of teachers, businessmen, priests, and other civilians. Hundreds of villagers have left their homes. Farms have been abandoned. Children get sick in the evacuation centers. It is never safe to travel in these parts of the island. Recently, a Catholic convent was bombed; a woman pastoral worker was killed.

It is not true, of course, that there is trouble all across the island, and that the majority of the people are dislocated in all the provinces. There is peace in most areas of the island; however, it is a situation that can drastically change if war escalates.

Why has peace been elusive in Mindanao?

When the Spaniards reached the Philippines in the 1500s and placed it under a four-hundred-year colonial rule, they planned to Christianize the people of the islands. Some of our ancestors resisted and fought war after war to oppose the colonial rule. This was especially true for those who had embraced the Islamic faith, especially in Mindanao.

Given their superior arms and technology, the Spaniards were able to gain a foothold in these islands which they named Las Islas Filipinas, from where the name Philippines came from.

The end of Spain's colonial rule in this country was the beginning of our people's experience of American imperialism. Spain sold the Philippines to the United States for $20 million by virtue of the Treaty of Paris of 1898. Like Spain, the U.S.A. wanted the Philippines as a colony that could serve as a base in gaining access to the bigger catch across the sea—China.

During their occupation of the islands, the Americans saw the rich potentials of Mindanao, an island rich with fertile soil, mines, forest, and other resources. They launched pacification campaigns to win over both the Moro and tribal people. Where they failed to peacefully win them over, they fought wars of aggression.

As part of the divine-and-rule tactic, they encouraged Filipinos from the central and northern part of the country to migrate to Mindanao. Thus was born the name—Land of Promise. It was to be the promised land for the landless peasants who dreamt of land of their own.

American agribusiness companies were also encouraged to come and set up fruit plantations. (They have remained until now and the land area used for planting cash crops, such as pineapples and bananas, has expanded. Meanwhile more and more farmers have become landless peasants.)

The problem in many of these areas were Moro and tribal peoples who were already tilling the land and tapping its resources. Naturally, there would be conflict over the land. Then and now, this conflict has raged. It has made Mindanao a bleeding land. Government has not been able to resolve this conflict. Many political analysts claim that government's intervention is part of the problem.

Thus peace remains elusive.

Growing up and being concerned with realities in Mindanao

My deceased father was from the central part of the Philippines, while my mother is from the northern part. Both came to Mindanao just before the Second World War, dreaming the dream of a better life in the promised land. They were part of the second wave of migrants who reached this island. They sought their fortunes here, believing that they could live peacefully and provide a bright future for their children.

I was born in a small town a few years after the war ended. This town was to become Davao City; today, it is the most prosperous city all across Mindanao.

Just before and after the war, the members of the Catholic Bishops Conference of the Philippines were concerned about the pastoral care of the migrants. They were also hoping that there would be more indigenous people who would want to be baptized in the Church. Since the number of religious congregations were forced to leave China, some of them were invited to have their missions in Mindanao.

Those who got assigned to Davao were the members of the PME Fathers from Quebec, Canada. Like most children in Davao, I was baptized by a Canadian priest, received confirmation by a Canadian bishop, and went to a school run by the Canadian Brothers of the Sacred Heart.

Thus early on I was exposed to missionaries and saw what their life was all about. I joined the altar boys group in our parish and went with the priests to the interior villages for Masses and sacraments.

In high school, I thought I had a vocation to the religious life. I submitted by application to the brothers before graduation. They accepted, but my father did not give his permission. So I went to the Ateneo de Davao University which was run by the Jesuits, who were both Americans and Filipinos. There I studied economics, sociology, history, and political science. I made friends with Jesuit Brothers at the university. In my senior year, I thought I was called to become one of them. But that did not work out.

I moved onto graduate school in Manila and studied economics and sociology at a time when young people all over the world—including the cities and towns in the Philippines—were marching in the streets. I got involved in activism and joined students in the streets protesting against the Vietnam War and corruption in government, supporting the peasants' struggle for land, and getting passionately involved with other social issues.

I finished graduate school just before Mr. Marcos declared martial law in September 1972. I came back to Mindanao after graduate school and took jobs offered by church institutions. I worked as a lay pastoral worker with the Maryknoll Fathers. This was just after the popularization of the spirit of Vatican II.

These were the pioneering years of building base ecclesial communities among peasant and fisherfolk communities. We initiated social action programs, including conducting literacy classes, organizing cooperatives, training leaders, and being engaged in rural development projects. I was also involved in organizing young people, especially out-of-school youth so they can be more actively involved in the development efforts of the parish. This we did through the community-based theater, where we improvised plays for the conscientization of the ordinary folks.

The day that martial law was declared, our group of churchworkers were arrested by the military. They claimed that what we had been doing was subversive. After our release, we just carried on with what we were doing and did our best to elude further arrest and imprisonment.

In 1976 I got elected to be the first lay executive director of the Mindanao-Sulu Pastoral Conference (MSPC) Secretariat. The MSPC was the communion of fifteen local dioceses that comprised Mindanao and the other small islands in the south. This was organized by the bishops and the heads of religious congregations. The Conference met once every three years. Bishops, priests, religious men and women, as well as laypeople attended these conferences.

Born in the wake of Vatican II, the MSPC was perceived to be the church institution that would provide the local dioceses the mechanism to renew their pastoral efforts through a sharing of resources and coordinating of common programs.

Mindanao, at this time, was seen to be the locus of the progressive Church in the Philippines. Whereas the dioceses of the northern and central part of the country were still locked into the pre-Vatican II mind-set, the ones in Mindanao took the needed risks and took the Vatican II pastoral thrusts and priorities seriously. Thus it was here that a pastoral conference such as the MSPC arose.

Given the martial law situation where things were worsening in the area of human rights, those of us in the MSPC Secretariat got involved in human rights advocacy work. We also helped the different diocesan groups in their programs to conscientized the people regarding the injustices and organize them to resist the efforts of government to silence them.

It was around this time that my ties with the Redemptorist community in Davao City were strengthening. As the members of the community became more committed to human rights and advocacy and justice/peace work, I spent more time working and coordinating with them. This included being with the theology students of the community who had more time to be involved in many rights activities. They also joined our theater group who staged plays so more people could get conscientized.

Spending more time with them, including living for days in the monastery, made me rethink my vocation to the religious life. I was very much impressed by their witness, by the quality of their community life, and their spirituality which encouraged active participation in supporting the struggles of the poor and the oppressed.

I thought that more than any other group of religious men in the area, they were the ones who internalized the implications of preaching the Good News to the poor and oppressed. They lived a simple life and sought to be in solidarity with the peasants, workers, tribal people, fisherfolk, and urban poor. Where it meant clearly manifesting an option for the poor, they joined marches in the streets side by side with the marginalized.

They also expressed openness in regarding the signs of the times in the light of the Gospel and taking concrete steps in witnessing to the Gospel values. This progressive theological and pastoral orientation was clearly seen in the way missions were conducted, in programs set up in the parish, and in the formation of the students.

The witness of a few who took a prophetic stance inspired me in my own work. In this context, I was drawn to consider joining the Redemptorists. I went through a discernment process. I consulted with a few of them about applying to become a member. I asked a Redemptorist to become my spiritual director.

However, in the late 1970s and early 1980s, the situation under the Marcos regime was worsening. It seemed inappropriate to go off to a formation program while so much needed to be done in the field of human rights. So I postponed joining the Redemptorists.

I got arrested in March 1983 because of my commitment to human rights and justice/peace work. I was subjected to psychological torture and kept incommunicado for a month. My family and friends searched for me in funeral parlors and killing fields. When they could not find me, they thought I was already "salvaged," a term meaning to be summarily executed. Such was the routine military practice at the time.

When I surfaced, the military charged me with subversion, then a nonbailable crime. I was to stay in prison for twenty-two months. This, I referred to later as my "first novitiate." I was acquitted by the court. As soon as I was released, I was accepted by the Redemptorists and began my formation as a postulant.

After I took my first vows in 1987, I was assigned to the community based in Iligan City, somewhere near the center of Mindanao.

The life of the Redemptorist itinerant mission community

Today I am a member of the Redemptorist Itinerant Mission Community (RIMC), the only community with a mission team based in Mindanao. We are an itinerant community, that is, we are inserted in the parish where we conduct missions along with our lay collaborators.

We have been an itinerant mission community for the past two trienniums. Most of our missions in the past few years have been in the northwest part of Mindanao.

Like other areas of the island, the majority of the people in this region are lowland farmers. The main crops they cultivate are rice, corn, and coconut; some also plant vegetables, coffee, and root crops.

The majority of them are poor, because most do not own the land they till. If they own land, their property is quite small ranging from one to five hectares. Given this situation, their average income level is also small, which does not suffice for their daily needs. Most have an average of six children, most of whom are afflicted with disease malnutrition.

This is especially so for the tribal people, known here as *lumads*. They are the indigenous people in this region, which constitutes a considerable section of the population. They are even poorer than the settlers. They have been driven away from their ancestral domain as the migrants arrived in this island. They have moved further to the hinterlands where their life situation is one of extreme misery.

The poverty of the people is further worsened by government neglect and indifference. There has never been an implementation of a comprehensive land-reform program. There has been very little government support to the plight of the peasants in terms of good farm-to-market infrastructure, adequate irrigation systems, easy access to credit, marketing assistance, and the like. In the rural areas very little resources is set aside for primary healthcare, schools, and other social services.

Part of the reason is that government is mainly in the hands of the elite who take advantage of their positions to further enrich themselves. Even as they hold key positions in government, they are also big landowners and rich businessmen. Some operate logging companies, mining firms, and rural banks.

This kind of political system breeds government corruption from the national levels down to the local levels. Government neglect is also evident in the extent of ecological destruction all over the island. Nothing is spared—

forests, seas, rivers, mangrove swamps, and coral reef—everything is subjected to ecological devastation. Dams and geothermal plants are constructed for hydroelectric purposes, but with very little regard to their impact on the environment.

This is the usual context of our mission work. We often give missions among these people. Given this reality, we feel very confident that we live up to the Congregation's call that we prefer "situations where there is pastoral need…with the choice in favor of the poor."[1] Indeed, we have been immersed among the most abandoned in this island as we seek "to encounter the Lord where he is already present and at work in his own mysterious way."[2]

There are five of us in the RIMC, three priests and two brothers. In our present mission, we work with six laywomen and three laymen collaborators. There are also three seminarians of the local diocesan seminary who spend time with us as part of their pastoral exposure program.

As a mission team, we have tried our best to be actively engaged in "the raison d'être of the Redemptorist [which is] the missionary proclamation of the Gospel."[3] And given the inspiration of the document that came out of the XXI General Chapter exhortation, we have strived to submit our mission methodology to "the process of inculturation."[4]

Being an itinerant mission community has greatly facilitated our ability to take steps toward living up to this challenge.

2. The Redemptorist Lay Vocation

When I joined the Redemptorists, I was convinced that my vocation was to become a lay brother. Until now I have not wavered in this vocation. In fact, as my experiences in this missions accumulate, the more I realize this is God's call for me.

The Redemptorist brothers have, most definitely, a contribution to make in nurturing and witnessing to the charism of the Congregation. As they become more actively involved in the conduct of missions, they themselves are better able to define their role. As a result, most people are also able to see how they are able to contribute to the realization of our missionary thrust.

This is the age of the laity. Vatican II and other pastoral documents have called on all of us to encourage greater participation of the laity in the life of the Church.

The Second Plenary Council of the Philippines (PCP II) considered a major breakthrough in the life of the Church in our country which was attended by 489 bishops, diocesan priests, religious men and women and lay leaders, reiterated that the laity are called "to mission...and...to evangelize."[5]

PCP II states that "Brothers affirm by their choice of lay religious life that many are the ways other than by ordination or matrimony that the Lord calls mature men to serve the Kingdom of God."[6] They no longer need to think that only those who are ordained to the priesthood have the dominant role to play in the work of evangelization.

In countries like the Philippines, where the religious culture puts such a high value to clericalism—especially in the most isolated rural villages—the brother's presence help to demytholize this religio-sociological reality. They are able to show that it is possible to remain unordained and yet become a religious. By their witness, they manifest that it is possible to take religious vows and yet remain a layperson.

The brothers are then able to convince the laity that they can take on very important roles in the evangelization work. By such witness, they are able to encourage the ordinary laypeople to take on greater initiative in doing mission work. This further makes them realize that they need not rely solely on the clerics for doing all the pastoral work.

With a new understanding of the lay religious vocation, they see that there is such a richness of roles and functions within the Church. This helps them to define a more active and meaningful role in the life of their base ecclesial communities, which are in the hands of lay leaders.

As more laypeople play dominant pastoral roles, the Church becomes less the medieval institution that it used to be—patriarchal, hierarchical, and clerical. With a far greater presence of the laity, the Church goes back to what it was during the time of Jesus and the early followers.

As Redemptorist brothers are members of religious communities who take time out during the day to pray, meditate, and celebrate the Eucharist, as well as spend days for recollections and retreats, they are able to bring other laypeople to a realization of the great value of prayer and liturgy. They are encouraged to deepen their being a worshiping community.

Considering the religio-cultural realities, the brothers can effectively serve to be the intermediary between the laity and the clerics, that is, the parish priest. Because of their nonordained status, there are a number of circumstances where the laypeople find it easier to approach the brothers. In this context, the brothers are able to serve as bridge and can help toward forging a sense of unity among all the members of the Christian community.

Gifts, talents, and skills that brothers bring to the work of evangelization

Within the framework of PCP II, the Church in the Philippines exhorts all the believers to consider that "it is from the perspective of God's gift of life in its fullness in the Kingdom that we view the Church's evangelizing mission in the temporal order."[7]

Given the "socio-economic and political problems [which] prevent the living of a life reflective of the Kingdom and thus cause the greatest anguish...social concerns are inextricably linked with our evangelizing mission."[8]

To this end, the vocation of the religious brothers is further affirmed, as they seek to "give public witness to the baptismal commitment to serve Christ in our neighbor...[and to] manifest how individual gifts (such as teaching, manual work, nursing, research, farming) can be placed at the disposal of the Church in the task of reevangelization."[9]

Mindanao's scenario provides the Redemptorist brothers with lots of opportunities to be part of a Church who serves the most abandoned. Precisely because they are not burdened with clerical duties and responsibilities and given the range of their academic, professional, and work backgrounds, they are in a position to offer a unique contribution in serving the needs of the poor.

As part of a mission team at the service of the local Church anywhere in Mindanao, they can do any of the following pastoral work:

- Teach catechism to adults and children
- Organize bible sharing groups where faith-life concerns are discussed and communal actions are decided on
- Set up community-based health programs where those interested are taught the use of herbal medicine and other oriental ways of curing the sick
- Help farmers develop organic farming and other environment-friendly farm technology
- Organize credit, consumers, marketing, and multipurpose cooperatives

- Set up nurseries of tree seedlings for reforestation
- Help organize ecological action appropriate in the areas of work
- Conduct literacy classes
- Set up community theater groups—reaching out mainly to out-of-school youth to improvise plays for conscientization
- Get involved in the production of audio and video and other audio-visual materials that can be used for educational purposes
- Do research, documentation, and publication on the impact of government development and big business projects on the lives of the poor and on the environment
- Do human rights advocacy work by documenting violations and working with lawyers to file cases in court
- Help in looking for safe drinking water and setting up water projects

There is so much work that needs to be done in a situation like Mindanao, if we are to be at the service of the poor. But there are so few who are able to do this type of work in the countryside, especially with the limited resources in government to hire good people. The ones they hire usually have little motivation to do their jobs well.

There are only a few nongovernmental organizations (NGOs) who are able to reach the isolated villages because their resources are so limited. Even if resources are available, there are only a few who will work in the countryside because of the risks involved—from being vulnerable to diseases to being harassed by the military. Where government is unable to do their work and nongovernmental organizations fear to make inroads, the only ones who could provide these services are church pastoral workers.

This is why, apart from a growing number of committed laypeople, the ones who have been rendering services in terms of the Church's mission in the temporal order have been the religious sisters and brothers. Precisely because of this dedication, there are young women and men who are attracted to join religious congregations. A few young professionals who discern a religious vocation are drawn to joining the Redemptorists if they see that they can use their gifts, talents, and skills in building the kingdom in the midst of poverty and powerlessness.

Being able to practice a profession—such as being a teacher, social worker, agriculturist and the like—or being able to use their skills in the service of the poor have led to a greater realization that brothers are laypeople. This distinguishes them from the clerics who are mainly called on to look after the sacramental and liturgical needs of the people.

Because the brothers do not have to undergo the long theological formation that clerics go through, they can pursue professions or accumulate skills that are useful in the missions. In this regard, they become more mobile and can offer a variety of services according to the gifts and skills that they possess.

This reality further helps to identify the specificity of the contribution of the brothers to the Church's mission. Since their work is not that different from other laypeople who are in the same profession or who have such skills, the brothers show that the work of salvation can take place within the secular world. This further highlights the fact that part of evangelization work involves being committed to integral and sustainable development.

The life of brothers in Mindanao

In Mindanao there is an association of all the religious brothers. The members of this group include De La Salle, Marist, Oblates of Mary Immaculate, Jesuits, Salesians, Franciscans, Carmelites, Maryknoll, Claretians, Sons of Mary, Brothers of the Sacred Heart, Redemptorists, and other congregations. Most are involved in the field of education; they administer and teach in Catholic schools. Others are engaged in campus ministry, media, ministry to the sick, skills training among out-of-school youth and pastoral work, namely taking care of the needs of convents and monasteries.

The Redemptorist Brothers in Mindanao are involved in the missions. The work they do is connected to building and strengthening base ecclesial communities. In the course of being lay missionaries, the brothers offer a variety of services to the people and to the members of the mission team. The brothers who are in this association meet once every two years. They also join the National Assembly of Religious Brothers in the Philippines, which takes place once every three years.

During these meetings and assemblies, they pray and join liturgical celebrations, share information regarding their apostolates and involvements, and plan activities toward promoting the vocation of brothers. Their continuing efforts have helped to make more people understand that the brothers' charism is one that "is urgently needed by the Church and which undoubtedly the Spirit bestows on every ecclesial community to enrich the work of re-evangelization with yet another of his transforming gifts."[10]

Within this varied mixture of religious brothers, the Redemptorists hold a special place. They are the ones who have the privilege of being in an itinerant mission community, with the great mobility to move from one isolated parish to another, to be with the most abandoned peasants and tribal peoples.

In terms of what they can do, the range is as wide as the sum total of their interests, gifts, and abilities which can all be gladly offered toward witnessing to God's love for his people.

A community of brothers

The Redemptorist lay vocation naturally is enriched in the context of our being a community of brothers sharing "in Alphonsian heritage, a common purpose, a fellowship resulting from coming together frequently in annual seminars and common retreats, apostolic group meetings and sharing experiences."[11]

The lay vocation of the Redemptorists is enriched because of the close contact of the brothers with those who seek ordination. Fortunately, changes have taken place in our communities that have helped the brothers in gradually getting rid of the feeling that the cleric-confreres are first among the equals and have greater access to privileges and opportunities.

There has arisen the greater possibility of setting up a community structure that "brings the members into communion with one another and promotes a spirit of fraternity."[12] Where this spirit exists, the Redemptorist lay vocation is also nourished. This is certainly true for two of us brothers who belong to our community.

There have been times when people we meet in the missions ask: "Why do you continue being a religious brother considering that your work is tough, the risks are enormous, and you face a lot of difficulties and disappointments?"

The answers come easy. We get a lot of support and affirmation from our confreres, especially the members of the Councils. We know that oftentimes they include us in their community prayers. They are proud of us and happy with what we do in the missions. Our family and friends continue to provide a lot of moral support. Their occasional visits to our mission areas are a source of encouragement.

The people in the mission areas—especially the poorest who live in the most isolated villages—have been very hospitable and generous. They've opened their homes and their hearts to us; they've empowered us by taking to heart the call for a radical discipleship. The depth of their faith in a loving God and their willingness to offer their lives for justice, peace, and the integrity of creation has evangelized us. The witness of our lay cooperators to their own vocation continues to provide us with an example; their affection and friendship keeps us going.

Our brothers in the itinerant community continue to inspire us by their commitment to be faithful to their vows and their total dedication to serve the most abandoned. The times we spend in prayer, liturgy, recreation, joint vacation, recollections and retreat, study, and other activities have deepened our brotherhood. It is from this spring that we drink; for this, we rarely experience thirsting for acceptance and companionship.

Last, we've been privileged to be face to face with God in the majesty of his creation. Mindanao—despite the violence—is a land of enormous beauty. This is especially true in the hinterlands where nature has not been totally ravaged by urbanization and industrialization.

There are mornings when we awake in villages and gaze at rainbows that seem like bridges crossing mountain ranges. There are afternoons when the soft winds play with butterflies fluttering through the wildflowers on the hills. There are twilights when fireflies begin their vigil by finding their places in the coconut trees. There are nights when we look out to moonlight gently gliding across the waters of a still lake.

3. As One Millennium Ends and Another Begins

There is much talk of the year 2000 in Mindanao.

When Fidel Ramos became president two years ago, he declared that his government's priority was moving toward modernization and greater economic growth. In an attempt to catch up with the tiger economies of Asia (Hong Kong, Korea, Singapore, and Taiwan) and the newly industrialized countries (NIC) of Thailand, Malaysia, and Indonesia, he has set up an ambitious economic program labeled "Philippines 2000." This was set up to make the Philippines an NIC country in the year 2000 and beyond.

One of the major strategies involved in "Philippines 2000" is to establish growth areas where regional industrial centers could be set up. This scheme arose from the meetings of the economic ministers under the Association of Southeast Asian Nations (ASEAN).

One such growth area connects Mindanao with East Indonesia, East Malaysia, and Brunei. The economic ministers seek to push a fast-track industrialization scheme in this area with the influx of foreign capital, the setting up of needed huge infrastructure and the adoption of state-of-the-art technology.

There is no doubt that gross national products of these regions will dramatically increase. There will definitely be an upsurge in banking, trade, and commerce. There will be greater wealth arising from increased productivity.

But will it lead to a better quality of life for the majority of the people who are poor? Or will only the elite—the big businessmen, key political figures, top military men, and government technocrats—benefit from such growth? What will this rapid economic growth mean for the environment? Will this lead to greater ecological destruction?

As modern history moves toward the end of this millennium, Mindanao is destined to move on to another stage. Whatever that destiny is, there is a place for the Redemptorist brother to be on the side of those who will remain marginalized as he witnesses to his Alphonsian charism.

In this land, the brother—by remaining steadfast in following the footsteps of the Redeemer—can be a symbol of hope. For in this land that still needs to live up to its promise of being a Land of Promise, his life and work can manifest that in the Lord, there is Plentiful Redemption.

Notes

1. Constitutions and Statues, Congregation of the Most Holy Redeemer, Rome 1982, (No. 5), p. 22.
2. Ibid., (No. 7), p. 23.
3. XXI General Chapter, Itaici (Brazil, 1991), *Final Document,* General Curia C.Ss.R., Rome, 1991, (No. 13), p. 12.
4. Ibid.
5. Acts and Decrees of the Second Plenary Council of the Philippines, January 20—February 17, 1991, Secretariat, Catholic Bishops Conference of the Philippines, Manila, 1992, (No. 402), p. 139.
6. Ibid., (No. 497), p. 170.
7. Ibid., (No. 238), p. 86.
8. Ibid., (No. 239), p. 86.
9. Ibid., (No. 497), p. 170.

10. Ibid., (No. 497), p. 171.
11. Statutes, Decrees and Electoral Law for Redemptorists of the Vice Province of Cebu, 1982, (No. 0011), p. 14.
12. Constitution and Statutes, Congregation of the Most Holy Redeemer, Rome, 1982, (Art. 3, No. 030), p. 88.

THE CHARISM
IN PRACTICE

20

PREFERENCE FOR THE MOST ABANDONED

Rodrigue Théberge, C.Ss.R.
Province of Ste-Anne-de-Beaupré
Translated by Raymond Douziech, C.Ss.R.
Province of Edmonton

I WAS BORN IN A SMALL rural village in 1941. My parents (still farmers, each in their seventy-seventh year) raised eleven children. I am the eldest. I did my primary studies in a country school, followed a classical curriculum at St. Alphonsus (Minor) Seminary, entered the novitiate when I was nineteen, and spent most of my twenties in the scholasticate. I was ordained on June 25, 1967, and subsequently spent thirteen years as director of formation at Saint Augustine (Pre-Theology) Seminary, Cap Rouge, Quebec, while also teaching part time. I had my doctoral studies in moral theology between 1981 and 1987. Since 1982 I have been a professor of moral theology at the University of Laval, Quebec City, in addition to being the pastor at the Basilica of Ste-Anne-de-Beaupré since 1987. I love priestly ministry and I am pleased that I can count on my confreres to give me the freedom and trust to carry out my ministry.

1. Introduction

Reviewers sometimes let themselves off the hook by stating that quoting sources or references are unnecessary to an evaluative review. This allows them to simply expound their own reflections without the fear of having to continually defend their positions. As I begin this paper, I take a similar stance as reviewers, and acknowledge that the following reflections are the result of my own intuitions. These musings I humbly offer as part of the grist of the grain and meal of other equally valid opinions of fellow Redemptorists around the world.

Like a composer I will attempt to develop variations on the theme: preference toward the most abandoned. My basic inspirations are shaped by the mold of my pastoral experience in Quebec. And the "zeal which consumes me" is Christ our Redeemer: everything else is dust in the wind.

Let us begin by asking the questions: What do we mean when we speak of a preference? Who are we talking about when we focus on the most abandoned?

2. Preference and the Most Abandoned

What kind of preference are we talking about?

At the beginning of another school year, certain clerical college professors are vaunting before their students that during their vacations they stopped at this one's place and that one's place where they were treated like kings. They also passed by other students' homes, but did not bother visiting. (It is obvious that these just happened to be the less wealthy.) The excluded students are forced to swallow their embarrassment and are left to curse the poverty that stigmatizes them like a mark of Cain. They are fully aware that their parents could not serve these connoisseurs the epicurean table of their richer classmates. Their only escape, their way to level the playing field, and their door to success is academic excellence. In a formation house for young men sixteen to nineteen, the priest director hovered lovingly over a small core of seven or eight candidates. Like a hen he would brood over his nest and willingly give his favored attention to them. In his eyes, they could do no wrong. However, toward the rest he would readily heap abuse for the least infraction. He never seemed short on anger when it came to reviling the "rotten apples" in the group. It is interesting to note that not one of his favored core was ever ordained, while vocations flourished with the delinquents.

In a major seminary there were certain professed members who were considered "perfect seminarians." There were others whose reputation was such that they inevitably caught the attention of the highest authorities. These "prominent" students were summoned to an audience with "the magi" as they finished their studies. Some time later, in the great upheaval within priesthood and religious life, the "saints" left for greener pastures while the "remnant" humbly continued the task of building up the kingdom! Reflecting on this turn of events, the sour cynics sang an unflattering Requiem to those who persevered chanting the refrain: "The best left!"

In a religious community, certain individuals held firmly the key roles. They had the monopoly of chapter votes. The remainder of the community was left to suffer in powerlessness, forced, as it were, to drink the dregs at the bottom of the barrel. "Kill the preacher!" Soon a new era dawned and these career superiors were upended by a new consciousness that permeated the community. In the end only the "hewers of wood" were left to repair the damage left behind.

In a diocesan parish, there was a nucleus of "committed" parishioners who held the parish priest hostage. They held the levers of power, to the point that they determined who had a right to receive the sacraments. Using sacred Scripture to back up their arguments, they would threaten to resign, en masse, from the parish if the parish priest did not listen or tried to accommodate the marginalized in the parish. Religion increasingly became something for the "elite," and those on the fringes became more and more the norm. There remained only Christmas and Easter when the Masses dared to assemble in spite of the poorly disguised scorn coming from the "practicing Catholics." At least the collection was up.

These examples, I hope, adequately give some answer to the question: What kind of preference are we speaking about? Each reader is also, no doubt, able to recall and glean certain situations where they were subjects of a preference made by others or can identify with those who were the objects of a preference.

Preference, an essential or incidental reality?

Where is the focus of our preference: in externals (preferring one thing over another) or in one's being (choosing a value to live by)?

A mother of a family had two boys. One was a priest. The other a barhopper. The mother would come alive whenever anyone would talk about "her" priest. However, she would let loose with the crudest language whenever allusion was made about "that other" son. The boy wallowed in such self-hatred that he lost all hope of ever winning back his mother's love. Deprived of maternal affection, he began to despise all that his mother valued. Completely turned off with life and filled with rage, he killed his brother. His mother is left tormented by the question: Why?

A teacher had a favorite among his students. He would often parade him before the class or the school. But the poor "cover boy" could not bear the continual harassment of his peers and began hating his mentor so much that he ended up killing himself.

A provincial superior had a coterie of preferred individuals who were the first on his list whenever there was a posting to give. However, he seemed unable to create a suitable job scene for the others and told them to fend for themselves. This generated such an apathy among the men that they lost interest and became deadened in mediocrity or anaesthetizing routines. Regular order agonized on its deathbed.

Certain elders of a rural village stood stoically withholding their tears as they buried the father of a large family. After the last sprinkling of holy water on the casket, the priest, a son of the deceased, took off his soutane and threw it on the coffin. With clenched jaw he yelled: "Here, take it. It wasn't me that wanted it, it was you!"

At a vocation display, a religious educator was commenting on the biblical passage where Jesus frees the two demoniacs and consents to send the demons possessing the demoniacs into a herd of swine. The swine rush over a steep bank and drown in the sea. Faced with this financial loss, the local townspeople beg Jesus to leave their neighborhood (Matthew 8:28–34). The teacher moralizing on the Scripture, declared: "You, young people, do you prefer farrowing filth to Jesus?"

There are many other possible examples that question the basis for our preferences—focusing at times on essentials, at other times on externals, and at times on both. It seems to be taken for granted that the human person is a totality, composed of body, heart, and spirit. Among these elements of the self are certain values: bodily, moral, religious and intellectual.

For a preference to be authentic, would it not need to encompass the whole person, body and spirit? I am only able to truly "prefer," "bring to the foreground," or "make as a priority" those things that are tied to my whole being: body, heart, and spirit. Does not the ebb and flow of daily life involve a cyclical movement from exterior to interior, and from interior to exterior? My whole being, thereby becomes, as it were, a visible record of my free choices.

Some preferences can appear quite insignificant and trivial in comparison to other choices which engage me in a much more definitive way and fashion who I become. However, none of these can be sectioned off from the totality of who I am. They all have their influence on my personality. They also reveal who I am and who I want to be.

Therefore, I can prefer blonds to brunettes, the plump over thin, a hot drink over a cola, maple syrup over blueberries, tennis over sailing, winter over summer, butter over margarine, heavy metal over Gregorian, being a nighthawk over being a morning person, ski-doing over snow shoeing, hunting over movies, sailboarding over jogging....And the list could go on indefinitely, depending on my tastes, my temperament, my family background, my cultural heritage, the milieu in which I live.

I can prefer reading to television, solitude to crowds, prayer over boring work, pastoral work over tanning sessions, social events over liturgy, the security of ritual over innovation, private confession over public confession, behind-the-scenes ministry over being on stage, personal confrontation over backroom gossip, proven principles over trendy ideas, order over chaos...depending on my emotional life or my intellectual interest these, too, can enhance the scope of my preferences.

My first cousin and elementary schoolteacher thought she was doing me a favor when she gave me a book entitled: *Notre Jacques Cartier* as first prize at the end of grade four. I was downcast, because I would have preferred the prize my cousin received as a last prize—a record called *"Le Grand Lustucru."* It seems to me he and I would have benefited much more from opposite prizes.

This little exodus on the human site of preferences may seem self-evident and thereby boring to the reader. Just as the reader may question whether preferences do engage the totality of body and soul, are essential or incidental, or should be placed on the perimeter as insignificant. Pascal once said: *Le malheur veut que qui veut fair l'ange fait la bête* ("Unfortunately many who try to be angels end up acting like fools"). He reminds us of the necessity to continually give flesh to our preferences.

When I prefer my horse to my cow, I would be ill-advised to starve my cow if I was expecting milk as part of my diet. My preference for my horse does not negate my other obligations.

For thirteen years, I was responsible for admissions and for formation in our intercommunity (pre-theology) seminary. As such, I traveled across the province averaging about fifty thousand miles annually to speak to graduates in the hope of finding prospective candidates. I would also address the graduates of the old juvenates. Oftentimes the candidates from the public system appeared to be less academically able than those who had gone through the juvenate because they were lacking basic academic skills. I found myself sympathizing and favoring the candidates from the public system. I wanted to give them the opportunity to excel, or at least to have the same advantages as the former juvenists. I found myself working hard to help them with their homework without, I hope, forgetting the needs of the others. As their French teacher and religion teacher, I had a stake in their successes.

"To bring to the foreground," "to make a priority," "to prefer," does not mean that I reject other aspects of my network of human relationships in the world.

A Gospel preference?

If the Gospel remains my reference point for sorting out my values, it deserves special attention. The Gospel obviously does not contain an abstract treatise that quotes sources as a reference for its content. Rather, it "brings to the foreground" God-made-flesh in our humanity. Just as it "brings to the foreground" the value of the human person. Both preferences go hand in hand.

The Gospel not only draws our attention to the lilies of the field, the birds of the air, the signs of the times, the wheat fields, the homes, the granaries, the herd of swine or flock of sheep, the dogs, the chickens or the fish in the sea, the yeast in the dough, the seeds for planting, the salt or the oil lamp, the beauty of the universe, money, the tax collectors or the ordinary folk, the political or religious institutions, but it places these within a particular time and space, where God takes on the form of "the carpenter, the son of Mary," the "son of the carpenter, Joseph" (Matthew 13:55; Luke 4:22; Mark 6:3).

Jesus "hides" the richest part of himself to enter fully into the humble realities of everyday living, from which he borrows those evocative images to proclaim the Good News. Jesus enters into solidarity with every child of the same God and Father; he enters into solidarity with the good and the wicked, the good seed and the weeds, the worker who is hired at the beginning of the day and the one who is hired at the last hour.

When Jesus begins his public ministry, he does not take on a new job. Rather, he follows up with the same work of gathering humanity into himself. How does Jesus perform as "carpenter for the reign of God"?

He walks in step with those whose bodies are hurting, whose heart is broken, whose spirit is crushed. "Jesus went around all the towns and villages, teaching in their synagogues, proclaiming the gospel of the kingdom, and curing every disease and illness. At the sight of the crowds, his heart was moved with pity for them because they were troubled and abandoned, like sheep without a shepherd" (Matthew 9:35–36; cf. Luke 4:17–44 and Matthew 11:4–6; 12:15–21).

What a perfect synthesis of the Gospel! Jesus develops this schematic framework of his preferences through every human encounter and all the events of his life. What Jesus is "bringing to the foreground," "preferring" is nothing less than the person in his or her total humanness. His preference echoes that of God who holds in his net "one hundred fifty-three large fish." This number represents all the known species accounted for by the biologists of that day and is a symbol of God's preference for all of humankind.

It follows that the preference of Jesus is totally inclusive. His mission will not exclude anyone from the opportunity of conversion. Even those who are shocked by his loving regard toward sinners and tax collectors (Matthew 9:12–13) are challenged to adjust their sights and see the inclusiveness of God's love.

Could anyone challenge this preferential attitude of Jesus? It is obvious that the Gospel preference is based on God's attitude toward all of humanity, it is in our world where God willingly inserts his beloved Son.

This union of heaven and earth does not inhibit Jesus from enjoying a party, good wine and a meal with friends, from washing feet or picking a head of wheat, from holding a child or touching a homemade stretcher, from friendship or tenderness, from riding an ass or writing in the sand, from putting his fingers into someone's ear or mixing his saliva with dirt, from the wood of the carpenter or carrying a cross, from falling or ending face first in the ground, from action or contemplation. Jesus lives his "Gospel preference" not only with his body but with his spirit and soul. There is no dichotomy in this complete in-the-flesh, incarnate insertion. The outstanding evidence is the Resurrection, which becomes a magnificent bursting forth of this union of body and soul, of corporeal values and spiritual values, of humanity and God. This is reinforced by the risen Jesus who asks Thomas to place his hands in his side and in his wounds, and when he invites his friends to join him for breakfast on the beach.

Preference, according to the Gospel, then, is centered on the human person, in his or her joys, sorrows, dreams, and failures. Preference is an attitude of the whole self imbued with the love of God and the love of neighbor. "I was hungry and you gave me food. Just as you did it to one of the least of these, you did it to me" (Matthew 25:31–46; cf Mark 12:28–34; Luke 10:29–37). No one is excluded from the reign of God!

A Redemptorist preference?

The coming of Jesus, both as son of the carpenter in Nazareth and as the risen Lord, completely transforms our understanding of human values. Christ's life, death, and resurrection will determine the preferential attitudes of the men and women who follow in his footsteps.

Alphonsus de Liguori would let himself be seduced by this Galilean who had conquered fear and death. Alphonsus would extend this story of love between Jesus and people.

For this Neapolitan there was only one Gospel, that of Jesus Christ the Savior. It was this Gospel that he asked the Redemptorists, as members of his Congregation, to live and preach to the countless without a shepherd.

As a committed Christian lawyer, Alphonsus felt duped in trying to exercise human justice. He was able to move beyond bitterness and mobilize his extraordinary giftedness to proclaim the tender justice and mercy of the Word made flesh who willingly died on a cross. He also tapped into his past experience of working with human anguish and despair to enhance his priestly ministry and his exceptional preaching skills.

Like the carpenter who was both from Nazareth and of the reign of God, the lawyer Liguori did not reject his legal background. In fact, he pushed it to its limits by proclaiming the name of the One and Only Defender of the law of salvation, Jesus the Redeemer. Jesus, who himself was duped and betrayed by Judas, was exercising justice for those without hope. Jesus, nevertheless, continued to show tender compassion even to the Good Thief (Luke 23:42–43).

Alphonsus's preference is that of the Gospel, a Gospel of freedom, the Good News of tender love from a Jesus who "will not break a bruised reed or quench a smoldering wick until he brings justice to victory" (Matthew 12:20).

If there is only one Gospel at the heart of the pastoral efforts of Alphonsus, there is also only one preference, the salvation of souls. "It is the love of souls that has made me write and publish: I have not published for love of money. What pains me most are the poor souls that are lost. I have no other interest in mind, none other than the glory of Jesus Christ and Mary. I write not to gain some vain renown as a scholar, but only to gain the glory of God and the salvation of souls."

Nicknamed the "lion of the bar," Liguori would devote all his energies and those of divine grace to "bring to the foreground," to "prefer" the salvation of souls to "the smoke screen of passing recognition" or the "folly of applauds." He would fight any battle to defend the "sheep without a shepherd." "I am ready to lose my head rather than tell a lie."

As a defender of "the truth as I know it before God," Alphonsus would show preference for defending the rights of ordinary folk to attain eternal salvation. This preferential attitude he expected from the members of his Institute who ought to "clothe [them]selves with compassion, kindness, humility, meekness, and patience" (Colossians 3:12). Today we translate *splanchnikos* as compassion, but the Greek word really means "of or relating to the viscera, entrails, tripe." It is significant that Liguori invites his confreres to love with nothing less than the "viscera of Jesus Christ." The compassion of God toward those who are lost without a shepherd ought to lead the Redemptorist to love like God does, that is, "with the viscera of God."

The preference expressed in this option presupposes in every Redemptorist a goodness and generosity which Alphonsus likens to the vocation of a wet nurse who must look after her own needs but also nurse her child with abundant milk (cf. Isaiah 49:15; Luke 11:27–28).

Some key guidelines can illustrate this preferential attitude. For example, the benefits of absolution infinitely outweigh the fruitless results of its refusal. Nothing is gained by playing heavy handed in the confessional: a single "Ave" is much more effective than a whole regimen of penances. Strictness only leads to despair, making allowances for human weakness is the golden rule in promoting the salvation of souls! If we have to choose between two penitents, we must begin with the one considered lower on the status scale! Everything that may be good to do is not by that fact necessarily good to legislate! "We will be held accountable to God for being too strict." From the time a child can distinguish between bread that we eat at home and eucharistic bread, the child has a right to communion! Of what value are sermons that are crafted like masterpieces and float like clouds over people's head without ever shedding a single raindrop? Incompetence or a superficial varnish of knowledge and holiness is dreadfully injurious to the Church. People will be influenced more by their eyes than by their ears!

While I was writing my dissertation, "Liguori and the Formation of Moral Conscience," a religious woman, gracefully approaching her eighties, would devour with great relish my daily writings. Often she would interrupt her reading and say over and over: "How come the Redemptorists have betrayed Saint Alphonsus with their strictness in the pulpit and in the confessional?"

Alphonsus himself would often complain that he was not being read by his confreres while strangers were fighting for copies of his works. He would plead with his confreres: "I do not assume that you must accept my opinions, but I do plead with you that before you reject my ideas, read my book and consider that what I have written comes after hours of work, research, and study. These works, my brothers, I did not write for a public hearing nor to attract praise, I have written these works solely for you, my brothers." Again: "I have the misfortune of seeing my books read by strangers, while my confreres do not read them under the pretense that they can get nothing worthwhile from my sermons!" He would also brood over meetings that were particularly exasperating: "Why is it that people who have nothing to say and do not deserve to be heard can at Chapter become Solomon and with one vote upset half a world!"

Alphonsus de Liguori did not hide when he was called "an ape" or "that unfortunate old man," because his adversaries, the Dominicans, had written that he would be damned for being the apostle of leniency! Rather, he channeled his natural fiery and irascible nature in defending the rights of the crippled to truth that would save. At seventy-five he was pained to see the effects of ignorance: "My God, where are we? Look at what our intellectuals know how to do in this Age of Enlightenment! Age of Enlightenment, yes; and in the meantime souls are heading to ruin; Naples is lost; no one goes to confession any longer, no one listens to the Word of God, and the laity theologize manipulating Scripture, dogma, and morality to their liking!"

The preference for Redemptorists is definitely a "lived Gospel" that brings to the foreground the benefits of salvation to the people who are without a shepherd. This preference involves the essentials and the incidentals, holiness and knowledge. It governs one's "viscera and entrails of mercy" in order to nurture oneself and give hope to others with "the Word of God broken fragment by fragment." Following Christ the Redeemer and Saint

Alphonsus, the preference for Redemptorists is the total defense of the rights of "souls" to the fullness of Redemption.

For the disciples as for Alphonsus de Liguori, this Gospel preference becomes even more pointed: "Go rather to the lost sheep of the house of Israel" (Matthew 10:6). Jesus, who "brings to the foreground" the Word of God, does not hesitate to proclaim: "I was sent only to the lost sheep of the house of Israel" (Matthew 15:24). Like Jesus, they can "rejoice with me because I have found my lost sheep" (Luke 15:6).

Preference toward the most abandoned

Possessing the "viscera, entrails, tripe" of compassion toward the most abandoned remains for each generation of Redemptorists a challenging Gospel preference.

Fortunately, the "abandoned" are not simply reduced to a sociopolitical, economic, ethnic, moral, or religious category. The abandoned include persons with AIDS, the bag ladies, the drifters, the homeless, those with cancer, the homosexuals, the prostitutes, the prisoners, the beggars, those on social assistance, the "Jesuits rounded up and abolished," the deprived, single mothers, single-parent families, the divorced or remarried, the alcoholics, the drug users, the young, the retired, the nonpracticing, and those who are on the fringes or marginal.

Can we simply let these people shift for themselves? Is it not incumbent upon us to journey with this flock without a shepherd, breaking the bread of the Gospel with them? What would it benefit to have eyes if they could not see or ears if they could not hear the spiritual suffering of a famished people?

The young Liguori did spiritual and temporal works of mercy. During his adolescent and young adult years, he associated with youth groups which visited the incurables, priests in prison, and cared for their needs. In his family, he sided with the slaves and had ample time to sensitize himself with the problems of the galley-slaves whom his father had command of on his royal ship. He was aware of the human misery in Naples and in his neighborhood. It was one of the motivating reasons that as a young priest of thirty he established his famous "Evening Chapels" in neighborhood areas. He also knew firsthand the life of ease of the aristocracy and the influence of their power.

It is very revealing that Master Liguori preferred a radical Gospel approach. Like Jesus who escaped the crowd that wanted him to be king (John 6:5), Don Alfonso left the bar to exercise another kind of law. He no longer followed the route of social, political, or economic litigation. He mounted a donkey in order to pitch his tent in the midst of those "far removed from Naples." Every Redemptorist is sufficiently aware of the providential events that upended the heart of Alphonsus when faced with this rural population deprived of the solace of the Gospel.

The priest Alphonsus would never again exercise his practice of law as he had for ten years. He would announce a law of freedom "of salvation through announcing the Gospel, by the teachings of Jesus, the humble carpenter of Nazareth who died on the cross of injustice." He would be completely seized by the Divine justice that flowed from the pierced heart of Jesus on the cross. He would henceforth never cease to preach, to write about, to make alive for others and to live out himself this Gospel of superabundant grace. This did not prevent him from partaking of some material goods. However, deeply influenced by the spirit of poverty, he would dispose of his meager revenues to assure basic subsistence for his men who were preaching without any honorarium.

He was able to strip himself of the ways of nobility to such an extent that he would pass as a stable hand. It was certainly not the sorry horse that pulled his episcopal carriage after he resigned as bishop that would give him any princely demeanor.

For nearly sixty years, Alphonsus de Liguori would deepen his roots in the small mountain villages. He would choose his foundations in such a way that they would provide the best pastoral outreach possible without yielding to the temptation of centralizing the mission. On the contrary, he wanted his missionaries to go to every village. He would truly make his own the command of Jesus: "Go out into the streets and lanes of the towns and bring in the poor, and on your shoulders the crippled, bring them to the inn before the synagogue, and take care of them" (cf. Matthew 22:9; Luke 14:23, 10:34–37; Acts of the Apostles 5:15).

Because of the way he was able to live with the abandoned, he was able to touch their hearts. He would recommend to them everyday ways to holiness without a lot of fancy frills. These were daily prayer, frequent participation in the sacraments, devotion to Mary, meditation (especially on the love of Jesus revealed through his passion), accepting the will of God in the demands of daily work, joining a lay group, and spiritual reading. Before such an ordinary and uncomplicated approach some "preachers of the day" made fun of Liguori who, they said, preferred "the humble chair of a catechist to a professor's lectern during his lessons on moral theology."

There is no argument that Liguori preferred, to "bring into the foreground," the spiritual riches of the Gospel to the abandoned people in the countryside. He allowed himself to be moved by the misery of their "soul." He clothed himself with the "entrails" of compassion. Through his simple preaching style, he showed them the ways of salvation. He wanted holiness to be attainable to these people "far removed from Naples," because in Naples people had access to spiritual resources. He would not abandon his country folk, even though as a man of seventy-five he saw Naples in ruin! It was a preferential choice which, however, did not preclude occasional visits to the city.

Why the most abandoned?

The etymology of *abandon* is very instructive: "to place under a ban or authority of another." The field is open to "the power of darkness" (Luke 22:53). *Abandon* is the establishment of an attitude that anything goes which becomes destructive of a human and social fabric; it is the absence and loss of leadership that in a former era could have maintained a better cohesiveness within society, a cohesiveness of shared common values. In short, *abandon* represents a time of dehumanization, a culture of death, a spiritual hopelessness. *Abandon* is the emptiness caused by the absence of a truly pastoral authority. The word *ban* is an interdict, a prohibition, or proscription imposed by someone in authority. A ban is also a public proclamation or edict, especially an official call to arms.

"To be abandoned" is simply to be forsaken entirely and giving up on anyone providing the basic needs for daily living. There is also a loss of power which is expressed in the word *banal*. *Banal* in French law was the authority by which a landed proprietor required his tenants to use his machinery, it was also the district over which he exercised authority.

A field that is left fallow is quickly overrun with weeds and is no longer productive. It appears useless. Likewise a building left uncared for ends up collapsing in ruins. A domestic animal that is not fed ends up dying. A human being uncared for and unloved becomes lonely and despairing.

It is relatively easy to imagine situations of abandonment, that is, places and people who no longer receive attention. We cease to consider these places or people as having value. We leave them in their sad state and discontinue feeling responsible for them. They no longer are "placed in the foreground," we quit giving them "preference" since they stop having worth.

Everyone knows that authority finds its root in author. Exercising one's authority ought to author another's growth and increase the value and richness of another. This growth and increase brings other benefits to the community. We have to "dig around it and put manure on it" (Luke 13:6–9). Then we can foster virtue.

This is precisely the kind of growth that Saint Alphonsus wanted to make possible for his shepherds in the mountains. They were people to whom civil and religious authorities had quit being concerned about because they were homeless, illiterate, and remote. The rare priests who ministered to them was equally ignorant or had lost any desire to evangelize. Alphonsus wanted to give all these people an opportunity to achieve holiness, to experience the richness of the Gospel and the Word of God. They had become a people who no longer recognized their dignity as children of the Father nor did they know that they had been saved by the tender mercy and compassion of Jesus, a simple village carpenter. Alphonsus wanted to promote within these people such a love of Jesus Christ that they would once again reclaim their beauty as children of God.

The salvation of these people, banished by society and by the Church, created for Liguori a sense of absolute necessity. He realized the inequities between the opportunity for spiritual resources in Naples and these people in the mountains. He decided in favor of these most abandoned. It is to these that he wanted to "proclaim the authority of salvation in Jesus." These people would once again walk along the path of perfection in the love of God and of neighbor because they had accepted the authority of Jesus.

These "most abandoned" had no one they could count on. They would, however, find a defender in Alphonsus who gave new meaning to the passages of Scripture: "To whom shall we go? You have the words of eternal life" (John 6:68) and "You give them something to eat" (Matthew 14:16). It was this priestly ministry of Alphonsus that attracted me as a young man.

According to my mother, "he always had that in his mind." For nearly a year after my first Communion, I would play "being the priest," trying to imitate the country parish priest. I could always entice my brothers and sisters to join in, after all I was the eldest of eleven. It is true that we did not know much beyond the concerns of the farm. At the end of elementary school, I was enrolled on May 29, 1954, in the regional diocesan high school. My parents would often use it as a threat when I was unruly, "If you don't smarten up you won't go to high school." As it turned out, I never did go to that high school. During the summer my parents and I went on a pilgrimage to Ste-Anne-de-Beaupré. Hearing about the minor seminary of Saint Alphonsus, my parents and I went to have a look and immediately I was given an entrance exam. As I returned to the parlor, my mother, always practical, asked: "Well, are you going to take him?" The positive reply forced me to make an immediate decision. In the end it was a five-dollar difference in tuition that confirmed a decision. My parish priest paid the twenty dollar room-and-board fee for several months. That gift seemed to make up for all those yearend prizes that would now go to my classmates in the diocesan high school. That is how I ended up with the Redemptorists. God alone knows the tricks he uses when it comes to a vocation.

It was only when I was nineteen that the separation from my family became most poignant. The twenty-third of July, 1960, marked the beginning of novitiate. That day is burnt in my memory. I remember vividly leaving home and going with my parents to the bus depot. I am positive that if I had returned to have one more look at the farm I would have stayed. A few days before my departure, my father suggested that I should go to the classical college in the area to avoid traveling so far. Also, I could be close to home and watch my youngest brother, a newborn baby, grow up. My father thought I was too young so staying home would give me time to mature. He also felt he was losing his right-hand man on the farm. Competition with my confreres helped motivate my decision to go.

Why become a Redemptorist and why persevere in my commitment to the most abandoned and those deprived of spiritual help? I have no other answer than it is a free gift, a call to follow Jesus and a love for souls. I do not see myself as outstanding. I am aware that religious life in itself has had little attraction for me. I recall categorically refusing the enticing offers the teaching brothers gave when they came hunting for vocations in our small school. In my opinion there was a lot of pious rhetoric when it came to speaking about the merits of religious communities. In the final analysis, I know that I am loved by the Lord of all kindness.

Pastoral activity with the most abandoned?

A government survey tried to measure the feelings of abandonment among rural people. Ten scenarios of social cutbacks were presented. Some seemed rather superficial to the life of a small rural area, others cut deep into the very core of its being. The municipality could, for example, lose its police station, its fire hall, or some small businesses without too much effect. However, when it lost its post office, its bank, its grocery stores, the area fell apart. The last stage of complete abandonment was the loss of the parish priest. When the priest was removed, it seemed like the last straw of total disintegration: the area no longer had any purpose.

In his stories of "Adagio," the famous Canadian Félix Leclerc speaks of this terrible rural anguish. He has the drunken Nazir aroused by the definitive departure of the parish priest and by the fact that he will no longer be able to buy his pew "number 181" in the Church. "No church to go to on Sunday, no place for the funerals of our dead, no baptisms for our newborn, no commandments, no laws, no anniversaries, no sacrament of marriage, no confirmation, no Communion, no Christmas, no Midnight Mass, nor New Year's Day, nor Easter, nor Trinity Sunday, nor the Assumption, nor Labor Day, nor All Souls' Day. You have no right to leave us without any defense, without any ideals, without education, without principles, without forgiveness. No law, no instruction, no vocations, no hope, no charity, no faith. We have become disgusting, dirty, base, abortive children. What are we going to do if you leave?" And the parish priest stayed.

This is no longer a fanciful story.

This is becoming more and more the reality in small parishes throughout the dioceses of Quebec. Even in urban settings the reception of the sacraments and religious practice is in a free fall. Nevertheless the phenomena within the city is less poignant because public transit and other modes of transportation make access to a neighboring church easier. This is not true in the rural areas where distances pose greater obstacles at least for the aged and those without a vehicle.

Could not Redemptorists, like Alphonsus, mount their modern-day beasts of burden to pitch their tents in these areas of spiritual abandonment? Can we truly call a group abandoned when, for example, physically challenged people have extensive media coverage to raise funds, when there are a number of social groupings or private initiatives to care for, to "bring to the foreground," the needs of persons with AIDS, street people, those on social assistance, the homeless, the prisoners, women who are victimized, the young, the sick, and so on? Is the mission of the Redemptorist to "bring to the foreground" these groups of people in areas where people are already sensitized to the pain and human tragedy of these various groups? Or, when the Redemptorist is merely joining supplementary forces where help already exists? In line with a Gospel preference and the preference of Alphonsus, is it not more urgent to be aware of the deep spiritual famine that so often accompanies other human pain?

Are there not many other religious communities who in their constitutions "bring to the foreground" the explicit reference in Luke 4:18 or its equivalent? And are there not other large fields to harvest which are without shepherds for the Masses (cf. John 10)?

Many people are feeling abandoned, stripped, when faced with the shortage of priests. The priest still represents the presence of Christ among people (Matthew 28:20). It is a blessing for the Church that many laypeople have been mandated by bishops to do pastoral work. Nevertheless the simple folk will still say: "It's not the same!" They are not easily seduced by fancy talk that tries to gloss over the situation. For example, using a "presider at Sunday worship" does not substitute for an absent priest. Theological babble does not convince them. What happens in the end is a general dissatisfaction and a diffuse indifference. They say: "That's quite a shift from what we were taught not long ago." As a result these simple folk are tossed hither and yon by conflicting ideas and the unreal lives of soap-opera personalities (1 and 2 Timothy 4). As in the Age of Enlightenment, so, too, in the Information Age, Jesus is no longer at the heart of everyday living. He has become one guru among so many others.

I have been the parish priest at Ste-Anne-de-Beaupré for eight years. I continually experience the same Gospel sorrow Jesus had when "seeing the crowds he had pity on them, for they were harassed and exhausted like sheep without a shepherd."

In fact, rightly or wrongly, many come to the basilica to satisfy their spiritual hunger because they cannot find any spiritual nourishment in their home parish. Ironically, at the shrine they see a line up of concelebrants. At least externally is there not evidence of vast priestly resources?

My parish, since its beginnings in 1658, has also been a place of pilgrimage. It remains so today. As a lay scripture scholar once said: "This is the only place where people can still come when in desperate need; for many this is their last resort."

Like every other Redemptorist who ministers at the basilica, I could go on at length about what happens here. There are always crowds of people in my church. I do not have to run after people. They spontaneously approach me with the weight of their wounds and infirmities. Anything you can imagine has probably been heard.

That is why it is so important to welcome people like a father or a doctor. As Alphonsus de Liguori vowed, he would welcome the most abandoned, who find themselves wandering on so many unknown roads.

Furthermore, the economic situation of my parishioners, according to recent government statistics, is significant. Among the twenty-three municipalities that line an eighty kilometer stretch along the St. Laurence River, my parishioners are at the very bottom of the economic ladder. Like a figure skater they only score a three without ever hoping to reach the podium with a ten. Stripped and mortified, my community can still be proud of its generosity—up to eight percent of its gross income goes to charity. In spite of this fact, some still criticize that these funds are not going to the Church. It is a pity! My parishioners just happen to have discriminating tastes!

There are many wonderful efforts made to welcome the crowds, even if it is only at liturgical celebrations. We have the conviction of Clement Hofbauer: "If we want to win simple people over to God we have to celebrate liturgy and public devotions with all the splendor and solemnity possible. By their pomp these external solemnities stir the heart and people are won in spite of their reticence. People learn more by their eyes than by their ears, they are seduced by their eyes."

To clothe oneself with the "entrails" of compassion can take on its fullest meaning when dealing with people who come from outside the parish boundaries. Whether it is for the reception of the sacraments or for the proclamation of the Gospel. This demands a concerted effort of both science and holiness. Do we succeed?

Those who come to me as "abandoned" are the young couples who have a baby to be baptized. It takes a barrel of honey to sweet-talk them into their first tentative desire for the freedom of a Gospel of hope and mercy. It is also single-parent families or other familial arrangements who present their children for reconciliation, Eucharist, and confirmation. One has to clothe oneself in "Gospel patience" (Matthew 13) in order to help them reflect on the spiritual questions of life. It is the young who have just been engaged and are seeking the sacrament of marriage. Often these young people have been estranged from the Church since their high school and college days. Again one must enter the spirit of the "wedding at Cana" to begin opening them to the unconditional love of the "invited Christ." It is people upset by the reality of death who need the "Consolation of Israel." One has to be aware of this prime time of grace for those who mourn and weep. And it is the countless anonymous individuals who are looking for a caring ear to hear their tale of woe—both of body and of spirit. As a young lad once said: "We feel alone and abandoned when we have no friends who love us or who listen to us."

How often did I repeat "ad nauseam" in my university courses that the image of the priest and the Church was different today from that of yesterday. However, since my concurrent appointment as pastor and professor, I have shelved this idea because it does not fit with my experience. It is not the professionals who come to the priest's office, but the ordinary folk who are lost and do not have the resources to pay for a psychologist. They come to the parish priest with the underlying expectation, more or less conscious, of a stereotyped priest of former days.

Hesitant about the time I give to my teaching, I have the joy of working with young adults who express in their own way the spiritual hopes of the most abandoned of our day. Is it good? Is it bad? I am not certain. I just know that I always find in this "pastoral work with the evangelically most abandoned" the realization of my youthful dreams.

In order to rediscover the pastoral relevance and the Redemptorist preference, it seems to me we need a total dedication to the point where "they had no opportunity even to eat" (Mark 6:31) and place in common scrutiny our knowledge and holiness (Acts 2:42-47). In my opinion it is only in this context that "the preference toward the most abandoned" has a chance of producing the fruits of a plentiful Redemption.

21

EXPLICIT PROCLAMATION
OF THE WORD OF GOD

John Byczkowski, C.Ss.R.
Province of Warsaw
Translated by Aloysius Rekowski, C.Ss.R.
Province of Edmonton

1. Why Did I Become a Redemptorist?

From the perspective of my religious life (about fifty years) and of my priestly life (forty years), I can only find one answer to that question. "God so wanted it!" Only that one answer can throw light on my Redemptorist vocation.

I was born in Cracow, Poland, on October 28, 1931, to a simple working class family in which all of life was permeated by faith and piety. From the time I was a child, I wanted to be a priest and a missionary. But I did not think of the Redemptorists, even though their monastery was near our home and I used to often attend their church. Having been nurtured in the atmosphere of the Eucharistic League, I was linked with the Jesuits and intended to enter the Congregation of the Jesuit Fathers. I remember on the day of my first holy Communion when I received a silver chain and medal from our moderator, a Jesuit. He placed it into my hands with the words, "To our future Jesuit." I also belonged to the Militia of the Immaculate, a movement started by Saint Maximilian Kolbe, whom I was privileged to meet but I don't remember anything from those meetings. Apparently, I was too much the small child to benefit from those encounters.

Meanwhile, in 1939, the Second World War broke out. We lived through it in great poverty and hunger, but in relative peace. In 1944, I finished the seventh class of elementary school. Further schooling seemed to be a great question mark. In Poland, at that time occupied by the Nazis, all middle and high schools were closed. I was unable to continue my schooling. Just then I received a call to personally present myself to the German Arbeitsamt (Ministry of Work). Such a call did not augur anything good, and I was very much afraid of it. But I had to answer the call.

The German official, though speaking a little Polish to me, received me, examined my documents, conversed with me a bit and asked what I intended to do now. I answered that I would like to pursue my education further for I wanted to become a priest.

"But you know that is impossible, said the official, all schools are closed." "In that case," I said, "I would like to stay at home and help my parents." And then very unexpectedly came his question: "And do you happen to know the Redemptorists?" "I do," I said, "for they have a monastery near my home." "In that case go to the Redemptorists," said the official of the German Ministry of Work, "they need such as you—they will take you under their care, they will help you get educated and become a priest."

The Redemptorists at that time (1944) conducted a secret minor seminary in Cracow for boys wanting to enter the Congregation. It was a very dangerous enterprise because if discoveried by the Gestapo, everyone could be sent to the concentration camp at Auschwitz. I do not know and I never found out where the German official had learned about this secret Redemptorist gymnasium. I do know, however, that he risked his own life to help me, so the manner of my vocation was resolved. For that, I am thankful to him to this day! Unfortunately, I do not know his name or his later whereabouts.

The very next day, I appeared at the door of the Redemptorists. After hearing my story, they feared that I might be a spy or under observation by the Gestapo, so they did not admit they were conducting a secret gymnasium and sent me away with a rebuff. After several weeks, during which time our family was observed and checked, I was called to the monastery of the Redemptorist in Cracow and told that there was a school (gymnasium) and that I might be given admittance. That very same day I passed my entrance exam and started classes in the minor seminary of the Redemptorists. The teaching, in view of the possibility of conspiracy, was conduced in small groups of five or six persons. The professors were Fathers of our Redemptorist Congregation. The director of the school was Father Stanley Solarz.

In 1945, the war ended, and we could now openly continue our studies. At first I wasn't certain whether I wanted to enter the Redemptorist Order. I was still thinking of the Jesuit, but slowly the atmosphere of the Redemptorist life began to draw me. Contributing to this were our meetings with other great missionaries like Fathers Szczurek, Grodniewski, Sochacki, who enjoyed such authority among us.

In 1947, I entered the novitiate and a year later took my first religious vows. I received my ordination to the priesthood on June 19, 1955. After finishing the seminary, I was directed to the Catholic University of Lublin (Kul) for further theological studies. After completing my studies in 1963, I began teaching religion to high school students in our monastery in Warsaw. I was also the chaplain to the students at the University of Warsaw and the replacement for the director of Ministry of the Health Profession in Warsaw. The director, Father Niedzielak, during the time of the struggle between the Communists and Solidarity, was brutally murdered in his apartment in Warsaw.

Late in 1963, I was sent to our major seminary in Tuchow. There I taught dogmatic theology until 1976, except for a break of several years to further my education at the Gregorianum in Rome.

In 1976, I left the seminary and became a "periodic" missionary. From 1990 on, I was perfect of the Tirocinium: namely the year's course to prepare our young Fathers for later missionary work. In our Tirocinium, there were not only Polish Redemptorist but also our young Fathers from the Czech Republic and from Slovakia.

I always regarded the direct proclamation of the Word of God as my main task and as my specific vocation. As a pastor in Warsaw, as a professor in Tuchow, and from 1976 as a full-time missionary, I used to venture out to preach missions and retreats according to my ability and the time at my disposal. I have conducted about four hundred apostolic works, counting not only missions and parish retreats but also retreats for priests, for religious men, and for sisters. I preached missions and retreats in Poland, Germany, France, and the Soviet Union. However, this was always in the Polish language and to Polish people living in those countries.

As is evident from this short curriculum vitae, I am not a theoretician of missions—I am rather a practitioner and want to write about the direct preaching of the Word of God as the expression of our Redemptorist charism. I do not mean to create a theory of missions. I do not want to tell anyone how to conduct missions nor how we in Poland conduct parish missions. I only want to tell how I see the realization of our charism in the life and work of a Redemptorist missionary.

2. Accumulation and Communication in the Realization of Our Missionary Charism

Father Boleslaus Slota, in his article "Redemptorists in Tuchow, 1893–1993" (pp. 227–242), asks how Saint Alphonsus expressed his ideal of spirituality in practice and how the Congregation founded by him realized it. He writes:

> The school of Redemptorist spirituality has two stages—accumulation and communication. They both spring from the definition of the Congregation and from its character and mission. In order to preach the mystery of Christ, one must first get to know it. The knowledge of and the love for Christ is for Saint Alphonsus the basic requisite for the preaching of the Word of God. Both these elements go to make up the totality of Alphonsian spirituality (p. 229).

Accepting in principle this distinction into two stages of accumulation and assimilation, we must note that *stage* is not meant to be understood completely in the sense of time, but rather as a certain aspect, a perspective into which the life and activity of a Redemptorist is assumed. At times these two stages will overlap. The personality of the Redemptorist will flow over into his missionary work. That which he is will spill over into the way he proclaims the Word of God on missions and retreats. But the apostolic works preached by him will also influence and shape his spiritual profile which can develop or destroy his own spirituality. That "accumulation" and "assimilation" keep going, or at least should last through the whole life and activity of the Redemptorist missionary. If we may speak here of stages in the sense of time, then only in this sense, that in certain periods in the life of a missionary, there will take precedence the stage of the formation of his profile by his upbringing, studies, and reflection. At another time, precedence will show forth those acquired and deepened values.

In order that such a symbiosis of accumulation and communication might occur in the life of a missionary, a certain dose of openness is needed in the psyche of the missionary, namely, that kind of docility or capacity to see and to hear, to understand and to accept, new values. A missionary so perfect and so satisfied with himself and his accomplishments that he can accept no new values or not be open to any changes will, in practice, be finished sooner or later as a missionary—and maybe even as a religious.

This missionary "openness" ought to go in two directions: one to the mystery of the Redemption, which we are supposed to proclaim; the other to the person to whom we announce this mystery.

The mystery of Redemption is not something to be likened to a stable, once for always defined and crystallized mathematical equation that one can learn by memory and ever afterward use it to resolve all tasks and problems. Our very understanding of the word *mystery* leads us to understand that we are dealing with an unfathomable depth, with an incomprehensible essence, and a multifaceted reality. That depth and richness of essence is a call to constant searching, many-sided contemplation and deepening through personal reflection. Redemption is the central truth of Christianity. It combines in itself the mystery of human misfortune, of weakness and sin, of passion and the debasement of the human person. At the same time, Redemption speaks of the worth of the person, of the greatness of his vocation, of the worth of his efforts and his exertions, even those not always or not immediately crowned with success.

On the other hand, this same mystery speaks to us of God, of his love, and the Son of God, who has come and will come, of the meaning of his life and death; of the Holy Spirit which is poured out into the hearts of people. All of that must permeate the thoughts and the consciousness of the missionary. Theological studies and taking advantage of suitable theological periodicals play an important role here. One cannot pass them by, for that risks closing oneself off and impoverishing the spiritual profile of the missionary, as well as the essence of his message. But they are not the most important elements of his life and work. Most important are his personal reflections and experiences. After he sees and lives the multifaceted mystery of the Redemption, then he will be able to live it and preach it. In view of the preceding, it is easy to see what an important role the various get-togethers of missionaries can and ought to play, organized with the purpose of exchanging their insights and reflections and their practical consequences. There, where these assemblies have fallen into disuse or have lost their role, we must try to revive them.

Besides this openness to the mystery of the Redemption, the missionary must be open to the mystery of the person of his listener. The silence of the listeners in the church is only apparent, in reality the person to whom we address the Word of God shouts to us and sometimes very loudly. He cries out to us by his presence or absence at our sermons; he cries out to us by his opening up to God or by his remaining closed; he cries out to us by his sin or by his conversion, by his discovering hope again or by his disenchantment, by his wanderings or by his search for the good, even if at times through crooked paths. If we do not hear that cry, if we close ourselves to the hope and the call of people, it will be hard for us to reach them. Even in full churches, we will be speaking only to deaf walls.

And here arises the question: How do we maintain and develop this openness to the human person in oneself? And the answer, so I think, can be only one: To hear and to understand today's person, one has to be with him. Sometimes there is in us some inner fear of the world surrounding us—for it is sinful, it is evil, it can threaten us, for it is bustling with all kinds of dangers, which lie in wait to entrap us. It could also come from a feeling of our own littleness and a fear that we will not measure up to people's hopes and expectations, that we will expose our own weakness. And so we sometimes "visit" that world with our missionary service. Or we come like some tourists who come with the Word of God in their valise, but soon leave it to go on to some foreign country and to foreign people.

In order to hear people and understand them, it is necessary to be with them—through contact with them, through wide reading in the spheres of sociology and psychology, and through a prudent use of the mass media. All of this must be accomplished by a constant inner desire to understand the other person, even if he thinks differently than we, even if he should conduct himself in ways other than our custom, our expectations or our desires. The constant readiness to help every person is the fundamental condition of missionary openness to another person.

In this way that "opening of oneself" to the mystery of the Redemption and to the mystery of the person joins and integrates the elements of accumulation and communication and permits the Redemptorist missionary to communicate effectively the charism of his vocation in his apostolic works. For this opening up and this integration to ensue the faith of the missionary is indispensable.

3. The Faith of the Missionary

When I speak of the faith of the missionary, I do not mean Catechism faith, namely, the acceptance of Catholic dogmas or the setting oneself up in relation to God as his partner in the task of saving the world. That kind of faith is taken for granted in every Catholic and, therefore, much more so in every priest and every religious.

Speaking of the faith of the missionary, I wish to say that he must believe in his missionary vocation, that is, he has been personally called and sent to announce the Good News to people and that in the call there resides the sense of his religious calling and the work of his life.

The missionary—one sent by Christ

The Redemptorist missionary is one who has heard Christ's call: "Follow me," who made that call his own and who followed Christ in order to announce the Good News of salvation to the poor. That following of Christ is realized in every act of service of the religious, but this charism of our spirituality is most pronounced in the formal proclamation of the Word of God.

Saint Alphonsus founded the Congregation in order that its members, taking Christ as an example, might announce the Good News to the people, especially the poor. In the days of Saint Alphonsus, there was no lack of priests in the Kingdom of Naples, but there were no priests for the ordinary people, the poor, those backward in culture and abandoned. One of the most important elements of the spirituality of Saint Alphonsus was "going out" to these abandoned people. Following Christ meant "walking with Christ," traveling with the Gospel. Following Christ for the Redemptorist and especially the missionary means "going to the people." That is why he is like Christ, an itinerant preacher. Even though he has his monastery, his room, his corner, his calling is to go out to people, because he is sent to them. "As the Father sent me, so I send you."

It is not easy to be "God's pilgrim," God's traveling preacher. Christ himself with sadness stated that the foxes have their dens, and the birds have their nests, but the Son of Man has no corner, where he might lay his head. It's this kind of Christ that the Redemptorist must walk with. It is that kind of a Christ that the world needed and needs today. So must the Redemptorist want to be, who in that way proclaims and realizes his vocation, his charism in the Church. To follow Christ, the Redemptorist missionary must go to the people to offer them that which Christ brought to humanity, namely, the treasures of God's mercy in the task of the Redemption of the world. And that precisely, what Christ brought—should characterize and modify the Redemptorist approach to people. Let other religious orders follow in the footsteps of Christ, bending over the sick and healing their ailments, or Christ concerned about proper order in the Temple, or Christ discussing with the learned scholars. A Redemptorist follows Christ going to and reaching out to the people, to tell them that "with him there is copious Redemption." That means that his salvation is for everyone, not only for those living in the shadow of the Temple but also for the "poor"—those abandoned, those caught in the snares of weakness and sin, the lost and confused; those who perhaps through their own fault have lost the way to the Father's house or have given up the search. That is why a Redemptorist, if he is to live up to his charism in proclaiming the Word of God, must be a man of hope.

The Redemptorist himself in his inner conviction must be a man of hope, that is, convinced that he has sheep whom no one else will discover. At the same time, he must be a man of hope for others, that is, show that hope to others, even to the most and furthest away from God. That hope of the Redemptorist should embrace not just individuals but groups, nations, indeed the whole human race. With the conviction that one can change the world, that one can help to solve the problems of people—of individuals as well as of society in general—and with the conviction that he, the Redemptorist missionary, is called to follow Christ in solving those problems and in building a better, more godlike world, therein lies his missionary optimism, his zeal for work and his perseverance, when his labors seem to be bringing him into spectacular results.

That hope, however, must have a missionary and a Christian character. It must be the hope preached and given by Christ. It depended on showing the way to the Father, the way that Christ offered to everyone, even to the lost, the straying prodigal sons. The way of Christ's hope is the way of return to the Father, the way of conversion. Such was the Good News of conversion proclaimed by Christ and it is with such a hope that Christ sends forth the missionary. The missionary goes to people, to announce and to bring conversion, and so the necessity of reminding the people of the eternal verities: of heaven, hell, the value of human life, judgment, sensitivity to sin, the possibility of forgiveness but also the necessity of penance. These truths may be unpalatable to modern man, they might be unfashionable even in the modern Church, but those are the truths Christ proclaimed. Therefore, the missionary, if he wants to preach the Gospel, the whole Gospel, unabridged and unfalsified, must proclaim all these truths. The missionary vocation is a vocation to hope, calling us to return to conversion, and this is the call, the vocation, the Redemptorist missionary must believe in.

The missionary—sent by the Church

Christ's call and mission reach the missionary through the Church. The missionary goes to the people commissioned by the Church and shows the way that leads to God through the Church. The way of return to God is also the way of return to the Church, to a sharing in its life through the liturgy and the sacraments.

Important consequences for the missionary flow from this. He goes to the people of God not as a private person, but as a messenger and a representative of the Church. This is why the missionary should always preach the doctrine of the Church—not his own personal views, not theological, community, or political discussions, not his own practices or devotions, but the teaching of the Church as it is proclaimed in the official documents of the Church. That might pose difficulties for the missionary, for he may be convinced that he can help people in a different way, that the official documents do not always answer the needs of the people to whom he is sent; that the yoke the Church imposes is unduly heavy, that the wishes of the Church are a bit too exalted. He should be convinced that he is going to the people as a messenger of that very Church, to announce the truths of the Church, to show the way for which the Church is responsible. The copiousness of Redemption flows out upon the people of God through Christ and through the Church, and through the missionary only to the extent that he proclaim the truth and show the way in their name, and not his own.

Since the return to God is at the same time a return to the Church, the task of the missionary is to lead people to the Church, to the liturgy and sacraments, to life with the Church and in the Church. That is why in our missions and retreats individual participation in the sacraments of penance and the Eucharist become important topics in our preaching, and concern about it an important element of missionary service.

The missionary—sent by the Congregation

When we ask how the charism of our Alphonsian spirituality is to shine through our formal preaching of the Word of God or of our missionary service, we make it clear to ourselves that our mission flows not only from Christ and the Church, but that it also reaches us through the Congregation. We go to the people not only with the hope of Christ, not only with the reaching of the Church, we go as Redemptorists, representatives of our Congregation. We must remember that not only are we missionaries but that the whole Congregation is missionary. That missionariness of the Congregation expresses itself most clearly, most observably through missions and retreats, but it does not flow therefrom that other forms of work in the Congregation are less apostolic, less missionary. Not the kind of service rendered, but the spirit that enlivens it decides whether it is an apostolic and missionary service.

In this understanding of our missionary preaching, we should always be accompanied by the awareness that in our apostolic endeavors we are never alone. The Congregation stands behind us, and through this sending (mission) the charism of the whole Congregation is fulfilled. We benefit from the offerings, the prayers, and the care and services of the whole Congregation. It obligates us to a fitting missionary posture at the time of our missions and retreats.

We missionaries represent the whole Congregation. People will judge not only us, but the whole Congregation by our apostolic work, by our dedication and our preaching. We need to remember that in order not to blemish the good name of our Congregation.

Every Congregation has some specific characteristics. Often they are difficult to define, but they surface very clearly in practice. In relation to our preaching of the Word of God, these characteristics are expressed (among others) in our devotions, for example, our eucharistic devotions, and our devotions to Our Mother of Perpetual Help. Our charismatic value in our Congregation is a certain style in our apostolic works, for example, the style of the life of the missionary—his simplicity, his poverty, his missionary dedication and sincerity. That charism, nurtured for many years in our Congregation, ought to be reflected in our missionary stance and in the style of our work.

4. Conclusion

In what way is the charism of our Congregation and the spirit of Saint Alphonsus to express itself in the direct proclamation of the Word of God, that is, in our missions and retreats? That's the question for which we are seeking an answer. The structure of the mission, the method of preparing and conducting it, the themes of the sermons, the devotions and the feasts—that all depends on the time and the circumstances and must be open to change. But in spite of this necessary changeableness, there must be in our missions something stable and unchangeable. There must be expressed in them the unchangeable charism of the Congregation. This will happen when —and only when—everyone in the Congregation and before all others who organize and preach the missions will be so permeated by the charism of our holy founder that, after the example of Christ, in the name of the Church and in the spirit of the Congregation, the missionary preaches the Word of God to the people. That is why I claim in a publication intended for the whole Congregation, we should not talk about how to conduct Redemptorist missions—for that is a changeable thing—but rather how to be a Redemptorist missionary, for that is unchangeable. At no time or in no place are we permitted to abandon certain traits of the personality of the Redemptorist missionary for that would threaten the loss of the charism of our Congregation.

As I said at the beginning, I am not a theoretician of missions. I do not want, therefore, to write a theoretical dissertation on this matter. But I have behind me several decades of work in preaching the Word of God and because of that experience, I want to tell what I see as necessary to be a good missionary in our Congregation. A good missionary, that means effective and happy.

And now, to sum it all up, I wish to say:

(1) The Redemptorist missionary must be open to divine and human truths and in that way to shape himself and his preaching. The personality of the missionary flows over into his preaching. On the other hand, his apostolic works fashion his personality.

(2) The fundamental characteristic of the personality of the missionary is his belief in his missionary calling—that it has meaning and value without regard to observable effects—that it is the way of salvation for himself and for many other people.

(3) The Redemptorist missionary follows Christ and together with him goes to people announcing the Good News of Hope, especially to those who have wandered furthest from God.

(4) The Redemptorist missionary preaches the entire teaching of Christ, even unstylish and unpleasant sounding truths. He preaches never-

theless the teachings of the Church and not his own theological opinions, whether ascetical or social.

(5) The missionary is sent by the Church and so tries to lead the people to life in the Church, to its liturgy and sacraments.

(6) The Redemptorist missionary draws from the whole treasury of the tradition of the Congregation and gladly cooperates with others in working for the good of all.

All of this is simple, but not easy. But such is our missionary vocation and in that consists our charism.

22

RELIGIOUS LIFE
IN A SECULAR SOCIETY

Josef Römelt, C.Ss.R.
Province of Cologne
Translated by Mark Miller, C.Ss.R.
Province of Edmonton

1. Introduction

I would like to describe why I am still a Redemptorist today in a society which distances itself from faith by offering the following reflections about the reason for religious life.

I am thirty-seven years old. I entered the Redemptorist community in 1977 with only a vague sense of my goal in life. I got to know the priests at the Redemptorist high school in Bonn. During the years of my novitiate and studies, my experience of life and faith deepened. My own wishes at the beginning were quite individualistic; I sought to enter into a safe and assured relationship with God in my own personal, religious way. Gradually, however, this attitude gave way to a conviction that I would work to further the Christian faith in the context of the Church and the Redemptorist community. To me, it became very important to come to terms with modern culture, to reflect upon and ponder its meaning for faith.

At the present time, I am a theology professor at the college seminary in Hennef, near Bonn (Germany), as well as at the Alphonsian Academy (Rome). Ultimately, it is a fascination with the God of Jesus, who is such a free and living God, that binds me to this present life. The meaning that I experience in this way of life satisfies me—albeit in the midst of many struggles and conflicts—more deeply than any personal creativity.

2. Making Sense of Religious Life in a Secularized Society

Today's society—at least in Germany where I live—is presently passing through a second phase of secularization. Secularization refers to a certain way of life, a "feel" for the meaning of life and its farthest horizons. This way is a life without God in this world. One need not understand this pessimistically as a world without hope. No, it means a life which is at home in a cosmos that we know has taken millions of years to arrive at its present form. It means being at home in an infinite space in which evolution has made possible thousands of life forms including, finally, humanity with its technological civilization. It means a civilized life which human beings have built through creativity and a wealth of ideas. Through its productivity and imagination, humanity has succeeded in fashioning a life that has become highly developed and complex, even in the midst of the multiple life forms of nature. It is a life with house, refrigerator, television, and automobile, with music and cultural exchanges, with books and computer systems, with the comfort of CDs and the information industry. The differentiation and pluralistic vigor of this life continually frees up new powers. The quality of life and intellectual intensity provide safety and, at the same time, push onward to ever greater innovations.

All the energy today is directed toward achieving a life of material certainty and human creativity.

Secularization refers to a life that has invested all its energy in building up this world's civilization. This way of life has today proven sufficient for the majority of human beings. It is a proud way of life: human beings fight for their self-realization. They wish to be full-grown and autonomous citizens within a free, democratic, and economically secure culture. They are prepared to be involved—to stand on their own two feet, to earn their own money, to enter animatedly into partnership and social involvement, to accept political responsibility. I also find this a very fascinating ideal. Every person is concerned with a bodily and spiritual vitality, striving to be fit, seeking to care sensibly for personal needs and the needs of others, and learning to settle conflicts honorably. It is the ideal of our society to master actively and through social confrontation, as human beings without cowardly fear, the occupational and human risk of our lives in order that a safer and freer culture can unfold to the benefit of as many human beings as possible.

Secularization means that God no longer plays a role in this life. Not that anybody arrogantly denies something Absolute, or a final horizon to this life, an ultimate spiritual depth or the truth of an all-embracing meaning to life. Many human beings sense, even today, that human creativity is a mystery-laden power, and that life consists of more than sex, career, and wealth. Many anticipate a true partnership, one which is so full of feeling and rightness, that spontaneity and spiritual vitality will not dry up. Over and above this, many people are looking, personally and in community, for an atmosphere of more deeply felt experiences: a cosmic harmony, a mental concentration that transcends everything, an ultimate energy whose protection can be so pleasant. They sense the fragility of our happiness and the persistent danger threatening all human development. They feel the limits of being human and seek a deeper validation of their existence—one which will not blandly dismiss as an empty promise the richness of their sense of protection or trust. Such sentiments easily connect with concrete notions of reincarnation and the immortality, with the truth of the stars and peace with nature, with ecological responsibility and pacifism.[1]

> *For many people today atheism is hardly a viable option; but there is also no longer any notion of Christian faith.*

The era of atheism as a totally conscious position that rejects every longing toward transcendence, whether intellectual or emotional—or even as a case of religious apathy due to work and the strenuous demands of making a living which leaves no room for deeper thought[2]—in my world appears somehow long past for many people. Paradoxically, that is far from meaning that the era of secularization has been overcome—at least not the era of distance from a transcendental God as understood within Christianity. On the contrary, there remains an odd mistrust toward all religious desires: the mistrust of any image of a God who stands beyond our feelings and experiences of infinity and harmony, of transcendent energy and security, or toward a God who precisely because of God's own freedom simply does not surface in our experience. For many human beings today, there is one rather vague feeling that nonetheless remains valid: if there is a God, then this God must raise a discernible echo within my own creative being. What could any God mean before whom or in response to whom one's own feelings of vitality and joy in life are silent? We are prepared to squander all our emotions on that God who carries our safety in his or her hands. But what is the point of a God who, as an Other, speaks in ways other than just through our own feelings? How am I supposed to understand a God whose voice sounds out the letters of a book, the Bible, or the customs of a believing community, the Catholic Church, or out of rational ideas about the world as created and humanity as a partner? Is God's closeness, then, some abstraction, communicated in contradictory ways, tiresomely hidden behind practices and traditions, sacraments and prayer formulas, and drowning in the chaos of Christian infighting?

Speaking from the Christian experience of belief, secularization means that precisely at this point of faith-connection many people are no longer—or are still not, or are not again—prepared to join in. They accept only one meaning—a meaning which is not tedious to achieve but rather is immediately present to experience and which engages experiences from the past, the present, and the future. This meaning is not simply handed on in verbal narration, nor is it experienced in signs whose inner meaning is truly open only to a structured community of faith. No, it is a meaning that is given without mediation. It is an original meaning, felt in immediate experience in all its fascinating richness.[3]

There are many people today who have a lively sense for the depth of life. Nor is it rare to find even radical claims of immediate openness to the transcendent. The care and intelligent sincerity such people show speaks to the concern they have to seek after the traces of the Divine in our life. However, they do not want to identify these experiences with the language expressed in the faith relationship of the ecclesial and Christian context. They sense a barrier between them and the Christian God, a barrier that they do not wish to climb over. They are cautious, hesitant, and sometimes downright negative.

What sense can there be in continuing to live as a Redemptorist in such a context—as a human being who feels himself united to the God of Jesus and who, out of this connection to the Otherness of God, undertakes to seek a Partner with whom he can experience in intimate nearness both security and the challenges of being human? What sense can there be to life as a Redemptorist, thereby renouncing any chance of having one's own family, which at least would offer the challenge of responsibility and the happiness of human procreation? Why shouldn't one make his own life so materially certain that he can use his money autonomously and independently, spending it for what he himself holds to be right? Why should he trust his money and his possessions to a community that devotes itself in common to the service of spreading the biblical message—and particularly within the Catholic Church? Why hide one's lifework in a life that requires the proper correlation of one's talents and habits to this particular community of priests and brothers within the Catholic Church?

Perhaps contrary to the modern trend, there is more at stake here than the desire to have an experience of religious elitism. The purpose of such a life is certainly not to intoxicate one's senses on the thought that one is doing with his life as a Redemptorist what few others do today. No one needs to convince himself that he will accomplish something special on the path chosen for God in religious life. Both the human challenges and risks of mature responsibility and the fullness of a Christian and human personality are found as readily in those states of life that arise in the venture of partnership, family, and career. It is not enough to believe that by means of the vows and entry into Redemptorist community one has arrived at a certain state through which only a select few human beings express their experience of the meaning and transcendent depth of our lives. How would such a feeling of a purely personal and religiously supported pride be different from these secular desires for faith where only the hard currency of one's personal experience of spiritual vitality, value, and self-consciousness counts?

The venture of a life for the God of Jesus

To live as a Redemptorist means that one is prepared to endure the risk and the gamble of putting one's life at the disposal of the God of Jesus within the tradition of a community of laymen and priests in the Catholic Church. This is a God who wants to speak to us in the many forms of Christian faith-experience expressed in the Bible, the sacraments, the Church's tradition and communal life. Such a life also entails a venture wherein one holds together one's own longing to experience the transcendental meaning of our lives and for human maturity and creativity through the words that Jesus spoke: "I am the way, the truth, and the life" (John 14:6). It is a matter of providing room within one's own feelings and thoughts for the interpretations and attitudes that others in the Christian faith community, in their search for happiness, have found through their encounter with Jesus Christ and have experienced as meaningful for their lives. Here, then, is the reason for living the life of the Redemptorist: to assimilate these thoughts and attitudes in a manner that is full of life and imagination within the context of modern life and to hand on or make available to others the power and the supportive security given by this process of faith.

Such a way demands a radical commitment and a serious readiness to allow Christ in; to turn over to him one's own doubt and uncertainties; to deal honestly with one's own fears, conflicts, wishes, and desires so that there does not arise simply a dead-letter faith or a clamoring for traditional forms and formulas, but rather a process of human growth and spiritual maturity. Only those who are prepared to examine their own limits, their human deficiencies, their biographical disjunctions, and their times of spiritual halfheartedness will experience the healing and freeing power of faith in the sense of Jesus' own experience of God. Only those who dare the honesty that allows the power of Jesus to work in their own life—not doing it oneself, nor precipitously laying one's own claim to it, nor taking credit in one's own self-assurance, but rather the honesty given (as gift) along extended pathways that really have no end—can be the connecting point for other human beings on their own journey of faith through an encounter with the Christian God.

Accordingly, it is necessary to pay attention to the unfamiliar experiences of meaning and of God which are alive in society and non-Christian religions, indeed, in the different Christian denominations. Because a person can envision only one perspective of the always larger and all-encompassing experience of God, tolerance and knowledge of the limitations of one's own state in life are part of the inner security and happiness that come with such a life. Nor are they to be confused with one's personal self-assertion or shortsighted fascination with the experience of one's own vitality. In a certain sense it is a modest life that is conscious of its own boundaries. The goal is service to the truth of the Christian God, rather than one's own self-affirmation. However, it is precisely because of this that such a way of life provides a person with self-awareness and a strong identity.

No fear of loneliness!

Today it is not always easy to survive the isolation within a society that seems to be less and less interested in a Christian way of life. Most often people will identify God's nearness with their personal success. Because our self-consciousness and awareness of our worth are often so fragile and sensitive, it is tiring to fashion our life in a Christian framework of experiential belief, much less want to go on, while surrounded by such a world. The inadequacies of ecclesial forms of expression and the limitation and weaknesses of our imagination can weigh heavily on a believer. But it is still in such concrete, historical form that the encounter with the God who works throughout salvation history presents itself. This is the God who, out of God's own freedom, confronts our longing right in the midst of our temporal, human existence.

Living in community

It is good during such an era to be on this journey in a community, together with other human beings who are searching in the same direction and somehow feel themselves called by the same ideal, even if the conceptions of the way to realize this ideal often part company. A shared community path presupposes a correct interpretation of the goals and patterns of life for the task of handing on Jesus' message in a vital way. To attain this common interpretation, honesty and an openness to conflict are very important within a religious community. It is important to share our wishes and plans, ideas and conceptions, and to share with one another our personality, as well as the deep processes of our human pathway and search in faith. For this openness to take place, there is a need for sensitive care in the interrelationships within the community.

Accountability and reliability make true community possible, regardless of how different and independent the individual members may be. For without this transparency of the confreres for one another on the basis of each one's independent and personal responsibility for his own journey, there will be no real experience of sharing a life together in the midst of this differentiated and ever more complex modern world. There will be no experience of being at home with one another, although this transparency can never be allowed to wound another by trespassing on the intimacy and ultimate autonomy of the individual: "Transparency is *the* great favour which establishes trust and furthers personal identity, and by which human beings can mutually reveal themselves to each other. 'Openness' belongs to 'transparency.' But this is not openness at any price. Rather it is a discrete openness which knows the value of a proper self-protection...."[4] The responsibility of the individual and the common responsibility of the confreres for one another and for their task: these provide the central, vital dynamism to bring God close through fidelity to the message of Jesus.

A life in the service of others

More and more often human beings are to be found who no longer wish to go along with the stress of living by means of experiences which are sustained through the tiresome striving with all the powers of one's own activity. These people are beginning to understand that the meaning of human life lies deeper than all human culture of the self. They are beginning to seek an Other for their own human longing. They are seeking an Other who does not simply manipulate the experience of meaning and happiness, implying nothingness, but rather carries them and gives them a supportive freedom.

It is worthwhile to be a Redemptorist today because the encounter with the God of Jesus Christ provides such an Other. We embrace the liberating life of Jesus in the name of our order. However, for others to be able to experience the genuine caring Other or God in us and our way of life, we must not behave as if we owned this experience of God. It would be ludicrous to try and dangle before others a haughty, human maturity or a self-assured, religious competence. That would be an affair whose dishonesty and hidden pomposity would blast itself apart. Not only would such a life be terribly stressful, but it would also be sad and, indeed, both infirm and incapable of truly living because of its constant duplicity against all that is human. And every person who is honestly searching would very quickly feel the helplessness of such self-alienation.

We ourselves are searchers. But because Christ invites us to himself and stirs the hearts of human beings through his Spirit, we are able to bring others with us on the long journey's search for him without manipulating them. Because Christ does not deceive anyone or override their autonomy or mature independence—and because he is the ultimate foundation of freedom and happiness—we are able to work in the service of his authentic power and approach others about him, as well as to offer them his way. "At this point," says Saint Alphonsus, the founder of our order, "it is almost impossible for a human being not to return to God." He adds, "Furthermore it is obvious that God also is helping us in other ways."[5] Perhaps we might then succeed in working together for a society in which violence and aggression do not prevail again; a society in which democracy and nonviolent solutions to social conflicts will truly and consistently be lived; a society which will not egoistically use prosperity and cultural development for oneself while protecting itself from the need of others. Rather a society will be fashioned for the worldwide development of all peoples and all places on this earth and for the participation of all human beings; a society in which each human being has the power to respect the rights of the environment and to enter into a realistic peace with nature; a society in which the human person learns to accept his or her limits as an individual and as part of a technological society.

Notes

1. See F. X. Kaufmann, W. Kerber, and P. M. Zulehner, *Ethos und Religion bei Führungskräften. Eine Studie im Auftrag des Arbeitskreises für Führungskräfte in der Wirtschaft (Fragen einer neuen Weltkultur 3)*, München, 1986.
2. See Karl Rahner, "Theological Considerations on Secularization and Atheism," in *Theological Investigations*, XI (London: Darton, Longman & Todd; New York: The Seabury Press, 1974): 166–184.
3. P. M. Zulehner, H. Denz, Hermann, *Wie Europa lebt und glaubt* (Europäische Wertestudie), Düsseldorf, 1993.
4. H. Stenger, "Kompetenz und Identität," in: H. Stenger, ed. *Eignung für die Berufe der Kirche*, Freiburg, 1988, pp. 131–133; this quote from p. 57.
5. Albino Luciani (Pope John Paul I), *Im Geiste Jesu. Das Beispiel des heiligen Alfons von Liguori*, Wien, 1981, p. 29.

23

WITNESSES IN TIME OF PERSECUTION

Volodymir Sterniuk, C.Ss.R.
Province of Lviv
Translated by George Perejda, C.Ss.R.
Province of Yorkton

1. Introduction

You ask about my thoughts and my story, about my vocation to the religious life, how I saw it, and how it turned out.

How it was… I have to say that a significant role is played by divine Providence: "Wondrous are the ways of the Lord; who can fathom them?"

I was born February 12, 1907, in Pustomiti, a little town near Lviv. My father was a Ukrainian Catholic priest, as were two of his brothers, Peter and Myron. My brother, Evstachy, also became a priest. I was brought up in a very religious and national atmosphere: both of my parents were related through marriage with national and cultural figures in the Ukrainian community, such as the Krushelnicky's and the Konovalets's.

My youth was spent in the difficult period of World War I, a time of great political and national unrest and renewal and disillusion for Ukrainians. For my schooling, I spent two years in a preparatory school in my hometown, two more years in Lviv, and four years in the first Ukrainian gymnasium (the juvenate, as it was then called) allowed in Lviv. I was in the gymnasium, and the superior was Father Ivan Bucko, not yet a bishop, of course. The Redemptorists used to come down to hear the confessions of the boys, to encourage them to join the religious life, and to go to Belgium to study.

Father Bucko said, "If they want you to go, if they want to send you to

Belgium, then go. If you decide to say in the monastery, good. If you decide not to stay, then you can always return home." So I went, in this fashion, with the Redemptorists, to Belgium. There I finished the gymnasium. In 1926, I stayed on for novitiate, and I've remained with the Redemptorists ever since.

I did my priestly studies in Belgium—two years of philosophy and four years of theology. In 1931, before entering my last year of theology, I was ordained a priest by Bishop Ladyka, who was visiting from Winnipeg, Canada, to recruit priests for his Canada-wide diocese. When I finished my theological studies, I went back home to Ukraine.

I soon found myself with other Redemptorists—Fathers V. Velych-kovsky, R. Bachtalowsky, Z. Kovalyk—doing apostolic work in Volhynia. After several years of apostolic work in the area, our confrere, Nicholas Charnetsky, had been consecrated bishop and was the apostolic adminis-trator for this missionary activity in this part of Ukraine.

You must know that work here, in the northwestern area of Ukraine after World War I and the redrawing of political boundaries, was extremely difficult—and the difficulties were caused, for the most part, by political and ecclesiastical policies that did not favor the emergence of a strong Ukrai-nian Catholic community. The Redemptorists had been allowed to come here from Lviv because they were seen as a lesser evil: because they had been organized and trained by Belgian Redemptorists who were originally Roman Catholic, they were thought to be more amenable to polonizing and ultimately latinizing policies.

But, as so often happens, the ways of the Lord confound the wisdom of men. The Belgian Redemptorists that came to Lviv at the request of Metropolitan Sheptytsky, who had earlier seen their work among the Ukrai-nians in Canada and was determined to have them work in his own country, proved themselves to be truly servants of the Lord's way, as was Saint Paul in similar circumstances, when working among the Gentiles. They, and the Ukrainian men who were attracted so bountifully by their apostolic work and witness, labored most worthily in the vineyard entrusted to them by the Lord, and thus earned the blessing of the Lord and of his people—and the persistent enmity of others.

This I know, from my many years of work and experience in that Volhynian vineyard, greater calamities were to follow in the wake of the German and then the Soviet occupations. In the prewar years of the 1930s, I was in Kovel, Ternopol, and Stanyslaviv working for our people.

World War II broke out on September 1, 1939. By the end of that same month, the Soviets, thanks to the agreement reached by Ribbentrop and Molotov, were in control of Western Ukraine. Although the full brutality of their presence would not be felt until after their second coming, after the German occupation, the Soviet authorities began a systematic persecution of the Ukrainian Catholic Church and its religious life, at every level. Not directly, as yet—that would come later—but indirectly, by making its activities as difficult as possible.

Like trying to pressure the Belgian confreres—for example, Father De Vocht, *ihumen*-superior of the Lviv house—as nationals hostile to the Nazi-Soviet Alliance, or Axis, to leave the country. Like imposing very high "taxes" on churches and monasteries, and thus threatening their closure; like occupying religious and church institutions and buildings.

During the winter of 1940, I think it was, the security division of the NKVD decided to move in with the Redemptorists: they took over the main floor of the monastery and allowed the priests and brothers to continue using the upper floor and the church. The presence of the NKVD in this Redemptorist monastery was not very pleasant, or very apostolic. It meant, really, living with the devil himself—and with constant surveillance of course. But *ihumen* Father De Vocht used to joke about it, saying: "If those three young men, with God's help, could survive in the blazing Chaldean furnace, then all the more reason for us Redemptorists to survive here amid the NKVD."

But somehow we did, though it was rather crowded, with about fifteen priests, brothers, and students on the upper floor. The devil only knows how many were crowded into the lower regions of this particular Redemptorist monastery!

The Redemptorist church by the monastery on Zyblikevych was, in spite of everything, a center of religious activity. It was not only Ukrainian Catholics but also many Orthodox that thronged there. Often, too, there were strangers, in civilian clothes and sometimes in uniform; many of them—women, for the most part—would come to confession and to holy Communion quite devoutly. In time, they came covertly, to have their children baptized and their marriages blessed. Many would show up on the feast of Theophany, Christ's baptism in the Jordan River, to obtain the blessed water. They would come with large bottles and containers in order to share the holy water with others who couldn't come. On Great and Holy Saturday, before Easter, they would bring their paskha-bread and baskets to be blessed.

In late June of 1941, the Germans turned on their erstwhile partners, and soon took control of our lands: they were in Lviv by the end of June. Under the German occupation, the situation became somewhat better. Many of the religious buildings and institutions that had been taken over or confiscated by the Soviets were returned and restored to their former uses. Seminaries were reopened, including our studendate in Holosko and our juvenate in Zboiska. We had several ordinations of our finishing students, mostly by Bishop Nicholas, who was living at our house in Lviv. We were able to go back to Kovel, in Volhynia, to work (but not Bishop Nicholas Charnetsky) and to Ternopol. During the Nazi occupation, and a bit longer, I served in Lviv at our monastery on Zyblikevych Avenue, now called Ivan Franko Avenue, and in the nearby church of Our Mother of Perpetual Help. For the most part, we were able to have regular services, to preach missions and retreats, and to do whatever was needed in these distressing times. As the Nazis revealed more and more of their true plans for the future of Ukraine, more and more evoked the resistance of the people.

Until 1944

The Soviets were approaching, again. Because there was no hope whatsoever of continuing missionary work after a renewal of Soviet occupation, Father Van de Maele returned to Belgium. Father Velychkovsky replaced him in Ternopol. It was there that the Soviets subsequently arrested him and dispatched him to prison in Kyiv, where he was confined for a long time. He was brought to trial and sentenced to die for the "crime" of being faithful to his Church. The sentence was later transmuted to ten years of hard labor in the laager camps of Vorkuta.

By the end of July 1944, Western Ukraine was again under Soviet occupation. For about three months, there was a relative calm in the storm that came upon our country—much like the eye of a hurricane—until the death of our ancient patriarch, Metropolitan Andrei Sheptytsky on November 1. Then, it seems, the ruthless winds of oppression and persecution really let loose.

The preparatory phase was an concerted onslaught of printed invective attacking the now-deceased Sheptytsky, the pope, and the Church. In other words, the Catholic Church in general, and most specifically, the Ukrainian Catholic Church.

Then, in one single night, between the tenth and eleventh of April,

1945, the entire Ukrainian Catholic episcopate was arrested, in a coordinated attack on the leadership of the Ukrainian Church: Metropolitan Josyf Slipyj, Bishops Khomyshyn, Liatyshevsky, Budka, and our Nicholas Charnetsky were grabbed by squads of GPU agents, whisked off to prison, went through months, years, really, of "interrogation," and then, of course, were found guilty of "collaborating with the enemy," of "anti-Soviet activity," and sentenced to long-term labors: five, ten years, whatever—as with so many others, these numbers usually turned out in reality to be much more.

Once they had removed the bishops and a few other key priests and religious, the Soviets could then proceed with their plan to abolish the Ukrainian Church. With three Judas priests, two of whom had been secretly consecrated Orthodox bishops as figureheads, they staged a gathering of coerced priests—relatively small, compared to the majority of clergy who stayed away—that dutifully, according to Moscow's dictates, agreed to the liquidation of our Church. Governmental agencies filmed this orchestrated performance—and officially there was no longer a Ukrainian Catholic Church in our land. All our churches and institutions were handed over to the Orthodox or appropriated by the government; and dissenting priests—that is, priests who remained faithful—were dispersed, many of them to parts north, and required to work menially, lest they be indicted as "social parasites."

I had been living and working at our Zyblikevych house. When that was taken away from us, I went to Zboiska, where our juvenate and novitiate were housed, but that, too, was taken away for governmental purposes. What purposes? The monastery was converted into an Intourist travel agency, and the lovely church served as their restaurant for travelers. The Zboiska buildings became the educational facilities for cadres of another kind of service.

Now I had to find a job and a place to live. Some good people got me work at a library. After a while, I became aware that the guardians of the peace were keeping an eye on me, and eventually I was arrested—reading a book in the library. They told me I was under suspicion of having contacts with underground anti-Soviet groups. Their version of the truth was different than mine....

They accused: "You're guilty of hearing the confessions of underground agents in private homes." Of course, among the faithful whom I did confess, there might have been individuals who worked for the underground, but how could I know or choose all those who came to me for confession?

So I spoke up, something like this: "Anyone who comes to me for confession does not have written on his forehead, 'I work for the underground.' All kinds of people come to confession. I don't pick and choose them; I don't fill out forms on them; I don't ask their names….Under the Russian Empire, by order of Peter I, their priests were ordered to inform on those who confessed. But you boast about having abolished czarist methods; so why are you acting this way with me?"

They were not very pleased with me, nor I with them. Eventually, they assigned me five years of imprisonment—up north, of course, where the climate is brisk. They didn't even bother about staging a court session. But they made sure I had a few knocks and bruises before they released me, to remember them by.

The days and the months of the five-year term passed in work, in prayer, in doing what I could for others. I made use of various possibilities to bring people the Word of God and to fulfill at least minimally the religious needs of so many lost sheep. Often I would have some kind of services in homes, in a familiar setting, even though I risked the unhappiness of various overseers.

On one occasion some good people asked me to have a service in the home of one of the inhabitants. As I was approaching the house at the appointed time, I noticed a divisional chief of the camp administration nearby, watching the house. Somehow, though, that didn't scare me off; I decided, maybe imprudently, to act decisively. I entered the house and, though the NKVD man was still around outside, I went ahead with the service. No disruption; nobody broke into the house. The NKVD angel outside may have decided that there was no violation of the legalities concerning religious cult: there were no children taking part in the service, which was strictly forbidden by law.

In any case, the service ended without incident. And I drew a very important conclusion: sometimes one just has to show resolution, determination. Without it that day, there would have been no service for the people. It was a good lesson for other days too.

In 1952, I was released, with the legal restriction to reside only in one area of our vast country—the area of my hometown near Lviv. I was going on forty-six years of age, and there was so much to do for our Church, shattered and shaken, for our people hemmed in with fear, terror, and misfortune. But what could I accomplish now? I used to dream in my boyhood years that when I went out into the wide world to seek knowledge and training, I would get an education, gain wisdom, and return to my own country to share all that I had learned with my people. But the years had slipped by and my heart ached because all my training would be of no use now to my people....

But that's the way it was, like it or not! *"C'est la vie!"* we used to say. One has to take oneself in hand and begin life anew. It wouldn't be easy, I knew: the times were cruel There had been strength enough, with God's help, to survive prisons and camp. I did not succumb then to the temptation. I can look openly into the face of our suffering Church and people: I did not betray them; I did carry the cross of Christ's suffering. I did not break. And I have returned with a clear conscience to my native threshold—not an invalid, not broken, but enriched with other kinds of knowledge, with precious, though bitter, life experience. So—be with me, dear God, in my continuing pilgrimage, in these new challenges and circumstances!

And the new challenge was this: all former Ukrainian Catholic priests and religious who had not yet reached the age for retirement and pension and who had not accepted serving the official Russian Orthodox Church were obliged to fulfill "work obligations"—in other words, they had to have some kind of job. For the most part, though, priests and religious had only their theological and religious training with no secular professional skills, so they had to find work that did not require special professional qualifications. You would find priests working as night watchmen, janitors, porters, messengers, orderlies; less often as bookkeepers, medics, accountants, and suchlike. Even those who had, for instance, pedagogical training and qualifications for teaching could not hope to find work as a teacher. Ministers of religion, and all the more Ukrainian Catholic priests who had also been catechist-teachers, were forbidden access to pedagogical work in an atheistic society—they might corrupt young minds with "religious myths and fables."

Father Volodymyr Sterniuk, former pastor of souls and missionary, became a worker in the labor department of the city of Lviv, in the division devoted to environmental greenery: in simpler words, I worked in one of the city parks. For a while, I had lots of fresh air! Then I worked as a kind of accountant. Then as an auxiliary in a medical-emergency service. In a word, I tried to do what I could, trying always to serve the spiritual needs of the faithful. The faithful were everywhere. And they found me, and I them. God be praised!

More time passed, and more of those who had been sent off for "Siberian holidays" appeared among us, including priests—not all of them, of course. Some did not survive; others were not allowed access to the city. Father Velychkovsky returned to Lviv in 1955, and again continued actively to carry out pastoral work. Discreetly, as we always did. In 1959, he was secretly appointed bishop of the catacomb Ukrainian Catholic Church. In January 1963, when Metropolitan Slipyj was released from prison, and on his way to Rome, Father Velychkovsky managed to meet him in Moscow before his departure. There, in a hotel room, he was consecrated bishop and entrusted with the care of our Church. Although our other bishops were no longer living, Metropolitan Slipyj had to leave the country, the canonical existence of our Ukrainian Church was maintained; and Vasyl Velychkovsky returned to his flock as bishop.

Vasyl—Kyr Vasyl, really, now, but we had to avoid using the title, of course—soon became aware that he was very much under suspicion and was being closely tracked. For the security of our Church, he had to prepare for the inevitable and to make sure that there was someone to replace him. He knew me, of course, maybe too well: we had worked together as Redemptorists in Volhynia and in Stanyslaviv and Ternopol, and Lviv, both before and after our Siberian vacations; and he had been my *ihumen*. In the summer of 1964, we spoke seriously of the need for an assistant bishop; and he succeeded in allaying my reluctances and hesitations; and I became even more his auxiliary and assistant. Three years later, I reached my pension age, and then I could use all my time for the care of our Church.

And there was so much to do! People everywhere, more and more, were becoming disillusioned with the false promises of the Soviet paradise, of the dead-endedness of life without God. At the same time, the older priests were dying out, and the rare candidates for their replacement had to be prepared for their formidable work. There were few books or resources. I tried writing some things, but they kept disappearing or getting lost in the many house searches and confiscations.

In October 1968, a new wave of antireligious persecution in Western Ukraine was initiated, especially against Ukrainian Catholics. There was talk that the official Russian Church had complained to the powers that be that there was too much resistance still from Ukrainian Catholics, even though they were supposed to be dead and nonexistent for more than twenty years. In any case, the penal squads were given orders to root out the remnants of the "nonexistent" Ukrainian Catholic Church—as a fitting tribute to mark the centenary of Lenin's birthday in 1970.

As a result, in Lviv itself, search warrants were issued and carried out simultaneously on the living quarters of eleven of our priests, including Philemon Kurchaba, Vasyl Velychkovsky, and myself. Anything that in any way resembled religion was removed: vestments, of course, and religious literature and pictures, crosses, icons, candles, wine; but also tape recorders, cameras, and any money at hand.

Then the arrests began. On January 2, 1969, Kyr Vasyl was arrested. Officially, believe it or not, he was sentenced and imprisoned for—in Kyr Vasyl's own words—"having written a pamphlet on the icon of the Holy Mother of Perpetual Help, because in it I supposedly slandered Soviet reality." Three years he suffered up north; they released him in February 1972, so he wouldn't die on them there and to get him out of the country. He died on June 30, 1973, in Winnipeg, Canada, where our confrere Metropolitan Maxim Hermaniuk had graciously made him welcome.

The searches and questionings went on throughout the entire year of 1969. Within the span of a few months, I went through three such searches myself. They were brutal—icons were trashed and trampled, documents destroyed, many items taken that were not recorded or itemized.

We survived; we kept on doing God's work, in God's good time. And, in God's good time, the times became better. We got through the 1970s. Gradually, there was more hope, more help, more confidence, in God and in the vindication of his truth. Then the winds of change really began to blow, truly the breath of the Spirit. The Golgotha of our Great Friday was definitely changing to the graying of Great Saturday, and the urgent and eager expectation of *Velykden*, the Great Day of our resurrection.

For which we thank God.

2. Our Most Holy Redeemer
...and our Holy Mother of Perpetual Help

Well, I am tired now, after all this talking and this remembrancing. But I shouldn't leave without sketching out at least a review of things Redemptorist, for the Redemptorists of Ukraine have been worthy companions of the suffering Savior and share in his Resurrection and in the resurrection of his Church. So, please, bear with me yet a little longer....

The Bolshevik occupation of forty years suspended—though never completely, I can vouch for that!—the missionary activity of the Redemptorists. During the underground years, the Fathers very cautiously and very bravely worked as well as they could for the spiritual good of the people.

Though, to be sure, there were losses. During the first Soviet occupation from 1939 to 1941, Father. Z. Kovalyk and Father M. Peretiatko were arrested. Father Kovalyk died in prison, and there are stories about that. Father Peretiatko, marvelously, ended up in Canada, with the Ukrainian Redemptorists working there. In 1945, Father Velychkovsky was arrested; from 1946 to 1950, Fathers Kutsach, Ivan Ziatyk, Pyliuch, Onyshcuk, Mysach, Potoreyko, Yurkiw, R. Bachtalowsky, P. Kozak, Pelech, the student Smal, and Brothers Avsentij and Ireneus were arrested. Father Joseph de Vocht, the last of our Belgians in Ukraine, and *proto-ihumen*, or major superior since 1933, was expelled by the Soviets on December 17, 1948. Before he left for Belgium, he handed over his duties to Father Ivan Ziatyk, who, on Good Friday 1953, was arrested, tortured, and clubbed to death in Siberia.

Since then, until the full emergence of our Church from the catacombs, the major superior was Philemon Kurchaba. In 1990, when the newly designated CSSR Province of Lviv held its first-ever chapter, with Father General Lasso proudly present, as confreres cautiously got to know one another, the young Ihor Wozniak—young in years, but a longtime product of the underground Church, and protégé of the indomitable Father Roman Bachtalowsky—was elected *proto-ihumen* and is now serving his second term of office.

After serving out their incarcerations, many of the Redemptorists returned to Halychyna, while others were forced—some chose, though—to remain in various parts of the vast Soviet Union. Which, in God's unfathomable way, proved its own wisdom: the Ukrainian branch of the Redemptorist tree now has been transplanted and taken good root far beyond Halychyna. The Lviv Province now has a mission station in Russia, in the Kemerovsk Province, in the town of Prokopievsk: Father Y. Spodar works there. There are vocations now from Siberia where so many latter-day martyrs nourished the soil with their blood and sweat, tears and prayers.

With God's continuing assistance and blessings, there will be other foundations, renewed life, and spiritual abundance among God's long-suffering children in our beloved Ukraine.

3. A Few Words About Formation

Until 1934, our young men went to Belgium for their priestly studies; that year, visas were no longer available to our students, so we set up our studendate in Zboiska, with Father Joseph Korba teaching church history and V. Malanchuk teaching philosophy. In 1936, the novitiate was established in Zboiska—the juvenate was already there—and the studendate was transferred to Holosko, another suburb of Lviv. Father Joseph Korba taught dogmatics; Father Roman Bachtalowsky, sacred scripture; Father M. Pyliuch, canon law; Father O. Dizitter, moral theology. In addition, Father Dizitter was prefect of students, and supervised their spiritual formation. Under the *ihumen,* Father J. Ghekiere, the studendate was enlarged with the addition of another building.

The work of the studendate was hampered by the World War II, and the first coming of the Soviets. Most of the students were evacuated to Poland, where they continued their studies in Tuchow; a few remained for much-interrupted studies in Holosko, until the Germans came. The students returned from Poland, and for a little while regular formation could continue. Our first fruits of the Holosko house of studies came when our Bishop Charnetsky ordained five candidates to the priesthood, in Lviv, on September 2, 1939.

In 1944, the Soviets returned. Repressions began the next year: regular studies came to an end, almost all the monasteries were taken over. In 1951 all religious were dispersed. The gray cloud of the underground had descended upon us.

Under such conditions, there could be no normal studies or regular formation. But the Fathers did whatever they could. Even for the few vocations we had during those dark days, they tried to give our young men the necessary and required training. Textbooks were few; various handwritten notes and papers were saved from numerous searches and confiscations. The main source of formation was the life and the learning and the living word and example of the teacher.

The first professors in this hard school were Fathers D. Lebiak, P. Kozak, and E. Pelech. Later, in the latter 1970s others began to teach: Fathers P. Dmuchovsky. P. Majik, V. Mychajliuk. The persisting novice master and prefect of studies was Father M. Lemishka, whom everybody called *Dziadzo*—the Old Man: during the entire time of the underground, it was he who provided the spiritual formation to all the novices and students.

After his death—God give him rest and reward!—the novice master and prefect of studies were Father E. Smal' and M. Vynnytskyj. At present, the novice master is Father M. Voloshyn, and the prefect of studies is Father V. Spodar.

In that long, difficult period—a time of enduring, surviving, patiently and prayerfully and hopefully—actual vocations really began to come to us only in 1966. "Regular" studies—if one can thus call them (referring to both terms, *regular* and *studies*) because the teaching Father would come to some agreed-upon building once or twice a week after finishing his allotted work; and on the other days each "student" studied on his own— began in 1976.

Thus it was, until full emergence from the underground—that is, until 1990. With the renewal among us of freedom, normal studies began in the monastery at Holosko, which was returned to the Redemptorist by the government. The first rector assigned to Holosko was Father C. Meniok, himself a product of the underground, with Fathers E. Pelech and V. Mychajliuk as professors. Beginning in 1992, students began to study in the Warsaw CSSR Province, in Cracow and Tuchow.

With the emergence of the Redemptorists, and the thawing of the Soviet Union and the proclamation of a sovereign Ukraine, the Redemptorists have regained almost all their former properties that survived the hurricane years. The monastery in Holosko, and on Ivan Franko Avenue (formerly Zyblikevych). In Zboiska, for several reasons, it is not advisable, so far, to reclaim our buildings there.

In Ternopol, a church was reconstructed for us to replace and restitute the one that the Soviets demolished in 1962; the Redemptorists then built their monastery nearby. In that same city, too, the Redemptorists, through their own efforts and at their own cost, with the generous assistance of good people, have raised a grand church, dedicated to the Holy Mother of God, Our Perpetual Help, to serve the spiritual needs of this bustling city. In Stanyslaviv, also through their own efforts and at their own cost, with generous assistance, they are building a church that may be adequate for the spiritual needs of the long-starved populace; a monastery is also in the planning there.

In Lviv, also, the state has relinquished two churches, both of which were in very sad shape—that's what happens after some forty years of usage as a garage or warehouse—but our confreres, and their good people, have been working on them. In Vinnytsi, too, the Redemptorists have established themselves and are building a church—and have much to do.

And so, life goes on....In God's holy light, in his abundant and great mercy, the Ukrainian Redemptorists will continue to give witness to our Most Holy Redeemer, now and forever.

In the Name of the Father, and of the Son, and of the Holy Spirit. Amen!

24

INSERTION IN THE
WAY OF LIFE OF THE PEOPLE

Guillermo Giraldo, C.Ss.R.
Province of Bogotá
Translated by Gary Lauenstein, C.Ss.R.
Province of Denver

1. Why Did I Become a Redemptorist?

My Redemptorist missionary vocation is not due to personal merit, nor was it initially by my own choice. I did not choose to become a Redemptorist. "You have not chosen me, I am the one who chose you, and I have destined you to bear fruit." By his own gracious, free willing of his love, the Lord called me to work for his kingdom in the Redemptorist family. I heard his voice, I welcomed his suggestion...I went in step after Jesus...I came, as the first disciples did...I saw where he dwelled and...I stayed with him. For that reason, I became a Redemptorist.

1.1 Or rather, why did the Lord make me a Redemptorist?

The Lord took advantage of simple circumstances to call me. Father Albert Ayerbe, Redemptorist missionary, came to our fifth grade class in my school in Pensilvania, Colombia, seeking vocation prospects. The song "*Dominique*," which he played on his harmonica, interested me more than the idea of becoming a missionary. I mentioned the visit of the missionary to the school to my mother; a comment which other children no doubt made that same day over their lunches. I had no intention of becoming a missionary, nor of "signing up." My mother piously presumed that I had insinuated

to her that I had a desire to go to the seminary, so she decided to go with me
to the parish to speak with the missionary. It was around seven in the evening
on a November night. The next morning Father Ayerbe would be traveling
on the bus. He had already looked over the academic records and grades of
the "candidates." I was not a bad student, but neither was I excellent. Without being able to verify any personal data, and to protect the seminary from
having a dull student in its midst, he gave me the guidelines of the seminary
to read and a list of things I should bring. My strong point was reading: I
favorably impressed Father Ayerbe, who, a few moments before he had to
go to bed, enrolled me as his last candidate for the seminary. Ten of us boys
left, bringing to a total of sixty students in the first year of studies at
Manizales.

Thinking about the call the Lord made to me, I believe it was a response to the Gospel dedication of the Redemptorists of that region. In the
fifties the Redemptorist missionaries spread throughout the rural areas where
we lived. Mom and Dad recall the very moving sermons of Father Argemiro
Gallego. They recall with emotion a great wooden cross that they raised at
the end of the mission on the hill named for the village of San Juan, where
I was born in May 1953. Without pretending to be Paul or Jeremiah, I could
say the Lord called me from my mother's womb. When the Redemptorist
missionaries were proclaiming the message of salvation in that area, the
Lord decided to choose me as a missionary of the Congregation and to
make the Congregation a gift to me. That is the way I see it now, in the light
of faith; and I gladly thank the Lord. I would not be able to make sense of
my life outside my Redemptorist family. From the age of ten, I loved and
belonged to this "beloved family of Jesus Christ." Since my entrance into
the minor seminary, I was formed in the demanding and caring traditions of
the Redemptorists. The love of God carries with it, from my boyhood, the
stamp of the Redemptorist Congregation. The Lord granted me the grace
of "being born again" and bestowed on me the Congregation, the gift of a
new family in the Spirit. In it I want to bring to completion the mission of
my life and to end in it my earthly journey. I beg of Jesus Christ the gift of
perseverance in the Congregation and the grace and joy of giving over my
life for the Congregation, following Jesus Christ in preaching the Gospel to
the poor.

I wanted to follow Christ as a missionary, so I joined the Eucharistic
Crusade. Every morning at six-thirty, I participated in the Eucharist. On
Thursdays I joined a group of other boys of the Eucharistic Crusade for the

adoration of the Blessed Sacrament. There the desire increased in me to serve Christ as a missionary. What idea could I have had, at my age, of the "Redemptorist charism" of religious life? The parish priest called my mother and advised her to have me switch to the diocesan seminary. He made an offer to her to pay for my lodging expenses and the costs of my formation, and warned her that religious would not be able to help their own families. My mother was indifferent to the suggestion of the pastor. It must have seemed less than honorable to her, because she wanted to give a son to God and it didn't matter whether I would be able to give her support. At that time Mom and Dad had fourteen children. Another four were born later. Luis Gonzaga, three years younger, is also a Redemptorist missionary. (Please note: he died in June 1995.)

Through the grace of God, I persevered. During minor seminary, we began to experience profound changes in the liturgy of the Church, in Church discipline, in the way of orienting and directing seminarians. The flourishing number of two hundred seminarians declined within months. We ended our time in the minor seminary with a good group: twenty-four made novitiate; sixteen made profession. When we went on to the major seminary, the great crisis hit us: at the end of our first year, thirteen classmates left. During the next year, everyone left. From that stage and its formative process only I remained, by the grace of God. I attribute my perseverance in the Redemptorist Congregation to two things: prayer and my commitment to the poor.

By custom, and even through a tendency to laziness in my temperament, I always fostered within myself a devotion to the Blessed Sacrament and devoted long hours to the presence of Jesus in the Eucharist. I am happy to be able to say that it was Christ in the Eucharist who helped me overcome all my doubts and crises when my classmates left. Even after my formation, I have spent my priesthood and my missionary work under the gaze of Jesus in the Eucharist. That is what I learned from my Redemptorist formators, reading about it in the works of Saint Alphonsus and admiring his great love for Jesus Christ in the sacrament of the Eucharist.

The second reason for my perseverance was my commitment to the poor. Since minor seminary days, I taught reading and writing and catechetics in the nearby poor neighborhoods. The same occurred in the novitiate and in the major seminary. Through the grace of God, I had a tangible preference for the most poor, a spirit that was inculcated in me in the seminary and through my reading about Saint Alphonsus and the history of the Congregation and by the very charism in which I was trained and instructed. The habit of being continually in chapel together with Jesus Christ and this link and solidarity with the poor are the two pillars which have given solidity to my perseverance in my Redemptorist vocation.

1.2 Why do I stay a Redemptorist?

"Stay a Redemptorist": beautiful expression! Because being a Redemptorist is not a static reality. It is a process of configuring oneself to Christ, evangelizer of the poor. Every day we become Redemptorists a little more. Every day the Lord repeats his invitation to us through the poor and the needy and in urgent pastoral needs. We, accepting his challenge, choose anew the charism, forcing ourselves to be more faithful to him. I believe that I stay a Redemptorist, first of all, through the grace of God which has given me joy in persevering. I also believe that I stay a Redemptorist by finding in this service to the poor a perennial, continual, fresh, and always current experience of the Gospel. Because, if there is more joy in giving than in receiving, in this charism there is opportunity for giving oneself totally to the poor without hope of reward and there is sufficient cause for achieving happiness, a sense of life—the full realization of one's wishes.

Evangelical service among the poor is always urgent. In the conditions of our continent, where poverty increases and people move to the cities leaving behind their fields, our charism continues having a special attraction and an unequaled vitality. I will say with Paul: "One thing I do, forgetting what has now passed, what remains behind, and I sprint forward to the goal; I wish to reach Christ Jesus who reached out to me first." As a gift of the grace of God, I hope for fidelity until death in the Redemptorist charism, not simply "staying" in the Congregation within the confines of institutions, but a "living" in it, seeking each day a greater dedication to the poor. Seeking to "reinvent" the charism of Saint Alphonsus in new circumstances and in a new epoc of history.

If the General Government is asking me for an article about "insertion into the circumstances of life of the ordinary people," it is because the Council feels I have had some experience with this. Before talking about the topic, I would like to give an accounting of my simple experiences of insertion.

In the minor seminary, I taught reading and writing in the poor neighborhoods near the seminary. Tutoring, catechetics, and help for the poor were my first pastoral work. In the novitiate I—and four other companions—was able to take charge of the poorest neighborhood in the nearby locality of Guacarí, a neighborhood where the prostitutes plied their trade. During philosophy and theology, I worked in poor neighborhoods near our seminary in Suba. The pastoral plan consisted of visiting homes, forming groups and making a network of Christian groups in these neighborhoods; it also consisted of bringing alms to the poor, distributing goods, taking many of the sick in the seminary's car to health centers or to the hospitals in the city. I alternated studies with pastoral work in the poor neighborhoods.

Ordained to the priesthood in March 1979, the Lord destined me for a team of itinerant missionaries with whom I worked for ten years. My experience of insertion among the poor was that of every Redemptorist missionary: share with the people; visit neighborhoods, villages, apartment complexes; take lodging with families; eat in their homes; live with the people in order that, with that advantage, one might announce the Gospel to them. I spent this period of my life using a style of insertion proper to the itinerant mission. I was never inserted for a very long time in any one area.

My period of insertion for a lengthy time in one area was experienced two years ago in poor communities in the city of Barranquilla, Colombia. The Bogotá Province of Redemptorists created a missionary team for urban pastoral work in poor areas, and we took up residence in the Colombian Carribean. Here we found large stretches of the city where people lived without any contact with the Church. There persisted what Puebla calls "a Catholic cultural matrix." Christian traditions were learned from radio or television or by family custom, but they have not been evangelized to any depth, which would help them to assimilate the faith in a personal and committed way. In other words: over a religious base that is only culturally Catholic, it is necessary to bring about first evangelization. The three of us missionaries who underwent this experience spent two years in one family's house, paying rent, living with the people, working with the communities in the marginalized areas where the poor people live. We are an inserted Redemptorist community. We live a full community life, but in solidarity with the style of life of the simple people of the sector. We are a community, but we do not have a canonically established house. The province does not always understand the extent of the work, because its fruit is not immediate but in bits and over a long period of time. On occasion there is a lack of understanding, but in general the experience is appreciated.

2. Why Speak of Insertion in the Poor and Marginalized Way of Life of the Common People?

The supreme norm for religious life is the following of Christ. The intention of Christ when he began to proclaim the kingdom of God was this: "The Spirit of the Lord is upon me, because he has consecrated me. He sent me to bring Good News to the poor, to announce liberty to the captive and sight to the blind. To free those who are oppressed and to proclaim a year of favor from the Lord....Today these prophecies which we have just heard are accomplished" (Luke 4:18f).

Since Old Testament times God decided in favor of the poor. He took as his own possession a poor people. He dedicated himself to being the liberator of a people in slavery. He was doing all this through his divine method of teaching so that they might discover their vocation of service to all nations and to awaken in that people hope for the Messiah.

Jesus assembled the new messianic people from among the poor and proclaimed the supreme happiness of the human being: "happy are the poor." After Christ, the Holy Spirit made an option for the poor in the new community of salvation—the Church: "Look, brothers and sisters, who have been called. There are not many wise people, in the sense of worldly-wise, among us, not many powerful people, nor many of the nobility. Rather, God has chosen the foolish of this world to confound the wise; God has called the weak of this world to confound the strong" (1 Corinthians 1:26–28). Christianity initiated from the place of the poor the mission of evangelizing the world. In spite of the long centuries in which the Church tried to evangelize from the pinacle of power, the Holy Spirit has not permitted that the word of prophecy fall apart and has pushed Christians to go out to the poor.

Our Congregation had its origin in that impulse of the Holy Spirit in favor of the poor, raised up in Saint Alphonsus, who, "as rich as he was became poor"; and although he was a brilliant Neapolitan gentleman, he mounted on a humble burro and rode off to his encounter with the poor goatherds of Scala. We owe our existence in the Church to an act of obedience to the Holy Spirit, who wanted to push forward a "process of insertion," inspired by Saint Alphonsus and taken up by his first companions. We continue this response of obedience, and we look in every moment to "reinvent the charism," inserting ourselves among the poor again.

Preference for situations where there is pastoral need, that is, for evangelization in the strict sense together with the choice in favor of the
poor is the very reason why the Congregation exists in the Church,
and is the badge of its fidelity to the vocation it has received (Constitution 5).

Indeed the apostolic work of the Congregation is distinguished more
by its missionary dynamism than by any particular forms of activity;
in other words, by evangelization in the true sense, and by service of
persons and groups who are poor and more neglected within the Church
and society (Constitution 14).

When Christianity became a mass movement, religious took on by
preference—though never in an exclusive way—the living out of Christian
radicalism and remained in the Church as a "sacrament," that is, as a visible
and effective sign of that radicalism. Thus religious have stuck to the original mission of the Church of "evangelizing the poor" and have helped the
Church to preserve that mission even to our day.

Our Congregation, following this line of fidelity to Christ and to the
Church, has made its preferential option for the poor, and has raised to
the level of one of its Constitutions this commitment which cannot be re-
fused:

Indeed the Congregation's mandate to evangelize the poor is directed
to the liberation and salvation of the whole human person. The members have the duty of preaching the Gospel explicitly and of showing
solidarity with the poor by promoting their fundamental rights to justice and freedom. The means employed must be effective and at the
same time consistent with the Gospel (Constitution 5b).

Redemptorists can never be deaf to the cry of the poor and the oppressed, but have the duty to search for ways of helping them, so that
they themselves will be able to overcome the evils that oppress them.
This essential element of the gospel must never be lacking in the proclamation of the word of God (General Statutes 09).

The option for the poor by the Church in Latin America is for our
Congregation, itself the standard bearer for evangelical radicalism in favor
of the poor, a challenge and a task: "We invite everyone, without distinction of class, to accept and make their own the cause of the poor, as if you

were accepting and making own your own cause, the very cause of Christ" (*Message of Pope John Paul II to the Peoples of Latin America,* n.3).

It isn't a hobby, it's not a fad, it's not "one among so many possible options." We Redemptorists ought—and we desire it with all our heart—to insert ourselves among the poor as the expression of fidelity to the Lord, who raised up in the Church, through Saint Alphonsus, the charism of service to the poor in situations of pastoral urgency.

Defining the term

The Church recognizes a growing situation of marginalization, dependence, underdevelopment, and poverty in the countries of the Third and Fourth World. The Gospel, as proclamation of and impetus for the kingdom of God, demands of us solidarity with those who live in poor circumstances and a search for ways to change. Religious life, knowing that we still lack a presence to those who live under marginalized and poor circumstances, remains disquieted wishing to take up its place among the poor, as a sign of its evangelical radicalism and of its obedience to the Lord and to the Church. Redemptorists, by the very nature of our charism, place ourselves at the heart of this common search of religious. Difficult questions are presented in this movement to go out to the poor and to be inserted among them: What exactly does insertion consist in? What objectives should be targeted? How does one do insertion? Where and when is it possible? What fields does it contain? What dangers does it present? In sum, how does one give orientation to our practice of insertion?

I would like to share what in more than sixteen years of missionary work in the midst of the poor—whether rural or the marginalized in the city—I have lived and grown in, along with other brothers of the community and of the Church. I want to share with you, my brother Redemptorists and with our lay collaborators, the fruit of my experience and reflection. I will expand and bring up to date here the reflections which I made in 1988 at the Conference of Religious Superiors of Colombia, during some days of reflection and prayer dedicated to this theme.

3. Principles for Giving Direction to Insertion

3.1 Insertion as part of the biblical concept of incarnation ...and especially of the person of Jesus

Insertion is not an option of the moment, an attitude urged on by a specific occasion. It is an option that springs forth from revelation itself. It is in this way that God wished to act in order to save the world: involving himself, inserting himself, accompanying a people in their process of liberation, becoming *Emmanuel*: "God-with-us."

God created a people by means of an old man and his sterile wife. Two people on the sidelines of life. He united himself to that people, even though they were exploited, oppressed, and were not-a-people. He, who calls things that are not so that they may be, made them his own, with a surprising nearness: "Which of the nations have gods as close as our God?" God's revelation is insertion in the world. It has to do with a universal, salvific insertion, from the starting point of an option made for a particular people. The God of Israel, while maintaining his sovereign transcendence, becomes incarnate in his people, battles alongside them in all their campaigns. The prophets, instruments of the God of the Covenant, saddened by the infidelity of the people, call them again to conversion and to fidelity to God who always has loved them. The God of the Bible is the God immersed in history, who becomes history.

The fullness of this insertion of God in history is Jesus of Nazareth, the son of Mary, God made man, inserted, involved in humanity: "true God and true man." The one who "pitched his tent among us" and who "had to seem like his brothers in everything in order to come before God our compassionate and faithful high priest."

Insertion is communion, restoration of broken relationships. It is salvation. Humanity is reconciled in Christ with God, and as a true child of God clings to him, who earlier inserted himself in the man Jesus of Nazareth, the son of God, born of a woman. The ultimate objective of the insertion of the Word into flesh is the bringing about of the communion lost by sin and the restoration of the kingdom of God: filial communion with God, fraternal communion, particpation of all in the goods of creation so that they are at the service of everyone and through their means we give glory to God and we arrive at eternal good. We go out to meet our poor brothers and sisters, because they are the face of Christ; because we perceive the great lack of solidarity and of meeting one with another; because we note great barriers which divide people, denying them fraternity. Because we perceive that even yet the kingdom has not arrived, and we call out with Jesus, "Thy kingdom come…thy will be done." We know that Jesus Christ has knocked down all the walls of division and that we Christians are in the world as stewards of reconciliation. Insertion as communion is, on one hand, revelation of the love of God: proclamation and announcement; on the other hand, transformation of reality according to the perspective of the revealed God. Insertion is total salvation or integral liberation from every servitude for service to the true and living God.

In Christ insertion is proclamation of the kingdom in a new way. John the Baptist, in continuity with the Old Testament, proclaimed: "Change and give fruit worthy of God so that he may welcome you into his messianic kingdom. The ax is laid to the root of the tree and the wrath of God is about to be unleashed over the unrepentant.…" But this bitter cry of anger and fear becomes in Christ joyful proclamation, "Gospel," happy news: God now loves you, even in the midst of your sins. "Love does not consist in our having loved first, but in that he loved us first." And "even when we were sinners, he sent his Son as propitiation for our sins." God has entered lovingly and graciously among us. Now the new commandment is not so much to love God above all things…but rather "to let oneself be loved by God more than by all things." "The Spirit of God is over me. He has anointed me and has sent me to bring good news to the poor, to proclaim freedom to captives and sight to the blind, to give liberty to the oppressed and to proclaim a year of grace from the Lord."

3.2 Insertion as a call to the Church

The Church is in the world a sacrament of the unity of people among themselves and with God, an instrument of reconciliation and of unity. She is the visible body of the risen Christ inserted and operating in the world. In the Church, Jesus Christ takes visible "body" according to the features of each culture and epoc of history, in order to take it on himself and to redeem it. The Church, continuer of the incarnation of Christ, inserts itself also in the world and enters into communion with men and women and their historical and cultural mediations.

It corresponds to every member of the Church to "incarnate the Church"; to be instrument of communion with God and with people, artificer of unity and constructor of peace, knocking down the walls which separate people. Pastoral work is before all else the task of the Church to proclaim and bring to completion the salvation of Christ, in the language, modes, the institutions of every time and place. To save is to create insertion, to create incarnation (since that is not redeemed which is not taken up), to destroy barriers, to knock down walls, to reconcile people freeing them for every dependency, the ultimate root of which is sin.

We religious make the Church present as a sacrament of communion. This is the mission that has been confided to us. The Church, by its discernment of charisms, has confided to each religious community a mission of insertion (service to the world), which no one could take upon himself. It is she, depository of salvation from Christ, who ratifies for each community and for each religious the gift of insertion bestowed by the Holy Spirit. The insertion of the religious is, before all else, insertion into the Church, to make real her insertion in the world, since in this way is brought about the historical insertion of the risen Lord.

Such insertion in the Church is not servile submission, but solicitous love. Sometimes a denunciation is needed, a prophetic word of criticism born from heartfelt love. Our founders give witness to us as much of their firm loyalty to the Church as their denunciation—in word and life—of all that they found in her in opposition to the Gospel. The life and preaching of Alphonsus and the first Redemptorists were a real testimony of this Gospel courage, in an ecclesiastical world where that kind of sensitivity had been lost. They were a "sacrament" of the love of the Church for the poor as an expression of fidelity to her Lord: "Whatever you do to one of the least of my brothers or sisters, you do to me."

The salvation which the Church proclaims is for all (universal) and embraces every human being (integral). But the Church does not become active except in the actions of each of its members. She needs "agents of insertion," prophets who bring her to the point of dislodging herself so that she can relocate among the poor. As religious, we are called to be a vital part of this dynamic of inserting the Church into the world. From its beginnings, religious life attempted to be the source of dynamism for Christian radicalism in an "unradicalized" mass. It has tried to be a "sacrament" (visible sign) of Christian radicalism. And today it has to be the same: ferment of radicalism, salt and yeast…spearpoint in fulfilling the options of the Church, which wants to be faithful to her Lord and spouse, Christ. If our Redemptorist religious life is not an expression of this radicalism of the

Church toward the poor, it is not faithful to Christ who wants her there, because it is there he loves his Church.

3.3 Insertion as part of incarnation in religious life

Religious life is election, consecration—setting aside. But oriented toward mission, incarnation, and insertion. And insofar as it is able to be incarnated, that is the extent to which it is set aside. Religious life cannot be disinterested in or despising of the world, but a lively desire, born of love, for sanctifying it and transforming it.

The axis of our Redemptorist spirituality is the following of Christ in the evangelization of the poor. Our spirituality is spirituality of solidarity and incarnation. This spirituality of commitment, of insertion, of solidarity, has enriched and complemented a shortsighted negative Christian spirituality, of flight from and spite toward the world. Theology today sees much better the interrelation between incarnation and eschatology. Final plenitude, a gift from God, does not fail to recognize temporal progress, the fight for justice and freedom, and this insertion not only is not opposed to contemplation, but enriches it and brings out its true sense.

3.4 Insertion from the perspective of liberating evangelization

For some time now there has been raised in the Church the question of the mutual relations between evangelization and human progress, evangelization and development, evangelization and liberation. The Medellín document put forward the question with sharp insight and tried to give answers. Paul VI (EN 29-38) tried to clarify these relationships even more, and Puebla maturely integrates all the aspects in a synthesis, fruit of various years of reflection and practice in the Church of Latin America: "liberating evangelization." Let us look at the Puebla document:

> We pastors of Latin America have the gravest reasons for urging liberating evangelization, not only because it is necessary to remember individual and social sin, but also because from Medellín til now, the situation has gotten worse in the majority of our countries (487).

> There appear to be two inseparable and complementary elements: liberation from all servitude to personal and social sin, from every

fractioning of humanity and society and from everything which has its roots in selfishness, in the mystery of iniquity; and liberation in order to progressively grow in being, through communion with God and people, which culminates in the perfect communion of heaven, where God is all in all and there will be no more tears (482).

If we do not arrive at liberation from sin with all its seductions and idolatry; if we do not help to concretize the liberation with which Christ conquered on the cross, we mutilate liberation in an irreparable way. We also mutilate liberation if we forget the axis of liberating evangelization, which is that which transforms the human being into the agent of his or her own development, whether individually or as a community. We mutilate liberation just as much if we forget the dependence and the enslavements which wound fundamental rights..." (485).

We are happy to see numerous examples of efforts to live liberating evangelization, in its fullness. One of the principle tasks in order to continue on with Christian liberation is the creative search for ways which do away with ambiguities and reductionisms (EN 32) in full fidelity to the word of God which is given us in the Church and which moves us to the joyful announcement to the poor, as one of the messianic signs of the reign of Christ (488).

In summary, the insertion of religious in marginal and poor circumstances has to be done from the perspective of liberating evangelization: integral liberation, which is liberation from sin, the transformation of the human person by his or her own development, and liberation from every dependence and slavery. This is a clear perspective of insertion for all religious in Latin America, valid and binding for us Redemptorists.

3.5 Insertion from the viewpoint of our Redemptorist religious charism

To each community the Holy Spirit has confided some charism for service to the Church and to the world. It is clear that religious should insert themselves in the Church and in her program of liberating evangelization, within the limits of their own charism. The insertion of a religious should not be able to cause one to lose his or her own identity. The religious will serve the poor and liberating evangelization more insofar as he or she is faithful to the charism confided by the Holy Spirit to his or her religious family.

These would be, to my understanding, the principal "Redemptorist characteristics of insertion":

- Preferential option for the poor and for those of humble condition and for situations of pastoral urgency (Constitution 5)
- As extraordinary service to the ordinary pastoral action of the Church (Constitution 14)
- Without losing our "itinerant" character: available and mobile. Ours should be an "itinerant insertion." Because we could run the risk, through insertion, of "reinstalling ourselves" (Constitution 15)
- In fidelity to the local Church, within its pastoral plans (Constitution 18)
- In community discernment, guided by authority, of the new pastoral methodology which demands insertion (Constitution 17)
- Respecting the culture, the language, the required processes for the authentic inculturation of the faith (Constitution 19)
- With the characteristics of the genuine Redemptorist: strong in faith, rejoicing in hope, burning with charity, on fire with zeal; in humility, persevering prayer, Gospel simplicity, available for what is arduous, denial of self (Constitution 20)
- For Redemptorists, insertion should not be an isolated option of "one" member or "some" members. It is a process that we should take up as a community. "To fulfill their mission in the Church, Redemptorists perform their missionary work as a community. For apostolic life in common paves the way most effectively for the life of pastoral charity. Therefore, an essential law of life for the members is this: that they live in community and carry out their apostolic work through community" (Constitution 21)

The charism given by God to a community is not static; it is enriched over the course of history and with new elements in each place and time. We ought to reexamine the significance of our charism in the light of the new options in the Church. With Vatican II, religious life rethought the various charisms in order to accommodate itself to the new demands on the Church. Now in Latin America, after Medellín-Puebla-Santo Domingo, we Redemptorists ought to rethink our charism in light of the preferential option for the poor and for liberating evangelization. This rethinking of the charism, done in the environment of prayer, discernment and in coordination with the ministry of authority (Constitution 17) does not betray our charism, but enriches it and makes it faithful to the Church.

3.6 Retaining religious identity in insertion

The insertion of religious could not deny the significance of their "being," since the religious is an earthly witness to the eschatological reality. By vows the religious is made capable of being in the world a visible sign of the ultimate realities to which all of humanity is tending. Since the final destiny of humanity is the full communion of human beings among themselves and with God, free from all slavery and dependencies, the religious sets about bringing to fulfillment in this time of earthly history, and in the best possible way, the eschatological reality of total liberation.

But the religious does not insert himself or herself only for earthly progress (though he or she does not exclude this from one's horizons) or for a partial program of liberation, but in order to make effective the kingdom of God which breaks forth and unfolds wherever the message of Jesus is accepted. The religious is a witness to the power of God, who, in the Spirit of Christ, now is acting to overcome all that lowers the human being, but who lives in hope of the definitive consummation. The religious is not so much a man or woman of work and progress, as a man or woman of God. Only to that measure is anyone truly committed in the cause of humanity.

4. Degrees of Insertion

Our insertion is not always equal or uniform. It can have various levels. I believe that there ought to be a certain variety of options, in the measure of the gift of God to each community and to each religious, in order of service to the poor. We will indicate here three degrees that the theologians of CLAR have pointed out to us. And we shall add another.

4.1 First degree: to live for the poor

A form of solidarity and poverty is to share what one is and what one has with others. Poverty is not so much not having, as sharing. The criterion for the validity of this attitude is service to the kingdom of God. In some instances, to divest oneself of goods and to leave off work in order to make a geographical and existential "exodus" toward the poor can do less to build up the kingdom of God than to remain administering wisely and prudently the goods of the kingdom for the service of the poor. This has special relevance when it has to do with communities that, in their long institutional history, have managed to increase their material possessions, fruit of their austerity, work and diligent administration. It is not licit, I believe, through insertion and solidarity, to leave behind works that build up the kingdom of God in favor of the poor and marginalized simply for the purpose of "not having" or "divesting oneself." However, the criterion cannot be fear of losing security, fear of losing privileges, fear of inconvenience, the incertainty before the future, because of a lack of faith.

To live for the poor is a demand that Jesus makes to every disciple and to every Redemptorist committed to "following Jesus Christ in the evangelization of the poor." This has to do with a commitment inherent to the following of Christ: "happy are the poor, because theirs is the kingdom.... Woe to the rich...." To opt for the poor, to orient everything to them, and to focus life and affection on them is not an "optional" or alternative thing, but a fundamental demand of the Gospel. We cannot be credible witnesses of the kingdom of God in the world without living for the poor, and without accompanying them, in whatever circumstances we find ourselves, in their struggle against inhuman conditions of misery born in sin and in unjust social structures.

4.2 Second degree: to live with the poor

Many Redemptorists, personally and institutionally, have dedicated themselves to an "exodus" toward the poor. We want to live located among the poor, and we want to work *among* them and *with* them. However, our way of life differs from that of the poor. There is a geographical solidarity, a nearness and a dialogue with them. But it is not exactly like they live. They live differently, they eat differently, they sleep differently.

In my opinion, these would be the criteria of validity for this option:

a) *The building up of the kingdom of God:* We position ourselves among the poor in order to build up the kingdom of God, the overcoming of sin and the restoration of brotherhood in justice and liberty—not in order to form a distinct class, or because we were not foresighted enough and the "repose of peace" drew people to us whom we have to tolerate.

b) *A special charism:* To live among the poor cannot be demanded of a whole community nor of all religious. A charism, a special gift, and a sensitivity is necessary in order to live among them with delight and generosity. To be able to serve the poor better, a whole institution cannot be among the poor, but it should support the charism of the group that desires to be among the poor.

c) *Community discernment:* Going to live among the poor should be done, I think, after discernment by the whole community. This can have nothing to do with a capricious exit by individuals maladapted to community life, but rather a lucid, well-thought-out and resolute decision. Without this community discernment, mediated by authority, "charismatic" persons and groups can make of their insertion among the poor a simple folly and take a quick withdrawal. Discernment is not always peaceful. There are struggles and even a prophetic attitude becomes necessary, but the Holy Spirit continues to guide the community who lives among the poor in an atmosphere of prayer and sincerity.

4.3 Third degree: to live like the poor

In this third degree of insertion, religious share completely in the lot of the poor and identify themselves existentially with them. They are like them in the same way as Christ, who "being God, empties himself of his status and passed for one among so many." And he lived not only for people and among them, but like people and like the poorest and most humble of them. "As rich as he was, he made himself poor in order to enrich us with his poverty." "He had to seem like his brothers and sisters in everything in order to be able before God to be our compassionate and faithful high priest."

It is an heroic degree of insertion. It is not a level that can be demanded of an entire community. Certain specific people, and at times groups, live it. It is a vocation and requires a special grace. The community and the ministry of authority should also discern this gift; sometimes it can be a temporary thing. It tends to be present more easily in religious communities that are just beginning and in small communities; and it is more difficult and contentious in communities with a long institutional history, which need to put people into internal ministries for formation, administration of goods, services of community facilitation, and so on.

The religious who lives this degree of insertion personifies the community sacramentally. That poor religious, identified with the real lot of the poor, is for the religious community their "sacrament" of solidarity and of presence among them. The majority of our founders, on a temporary basis or permanently, heroically lived just such a degree of insertion. They became poor among the poor. They stripped themselves of even what was necessary, suffered hunger, thirst, nakedness, a lack of roof and bed. They were humiliated; begged like the poor; changed their clothing; abandoned their lineage, their culture, and their education. They left behind human wisdom in order to clasp the wisdom of Christ. Craziness and scandal to many, but the strength and power of God to those who believe. That was the way it was, and to a heroic degree, for our Father, Saint Alphonsus.

4.4 Fourth degree: to give one's life for the poor

The highest degree of solidarity and insertion is "to die for the poor," to give one's life for them. Jesus said: "No one has greater love than this: to give one's life for one whom he loves." To die for the poor is the summit of solidarity with them. In regions of the Third and Fourth World, many religious have achieved this supreme degree of love til death. Especially those who work for human rights are in a position to be critically close to this degree, through their great risk of death in defense of the poor. There could be, on occasions, a much higher degree of insertion in a brother dedicated to the fight for the rights of the poor and who is risking his own life than in another who lovingly shares with them, living "like them."

5. The Methodology of Insertion

Besides needing a theological basis, insertion requires a "strategy of implementation" to become real. We need to respond to the questions: What are its objectives? What are its means? What are the attitudes involved in insertion?

5.1 The objectives of insertion

Insertion among the poor is not an option exclusive to the Church. Various groups of varying ideologies have their own insertion into the way of life of the poor. It is worthwhile, therefore, to ask oneself what objectives identify the insertion of the Redemptorist religious among the poor?

5.1.1 The main objective is announcing and bringing about the kingdom of God

Proclamation of the abundant redemption in Christ. The Redemptorist enters the way of life of the poor in order to proclaim the love of God manifested in Christ. In order to invite human beings converted to Christ to form a brotherhood (Constitution 12); to live the kingdom like brothers; to put in motion effective processes of integral liberation, that is, inculturation of the Gospel and achievement of human progress in small groups facilitated by laity. Those are the pastoral options of Santo Domingo (nn. 287–301).

a) The kingdom is frustrated by sin which, beginning in a personal reality, affects social structures and creates unjust situations.

b) The kingdom now has been initiated in Christ. By his incarnation, by his saving message, by his death and resurrection, and by the sending forth of the Holy Spirit in the Church. Where the message and person of Jesus is accepted, the kingdom keeps increasing patiently, but with total efficacy.

5.1.2 Through liberating evangelization

"Within the conditions of poverty on our continent, generated by unjust structures, and not only through marginalization and underdevelopment, activity on behalf of the kingdom of God ought to pass through evangelization and an evangelization which is liberating, within the lines which the Church in Puebla has drawn up" (cf., SD nn. 480–489).

a) As explicit announcement of the word, liberating evangelization is for many communities explicit proclamation of the Word of God in ordinary and extraordinary form. We proclaim the kingdom of God, which calls us to be sons, brothers and masters, free of all dependence; and from this announcement we denounce every situation in opposition to the kingdom which enslaves and oppresses the human person. A word proclaimed thus is a force of conscientization for integral liberation and for organizing the poor who look to overcoming all their dependencies.

b) As concrete attainment of the kingdom, it is the love which is truly effective that religious show when they encourage people and communities, be it through attention to their problems, be it through the struggle for development, making the poor "artisans of their own development," be it by promoting a consciousness for liberation from every dependence with the use of effective means according to the Gospel in order for them to organize themselves and to achieve liberation; and, finally, involving oneself if it is necessary in the defense of human rights.

c) Under the inspiration of a spirituality of incarnation: the testimony of God and the life of prayer are the greatest treasure of our consecrated life. This treasure should be present in our insertion: "They are especially called to live in intense communion with the Father, who fills them with his Spirit, urging them to build up an always renewed communion among people. The consecrated life is thus a prophetic affirmation of the supreme value of communion with God among people and a very distinguished testimony that the world cannot be transfigured nor offered to God without the spirit of the Beatitudes" (Puebla n. 744). "Let the members ever take to themselves the exhortation of Christ the Redeemer: 'they ought always to pray and not lose heart' (Luke 18:1). Let them imitate the disciples of the first community in the Church....Indeed, they will make every effort to have Saint Alphonsus's spirit of prayer in their own lives" (Constitution 26).

It should be noted that this is the type of insertion which also is proper to contemplative communities. They also participate in the preferential option for the poor. From their reserve, they build up the kingdom of God together with those who build it up in the active life. "Contemplative communities are like the heart of the religious life. They inspire and urge everyone to intensify the transcendent sense of Christian life. They are themselves evangelizers, since 'being contemplative does not mean cutting oneself off radically from the world or from the apostolate. The contemplative community needs to find its own specific way of understanding the kingdom of God'" (Puebla n. 738).

5.1.3 With the conditions which the Church puts on it

Pope John Paul II, in his innaugural discourse in Puebla, made clear the conditions under which one does liberating evangelization:

a) *At the level of content:* Fidelity to the Word of God, to the living tradition of the Church and to its magisterium.
b) *At the level of attitudes:* Sense of communion with the bishops and with the other sectors of the people of God. Their contribution to the effective building up of the community; the way they launch with love their solicitude for the poor, the infirm, the dispossessed, the abandoned, the oppressed. Finding in them a poor and suffering Jesus, the form in which they might work to remedy their needs and attempt to serve Christ in them.

5.2 Attitudes behind insertion into the way of life of the poor

Insertion is a process for entering into communion with the marginalized and poor of the world, which is not done with a single blow. Generally, it is a slow and painful process of getting ever closer to them. I want to note here the attitudes which, according to my way of thinking, ought to accompany that process of insertion.

5.2.1 The attitude of community discernment

The whole community, at times pushed forward by prophetic forces within itself, ought to review its own attitudes and its situation in light of the Gospel, in light of the intuitions of its founder and its initial group, and in light of the options of the Church in each time. This process of discernment will help each community to look for lines of commitment among the poor. Beginning with Vatican II, all communities have "rethought" their charism in order to fit it to today's world, to the preference of the Church for the poor and for liberating evangelization.

5.2.2 Attitude of dialogue and encounter

We cannot bring about insertion in a vertical environment, one of imposition, creating divisions and walls; and thoroughly establishing distances and differences. In order to be evangelical, insertion has to clothe itself in simplicity and a spirit of communion and dialogue. This attitude of dialogue and encounter demands from us

a) having faith in the poor, such as God had, who identified himself with them. Insertion is born from faith: faith in the capacities of the poor, firm certainty that exodus to the poor is the road for better implanting the kingdom of God. "For God nothing is impossible"; "everything is possible for the person who believes." Only faith can transform situations of marginalization, of underdevelopment, of dependence. Without this attitude of faith, it is impossible to get close to the poor and to grow with them. It is necessary to remember that "integral liberation," beginning with human effort, is also a grace of God and must be awaited as a gift. Saint Alphonsus and the first missionaries give us an example of this faith. Faith is a force capable of overcoming every "limiting situation." Jesus called people to this faith to fulfill the most demanding commitments.

b) going out to meet the poor: "God so loved the world that he gave his only Son." So much does the religious love the Lord, present in the poor, that he goes out to meet them and makes himself like him. Jesus, whom the religious has made the center of his life and its purpose, is present in the poor. The religious goes out to meet Jesus in the environs of the poor and there adores and serves him. Without that sincere love, born from faith in the presence of Jesus in the poor, every effort at insertion will end up being myth, external appearance, something showy and, for lack of real ties...will result in a quick retreat. Insertion needs to grow out of the contemplation of Jesus Christ identified with the poor. That is the purest fount from which comes forth true insertion.

c) waiting for an answer. The love offered by the religious requires a response of welcome on the part of the poor. If the poor do not accept us, insertion is not possible. Insertion is not forced on anyone, nor is it a dominating presence come to conquer in order to attract the poor and subjugate them, albeit for their own good. No. It is the power of love which conquers, because it comes close and gives itself and stirs a grateful response, moved by the same God who is love and is born where one serves and loves.

d) growing in communion: having arrived at an encounter with the poor, to walk together with them, bringing about "liberating evangelization," without impositions, without artificial interests, attempting growth in truth and the formation of the Christian community. To knit a network of small communities, which inculturate the Gospel, brings about human development. The objective of our insertion is not "to become a protagonist," but rather to accompany the humble people in simplicity on their journey to the kingdom: a search for God as Father and an offering to one's brothers and sisters, as children of the same Father. The religious incarnates himself in the situation of the poor and makes it his own and brings to the poor all that the Lord has given him for the building up of the kingdom. But the religious also allows himself to be taught and transformed. The religious is not a teacher but a brother. Every attitude of insertion inspired by superiority and a pretense of being more than the poor is a prideful lie and against the Gospel. Only generous love, simplicity, humility, dialogue, kindness under every test, can create communion, tear down walls, and be a force for liberation.

e) accepting conflictivity. Sin conditions the process of entering into communion with the poor and exposes it to conflictivity. The concrete demands of love lead to many confrontations. Insertion does not happen without the cross, without contradiction, and without sacrifice. The life and work of Jesus is the paradigm for this situation of conflict: his proclamation ended in martyrdom.

f) respecting the language and the culture. Each human group has its way of expressing its understanding of life and its relationship with others, with the world, with the transcendent. This way constitutes its language. Insertion asks that one adapt to this language, this peculiar manner of expressing and pronouncing the world. Christianity accepts the good from everything human and purifies it of the inhuman inherent in it because of our sinful condition. Insertion is, then, also the study and knowledge of the language and of the culture in order to make them grow in the Gospel. We religious ought to also make valient contributions to the culture, keeping in mind that the culture has to be harmoniously evangelized and that one has to integrate positively and creatively new elements. The mission of the Redemptorist is not to care for the culture as if it were a museum fossil, but to protect it and help it to grow as an instrument of communion among people and of transformation of reality for integral liberation.

g) special attention to be given here to popular religiosity or the religion of the people, "the collection of deep beliefs sealed by God, basic attitudes which derive from these convictions and the expressions which manifest them" (Puebla n. 444). This religion of the people ought to be positively assumed into the process of insertion. The following criteria, I believe, can be used to evaluate it:

- Reject those practices and forms of religiosity that degrade the person, which impede his or her exercise of liberty, which create dependency or irresponsibility, immaturity, and induce fatalism or incite disunion.

- Respectfully accept those practices that perhaps do not now correspond with our more evolved religious language, but are at the level of understanding and living of faith of certain human groups. We accept with love their own form of expression and we accommodate ourselves to it without imposing our "modern" forms, in order to express the same values.

- Promote those practices that genuinely express the values of the Gospel in contemporary language and which encourage the faithful to commitment to their brothers and sisters, in their situation and with God.

- Create in communion with the people new forms of expression, in accord with recent cultural forms and the present-day language of faith.

5.2.3 Attitude of penitence and continual conversion

In insertion among the poor, we remain exposed to the temptation to infidelity and flight. In every exodus the pleasant fragrance of the shores of Egypt continue to tempt. We need to "keep watch and pray that we do not fall into temptation…since the spirit is willing but the flesh is weak." Perseverance is a gift of God that strengthens us through the Holy Spirit and which we obtain through prayer. Only he can keep us faithful to the end. Without this strength of God obtained in prayer and in the practice of the sacraments, insertion cannot endure. Through lack of this penitential spirit and lack of continual conversion many experiments in insertion have failed.

5.2.4 Attitude of patient waiting

The full communion of all people and liberation from every servitude is an eschatological gift from God, which also takes into account our human struggle. Now we try to achieve it in the best way possible, but it will be fully accomplished only when the new world and the new heavens come into being; and the Lord dries every tear from every eye. Illuminated with this hope, the religious dispels every sadness, soothes anxieties and frees his energies for the commitment. Already we have received by way of pledge the Holy Spirit who comes to walk with us. Seen thus, insertion is not painful martyrdom, but daily celebration of the power of God that erupts into our world every day and goes on saving it with power until its full manifestation.

Unfailingly, the poor religious is a happy religious. Inserted into the lifestyle of the poor, he can breathe the gentle liberty of Christ who said: "Take up my yoke which is light"; "he who gives up his life for me and for the Gospel, gains it." This is the living testimony of many who have surrendered themselves without reservation and have enjoyed an unconquerable freedom and peace. How many religious, by contrast, live frustrated, alienated, in discord and envy, enclosed and imprisoned, in the "castles" which they have constructed to make themselves happy by being away from others. Happiness is not to be found in the "refuges," but in the desert, where God leads his beloved and speaks to her heart, and the beloved does not call out "my idol," but "my Lord."

5.2.5 A martyr's attitude

Religious life took the place of the lost vocation of the martyr of the early Christians when faith became a massive cultural phenomenon and lost the dimension of personal commitment. It began as a vocation of martyrdom, that is, as a vocation of exhaustive self-surrender, of radical gift to

Jesus and his kingdom. In insertion, we religious have a magnificent opportunity to put value back into our "vocation of martyrdom" as a vocation of Christian radicalism.

When it was the poor who were evangelizing, Christianity began with the vocation of martyrdom. It was the normal vocation of every Christian in the first centuries. And it would be the normal attitude today, if we wanted to evangelize as poor people. The vocation of martyrdom has been frequently absent from our Redemptorist religious life, and we ought to recover it. We urgently need it in order to invigorate the commitment of insertion, because for a deep and effective insertion our total self-surrender is necessary, with the willingness to give one's life; firm willingness to follow Christ crucified and generous self-offering and the freedom to be crucified with him. Without this vocation of martyrdom, without this willingness to follow Christ crucified, the insertion of religious in the lifestyle of the marginalized and poor, will be a passing flash, momentary myth, or a show to satisfy egoism at the cost of the poor.

5.2.6 In communion with laypeople

It is the time of the laity in the Church. It always has been, theologically speaking. But now the dedication of the laity in the Church surges forth with new vigor. Faithful laypeople, called to bring the law of God into the heart of the world, to transform the whole social order, have a relevant role to play in the process of insertion. As Redemptorists, we ought to open ourselves to an effective work in solidarity with them. In communion with committed laypeople, we will be able to achieve our goal in a more coherent way on the path of insertion.

25

THE MINISTRY
OF RECONCILIATION

Raphael Gallagher, C.Ss.R.
Province of Dublin

1. Why I Became a Redemptorist

My vocation story is a rather ordinary one. I grew up in an Ireland where the Church was a central part of life and where becoming a priest was socially acceptable. It was a normal thing to think about doing: it was as usual *then* to think about becoming a priest as it is now *not* to think about becoming one. Both my parents were teachers, and there were always priests visiting our house. I thought about becoming a diocesan priest, but not very seriously; the fact that I had been sacked as an altar boy by the local curate for some youthful misdemeanor may have left some subconscious feelings about the local clergy.

When the Redemptorists came to give a mission in my parish they seemed different, even rather exotic. Rural Ireland of the 1950s did not offer much excitement, apart from the local football games, the annual visit of the circus, and the parish mission. I probably joined the Redemptorists because they were different from the local clergy, and they seemed to offer all sorts of exciting possibilities of converting the whole world. My years in the juvenate were happy ones: I liked studying and we had very good teachers. Despite being in the juvenate, I don't think I got to know all that much about the Redemptorists, apart from being told what a wonderful life it was. I was happy to believe that, and I was accepted for the novitiate. There was a sort of natural progression from rural Ireland, a good Catholic family, the chance of secondary education in the juvenate to joining a Congregation that was well-respected in Ireland. Only one person tried to dissuade me from joining the Redemptorists: a diocesan priest whom I knew could not understand why I wanted to join a religious congregation that had such poor intellectual standards.

The difficulties with my vocation began when I joined the Congregation. The studendate years of the 1960s were very troubled ones. Most of my companions left: from my novitiate year, six of us were sent to study at Galway University: I am the only one of the six still in the Congregation. I stayed because I was excited by the possibilities of the Second Vatican Council, and I saw the Congregation responding to that (even if, in my student fervor, I thought progress should have been faster). But I did not find it easy to stay, particularly when most of my friends had left.

With the grace of God, I am still here. Because of my upbringing in rural Ireland and my formation in a fairly closed studendate, I had to do a lot of my growing up after ordination. On a human level, I think I received the most support in this process from the people I met in pastoral situations. After ordination I was assigned to study moral theology, and I began to be in contact with a wonderful variety of people who had all sorts of interesting moral dilemmas. I got great support from the Redemptorists in all of this: but, very importantly, I got great encouragement from the people whom I was meeting. They expected certain standards and commitments from me as a Redemptorist priest, and they expected me to be faithful to my vocation. I like being a Redemptorist because the way of life in the Congregation keeps me in contact with people who are trying to make sense of their lives: some of these lives are boring, some are anything but ordinary. I have to study and pray about how to respond to their problems (I am better at the studying than the praying), and I remain happy in my vocation in a Congregation that, with all its difficulties, is still capable of being interested in telling people about redemption in a rather chaotic world.

2. I Confess…the Love of God

2.1 We acknowledge our sins

We, as Christians and as Redemptorists, are sinners: we are a Church of sinners, and a Congregation of sinners. Any reflection on the ministry of reconciliation should begin with that point. No doubt, the Church and the Congregation are also holy, but we will not make progress in how we are to be ministers of reconciliation unless we first acknowledge our personal contribution to the sinfulness of the Church and the Congregation.

To acknowledge our sinfulness is, fundamentally, a positive thing because we are accepting the need for God's healing and forgiveness. Sin is a negative reality only when we are so convinced of our own righteousness that, in our self-sufficiency, we look down on others and ignore God: this is clear from the parable of the Pharisee and the tax collector (Luke 18:9ff). When we are prepared to own the reality of our sins, we can move to the next step of disowning our sins. Redemptorists are very good at naming the sins that others commit, but are shy about saying how we ourselves have sinned. I think a number of our present difficulties in the ministry of reconciliation begin precisely with this point. Why should people come to us for the ministry of reconciliation if they do not witness the struggle for reconciliation in our own lives? And how can there be a struggle for reconciliation if we, in the first place, do not confess how our sins lessen the credibility of the Church and the Congregation?

For many people, the Church appears to be an unforgiving place. People in second unions or homosexuals, to take obvious examples, stay away from the Church because they feel the Church has no place for them, or that they have to be "converted" before they come to the Church. There is a telling paradox in this: some people will experience reconciliation outside the official confines of the Church rather than within the Church. The impression given is that people have to be holy and converted before they can belong to the community of the Church: this, if true, is indeed a scandal. The ministry of reconciliation to those who have strayed from the commandments of God and the community of the Church will be more effective if we can show, in a public way, how we are sinners and in need of reconciliation ourselves. We acknowledge our sins, not out of morbidity, but out of a sense of the need for forgiveness. The more we do that, the more we show that we are a Church of sinners. The ministry of reconciliation begins at this point. There are those who will say that such a view is too soft, and that we should begin our ministry of reconciliation with the loud and clear denunciation of the sins of the people that we see all around us. But what causes the greater scandal: our acceptance of sinners or our rejection of them?

2.2 The crisis in our day

The crisis of the ministry of reconciliation within our Congregation began with the decline in the number of people celebrating the sacrament. This happened because reconciliation was identified, almost totally, with a particular sacrament. It might be interesting to analyze our own response to this crisis. If the crisis is judged to be fundamentally the decline in the sense of sin, then our response will be a campaign of more vigorous preaching and catechesis: if the crisis is judged to be primarily the poor celebration of the ritual of penance, our response will be a liturgical updating along the possibilities of the 1974 reform of the order of penance within the Church. But what if the crisis is not a theological one about the nature of sin or a liturgical one about the celebration of rites, but a pastoral one about the experience of God through the community of the Church? It is my view that this is the aspect of the current crisis that should interest Redemptorists.

There is some consolation in the fact that the ministry of reconciliation has always been in crisis. Of the seven sacraments, it is fair to say that the sacrament of reconciliation has undergone the most changes in the way it has been celebrated within the Church. One way of interpreting the changing ways in which the Church has celebrated the sacrament of reconciliation is to see each development as a response to a pastoral crisis: at each stage of the crisis the Church's answer to abandoning sinners and leaving them unreconciled was a definite "no."

The first crisis arose out of a belief that sins committed after baptism could not be forgiven: a pastoral practice gradually developed that allowed the reconciliation of postbaptismal sinners. The second major crisis arose when the conditions implied in this pastoral practice proved impracticable as the Church moved out of the Mediterranean area into the new cultural sectors of northern Europe: a new pastoral practice developed (often against the wishes of local bishops). But, in time, even this practice became too harsh: by the Middle Ages we have the development of a pastoral practice that allowed frequent forgiveness of sins through private celebration of the sacrament in the presence of a priest. The Reformation rejection of this practice provoked a further crisis: the Church insisted on the proper formation of priests to ensure a more beneficial celebration of the sacrament. And today? The crisis seems to revolve around this point: while the theology of the Church has limited the expression of reconciliation to one particular sacramental rite (individualistic in nature and surrounded by precise canonical rules about the material integrity of confessing sins according to their number, kind, and species), the practice of the people has increasingly been an abandonment of the rite of penance as the normal form of reconciliation. If my interpretation is correct, there is a broad pastoral similarity between each of the crises of reconciliation in the Church. A practice evolves that allows a way of reconciling sinners: cultural conditions change and the once-helpful practices become a hindrance to the experience of being reconciled with the Church.

2.3 Reconciled through the community

Besides the pastoral similarities between the various crises of reconciliation, we should note also the two nonnegotiable elements of the Church's ministry of reconciliation: those of binding and loosing. The Church must face the fact of sin in its members, confront them with it, and challenge them to return to their baptismal commitment: the Church binds us to the community in this sense. But if the members of the community repent, and prove the sincerity of their good intentions, they can again be reconciled with the community: in this sense the Church looses us from our sins. This binding-loosing always happens in a reconciling community. True, this community dimension is very weakly seen in the rite of individual private confession: the priest, rather than the community, assumes the predominant role. But the principle is the same: we are reconciled and loosed from our sins through the experience of a reconciling community. The ministry of reconciliation, therefore, has as its starting point the building up of the Church as a community that welcomes sinners. There are many interesting possibilities here for Redemptorists.

Individual auricular confession has been our traditional means for doing this, and Redemptorists are justifiably famous for this particular ministry. There are some aspects of reconciliation that this form of the ministry will continue to nourish: the self-disclosure that is necessary for healing, the personal encounter with Christ, and the chance for receiving spiritual guidance. I am presuming that this form of the sacrament of reconciliation will continue, and will be valued by Redemptortists. However, it would be foolish to ignore the lessons of the declining practice of this form. We know that this particular rite of reconciliation is historically conditioned, and that it is not an absolute requirement (other rites of reconciliation are allowed in cases of the "physical impossibility" of receiving private auricular confession). I shall return to the Redemptorist celebration of auricular confession, but for the moment I wish to concentrate on another question: if the Church cannot dispense with the requirements of conversion (the process of binding and loosing), what should our attitude be to those many people who no longer frequent the canonically required form of the sacrament?

In a Church that no longer confines its ministry to priests and which provides many ways for people to share their faith, to challenge one another and to support one another in the Christian way, Redemptorists should explore new forms of reconciliation. This can be done through our regular apostolates: missions, retreats, novenas, adult education programs, counseling, and spiritual direction. With our tradition of caring for the most abandoned, we could give attention to groups that need special attention: those who have been away from the Church for a long time, those who have had bad experiences with the institutional Church, and those who have a very poor formation in the Christian way of life. Without touching the precise sacramental question of reconciliation, I think there is more scope here than we may imagine. I take it as a theological truth that the person who sacramentally reconciles the penitent with the eucharistic community should be the person who is commissioned to preside at the Eucharist. But the priest is not the Church: we should, therefore, be able to explore ways in which all the members of the Church should exercise their role in building up the Church as a reconciling community.

When looked at in this way, we can see that the ministry of reconciliation is wider than the question of having more confessions. Concentration on sacramental confession and absolution can obscure the possibilities of other forms of reconciliation. The apostolates of ecumenical reconciliation between the Churches or of peacemaking in politically divided communities are not strictly sacramental: but are they less ministries of reconciliation for that? Abuse is always possible: as it is possible to abuse private confession through a routine use of the sacrament relying on its presumed *ex opere operato* effect, it is possible to abuse new forms of reconciliation through a routine that presumes that "grace is cheap."

In these senses no ministries of reconciliation, old or new, will guarantee success. But, equally, no rite will make sense unless it is performed within the experience of the Church as a community that itself seeks reconciliation. I think it is this dimension that is now most pastorally needed, for this reason. The credibility of the Church is a necessary component of sacramental credibility, because sacraments are celebrated in the Church and the reality to which they point should be lived within the Church. I have experienced the private celebration of the sacrament of reconciliation where all the canonical requirements were followed, but I lacked the sense that the penitent experienced a reconciliation with the community: I have experienced the public celebration of the sacrament of reconciliation where, again, all the canonical rules were observed, but I lacked the sense that the penitents had been adequately prepared for the reconciliation with the community.

I grant that the present crisis of the sacrament of reconciliation within the Church involves delicate theological, liturgical, and canonical questions. While these are being studied, Redemptorists can make a useful contribution on the pastoral level, by exploring ways and means of promoting reconciliation: within the Church, between the Churches, and with those who are alienated from the Church. This building-up of the Church as a reconciling community could be an important ecclesial service as we await the developments of whatever precise forms sacramental reconciliation may take in the future.

2.4 The celebration of the sacrament

The declining numbers frequenting the sacrament of reconciliation has undermined the confidence of many Redemptorists in this ministry. This loss of confidence has been reflected in our attitude to moral theology which was, in the recent past, almost totally focused on our preparation as good confessors: moral theology is now concerned with the broad questions of Christian living, rather than having as its focus the practical, juridical, and administrative aims of the celebration of a particular form of the sacrament. A further cultural factor has affected our self-confidence about the sacrament: the growth of nondirectional counseling and the contemporary therapeutic sciences. It is not a surprise that many Redemptorists now ask: If people are staying away from the sacrament, if moral theology has changed its focus, and if there are so many new possibilities for people, why bother with the ministry of sacramental reconciliation?

The recovery of confidence is this ministry is, fundamentally, a recovery of confidence is the core truth of what is celebrated in this sacrament: it is the rite in which, through the ministry of the Church, we are reconciled to God and the Church when our serious sins have impeded the freedom Christ won for us in our baptism. If we do not accept this truth, there is no point in the ministry of sacramental reconciliation.

The difficulty for Redemptorists is, I trust, not a rejection of this theological truth: our difficulty today is linked with the moralistic tradition that we inherited and which has made it difficult for us, in practice, to celebrate the sacrament as a moment of healing love. A legalistic emphasis on our own role in the sacrament and a courtroom type of enquiry into penitents' lives have shaped our approach. There is a great irony in this. No one did more than Saint Alphonsus to emphasize the various roles of the confessor (father, physician, teacher, judge): to have reduced our concern to one role (that of judge) has been a betrayal of our tradition.

When we are celebrating the sacrament of reconciliation, we are not an attorney trying to give an exact reconstruction of the crime, nor a psychiatrist deciding on a client's accountability, nor a therapist ridding a person of unconscious inhibitions and complexes. All these are very useful things to do: but they are not of the essence of the particular sacramental purpose of reconciliation. What we are celebrating is the mystery of God's love for the repentant sinner. Everything we do in the sacrament (no matter which of the accepted rites we are following) is in view of making this love of God clear in the signs we use. The material integrity of the sins we confess, for instance, is always in view of the formal integrity of the core religious sign of the sacrament: be merciful to me, a sinner. The decline in the number of confessions may, in fact, be having a positive effect for us: it is enabling us to recover the precise sacramental purpose in a clearer form. I would propose the following general practical guidelines to help Redemptorists in this process.

a) The motivation we propose for sacramental reconciliation should be the desire of God to love each person. I accept that there are other theological and canonical theories that can be given: for instance, a theology of satisfaction to an offended God or a canonical requirement to frequent the sacrament. Redemptorists should stress the initiative of God who, through loving us, wishes us to respond. This sense of reconciliation being the "work of God in us" is more likely to keep the sacramental purpose in focus.

b) The celebration of the sacrament (in any rite) should focus on the reconciliation of a sinner, through the community, with God. In practice, this means that the sacramental celebration is not appropriate for counseling or spiritual direction. These are, indeed, very useful means for Christian growth, and should be encouraged, but not usually within a sacramental celebration. I say "usually": the needs of the repentant sinner are always paramount, and if we judge that the sinner will not avail of the necessary counseling or spiritual direction except at this particular moment of the sacramental celebration, we could make an exception. Receiving the sacrament could, for instance, be part of a program of spiritual direction, but it is not itself properly seen as spiritual direction. The grace of the sacrament of reconciliation is to become more Christlike members of the reconciled community through the forgiveness of our sins.

c) In facilitating a good celebration of the sacrament, Redemptorists should focus on the link between conscience and the love of God. The examination of our conscience is an intrinsic part of the celebration of the sacrament, and we know of the various methods for doing this. The problem with many of these methods is that they concentrate on lists of things that are wrong and ignore that conscience is a call to love God in the first place: it is only then that conscience is the call to do good and avoid evil. This is clear from the descriptive definition of conscience in *Gaudium et Spes* (par. 16).

d) The Redemptorist celebrating the sacrament of reconciliation with others is himself a sinner. If possible, I find it useful to begin a celebration with a prayer that God will be merciful to me, a sinner. This is not just for the sake of appearances, but it can help the penitent toward an appreciation of the nature of the sacrament, which is to build up the Church as a community of reconciled sinners. Too many people celebrating the sacrament have a wrong idea of the role of the priest: we are not the judge of a person's life (God is), and by acknowledging our own sinfulness before the penitent we may help in locating the process of judgment more correctly: the person accepts judgment on his or her past life, a judgment made in conscience and before God.

e) Most sacramental celebrations will represent a stage of reconciliation in a person's life rather than a final conversion: the sacrament of reconciliation is better seen in the image of springtime than harvesttime. I am not, hopefully, being pessimistic about the nature of sin or unduly weak-minded about the recidivist possibilities of many sinful habits. But realism about our sinful nature can have a beneficial effect on our appreciation of the need for the continuing grace of God and the support of the community in our process of conversion.

Because God loves us, we wish to have our sins forgiven and to receive the grace of the sacrament and the support of the community in our ongoing struggle to remain faithful as reconciled sinners. It is this combination of an appreciation of God's love and a calm realism about the perversity of our human nature that should characterize the Redemptorist celebration of the sacrament of reconciliation. Redemptorist and penitent are both under the sign of the merciful judgment of God. Both should seek the truth of the penitent's sins, always with a respect for conscience and in view of creating that sense of Christian freedom which is essential for the liberation from sin. Just as we could begin the celebration of the sacrament with a prayer acknowledging our own sinfulness, the sacramental rite could conclude with a prayer said jointly by Redemptorist and penitent: "Lord, be gracious to me: heal me, for I have sinned against you" (Psalm 41).

2.5 A necessary ministry

Two developments have been noticeable in the Congregation in recent years, and there is probably a connection between them: the decline in the numbers availing of the sacrament of reconciliation, and the emphasis on the Eucharist as the primary (almost sole?) rite of reconciliation in our ministry.

The decline in the sacrament of reconciliation is difficult to analyze precisely: but I have argued that it has happened for pastoral reasons (rather than for theological or liturgical reasons, in the strict sense). So much was reduced to a short and canonically rigid rite, it was almost as if the Eucharist were reduced to the consecration and Communion. People have stayed away from the sacrament of reconciliation because it was unclear to them how it was a necessary part of being reconciled with God through the ministry of a forgiving community. So the people would not be totally deprived of the experience of reconciliation, we began to emphasize the reconciling function of the Eucharist. It is, clearly, true that the Eucharist is the core symbol through which the community of the Church is built up (Constitution 12), but are we pastorally wise to rely on the Eucharist to achieve, within an hour, all that we expect it to do? I think not, and that is why I have argued for an exploration of new forms of nonsacramental forms of reconciliation, as well as for a more focused Redemptorist expression of the method of celebrating the sacramental rite of reconciliation itself.

The motivation for proposing both developments is the same: how can we communicate the desire of God to reconcile sinners to himself? I cannot see how we will understand how this can be done, in our day, unless we are willing to take the risk of getting to know and understand those in need of reconciliation. Society can be harsh in the way it excludes people who are not "acceptable" for social, economic, or sexual reasons. The Church, too, can be harsh when it seems to demand full reconciliation as the very means of entry into the community, when the community itself is sinful and in need of reconciliation.

The resolution of the problem of reconciliation will not be easy, and Redemptorists should not act as if they were independent of the Church, universal and local. But our charism within the Church gives us a useful access to those who are experiencing difficulties in reconciling certain lifestyles or actions with a Gospel way of life. Some of these will, undoubtedly, remain irreconcilable, while others may not prove to be so: for instance, the Church, at one stage, deemed the lifestyles of being a soldier or an actor to be incompatible with membership of the Christian community. The Redemptorist commitment to ministries of reconciliation, both sacramental and nonsacramental, is an aspect of the Church's desire to seek every possible means, compatible with the Gospel, of reconciling the alienated. "In the midst of conflict and division, we know it is you who turn our minds to thoughts of peace. Your Spirit changes our hearts: enemies begin to speak to one another, those who were estranged joined hands in friendship, and nations seek the way of peace together. Your Spirit is at work when understanding puts an end to strife, when hatred is quenched by mercy, and vengeance gives way to forgiveness" (Second Eucharistic Prayer for Reconciliation).

26

REDEMPTORIST CHARISM AND THE MORAL PROPOSAL

Marciano Vidal, C.Ss.R.
Province of Madrid
Translated by Stephen Rehrauer, C.Ss.R.
Province of Denver

ONE OF THE PRINCIPAL FUNCTIONS, and a basic trait, of the Redemptorist charism is that of bringing together theological reflection, pastoral ministry, and moral theology. The General Chapter of 1991 pointed out that moral theological reflection constitutes "one element of the Alphonsian heritage" and that "it is a characteristic trait of the Redemptorist tradition" (*Final Document,* n. 20). The General Constitutions and Statutes relate this option for moral theological reflection to the "missionary purpose of the congregation" (Constitution 90), and to both "the history and character of the Congregation" (Statute 023).

My proposal in the following pages is to comment on this moral dimension of the Redemptorist charism. I will do so by means of two approaches, each of which may serve as a distinct literary genre. My first approach will be that of a narrative theology in the first person, and the second will bear the character of a more general theological exposition, although no less involved for this reason.

1. My Biography As a Moral Theologian

I was born in 1937 in San Pedro de Trones, a small town in the province of Leon; geographically, linguistically, and culturally near Galicia, a province within the broader Spanish environment. Recognizing these human roots, I have attempted to broaden and deepen the horizon of my "human home" in such a way that I am clothed with the desire to become, and I have the impression that I am in fact, basically a citizen of the one world, rich in its plurality but convergent in fundamental values.

Like all human beings, my family life gave me my primary and decisive inspiration. No stranger to difficulties and limitations, I am content with the human and Christian equipment provided me by my family. With respect to the Redemptorist life, I can say that Alphonsian spirituality and the books of Saint Alphonsus were always near at hand during the first stages of my life in the family. It was customary in our house to read from the books of Saint Alphonsus, such as *The Glories of Mary* and *The Preparation for Death*; it was also customary to make visits to the Blessed Sacrament in the evening, following the book of Saint Alphonsus. This Alphonsian environment has its explanation in the fact that my father had tried to become a Redemptorist brother, even though he was not able to fulfill this desire for reasons of his health.

I entered the juvenate at the age of twelve. I made my novitiate, professing first vows on August 15, 1956. I carried out my studies of philosophy and theology in the studendate at Valladolid, during an epoch of flourishing vocational numbers and of notable intellectual unrest. I was ordained to the priesthood on September 9, 1962.

I attained my more specialized academic preparation first of all at the Pontifical University of Salamanca, earning a licentiate in theology. In addition to this, I took courses in clinical psychology at Complutense University in Madrid without actually earning the licentiate. It was at the Alphonsian Academy of Rome where I accomplished the most qualified preparation for the field of moral theology. This happened in an era of great euphoria for theological studies. It was the second part of the decade of the sixties, the Second Vatican Council having just ended. I hold as one of my most privileged experiences that of having been present in the plaza at St. Peter's at the closing ceremony of the Council. I obtained my doctorate at the Alphonsian Academy under the direction of Professor A. Humbert, presenting a thesis concerning "The missionary discourse of Matthew 10." I can never forget the figure of Master Bernard Häring, from whom I drank the enthusiasm for the *renovation* of moral theology, according to the orientation given by the Second Vatican Council in the decree *Optatum Totius* (n. 16), which I have quoted and explicated so many times in my classes and in the conferences that I have given.

I have dedicated myself to the work of renewing moral theology for almost three decades. I have done so by means of academic activity, publications, university courses, and the various positions of responsibility that I have held. I will briefly highlight these facets of my intellectual biography, but first, I cannot omit the fact that during my first years as a priest I complemented my education with the ministry of the missions. They were two years of intense pastoral ministry replete with the fervor of the Redemptorist mission. In addition, I had the joy of collaborating in the renovation of the *content* of missionary preaching, working side by side with the great missionary Father Luciano Del Burgo. The result of our work together was published in books that served many missionaries to take the step in the content of their preaching from the "traditional" mission to the "renewed" mission. Having made this slight digression, I return now to my labor as a moral theologian.

Academic activity: I have developed my academic activity first of all at the Pontifical University of Salamanca, and later at various theological centers of Madrid: at the Instituto Superior de Pastoral, at the Seminary of Madrid, at the Instituto Superior de Ciencias Morales, and at Comillas Pontifical University. Presently, I work exclusively at these latter two centers, where I am a full professor. I also impart an intensive course every two years, as an invited professor, at the Alphonsian Academy of Rome.

Of the indicated centers, I wish to point out the importance that the Instituto Superior de Ciencias Morales and Comillas Pontifical University have had for me. The first is a center directed by the Spanish Redemptorists, founded in 1971. It was an important decision of the Spanish province, a decision taken in provincial chapter. I am pleased to think that my great interest, enthusiasm, and effort were part of the driving force that caused this initiative to arise and be assumed by the province. I began to teach at Comillas Pontifical University, run by the Jesuits, in 1971. Contact with the members of the Society of Jesus has reminded me of the ties of Alphonsus, the moralist, with the Jesuit authors of his era. I also have learned a great deal from the Jesuits. I hope that the presence of the Alphonsian spirit in the university will be a positive force for both institutions. In fact, our Redemptorist center for the study of moral theology is incorporated into the Jesuit university. Every two years I give a course there concerning the history of moral theology, in which I have the opportunity to emphasize the ties of Alphonsian moral theology with the Jesuit spirit. I have published a brief study concerning "the relationship between Saint Alphonsus, the moralist, and the Society of Jesus."

Extended university activity: My extended university activity has been fairly intense, stretching throughout many different countries. I have taught courses in many European countries, above all in Portugal and Italy, and for pastoral ministers of emigration in other European nations. I have directed courses and workshops for missionaries in Africa (Angola, Zaire, Kenya) and in Asia (Korea, Japan). My activity and my presence have been more intense and extensive in Latin America: Mexico, Guatemala, El Salvador, Puerto Rico, the Dominican Republic, Venezuela, Colombia, Ecuador, Peru, Paraguay, Uruguay, Argentina, Chile, Brazil. All of these contacts have helped me to develop a more open sensitivity, which is pluralist and incarnated in these various situations of Christianity.

Positions of responsibility and initiatives: Regarding my positions of responsibility and initiatives in the field of theology, I will enumerate the principal ones. I have been and am currently the director of the Instituto Superior de Ciencias Morales, a center dedicated to research and the instruction of moral theological reflection in the second and third academic cycles (the levels of licentiate and doctorate). I have been director of the Interfacultative Institute of "Matrimony and Family Life" of Comillas Pontifical University, a center for whose coming into existence I am responsible. I am a member of the editorial board of the magazine *Concilium*. I am a founding member of the European Association of Theologians and have been vice president of the Spanish chapter. Among the initiatives in which I have actively taken part, I am proud to have collaborated in the preparation and the realization of the first three International Congresses of Redemptorist Moralists: in Aylmer (Canada) in 1989, in Santo Domingo (Dominican Republic) in 1992, and in Pattaya (Thailand) in 1995.

Publications: I believe that one of the most distinctive traits of my personality as a theologian is that of my publications. I am a contributor to many national journals (*Moralia, Sal Terrae, Razón y Fe, Miscelánea Comillas, Iglesia Viva*), as well as to foreign journals (*Studia Moralia, Le Supplément, Rivista di Teologia Morale*). I have collaborated in collective works, the most recent being *Moraltheologie im abseits?* (Herder, 1994); *In Christus zum Leben befreit* (Herder, 1992); *Historia: memoria futuri* (Alphonsian Academy, 1991); *De dignitate hominis* (Herder, 1987). I have also edited a number of collective works in Spanish, the most notable of these being *Conceptos fundamentales de ética theológica* (Trotta, 1992), in which forty-four specialists in philosophical ethics and moral theology from Spain collaborated. Insofar as my own works go, I have published about divergent fields of moral theology: bioethics, ethics of marriage, fundamental ethics. I have dedicated two critical studies to the moral theology reflected in the *Catechism of the Catholic Church* and in the encyclical *Veritatis Splendor, La moral cristiana en el Catecismo* (PPC, 1992), *La propuesta moral de Juan Pablo II* (PPC, 1994). I have made incursions into the history of moral theology, specifically in the area of the moral thought of the eighteenth century revolving around the figure of Saint Alphonsus: *Frente al rigorismo moral, benignidad pastoral* (PS, 1986), *La familia en la vida y en el pensamiento de San Alfonso* (PS, 1995). However, my principal work remains the four-volume manual of theological ethics, with more than three thousand pages, entitled *Moral de Actitudes*. I have procured the revision of this manual in successive editions for the purpose of maintaining it up to date. It is currently in its ninth edition. Finally, I would point out that almost all my books have been translated into Italian and Portuguese. I regret not having had the luck of seeing my works published in English yet, the language which is today the most universal among authors for communicating the ideas they formulate.

Interests: To bring to a close this short intellectual autobiography I want to point out the constellation of interests that has occupied most of my time as a moralist. In the field of moral theology, I have been concerned and continue to be concerned with four issues and/or fundamental orientations:

- The internal renewal of Christian morality both as a "theological science" (epistemological, moral-theological) and as the "Christian way of life" (seeking a way of pastoral benignity between rigorism and permissiveness)
- The dialogue between moral theology and the anthropological sciences, and with the reality of the secularization of Western culture, particularly that of Europe
- The inculturation of the Christian ethos in cultures that have been neglected by theology and which have a notable future for Christian faith, particularly African and Asian cultures
- The exposition of the Christian ethic as a force for liberation, looking to the situation of the Third World, above all to Latin America

I must confess that I would not be sensitive to these four orientations were it not for the luck of knowing Christian communities of the whole world and if I did not have the opportunity to direct the work (licentiate and doctorate) of students who come from diverse areas, cultures, and countries.

The description I have just given of my journey as a moral theologian not only explains *how* I became initiated into the Redemptorist charism but also *why* I have remained within it and why I continue to remain a part of it.

I believe that one does not "enter" once and for all at a precise moment into the charism of an institute. I consider myself privileged to have been entering little by little into the Redemptorist charism. Already in the family, I had the first taste of this charism due to the already-mentioned Alphonsian spirituality that I saw in my father and to the presence of Redemptorist missionaries preaching in my parish. As a child, I saw many illustrious Redemptorists, among them I remember Fathers José Pedrero (who would later become a consultor general), Julio de la Torre (later professor of the Alphonsian Academy) and José Suescun (professor of the studendate at Astorga and Valladolid). Initiation into the Redemptorist charism proceeded in the juvenate at El Espino. It became an option in the novitiate at Nava del Rey. It deepened intellectually and spiritually in the studendate at Valladolid. From the moment of priestly ordination until now, the Redemptorist charism has been entering into me. I can rightly say it has neither caused me discomfort nor has it been any problem for me.

The foregoing affirmation explains *why* I remain. I feel comfortable within the Redemptorist charism. My form of understanding and of living the Christian experience fits perfectly within the parameters of the charism. I want to highlight those aspects of the charism which best define, give meaning to, and orient my Christian lifestyle. They are the following:

- an *anthropology* of simplicity, of normalcy, of contained optimism, of shared debility
- the concept of a *God* who is open to everyone, rich in mercy, exaggeratedly understanding a down-to-earth *Christology*, evangelical, tempered by the presence of the *Holy Spirit* and by the continual nearness of *Mary*
- a *spirituality* of affect, which "makes us remember" Christ and is projected outward in efficacious practices of charity

- a *pastoral praxis* that rests upon the options of missionary urgency, of preference for the weakest, and of strategies of evangelical confidence in the Word

I remain in the Redemptorist charism through a species of *vocational connaturality*. I sense this connaturality intensely in my work as a moral theologian. In the second part of this reflection, I will try to describe how the Redemptorist tradition of pastoral praxis and reflection is related to moral theology.

2. The "Alphonsian Spirit" in Moral Theology

I believe it is possible to speak objectively about a *Redemptorist tradition* within Catholic moral theological reflection, as well as within pastoral practice, above all in terms of our preaching and our presence in the confessional. At the end of the twentieth century, this awareness of a Redemptorist tradition in moral theology has attained both a *critical character* and a *universal amplitude*. The critical character is the result of the studies realized concerning the Alphonsian moral tradition and concerning its ecclesial reception with occasion of the bicentennial of the death of Saint Alphonsus. Its universal amplitude has been seen in the three International Congresses of Redemptorist Moral Theologians, celebrated in Aylmer (1989), Santo Domingo (1992), and Pattaya (1995).

It is more difficult to describe the shape of this Redemptorist moral-theological tradition. Without a doubt, it is born and is fed by the Alphonsian writings. However, it is also conditioned by the ongoing reception of the morality of Saint Alphonsus in the Church and in the Congregation. This reception has not always taken the same form so we can speak of "traditions" (or of "subtraditions") within the shared Redemptorist tradition. For example, the Redemptorist tradition expressed in the manuals of moral theology edited by Redemptorists of the nineteenth and the first half of the twentieth centuries, and the tradition which arose out of the moral theological work carried out at the Alphonsian Academy of Rome during the past decades, are very different in character. While the former attempted to be faithful to the "letter" of Alphonsian morality, proposing a more rigorist interpretation, the latter has attempted to situate itself within the "spirit" of Saint Alphonsus, projecting this in terms of an interpretation which is more open and benign. On the other hand, tensions in pastoral practice have also existed with relation to the Redemptorist moral tradition; evidently, there exist rigorist tones in both preaching and in penitential practice; however a closeness to the people has never been lacking, and there has always been an option for the salvific character of all pastoral practice.

The preceding annotations indicate that it is necessary to study in greater depth both the meaning and the historical trajectory of the Redemptorist tradition in moral theology. I do not intend to do so in these pages. I only want to make reference to the "Alphonsian spirit" that must animate this tradition, which, when all is said and done, constitutes it, defines it, and makes it what it is.

In continuation, I would point out the most decisive traits that characterize the moral theology of the Alphonsian cradle. By adopting this orientation, I am distancing myself from a "literalist" reading of Alphonsian moral theology. What is valid in the moral thought of Saint Alphonsus is not found in the concrete contents, that is to say, in the concrete resolutions of the proposed cases. These refer to questions concerning the reality of another epoch and they are formulated according to moral categories that contemporary theological moral reflection has left behind. What is valid and permanent in Alphonsian morality is his "spirit," that is to say, the basic orientations that condition all the work of his moral casuistry, and which, with the normal historical adaptations, can continue to function in configuring a particular moral "tradition" within the Church, in theological reflection as well as in pastoral practice.

Pastorality: Alphonsian moral theology is born in pastoral practice and is directed toward pastoral application. The first edition of the *Theologica Moralis* (1748) constitutes an edition of the *Manual of Busenbaum* throughout which Alphonsus made his own annotations, incorporating them into the body of the original work. Tannoia points out that the passages proper to Alphonsus had their source in the moral cases that were coming up in his pastoral activity. Alphonsus himself noted in the prologue to the second edition (and he repeated this up until the ninth), that many of the contents have their origin, not in the reading of books, but in pastoral practice.

Both the contents and the form of treatment of the themes are conditioned in Alphonsian moral theology by the orientation which pastoral practice imposes. He frequently remits to the "scholastics" the questions that seem to him to lack pastoral relevance. Rather, he deals at length with those which are of notable interest for the pastoral practice at that historical moment.

It is possible to affirm that the Alphonsian moral theological discourse is ruled not by the principle of academic purity (intellectualism), but by the criterion of coherence with pastoral practice. This practicality, identified with pastorality, constitutes a key for the explication of Alphonsian moral theology.

Salvific character: The criteria of "pastorality" revolutionizes the concept of moral theological science. Moral discourse does not consist in the search for an aseptically objective truth, but rather for the truth which saves. Because of this salvific condition of the moral truth, Alphonsus made a methodological choice in favor of casuistry, overcoming the allurements of the pretended evangelical radicality proposed by both tutiorists and filo-jansenist moralists.

Alphonsus considers moral theology to be a science ordered toward salvation. He does not understand moral theological reflection as a simple search for the objective moral truth, and even less as an exercise of the discursive capacity of the human mind. For him, morality "is directed completely toward praxis." This "practicality," a criterion that guides his work in the field of moral theology, is identified with the search for the concrete truth which saves.

The salvific dynamism of Alphonsian morality is at work in the whole complex of his moral theological project. In concrete, we can see it

- in his rejection of excessive rigorism, which carries within itself a condemnatory tendency
- in his pastoral acceptance of the reality of inculpable ignorance that impedes formal sin
- in his application of the moral criteria according to the concrete situation of the person, seeking not the formal perfection of the application of a system, but rather the personal perfection of the situated subject

The articulation of moral theology in a "unified project of the Christian life": It has become customary to divide the Alphonsian literary corpus into four or five large blocks: dogmatics (and apologetics or controversies), moral theology, pastoral writings, and spirituality. This division is patently artificial and distorts our understanding of Alphonsian thought. There is a much greater unity to his writings than what is expressed by this way of grouping his works together.

It is apparent that the relationship his moral writings have with the rest of his theological, spiritual, and pastoral works does not leap out at us. Liguori composed his moral theology in an era when dogmatics and spirituality were considered to run along two parallel courses. Because of this, his strictly moral works do not form a direct and immediate unity with his spiritual writings. The unity, however, does exist. It must be sought in more profound areas, in those which breathe the unique and same Alphonsian spirit. One can rightly speak of an "Alphonsian corpus," in which dogmatics, moral theology, spirituality, and pastoral theology are all integrated. In the "corpus Alphonsianum," all of the works converge to offer a proposal for the Christian life destined for the people. In this way, the spirituality completes the moral vision offered in the writings cataloged as "strictly moral" according to the categories of the eighteenth century.

To discover both the historical meaning and the modernity of the moral message of Alphonsus, it is necessary to take into account not only the writings catalogued as strictly moral but also those works which expound the "morality of Christian perfection," those which complement the "morality destined for the confessor." The book *The Practice of the Love of Jesus Christ* is the most polished exposition of the "morality of perfection" as Saint Alphonsus understood it.

If understood in this way, the morality of Alphonsus is revealed as an authentic pedagogy of the Christian life. This morality is a preferentially positive sign, it has a pedagogical-educational formulation, it flows out of the river bed of the virtues, and it is inserted into the whole of the Christian mystery. All of these traits are harmonized into one: moral theology is understood as *the practice of charity.*

Pastoral benignity: I believe that the historical significance of the moral works of Alphonsus as a whole is sufficiently expressed by the expression which indicates a twofold movement of rejection and acceptance: away *from rigorism* (rejection) *toward benignity* (acceptance). That is to say, the step or conversion from moral rigorism toward pastoral benignity is the fundamental key for the understanding of the Alphonsian moral labor: of its genesis, of its configuration as a literary work, of its confrontation with other stances in the eighteenth century, and of its ecclesiastical acceptance during the nineteenth and twentieth centuries.

This understanding of Alphonsian morality from the trait of pastoral benignity is found already in the work of Tannoia, when he says that the moral theology of Alphonsus "avoided the two extremes of probabilist laxism and of tutiorist rigorism." However, the expression "pastoral benignity" is of recent coinage. I feel privileged for having been one of the first and one of those who with greatest insistence has characterized Alphonsian moral theology as a morality of pastoral benignity. Pope John Paul II used the expression "pastoral benignity" in his apostolic letter on the occasion of the second centenary of the death of Saint Alphonsus.

Alphonsian benignity has nothing to do with *laxism*. The expression which, according to Alphonsus, qualifies his option for benignity is that of *the just mean*. Between the two extremes of laxism and of rigorism, Alphonsus builds a secure highway out of the benignity demanded by the Gospel. It is what he will call "the middle way," a position of prudential equilibrium which sustains

- in order to offer a moral theological escape from the irreconcilable theoretical arguments between rigorist (probabiliorists) and laxist (probabilist) moral theologians
- in order to open up a way to salvation and liberation of the Christian conscience, enslaved by merciless rigor or by hopeless relaxation

Both the rejection of rigorism and the option for benignity have in Alphonsus the same motivation: his understanding of Christianity as both the invitation and the way to salvation. This salvific understanding of moral theology, and the consequent option for salvific benignity, is supported by an anthropological and theological conception bearing the same shape. It has a clearly salvific orientation. Christianity is understood and lived by Alphonsus as an abundance of salvation. This quality is so characteristic of his thinking and of his life that there is no need to subject it to a detailed analysis or proof. It is enough to remember that it is the support and justification of the Alphonsian option for benignity.

I believe that the historical significance of Alphonsus as a moral theologian resides in his having been the most qualified representative of those who explicitly and efficaciously opposed the rigorist distortion of the Gospel, and he provided the rediscovery of a benignity born in the abundance of Christian salvation during an era of profound crisis for Catholic conscience.

Our own era is also a time of profound moral crisis. Moral theology can continue to offer a message of salvation to the world today if we are capable of entering into his spirit of benignity, and in so doing overcome the temptations of moral rigorism, which are still lurking today, waiting to ambush the conscience of Christians.

27

RETREATS ACCORDING TO THE ALPHONSIAN CHARISM

John Kane, C.Ss.R.
Province of Oakland

1. Biographical Background

1.1 Why I became a Redemptorist

There were three experiences that led me to become a Redemptorist:
growing up as a boy in a Redemptorist parish; coming under the influence
of Father John Zeller, my novice master; and the six years I spent at the
house of studies in Oconomowoc, Wisconsin.

As a boy I grew up in a parish conducted by Redemptorists, Holy
Redeemer in Portland, Oregon. During that time, I got to know very well
the community of priests and brothers at Holy Redeemer through serving
Mass, meeting them in many informal ways, and from their visits to my
family home. When it seemed to me, at an early age, that God might be calling
me to be a priest, I never for a moment doubted that I wanted to be a
Redemptorist. As I look back, after a period of more than sixty years, on
those Redemptorists of my youth, I still feel for them deep gratitude and
affection. They remain among the most significant people of my life.

After attending the preparatory schools of the congregation, first at
Oakland, California, and then Kirkwood, Missouri (years filled with joy
and pain, typical of adolescence), I went on with my classmates to the novitiate of the St. Louis Province at DeSoto, Missouri. There I was to come
under the influence of one of the most remarkable men I was ever to meet,
Father John Zeller.

It is not easy to describe Father John, which may be why, to this date, no one has attempted to write his biography. One has to learn to recognize opposites in him. He was, on occasion, so childlike and simple, one might think he had never read a book in his life. On the other hand, he was such a profound student of the Scriptures that, as he spoke, one listened in awe, as one might have to the Hebrew prophets or to Jesus himself. He brought us to love Saint Alphonsus, by a display of such thorough knowledge of our founder's life and writings (which he meditated on every day), as no one ever after was to equal. Yet he could shock us, too, by reciting in vivid detail the history of the failures of the Congregation and the scandals of some of its members. Again, we felt he really cared for each of us; yet few, if any, did he ever allow to get close to him.

During the year we lived with Father John, we came little by little in intuit his unbelievably joyful secret: that the price of total commitment to God, by the vows of religion, is in the end not death but life, and that, with Leon Bloy, "there is only one unhappiness, not to die among the saints."

After novitiate came the time that I have always considered the happiest of my life, the six years at the house of studies at Oconomowoc, Wisconsin, for what it was and for what it promised. It was a distinct pleasure—I do not hesitate to say privilege—to live during those six years with the students, sometimes numbering over one hundred. All were of one mind; they wanted, more than anything in the world, to be Redemptorists. It was good to be with them, whether in the classroom, the chapel, or at recreation. The future was to confirm how talented many of these confreres were: from their ranks came bishops, provincials, teachers, missionaries (at home and in Brazil and Thailand), parish priests, and those in special ministries of all kinds. We were glad to look forward to sharing our future together.

For me personally this time was a time of awakening. Until this period of my training, studies had meant hardly more than what was required to pass on to the next stage of preparation for the priesthood. They seldom held any interest for me in themselves. But at this period books came into my hands that broadened my mental horizons and moved me deeply. I can remember, as if it were only yesterday, such authors as Maritain, Gilson, Guardini, Gerald Vann, E. I. Watkin, Karl Adam, Dom Marmion, Edward Leen, Mortimer Adler, and most of all the classical writers on the spiritual life, John of the Cross, Teresa of Avila, Eugene Boylan, enlightening me in ways I would previously not have thought possible. That side of Alphonsus that is author, preacher, and scholar, I began to see as an ideal. The text in the old rule "they shall spend their lives among books" took on new meaning for me.

Hardly more than fifteen years after my time, the life and many of the ideals prized by my generation at Oconomowoc were considered to be in need of radical change, and so, as a house of studies, it was abandoned.

I can only reflect that, though few things are perfect or destined to endure for long, the only changes I ever wanted during my time there were minor. At any rate, on June 22, 1944, when I joined my seventeen classmates in the seminary chapel, my twelve years of Redemptorist training had prepared me to say yes to ordination with great joy—and with no reservations.

1.2 Why I remained a Redemptorist

It is not likely that ever again, in America at least, will it be the ideal for religious orders to multiply small seminaries or even novitiates. Such a policy is not only a drain on personnel and finances, but a threat to the high standards required for the education of clerics. At two different periods during my priesthood, I was put into this situation by obedience: once for seven years as lector; at another time, as rector for eight years. Despite some very notable exceptions (all known to the province at large and deeply appreciated), the faculty at Holy Redeemer College (our minor seminary) was seldom well trained or very highly motivated. Shortly after Vatican II, the school was closed. The reaction among the confreres varied from relief, to regret, to anger. Looking back it was simply the beginning of changes that would go on shaking the foundations of the Church in America until the present time.

For me, I had preaching, my first choice, to take up again. I had been on the mission band for eight years, a ministry to which I am very much attracted. Now I was appointed to preach retreats at Picture Rocks Retreat House in Arizona. After six years, I requested, and was given permission, to organize the ideals of Father Bernard Häring into a working house of prayer. The twenty-one years of its existence have known both struggle and blessings. What at first was a dream has become a reality. It has been made such by the wide variety of people (priests, religious, and laypeople) from all over North America and beyond, and by confreres from my own province and most of the English-speaking provinces.

Because of age this will undoubtedly be the last full-time ministry I will be engaged in. If so, I will be able to look back on my life as a Redemptorist as one that surpassed my expectations. It has allowed me to do, in my favorite phrase, not so much what pleased me, but "what I believed in with all my heart." I could not have asked for more.

2. Introduction

The question this essay raises and, in some tentative way, will attempt to answer is: What is a retreat according to the Alphonsian charism?

It is a question of concern to all Redemptorists: to those who conduct retreats (a ministry commended by Statute 020); to those who make retreats (each Redemptorist is requested to made a retreat of eight days each year, and of one day nearly each month by Statute 029), and to newly appointed superiors [these are asked to make the spiritual exercises at an opportune time after their appointment (Statute 095f)].

For an answer to this question, one must look to Saint Alphonsus (his writings and his life), and to the Constitutions and Statutes, which bring to us today the Alphonsian charism.

3. Saint Alphonsus

To return to Saint Alphonsus, at this period of time, has its difficulties. Many today who have tried to adjust their lives to the norms of Vatican II have done so by turning away from what has come to be referred to as the Tridentine Church—the Church under the spirit and letter of the Council of Trent. As a consequence, interest in the writings of Saint Alphonsus, as one identified with the Church of that period, has considerably cooled. The reason is that many of our concerns today (ecumenism, the new liturgy, ecology, the role of the Church in such documents as *Lumen Gentium* and *Gaudium et Spes*, the place of women in the church, and religious obedience by consensus) are ones Saint Alphonsus would have no answer for, simply because they were questions which he, in his lifetime, was not obliged to face.

It is perhaps time, however, to bring some balance to the way we think about Saint Alphonsus. For two hundred years after his death, Alphonsus was widely read and much appreciated. In many areas of the world, his books were highly prized classics. He was given by Pius IX the highest rank that can be given a writer in the Catholic Church, that of Doctor of the Church. If he is not as popular as he was once, this in time may be reversed. After all, the fate of falling in and out of favor is a fate not escaped even by Augustine and Aquinas. In a real sense, in making Saint Alphonsus a Doctor of the Church, the Church is saying that his writings transcend his own age, and are for the ages.

Constitution and Statues

When Vatican II began in 1962 few, if any of us, could have guessed that the Church would have faced the world, in the very midst of its unprecedented change, and come up with a vision of how to plunge itself into this world and carry on its mission. Not only would Saint Alphonsus have been unprepared for the conclusions of that Council, but neither were those of my generation, whose training in theology had been completed just twenty years before. It would take the Congregation a great deal of time, work, study, anguish, loss of members, a prodigious amount of travel, and growing old to come to grips with the aftermath of this Council.

But during the last thirty years, in the great number of general and provincial chapters held, we have, with our present Constitutions and Statues come, at least in theory, from the Church of Trent to the Church of Vatican II. This altogether remarkable document states what, for us today, is the Alphonsian charism. It is from this document, as well as from the writings and life of Saint Alphonsus, that an answer is to be found to the question: What is a retreat according to the Alphonsian charism?

4. A Retreat

I have been asked to reflect on this subject not so much objectively, as a scholar might with a plethora of footnotes, but subjectively, as one reflecting on his own experience. This I will gladly do. What I have to say will fall under five headings:

- a time for silence
- a time to absorb God's Word
- a time to encounter Jesus Christ
- a time of prayer
- a time to face sin and conversion

The retreat: a time of silence

Saint Alphonsus was accustomed to refer to the retreat as a time spent in the *strictest silence*. I questioned that at one period in my life, but all in all, from my experience of many years, and especially after the experience of my twenty-one years at the house of prayer, I have come to agree. The best retreat *is* the one made in silence. There are reasons for this.

Jesus obviously showed a preference for silence: "In the morning, long before dawn, he got up and left the house and went off to a lonely place and prayed there" (Mark 1:35). It is a matter of experience that without silence, words lose their meaning; without listening, speaking no longer heals; and without a lonely place, our actions quickly become empty gestures.

Silence, paradoxically, can be the cure for those who often prefer to turn from it. The kind of person, whom I have in mind, is one for whom work has been a preoccupation. For him, there is a noticeable reluctance—*in certain cases, an actual incapacity*—to take up even the most basic acts of spiritual practice, like reading the Scriptures, reflecting on what has been read, or praying for more than a few moments. The lives of such people are usually flat; for them there are no peaks of joy, sorrow, compassion, or wonder. As a consequence, even to attend liturgy is little more than an arid duty. This kind of person, in the fulsome meaning Scripture gives to the words, no longer knows how "to think in the heart."

Father Thomas Merton, American Trappist monk, spent a great deal of time in pursuit of the significance of silence and solitude, in relation to the psychological and spiritual growth of such a person as I have been speaking about. He once said:

> Solitude is necessary to some extent for the fullness of human living....All need enough silence and solitude to enable the deep inner voice of their own true self to be heard at least occasionally. When that inner voice is not heard, when man cannot attain to the inner spiritual peace that comes from being perfectly at one with his own true self, his life is always miserable and exhausting. If man is constantly exiled from his home, locked out of his spiritual solitude, he ceases to be a true person.
>
> *The Silent Life*, p.143

To conclude, when Saint Alphonsus asks that a retreat be carried on in strict silence, I feel he is in the tradition of those highly gifted spiritual leaders *from both East and West* who take seriously what it means to make a retreat.

The retreat: a time to absorb God's Word

The document that was, perhaps, the most practical of all those to come from Vatican II was *Dei Verbum*, that on divine Revelation. The members of this Council, enlightened by the Spirit and heartened by the great advances being made in Scripture study, set the Church in a biblical direction that has not prevailed since the age of the Great Fathers of the Church.

The practical results were these: the Scriptures would no longer be a book that the Church would only reverence. It would be a book that would be used—*as no other book.* The memorable symbol for this was the ceremony that took place every day during the Council, when the only book set before the Council Fathers, as they met in the great aula of St. Peter's, was the sacred Scripture.

What this came to mean, in a practical way, was demonstrated by those who wrote and approved the various constitutions, decrees, and declarations. These are all steeped in the spirit, and often the very words, of the Bible.

This spirit has continued since that time in the Church, in writings of the pope and bishops, in the three-year cycle of readings for the liturgy and in the fact that all the theological disciplines have been renewed through biblical studies. One can note, with pride, that our Redemptorist Constitutions and Statues and the *Communicada* from our central government, are written in this same spirit.

We are illumined by sacred Scripture itself on what it means, in the fine phrase of Pope Paul VI, to "absorb the Word of God." The Word of God has the power to take us to the very center of our being. "The word of God is living and effective, and sharper than any two-edged sword, penetrating even between soul and spirit, joints and marrow, and able to discern reflections and thoughts of the heart" (Hebrews 4:12). It brings truth and freedom: "If you remain in my word...you will know the truth, and the truth will set you free" (John 8:31). It brings us to the deepest relation with God: "To those who receive the Word are given the power to become the children of God" (John 1:12).

History reveals periods in the Church, when sacred Scripture was not cultivated, when certain regions of the Church organized themselves and ruled, in the main, by canon law. Happily *Dei Verbum* prescribes a different course: "The entire Christian religion should be nourished and *ruled* by Sacred Scripture" (n. 21).

Benedict XV, Pius XII (in *Divino Afflante*) and *Dei Verbum* present us with a truth that is calculated to make every honest Christian turn to the Scriptures. This truth is to be found in the famous statement of Saint Jerome: "Ignorance of the Scriptures is ignorance of Jesus Christ" (n. 25).

The full meaning of "to absorb God's Word" is to receive it into one's consciousness. C. G. Jung, after years as an analyst working with people who referred to themselves as Christians, charged nearly all of them of not being Christian at all, but pagan because they had never allowed Christianity to penetrate to their innermost being. Religion was for them an outer reality only—never an inner one.

Saint Alphonsus knew those in the Kingdom of Naples, priests and nuns among them, for whom faith was an outer, not an inner, reality. It saddened him. But it became his lifework to help them to become the good soil into which the seed of God's Word might take root and bear fruit.

One stands in awe at what Saint Alphonsus offered of himself to the service of the Word of God:

- *his very being*, so full of passion and drive
- *his gifts as preacher and writer*, which attracted people in such remarkable numbers
- *his practice of asceticism*, so frightening, by contrast, to us who are well fed, well rested, and in good health
- *his prayerfulness*, rarely less than six hours of duration
- *his intelligence*, equal to the highest of the day, offered in service to the lowly as to the lofty
- *his affectivity*, poured out in such fullness in his written prayers to the Father, Jesus, the Holy Spirit, and Mary
- *and his learning*, the fruit of a lifetime of dialoguing with the great texts of the Scriptures, the Doctors of the Church (Augustine, Aquinas, Teresa of Avila, John of the Cross, and Francis deSales), and the writers of his own day

Yes, one stands in awe.

There must have been moments when Saint Alphonsus was relaxed.

But I keep seeing that side of him which was a kind of holy restlessness, the side of him that wanted to get his agenda completed before the night came "when no man can work" (John 9:4). He seems to have been as convinced as anyone ever could that "the kingdom of heaven suffers violence, and the violent are taking it by force" (Matthew 11:12). As for his love for the Word of God, Alphonsus was brother to the prophet who said, "When I found your words, I devoured them; they became my joy and the happiness of my life" (Jeremiah 15:16).

Admiration for Saint Alphonsus may not be enough for the retreat preacher. But without it, he may never be moved to work under his charism.

The retreat: a time to encounter Jesus Christ

There is every reason to believe that Jesus Christ came to earth to be "on our side," on the side of humanity. This seems to be clearly what Paul is saying: "Though he was in the form of God, he did not regard equality with God something to be clung to...he emptied himself..."; he came "in human likeness" (Philippians 2:6–7). Also, "he was like us in all things, except sin" (Hebrews 4:15).

Yet, in the theological climate in which I grew up, Christ, insofar as our consciousness was concerned, had been allowed to pass back to the side of God and be, in effect, God alone. I suspect that this focus on Christ is still, to some extent, present in the Church.

Gradually over twenty years—through reading such authors as Marmion, Karl Adam, and sad to say, what I only came to lately, the New Testament—the person of Christ and his place in the spiritual life began to enter my consciousness. The book that illumined me most on this point was *In the Redeeming Christ* by F. X. Durrwell. It has been some thirty years since I first read the passage in that book that ever afterward I have been thankful for, and which I have shared with retreatants ever since:

> What the believer affirms, the object toward which he makes his "leap of faith," is not merely a truth of reason or even a series of truths. The Apostles were not teaching doctrines, propagating religious ideas. They were heralds, the witness of a *person*...."What we preach is Jesus Christ our Lord" (2 Corinthians 4:5).

When it was a question of getting them to deny their faith, what they were asked to renounce was [not doctrines but] a person, Christ (pp. 82–83).

One further thing I have learned—that this same person, Jesus Christ, the object of faith, *dwells* in the baptized person, and when love is present, Christ will love in return "and reveal myself to him" (John 14:21). In the Eastern Church where spiritual writers who, by preference, spoke of their *experience* of Christ and who were not apparently as much threatened by Inquisitors as in the West, to modify their expression, have agreed upon a theology to explain what it means for Jesus "to reveal" himself to the one who loves him. It is explained in the context of the Jesus Prayer:

> Although the baptismal Christ and the indwelling Paraclete never cease for a moment to work within us, save on rare occasions, most of us remain virtually unaware of this inward presence and activity....To pray is to pass from the state where grace is present in our hearts secretly and unconsciously, to the point of full inward perception and conscious awareness when we experience and *feel* the activity of the Spirit [of Christ] directly and immediately.
>
> *Power of the Name* (K. Ware), p. 3

In the New Testament Scriptures, and in the theology of the Jesus Prayer, I have found a way to Christ that has been one of the great graces of my life. It is what I, and those who minister with me here at Desert House of Prayer, attempt to communicate to all our retreatants—whether Catholic, Orthodox, Protestant, or other. Their interest has always been of the highest.

The retreat: a time of prayer

Under this heading I wish to indicate what kinds of prayer the people who come to Desert House of Prayer—priests, nuns, laypeople (most of these are men and women of some education)—*as a matter of fact,* actually engage in. These, most often, are of three kinds: liturgical, personal, and devotional.

Liturgical: The Eucharist is the heart of our life of prayer. It is prepared for each day by those who will have a role to perform as lector, homilist, or music leader. One of our goals is to expand our understanding of *true pres-*

ence to include not only the Eucharist but also the assembly (the people of God) and the sacred Scripture, as the Vatican Council II teaches. At our house of prayer, we are under no hurry to move things along. Our contemplative prayer teaches us to be still at the proper times—*and savor the moment.* We also celebrate the liturgy of morning prayer and evening prayer. The psalms are set to a simple chant that is led by a cantor. This approach to the Liturgy of the Hours is well received.

Personal: Every one who makes a retreat with us engages, in one way or another, in the four classic steps of prayer: serious reading (*lectio*); reflection (*meditatio*); praying over what one has read (*oratio*); and resting in the Lord (*contemplatio*). Many of our retreatants ask for guidance during their stay with us, which we are always glad to give. We attempt to help them decide how the Holy Spirit is leading them.

Each day we offer two periods for praying the Jesus Prayer. Generally, those who join us in this prayer are in one or the other of two stages of progress: (1) the majority will probably be in the first stage, in which the recitation of the Jesus Prayer will lead them to rest in God without a constantly varying succession of images, ideas, and feelings. (2) The second stage is where God becomes more active in their prayer and they become receptive. Their prayer ceases, to some extent, to be "their prayer" and becomes, to a greater or lessor extent, the prayer of "Christ in me."

For years there has raged a debate as to whether or not those in active ministry should consider the practice of contemplative prayer, which is the kind of prayer I have just briefly described. It was maintained by many that this kind of prayer was only for those in contemplative orders. This debate, in recent years, has come to all but a halt. It is believed now, for the most part, that God gives the graces of prayer to whomever he wills, independent of the style of ministry one might be engaged in. Further, now that the subject of contemplative prayer has been taken up in the new *Catechism of the Catholic Church*, possibly the debate will be remembered in hardly more than a footnote, if it is remembered at all.

Insofar as Redemptorists might be concerned, Alphonsus both prayed contemplative prayer and taught it (*Saint Alphonsus de Liguori by Frederic Jones,* p. 350). He alerted young confessors how to be prepared to notice it when directing penitents (*Praxis Confessarii*, Ch. IX). If contemplative prayer is in itself the highest of all forms of prayer, it was wise of Saint Teresa to advise all to pray for it.

Devotional: Some of our traditional Alphonsian devotions, with some variations, are still welcomed and practiced by modern retreatants.

- *Devotion to Christ crucified:* Every Friday, when compatible with the liturgical season, we reinact the Good Friday symbol. The crucifix, resting on a purple-covered pillow, with a candle on either side, is placed on the floor before the altar where it remains all day. The Mass, when allowed, is that of The Most Precious Blood of Jesus. Friday is also a day of mitigated fast—added to our prayer for the concerns of peace and justice.
- *Prayer before the Reserved Sacrament:* Beginning each Saturday evening and extending until Sunday morning, those who desire spend an hour before the Blessed Sacrament praying as we wish: but there is also the thought that the hour with the risen Lord will help prepare us for Sunday, the day of the risen Lord. Each Sunday at Desert House is a day of celebrating the Resurrection, ending with our evening meal, which is always a little more festive than usual. What better reason for rejoicing than the world-shaking hope that there is no more death, only life.
- *Our Lady:* We celebrate all the feasts of Mary as they appear during the liturgical year, the women with us often adding to our festivities in very creative ways. Likenesses of Our Lady, in painting and sculpture, especially of Our Mother of Perpetual Help, sweeten nearly every room in our home. We recite the Angelus, with bell, twice each day. Other devotions, like the rosary, are said in private.

Bernanos, in his *Diary of a Country Priest*, wrote of those "innumerable people who find, to their dying day, sheer, robust, vigorous, abundant joy in prayer." This seems to indicate that if genuine prayer is integrated into one's life, such a life might be really worth living.

The retreat: a time to face sin and conversion

Sin: Sin touches everyone's life. It is present in individuals, in the world, in the Church. A retreat that did not touch sin and conversion would be seriously incomplete.

Sin is in the individual: In each person sin upsets the delicate balance between the mind and the will, as Paul taught: "I am carnal, sold into slavery to sin. What I do, I do not understand. For I do not do what I want, but I do what I hate" (Romans 7:14). There is not one of us so confirmed in grace but we can say with Peter, "I am a sinful man" (Luke 5:8). For each man the saddest effect of sin is death: "by sin death came into the world" (Romans 5:12). It is both a measure of the mercy of Christ and the tragic evil of sin that to take sin away, Jesus had "to give up his life as a ransom" (Mark 10:45).

Sin is in the world: There is one sense in which the world was so dear to the Father that he "sent his Son to redeem it" (Jn 3:17). But there is also that side of the world that is "aligned to Satan" (1 John 3:8–9). We are confronted every day with some aspect of this side of the world. I have learned, from a very respected confrere, that it may be tragic for one who wishes to preach the Gospel, to be ignorant of the tangible evils of our times. He has taught me that one must be aware of these evils in a conscious way, rehearse them over and over in the memory so as not to let them slip out of consciousness, especially at the time for celebrating the liturgy. Because nearly all of these injustices concern the poor, to preach against them, and to work toward eliminating the evil structures that cause them, is one positive way for a Redemptorist to keep faith with the poor.

Sin is in the Church: Because we who make up the Church are sinners; the Church is not only a communion of saints, it is also a communion of sinners. During the late Council, there was some talk of the council members dressing in penitential garb and processing through the streets of Rome, in penance for the sins, past and present, of the Church. If the plan never materialized, it does not mean that the instinct was not sound.

Conversion: Constitution 10 states: "Redemptorists have, as their special mission in the church, the explicit proclamation of the word of God, to bring about fundamental conversion." How does one today preach turning away from the evils of sin, whether in the individual, the world, or the Church? Personally, I think one direction can be found in observing the qualities of those leaders of our own day who have moved hearts for the better. Tentatively, I suggest these following qualities:

- *Love:* I have especially in mind the love so characteristic of Pope John XXIII. Somehow, everyone who met him, and even those who saw him on television, felt they were loved by him. And of course they were.

- *The will to risk one's life and reputation, if need be:* I have in mind, as an example, Archbishop Oscar Romero. He must certainly have been frightened to learn that he would be murdered, if he kept speaking out as he did against his repressive military government. But there is no sign that he backed down from his commitment to bring justice to his oppressed people.

- *The need to be positive:* It seems to me that prophets of doom, no matter how eloquent, never manage to touch human hearts for the better. Pope John XXIII held before the Church a very positive goal: "Let's open the windows and let in some fresh air." Dr. Martin Luther King, Jr., likewise was positive: "I dream of a world where my children will be judged for their character, not for the color of their skin." So, too, are our Afro-American confreres positive in the slogan emblazoned across their vocation poster: "Come help us preach the Gospel *with power.*"

- *The need to be well-informed and articulate:* People who are neither of these are not likely to move anyone to conversion. Bad preaching, to cite an example, may be the worst enemy religion has—a fact, it is clear, that Alphonsus totally subscribed to and made clear to his confreres and later to the priests of his diocese.

- *The need to be supported by a community:* There will be times ahead, as there have been in the past, when a confrere will feel the necessity in conscience to speak out, in love and risk, against the conduct or ruling of those in authority (in state or Church). It will be impossible for the individual to do this without the support of his community—for psychological and spiritual reasons, not legal—a fact abundantly confirmed by the history of our time.

28

THE LAITY DISCOVER
THE REDEMPTORIST CHARISM

Alicia von Stamwitz
Province of Denver

SOMETHING NEW IS HAPPENING in the Congregation. From among the many laypeople who collaborate with Redemptorists, a growing number are stepping forward and asking to enter into a new kind of relationship with the Congregation. Through contact with the Redemptorist community and participation in the Redemptorist mission, these laypeople have become attracted to the charism of the Congregation. Consequently, they are asking for Redemptorist formation and the opportunity to share in Redemptorist apostolic life. They are pursuing a more dynamic, interdependent model of lay association with the Congregation.

In this article I will present my own story of how I became attracted to the mission and charism of the Congregation, a brief review of Saint Alphonsus's involvement with laypeople, testimonies from lay collaborators in various regions of the Congregation, and a summary of recent developments in Redemptorist-lay collaboration. From these combined points of reference, we can begin to chart a course for the future.

1. Common Mission

I have known the Redemptorists since 1980 when I started working at Liguori Publications. My university studies had prepared me to be a schoolteacher, but after I wrote a freelance article for the *Liguorian* magazine, the Redemptorist editor of the magazine urged me to change careers. I enrolled in a thirty-credit journalism and communications program at Washington University in St. Louis, Missouri. Since my husband had just graduated from law school we had no savings for my tuition. The Redemptorists paid for my first classes and helped me obtain a scholarship from the Catholic Press Association of the United States and Canada for the remainder of the program.

When my daughter Teresa was born in 1983, the Redemptorists supported my decision to change to a part-time work schedule to care for her. My hours were flexible and they loaned me a word processor to write articles at home. My second child, Maria, was born in 1985. I continue to work part-time in my current position as associate editor of *Liguorian*.

During my first ten years at Liguori Publications, I knew the Redemptorists primarily as professional associates and friends. But after 1990 a series of events drew me into a more profound relationship with the Congregation.

In July 1990 the St. Louis Province Redemptorists returned four middle-class parishes to diocesan clergy. In a letter to the confreres, the provincial explained, "The personnel freed by these decisions will strengthen our remaining commitments and allow us to make new initiatives among the poor marginalized minorities." Soon after, the province accepted responsibility for two abandoned inner-city parishes in Chicago. The new parishes were in an interracial neighborhood with much poverty, crime, and gang violence.

This was the first time I heard about the province's newly reformulated apostolic priority statement in favor of the economically poor, the marginalized, and ethnic/minority groups (April 1989 Provincial Chapter). Later, I read about the major theme of the sexennium for the Congregation: "To evangelize the poor and be evangelized by the poor." But it was the concrete witness of the St. Louis Province that had the greatest impact on me.

In June 1991 the Redemptorist superior general, Father Juan Lasso de la Vega, visited the United States. He came to St. Louis to attend the North American Youth Congress. I happened to be there as an observer, representing Liguori Publications. Father Lasso's keynote talk was electrifying.

Addressing the young people and the Redemptorists together, Father Lasso spoke of our Christian mandate to make a radical, personal commitment to the poor and our common mission to renew the Church—laypeople and vowed religious *together* taking responsibility for the future of the Church. Then he invited the Redemptorists and laypeople to form apostolic communities together:

What I propose to you, as a friend and brother of all of you, young people and Redemptorists, is that you try to form apostolic groups together, that you combine your forces and also your lives. That in your parishes or groups you, young people and Redemptorists, take on a common project. I am convinced that our calling and our mission are very similar, and mutually complement each other.

Although my husband and I were already members of a small Christian community in our inner-city diocesan parish, Father Lasso's proposal interested me. His description of the Congregation's mission and vision was very appealing. But there was no precedent in the St. Louis Province for a religious-lay apostolic community. I needed more information about the Congregation and its founder to make this decision. I wanted to be sure that my ideals matched those of Saint Alphonsus and that there was a place for laypeople in the Congregation.

2. Saint Alphonsus and Laypeople

I began to read biographies on the life of Saint Alphonsus. I was particularly interested in Alphonsus's contact with laypeople. When I read about Alphonsus's "Evening Chapels" I stopped short: here was a religious who was not afraid to turn over the reins to laypeople over two hundred fifty years ago. Alphonsus trained ordinary laypeople to become catechists and preachers and to lead small Christian communities in the poor neighborhoods of Naples. Théodule Rey-Mermet writes,

> ...these groups became a "grass roots" movement for education; for social improvement and the reformation of morals; for mutual help and sharing with the poor....The people in charge—and this was a daring idea far ahead of its time—were laymen....The leader of each fraternity was a manual laborer, a poor man, an *ignoble* person like all the other members, and the priests were simply "assistants." For Alphonsus knew that these poor baptized people possessed the Holy Spirit, too. He also knew that they were the only people who possessed the necessary down-to-earth experience and who knew the right words to communicate with proper authority: They knew what they were talking about, especially when they talked about sin and mercy.[1]

Moreover, Alphonsus valued laywomen as spiritual leaders at a time when laywomen had no power or place in the institutional Church. He set up a school of formation for women, directed by a laywoman. Although Alphonsus did not fail to visit the school, it did not last. Rey-Mermet explains:

> Why didn't it last? Because the *Cappelle* were not intended for an economically independent world but for "outcasts."...The men could come to the meetings after their day's work; but for the women of the *bassi* and the slums, who had children with whooping cough, croup, and other miseries, the day's work was never done.[2]

In each biography I found evidence of Alphonsus's unorthodox openness and attention to laypeople. Two final examples: (1) Alphonsus wanted Redemptorist houses to be places of ongoing contact with laymen, who were invited in for spiritual exercises and retreats:

> Like the house at Villa degli Schiavi, the house at Ciorani was made large enough to accommodate retreatants....The retreat work of the fathers was to meet with great success, for the letters of Father Sportelli reveal that there were as many as fifty-four clerics making retreats there at one time and as high as 114 laymen. The missionaries themselves often had to sleep on boards, or chests, or on the ground, because of the crowds that came to take part in the spiritual exercises.[3]

(2) Alphonsus's program for the "continuous missions" included regular community prayer with laypeople. Twice a day, the community made its meditation together with the people in Redemptorist churches. This is how Clement Hofbauer, the second founder of the Congregation, first came into contact with Redemptorists:

> One evening [Clement and Thaddeus Huebl] agreed to hear Mass on the following day in the church whose bells should be the first to fall upon their ears. At an early hour an unpretentious little bell invited them to the unpretentious little church of San Giuliano, quite near. They entered and found a community of religious making their morning meditation....Clement was impressed, very favourably impressed. On leaving he called an altar-boy and asked who these religious might be. There came a strange reply. "They are Redemptorists," said the lad, "and you will be one of them."[4]

If Clement had not had this intimate experience of Redemptorist spirituality, the Congregation might look quite different today. Clement later carried the Redemptorist charism north and became "the most influential priest in the entire Austrian Empire," in the words of the then papal nuncio to the pope. His enthusiastic association with groups of dedicated laypeople triggered a renewal of Viennese society.

3. The Redemptorist Charism

As I read about the early history of the Congregation, I instinctively matched recurring ideals and themes with my concrete experience of the Redemptorist community. Gradually, I gained a sense of the Redemptorist charism. Like a regional accent, I think a charism is more easily recognized than described. But I picked out two characteristics of the Redemptorist charism that were especially attractive to me.

First, a distinctive mark of the Redemptorist is that he is willing to go to the outer edges of humanity to reach those who are rejected and forgotten in our world. Just as Christ did not sit in synagogues waiting for the people to come to him, so the Redemptorist does not confine himself to traditional places and forms of ministry. Rather, he goes out to distant villages and dark street corners seeking direct and personal contact with the abandoned poor. He thereby becomes a living reminder of the Son of Man who came *to search out* and save what was lost (cf. Luke 19:10). His presence alone is a prophetic word among the poor, announcing "God-with-us" to people who have lost hope.

Second, the Redemptorist recognizes the transforming power of genuine community:

> The chief object of their preaching is to lead people to a radical choice regarding their life—a decision for Christ—and draw them firmly and gently to a continuing and total conversion. The conversion of the individual, however, is brought about in the ecclesial community. And therefore the object of their whole missionary activity is to raise up and develop communities that will walk worthily in the vocation to which they are called, and exercise the priestly, prophetic and royal offices with which God has endowed them (Constitutions 11,12).

The Redemptorist lives in community because "genuine community life is an evangelical witness in itself, and as such is a vital part of our mission of evangelization,"[5] and "apostolic life in common paves the way most effectively for the life of pastoral charity" (Constitution 21). It is the community that animates and sends out the missionaries; it is the community that revives the missionaries when they return home weary or discouraged.

After this period of reading and reflection, I concluded that there was sufficient precedent for Redemptorists and laypeople to form apostolic communities together. With the blessing and encouragement of my husband and the members of our small Christian community, I made a commitment to help launch a Redemptorist-lay apostolic group in St. Louis. The Ordinary Provincial Council later designated a Redemptorist community in St. Louis to serve as the center for this lay group. Today laypeople regularly share in this community's prayer life and family life. They support one another and the Redemptorists in their common mission to evangelize the poor. Some of these laypeople are receiving formation in Redemptorist history and spirituality, hoping to become candidates for the newly established category of Lay Missionary of the Most Holy Redeemer.[6]

4. Testimonies of Lay Collaborators

After my 1992 appointment to the General Secretariat for Collaboration with the Laity, I began to hear the stories of other laypeople who are attracted to the mission and charism of the Congregation. Before writing this article, I contacted thirty laypeople from various regions of the Congregation and invited them to respond to three questions:

- How did you first come into contact with the Redemptorists?
- How long have you been active in the Redemptorist mission and/or involved in Redemptorist community life? What is the nature and extent of your involvement?
- What is your dream for the future of Redemptorist lay collaboration?

I received twenty responses. Although the respondents do not represent every situation in the Congregation, I hope the following excerpts from seven testimonies will give an initial idea of the spirit and perspective of our lay collaborators.

4.1 A laywoman from Naples Province, Italy (0200)

I know the Redemptorists because their formation house is in my parish and the Redemptorist students work among the children and youth of my neighborhood. I have been active in Redemptorist youth ministry for eight years. I began to participate in missions in 1990.

My decision to collaborate with the Redemptorists came from my growing consciousness of their charism and then my identification with their pastoral priority for the most abandoned—specifically, for the abandoned youth who are my special preoccupation and passion.

My dream is that lay collaborators will continue to be more and more involved in the planning and work of the mission and/or of other common pastoral activities. Then that laypeople may have a stable means of participation in the Redemptorist community, one which maintains and respects the autonomy of each and the real differences between religious life and lay life.

4.2 A layman from CEBU Vice Province, Philippines (1302)

In 1974 a visitor came to our house in Pangi, Mandug, Davao City and introduced himself as a Redemptorist seminarian. He explained about his mission activities in our place. He was very respectful and genuine in the way he approached people. The works initiated by this seminarian became part of the life of the people in the barrio. Moreover, there was ongoing formation for lay leaders like me. This seminarian was later transferred to another place, but his ways as a Redemptorist took root in my life through the formation process he initiated.

One trait of the Redemptorists that really attracted me is their integration and living with the poor people. They preached and taught the barrio folks about Christian responsibility and awareness of the real situation in the country.

I've been working with the Redemptorists almost twenty years now. As a parish worker I visit the different member-communities of the parish, conduct seminars for leaders, organize new communities, attend meetings in the parish and in the diocese, and participate in the regular assembly of all Redemptorist lay collaborators in the Vice Province of Cebu.

I dream to be fully part of the life of the Redemptorists as their lay collaborator and to benefit from this relationship as befits my role as a lay member of the Church.

4.3 A laywoman from Warsaw Province, Poland (1700)

I grew up close to the Redemptorists. I live in Tuchów where there is a Redemptorist monastery and seminary. My uncle has been a Redemptorist for thirty-five years; my cousin, a Redemptorist for three years. Also, I am a member of an Oasis group of the "Light-Life" movement, which is led by Redemptorists. Thanks to this group, I learned how to live with faith and love; I realized that we cannot be passive Catholics, but that the *laity* also must tell everyone about God.

At first I did not know how to carry into effect my new conclusions, but then in 1991 a Redemptorist asked me to join a group called Young Missionary Group–East, and I agreed. As a member of this group, I travel with Redemptorists and other laypeople to the East in order to evangelize the territories of the former Soviet Union and other republics. We organize prayer days for children, youth, and the elders during the Christmas and Easter holidays.

This was the beginning of my adventure with the Redemptorists—I can say it has been amazing. The Redemptorists have something special. They make others become enthusiastic and they encourage the work, even when it is not easy.

4.4 A layman from Edmonton Province, Canada (2900)

I am a married man and father of four children. After twenty years of working for the government in youth recreation programs, I was offered a job as a full-time youth minister and pastoral assistant in a Redemptorist parish. The Redemptorists later helped me obtain a theology degree, and they continue to empower and encourage me as I minister to our parishioners.

I have been collaborating with Redemptorists for over six years now. Each year I become more appreciative of the Redemptorist charism. My dream for the future is to see Redemptorists leading the way by example toward full collaboration between all laypeople and all religious orders, for it is then that we, as laypeople, will be able to exercise fully our responsibilities as equal partners in caring for God's Church.

4.5 A laywoman from Bogotá Province, Colombia (2800)

After receiving a university degree in mathematics, I decided to commit two years of my life to missionary work. Through a friend involved with IMSA (Alphonsian Secular Missionary Institute), I found out about an inserted Redemptorist community in a poor barrio in Bogotá. After visiting the community, I was invited to share in its apostolic life as a lay missionary.

Since then, I have had an ongoing experience of discovering God among the poor and of admiring ever more the Redemptorist charism. Three priests and eight theology students live in the house. My bedroom is in a separate house (I rent a room in a house nearby), but I live with the Redemptorists in the sense that I share everything with them: prayer, meals, household duties, celebrations, retreats, and theology studies.

I was very happy to find out that the last General Chapter established the category of Lay Missionary of the Most Holy Redeemer, so thanks to this, people like me will be able to assume and live the Alphonsian charism.

4.6 A layman from Manaus Vice Province, Brazil (1202)

I met the Redemptorists when I was a child. My parents worked at collecting Brazil nuts, and a Redemptorist and his helpers walked through two hundred meters of mud to visit the property where we worked and lived. Their stay of three days brought a lot of happiness for all the workers because of the wedding celebrations, baptisms, confessions, Masses, and games with the children. I have never forgotten this blessed first encounter.

When my family moved to the city of Codajas, we became members of the Redemptorist parish. Since my confirmation, I have dedicated myself to pastoral work in the Church: in youth groups, catechetics, rural and city base ecclesial communities, vocational groups, and human rights groups. Today I am a regional coordinator for youth ministry.

My dream is that Redemptorists and laypeople will develop a closer relationship in order that there might be an awakening desire among children, youth, and adults to know and to live more intensely the way of Jesus Christ, whether as laypeople or as Redemptorist brothers or priests. Thus will the Redemptorist family grow, and opportunities for this indispensable collaboration increase, so that we might expand the kingdom of God.

4.7 A laywoman from Dublin Province, Ireland (1300)

I was a college graduate and I had been a member of a Redemptorist parish youth group for six years when I chose to collaborate with Redemptorists in youth ministry. I now live in a mixed community of religious and lay, male and female, called Scala. It is an open house primarily engaged in youth ministry, though we also give missions. I am not quasireligious nor do I intend to become a religious. Living with religious in community has led me to discover my own differing yet complementary identity as a layperson.

I believe mixed communities are part of the future of Redemptorist-lay collaboration and the Church as a whole. Yet there must be support for collaborative living at a grassroots level if it is to survive and flourish, that is, support from Redemptorists in all the houses of a particular province. At this present time, mixed communities are supported at the General Government level but not by all Redemptorists at the local level.

Finally, since I was unable to obtain a testimony from a layperson in the region of Africa, I would like to reprint a portion of a letter that appeared in the July 1994 issue of *C.Ss.R. Communicationes*:

4.8 A Redemptorist from Niamey Vice Province, Niger (0404)

Not long ago we started a small group of lay missionaries in response to the call of the General Chapter. The group consists of ten laypeople, [another Redemptorist], and myself and is called The Mission Team of St. Alphonsus. Several times a week, the team spends the night in a parish and holds meetings in the compounds with Christians and some Muslims whom we visit, a sort of "evening chapels" in the style of those of Saint Alphonsus. This little group is working with great enthusiasm.

5. Charting a Course for the Future

The testimonies of these laypeople reflect a new reality in the Church. Prompted by Vatican II, laypeople have reclaimed their baptismal right and responsibility to actively further the growth of God's kingdom. As they become more deeply involved in the Church's mission, often working side by side with religious, they are discovering religious charisms. Most of these laypeople cannot be professed members of religious orders; nevertheless, religious charisms are animating their spiritual lives and apostolic work.

This reality, evidenced in the preceding testimonies, is "new wine" in the Congregation of the Most Holy Redeemer. The last General Chapter in Itaici affirmed this significant development. The Chapter made a number of recommendations promoting Redemptorist-lay collaboration, and it reached two important decisions:

> The General Chapter establishes in the Congregation the category of Lay Missionary of the Most Holy Redeemer as an active co-worker and participant in the apostolic life of the Redemptorist Congregation. The General Government should prepare general norms which will apply to all units of the Congregation. (F.D. 60a). The General Chapter inspires our communities to open themselves up to the laity, so that they may have a greater share in our experiences of life, work and spirituality (F.D. 60b).

Regarding the new category of Lay Missionary of the Most Holy Redeemer, the General Chapter's intent was not to create an elite or isolated society of laypeople devoted to the Congregation. Rather, its intent was to encourage structures by which lay collaborators might be strengthened for *missionary action*: that is, by offering lay collaborators Redemptorist formation and a stable means to share in Redemptorist apostolic life.

Regarding the second directive inspiring communities to open themselves up to the laity, some Redemptorists and laypeople have responded to this directive by forming "mixed" communities in which Redemptorists and laypeople share one residence. Although this is an option, it is an exceptional option. The point of the Chapter's directive is to encourage new initiatives whereby laypeople can share regularly in *some moments* of Redemptorist apostolic life—a modest goal that can be realized in every unit of the Congregation. Two Brazilian confreres expressed this ideal beautifully:

> We are very loved. We ought to invest more in our lay people who love us so much. Many laypeople are already profoundly tied in with our missionary ideal. We think the time is right to associate them with us in more stable ways....There are hardly any laypeople who participate in our day-to-day community life. Here, on this point, we can be more creative and more open: we can invite laypeople to participate in our

common prayer and reflection, we can invite them to retreats, anniversary celebrations, and parties. It would be good if our lay collaborators could have a rich taste of our common life.[7]

Many good things are already happening in the Congregation with respect to Redemptorist-lay collaboration. The General Secretariat for Collaboration with the Laity is working to spread the news about these developments through reports, regional meetings, a newsletter called *Together*, and other means.

At the same time, areas of tension and ambiguity are surfacing due to our inexperience and the newness of Redemptorist-lay collaboration, for example: confusion regarding the concept of "equal partnership" with lay collaborators (F.D. 58a); questions regarding the decision-making power and rights of lay collaborators, especially at the vice provincial level; ambiguity regarding the juridical status of Lay Missionaries of the Most Holy Redeemer; tension among some brothers regarding the prominent position accorded to lay missionaries in some units of the Congregation; uncertainty regarding the Congregation's financial obligations to long-term lay collaborators. Given time, discernment, and the experience of collaboration itself, these tensions will gradually be resolved and the ambiguities clarified. In the words of a Native American saying, "We create the path by walking."

Conclusion

I would suggest that the desire of a growing number of laypeople to participate in Redemptorist apostolic life is a positive development. The loyalty and love of these laypeople is a gift to the Congregation. Their dream of a more dynamic association with the Congregation is a prophetic sign and evidence that the Redemptorist charism is vital to the Church today.

For years Redemptorists passed on their charism to professed religious, but perhaps the time has come to develop a new model. While respecting the differences between religious life and lay life, it may be possible to share the Redemptorist charism with laypeople who will treasure it. In the end, perhaps laypeople will do more than discover the charism; perhaps they will also reflect a new dimension of the Redemptorist charism as it finds fresh forms of expression in their lives.

The way forward is not self-evident and will not be easy. Nevertheless, a closer association between Redemptorists and laypeople presents the Congregation with a unique opportunity for growth, and thus for greater service to the Church and to the world. It is imperative that the Congregation continues to integrate and guide the tremendous energy and hope of its dedicated lay collaborators.

Together, may Redemptorists and laypeople continue to bring the good news of Christ's plentiful Redemption to the most abandoned and the poor among God's people.

Notes

1. T. Rey-Mermet, *St. Alphonsus Liguori: Tireless Worker for the Most Abandoned* (Brooklyn: 1989), pp. 181–182.
2. Ibid., p. 180.
3. D. F. Miller and L. X. Aubin, *Saint Alphonsus Mary de'Liguori* (Quebec-London: 1940), pp. 107–108.
4. John Carr, *St. Clement, C.SS.R.* (London: 1939), p. 44.
5. *Communicanda N. 11*, "The Redemptorist Apostolic Community, 1988, 1
6. XXI General Chapter (1991), *Final Document 60a.*
7. Cf. *Report on Lay Collaboration in the Congregation of the Most Holy Redeemer*, General Secretariat for Collaboration with the Laity, October 1992.

29

A MISSIONARY CHARISM
FOR THE THIRD MILLENNIUM

Francesco Chiovaro, C.Ss.R.
Province of Naples
Translated by Walter H. George, C.Ss.R.
Province of Denver

1. Why Did I Become a Redemptorist?

To Redemptorists of my generation, the event has been the Council. Not so much because of the texts promulgated, but for the Christian energy released by Vatican II.

We were in our thirties and were irrepentant dreamers. We dreamed of a new Christianity, of a new evangelization that would take on the real demands of a world which, in the aftermath of war, was experiencing rapid transformation. Our passion as Redemptorists was to proclaim the Gospel to the world—not to an abstract world, but to this world, to our world, the world to which we had been sent and with which we stood in solidarity.

The study of Church history had led me to a certain detachment from the way, objectively out of date, in which the Gospel was being proclaimed— if indeed it be the Gospel?—to contemporaries. I admired the monumental structure and order of the Church, and of the Congregation, but I did not feel involved: human, too human. People would ask me, "Why do you continue to be a part of it?" They spoke, of course, in terms of structure: if you do not agree, get out. And I responded: "But I, too, am the Church, I, too, am the Congregation. I cannot leave myself."

Besides, it seemed to me that there was a formidable advantage here: there was nothing to lose. Religious profession impressed me as gradually taking, more and more, the shape of an extraordinary form of Christian liberty. I knew there was a price to pay as well; but it was worth it. What would it matter where I was, or what I was doing? As long as always and everywhere I would be able to spend my life freely for the Gospel.

There was a risk of subjectivity. I have always loved the Church and the Congregation. I thought I loved them in the right way. But the pressure of so many invitations to change or to leave resulted in generating doubt: what if I were mistaken? And what if my evangelical dreaming was an illusion? In 1957, I listened to a conference of Father Henri de Lubac. The, then recently, condemned theologian developed a single idea: stay in the Church, above all if you are not in agreement with the Institution. Contest, but stay. Shatter the stained glass, open doors and windows, but stay. Do not delude yourself that you will be able to change the Church by abandoning the Church. It was for me a healing viaticum. Six years later, it seemed as if the dream would come true.

"Behold, I make all things new"

Only those who lived through the conciliar springtime can fully appreciate the upheaval provoked by the Council. People liked to quote Gregory VII: *"Dominus non dixit: Ego sum traditio, sed veritas."* Father Yves Congar loosely translated the phrase, more or less, like this: "Everything that has changed can be changed." Traditions patiently embedded in the depth of our souls crumbled like the walls of Jericho. The world with its joys, its pains, and its hopes became in immense evangelical field for the sowers of the Word. A heady feeling possessed us, at the same time euphoric and intimidating. We had the impression we were assisting at the opening of a new age, of at last being able to work on the renewal of the Church of God. We felt unprepared; but we had confidence in the Spirit.

To us Redemptorists it seemed that for the first time we had left the periphery of Christianity. The Congregation, in a Church that had rediscovered its missionary nature, seemed to have become a driving force, at the center of a Christianity renewed and committed to the realization of the kingdom of God. It is almost impossible to express today the faith and the hope that inspired us in our thirties. They were years of great optimism in every field of endeavor: it was as if we were emerging from a tunnel.

The extraordinary General Chapter (1967–1969) was born of that enthusiasm. The Chapter was quickly transformed into a great scaffolding, dedicated to the single task of trying to reconstruct a Congregation faithful to its originating charism but, above all, evangelical and sensitive to changed conditions in the Church and in the world. The new Constitutions, elaborated and approved almost unanimously by the Chapter, constituted the best witness of that climate and effort. The Second Vatican Council had supplied the basic foundation of the project and encouraged the audacity to make it come about.

I worked in the archives of the Sacred Congregation of Rites from 1963 to 1967 and taught the history of Christianity in the faculty of theology for laymen of the University of San Tommaso in Rome. I detested the work in the archives, but must acknowledge that being part of the Roman curia permitted me to accompany the work of the Council regularly, and with a passion. Teaching, however, stirred my enthusiasm. For a Redemptorist, the occupation was usually considered out of line, if not beyond the pale. I had never imagined that being a Redemptorist would mean classifying files and speaking of pontifical finances during the Avignon period. The mission, the Redemptorist charism (as it came to be called at that time), seemed for me a dream stored away for the moment in some file drawer. In the new conciliar climate and even more during the Extraordinary Chapter, I took care to restore the Redemptorist side of my life.

One day a student has asked me if the Second Vatican Council could be considered a "great council." I said that it would be the post-Council that would give him the answer: the texts, certainly innovative but objectively equivocal, lent themselves to multiple interpretations. It would be the survival of the spirit of the Council and not the letter of the Council; it would be the men of the post-Council, the intelligence and the energy that they would dedicate to advance the "aggiornamento," that would determine the greatness of the Second Vatican Council. It was the prudent response of an historian who refuses to forecast the future, but in my heart I knew that things would never again be the same.

2. Why the Year Two Thousand?

Thirty years later we still do not have an answer to that question, at least it seems to me. We are now in midstream, facing a strong temptation to turn in on ourselves, or, at most, to content ourselves with apparent, yet superficial reform.

There were, at the close of the Council, two ways of interpreting the event. The more optimistic saw in the Council a starting point, a *terminus a quo* toward the full incarnation of the Gospel: a first step anticipating Vatican III. For others, Vatican II, in contrast, was prospectively the end of the line, the *terminus ultra quem non*: the Church could not advance beyond this point. The most optimistic thought of Vatican II was an unanticipated irruption of the Spirit, the new Pentecost foreseen by John XXIII. And who could deny it? The others saw it as a king of cyclone which had hit the old structures. And it certainly was this as well.

In the name of the Council, each chose where to take their stand. In this phase of postconciliar stalemate—and delusion—what sense does it make to speak of the year 2000? Objectively, none whatsoever. I see no difference between 1999 and 2001. A century from now historians of the Church and of the Congregation may discover that certain changes of direction, certain reconsiderations, certain renewals occurred in 1963 or 1967, or unforeseeably in 2013. Scarcely in the year 2000.

Of one thing it is possible to be certain: there will be no Christianity of the third millennium anymore than there was of the first millennium, nor of the second millennium. The turning points of history, for those to whom they are significant, do not coincide with the millenniums. I do not dare think of the third millennium in global terms.

With this restriction, the date—2000—remains important from a psychological point of view, as a time to pause and to reflect: the beginning of the third millennium is an opportune moment to reflect on the meaning of the Redemptorist presence in the near future.

Dreams for the Congregation of the year 2000

Among us Redemptorist, preparations for the year 2000 began some time ago: at least in the years of the generalate of Father Leonard Bujis. Since then there has been much talk of "Redemptorist identity," of "charism," of "characteristics," and of other matters that were unthinkable before the Second World War. A sign of the times: it denoted that we were in crisis, as were almost all other religious institutions, as was the Church herself; that the traditional image of Redemptorist, at least the image of recent tradition, had turned opaque, so that in it Redemptorists no longer recognized themselves; that we were unable to reconstruct it in order to find ourselves a spiritual identity; that we could not find our place in the Church; that we could not establish a goal for our apostolate. It then became evident that we were in an intolerable situation. An exodus took place.

The idea of exodus has become familiar even if all that is and was obscure in the image instilled fear. No one could pretend to know what direction the Congregation would take tomorrow. Not even Moses knew what the "Promised Land" was like. The temptation to return to Egypt was constant during the passage through the desert. It took courage to push forward, especially when "forward" would not let itself be clearly defined. And it took imagination: it helped to imagine the Promised Land as a place of "milk and honey." The future is conditioned on the aspirations of the present.

We imagine the new millennium, then, as a journey to a new house to which we have been called to live. We need to move. We are moving. As with every move, we need to choose what to take with us and what to leave behind. I do not see that I have the competence to prepare an inventory of the vital energies and the dead weight in our Congregation. In a general way, I dare to say that to move ahead expeditiously; it is not necessary to weight one's self down with a lot of baggage. It is better to run the risk of leaving along the way some part, even an important part, of our patrimony than to risk paralysis by dragging along all the rubbish accumulated in the old house.

I have asked to set aside the role of historian and to imagine the vitality of our missionary charism. I will try because my personal experience and the history of the Congregation have convinced me of the vitality and of the creativity of our charism. I will try also because I want to continue to dream.

3. The Obligation to Mission

When we speak of missionary charism, it is not as if it were but one of the things to save. Here what is at stake is the very being of the Congregation. Hence the Congregation of the third millennium will be missionary, or it will cease to exist. Slowly but surely we have become aware of this. Being missionary is being who we are in the Church. Among other things, this implies that we are not called on to do everything in the Church.

Continuing the image of the exodus, I would like to call attention to the first requirement for mission: mobility.[1] Since the beginning of Christianity, mobility has been a basic characteristic of the missionary. Ease of travel in the modern world has made this characteristic more dramatic. The very term *mission* has lately acquired a meaning in common usage. For us, however, mission is not limited to the sense of moving on from one place to another. Apostolic mobility implies a particular way of being part of the Church. The Church will always need someplace to take root. For this reason, the local and the universal Church will always need a minimum of permanent structure. Missionary mobility, on the contrary, does not allow planting roots: we cannot be part of the permanent structure of the Church, even of the pastoral structure. An itinerant institution cannot accept offices in government within the Church community.

Now and then the Church requests that some structural support be taken on: but this support will be exceptional and temporary. Missionary mobility also includes this: taking a position on the frontier of the institutional Church. The outside edge: laying the foundation of Christian community. The inside edge: stirring to life a community at risk. Our residence, which we no longer build to last forever, will be missionary outposts.

In the past one of the reasons that has spurred the Congregation to integrate itself more and more into the ordinary pastoral structures has been the fear of remaining without work. And it is true that as long as we understand mission in the traditional sense, the danger exists of becoming idle shepherds. But the mission is no longer identified with a technique of preaching. In a Congregation that exists in diverse geographical and cultural contents, missionary proclamation will assume various forms and methods, adapting itself to the demands of the local Church. The principal concern of members of the Congregation, particularly of superiors and chapter members, will be to define forms of mission without falling into the mania of changing for changing's sake. Unchangeable alone will be the message, under every circumstance, of the plentiful Redemption of God in Jesus Christ. In this way a plurality of forms of pastoral will lead to tolerance and to respect. No one in the Congregation of the year 2000 will think that he possesses the monopoly on mission: *dummondo Christus annuntietur*.

Mobility is an indispensable condition, but it is not the purpose of mission. The mission is the proclamation of the Gospel. Redemptorists of the third millennium will all be biblical scholars, or almost so. I want to say that they will have understood the importance of the Word and the need of involving themselves in the hearing of the Gospel. Their spiritual and cultural formation will be centered on the sacred Scriptures. Study and meditation on the Bible will make Redemptorist men free to proclaim the Word.

Those whom the mission addresses

Luke will probably be the Gospel preferred by the Redemptorist of the year 2000, the Gospel of the poor, of the little ones, of the weak, and of...missionaries. The conscious dedication of the founding motto—"to evangelize the poor"—is the choice that justifies and qualifies the Congregation. We are talking about the central nucleus of our charism. To be in favor of the "poor and the abandoned" means to come to grips immediately with the world we want to evangelize, with its problems and with its hopes. It is our way of being modern.

One of the great problems of the next decade, if not of the coming millennium, will be exclusion, something quite different from marginalization. Marginalization can be understood as the unintended result of a society geared to progress. The marginalized are all those who could not succeed in keeping pace. Exclusion is something much more malevolent: a perverse tendency to exclude from the benefits of the culture, from socioeconomic progress, even from respect, a large strata of the population, whole countries and continents, sacrificed to the idol of profit. The field of our apostolate has not only not been restricted, it has been immensely extended.

To insert ourselves into this field, we do not have to start a revolution. It is enough that we look to our initial charism. The ecclesial, cultural, and socioeconomic fortunes of this close of the century refer back to the classic definition of the recipients of our apostolate: "the abandoned poor." Once we have justly put the emphasis on poverty, we have uncovered the tragic dimension of the abandonment that is its most degrading consequence. In a world that creates exclusion, the Redemptorist will be defenders of human dignity and witnesses to Christian hope.

What the Congregation of the third millennium looks like and its apostolic efficacy depend on the seriousness with which we assume this prophetic aspect of our charism. Not that the Congregation has not concerned itself with the "abandoned poor" up to now; the vital moments of her history have always coincided with this preoccupation. But a new and more conscientious awareness is demanded of us in a world that imposes new forms of poverty and of abandonment.

Meanwhile, we have also overcome the anxiety caused by a smaller number of confreres. Given the immensity of the task, we have taken on, we will always be few, like the ferment in the dough. We need collaborators. The Redemptorist charism should become an evangelical movement that embraces as many as feel attracted to our mission. Redemptorists of the third millennium will think of the mission as a gift to be shared with all those who are concerned with implanting the kingdom of God in a disinherited world. The vitality of the Congregation extends also to this: a demonstrated capacity to arouse vocations among the laity.

They style of mission

More than once I have told the story of how I discovered the "Redemptorist style." It was at the beginning of the General Chapter of 1967.

The month of September was exceptionally warm in Rome. All the capitulars agreed on the need for an afternoon siesta. I needed to prepare an intervention: an *expresso* would be the way of not giving in to sleep. There were only the cashier and a waiter in the Café of the Domus Pacis. "What kind of religious are you?" the girl at the cash register asked. "Redemptorist," I replied. "Redemptorist?" she repeated. A pause, and then, "You're a different kind!" "Different, how?" I asked in turn. The young lady tried to put her impressions in words: "We have seen so many religious this year! But it is so difficult to find people like you. Never a protest, never a complaint. *You are content with everything.* You are the simplest and least complicated people that I have ever seen."

Only a few years later, rummaging through our general archives, I accidently came upon a letter of the Pious Worker Gerolamo Sparano to Monsignor Lucci (today Beato Antonio Lucci, O.F.M.Conv.), bishop of Bovino. Sparano recommended the foundation of the house in Deliceto. The letter intrigued me because it is one of the first "external" documents on the Congregation so I copied it. Although it occurs to me that it has already been published partially by Father Tellería and completely by Father André Sampers in *Spicilegium Historicum C.Ss.R.*, 5 (1957) 265–266. Sparano writes among other things January 15, 1745:

> So it is that the work…and the lives led by his [Alphonsus's] companions is very exemplary and mortified. The Institute holds missions every year, and in the dioceses where they live, marvelously instruct the people in Christian doctrine, sanctify them by the frequentation of the sacraments and the Word of God, and with exercises of prayer and meditation. They are men who are theologians, or at least moral theologians, preach quite well, *and what is more, content themselves with anything,* not running after self-interest or magnificence.

It was the image of themselves that Saint Alphonsus and his first companions gave in the environment in which they lived: the same that the cashier of a Roman coffee bar had caught. What we have here must be a genetic characteristic of Redemptorists.

There you have it, and if I were to propose saving any single jewel of our tradition, it is certainly simplicity that I would choose. In the market of spiritual values, it is of solid worth. Besides, not only does it not stand in the way of our progress into the future, but it eases us along more effectively.

Notes

1. The author in the original Italian text uses the word *itineranza* [translator's note].

Conclusion

TO PROFESS
CHRIST THE REDEEMER

Domenico Capone, C.Ss.R.
Province of Naples
Translated by Joseph Tobin, C.Ss.R.
Province of Denver

FATHER DOMENICO CAPONE (1907–1995) was born in Siracusa (Sicily) and entered the Congregation of Redemptorist missionaries at a very young age. He was twenty-three when he was ordained. Then he worked for a short time as a professor in the formation program of the Province of Naples. In 1942, he received a doctorate in philosophy from the Gregorian University, having successfully defended his thesis "The Truth of the Human Act." He began his teaching career at the Alphonsian Academy in 1950, dedicating the rest of his life to lecturing and to scholarly research in the field of moral theology.

Capone never attempted to veil his immense affection for Saint Alphonsus, to whom he dedicated the majority of his historical studies. In addition to his voluminous writings on Alphonsian moral theology, we may also highlight: *The First Contact of Saint Alphonsus with Philosophy* (1940); *The Image of Saint Alphonsus in Portraits and Iconography* (1954); *The Sources of the Ascetic Works of Saint Alphonsus* (1960); *The Roots of Redemptorists and Redemptoristines* (1985).

By the last years of his life, Father Capone had achieved a sort of identity between what he wrote and who he was; this was a theological-spiritual synthesis centered on the person of Christ the Redeemer. He used to say: "Christ is the heart and the face of our Congregation. It is from him that we take our name, Redemptorists, a name which should not be an adjective but rather, a noun....Our very being implies a participation in the filial relationship of Christ and, because of the transforming work of the Spirit, this relationship is expressed and made flesh in us and—by means of us—is a missionary radiance in the world as well."

* * * * *

The following is a translation of the homily given by Father Capone on December 11, 1993, the celebration of the seventieth anniversary of his religious profession.

Most Reverend Father General, Father Provincial,
Father Rector and my confreres:
This celebration, on the occasion of the seventieth anniversary of my religious profession, wishes to be an exhaltation of that which unites us with all who have gone before us, from Saint Alphonsus until our own times.

We do not profess the vows as some sort of inherited formula aimed at our personal perfection. We profess a person: Jesus, who is proposed as the loving will [*eudokia*] of God to save and the mission of the Father. That is to say, we profess Jesus Christ as "Good News" for the poor, the marginalized and the suffering (Luke 4:18). We profess Christ, the Mystery of the Father (Colossians 2:2), in whom and under whom is gathered all history (Ephesians 1:10). Our profession, thus understood, is an ontological concept!

Our profession conveys the sense of Luke 12:8: "Whoever openly *declares himself* for me before others"...*Omologeo* here signifies: to agree with, to adhere and bear witness to a dynamic reality which has become an internal and personal union. Therefore we profess the person of Jesus and that is the reason we call ourselves Redemptorists. The person of Jesus, the saving mystery of the Father, thus becomes the keystone of our identity and charism—our very name, both as individuals and as a community.

In this sense, the text of Constitution 23 is fundamental for our identity: "Since the members are called to continue the presence of Christ and his mission of redemption in the world, they choose the person of Christ as the center of their life, and strive day by day to enter (here again is the sense of *omologein* of the Gospel of Luke) ever more intimately into personal union with him. Thus, at the heart of the community, to form it and sustain it, is the Redeemer himself and his Spirit of love. And the closer their union with Christ, the stronger will become their union with each other" (cf. also Contitution 25).

So, "the members are called to continue the presence of Christ." But how? The answer is decisive for our identity.

The text of today's first reading comes to help us: "The Spirit of the Lord is upon me for he has anointed me. He has sent me to bring good news to the poor...to announce a year of favor from the Lord...I exult for joy in the Lord, my spirit rejoices in my God, for he has clothed me in the garment of salvation, he has wrapped me in a cloak of saving justice" (Isaiah 61:1,2,10; cf. Luke 4:18–19).

Jesus Christ raises this same hymn to the Father, for he has sent him into the world as Redeemer. It is the Father who, with the fullness of his Holy Spirit, clothes Jesus *with the garment of salvation and wraps him in a cloak of saving justice*, so that he might become salvation and justice for the world.

Although I cannot remember the exact citation, Saint Ireneus writes that the Holy Spirit lives in Christ in order to pass from him to dwell among human beings. In this way each person, according to his or her own vocation in life, opens himself to Christ through the Spirit.

Constitution 23 reminds us that we are called to continue the presence and the saving mission of Jesus in the world. Then, we must truly open ourselves to the Holy Spirit, who will transform us at the very core of our being, sharing with us the same anointing by which Jesus is Redeemer. Thus we take from him the name and the identity of Redemptorists.

It is by means of this profound transformation that Christ shares with us his garment of salvation and the cloak of saving justice with which the Father has clothed him. The Father offers this same favor to us, as individuals, as communities, and as an entire Congregation, so that we may be effective and transparent instruments of his will. In this way—and only in this way—will we be able to continue authentically the presence of the Redeemer in the world. This is what it means to *profess Christ* and, consequently, to preach Christ.

Our Congregation has become increasingly more conscious of the nature of our Redemptorist identity and our religious profession. The most recent General Chapter has affirmed this thinking with a doctrine that is at the same time theologically exact and spiritually rich: "The center of Redemptorist spirituality is Christ the Redeemer, as he reveals himself above all in the mysteries of his Incarnation, Passion, and Resurrection, which we celebrate in the Eucharist. These lead the Redemptorists to be his living memorial and to continue his mission in the world" (XXI General Chapter [1991], *Final Document*, n. 36).

Research into our origins leads us to recognize that *viva memoria* is not simply a recollection of the Lord's mysteries nor an imitation of the Lord as a model for the spiritual and apostolic life. We are not simply asked to open ourselves to the Lord, accepting him as a paradigm for our spiritual life (although this might have some use as a pedagogic or ascetic tool). We are called to open ourselves to the Lord in order to assume him—or better said—to be assumed by him in his Spirit. He then becomes operative within us and within our community, uniting us in a love that is truly centered in God, and at the same time, is apostolic.

We have to take seriously the real presence and action of the Holy Spirit within us and our communities by virtue of the resurrection of the Lord. This means we take seriously the truth of the mystery of Christ. Our own Father Durrwell has seen this very well! This is our foundational principle.

So it can be seen that *viva memoria* is not to remember, but to celebrate a living presence. Preaching thus becomes our particular way of celebrating but, like Jesus, a preaching-celebrating that takes place among the poor. This was the intention of Saint Alphonsus, clearly a charismatic founder. It is vitally important to insist on this concept: that preaching is a celebration of the mystery of Christ. Everything within us becomes a celebration and proclamation of the mystery of Christ.

That was how Saint Alphonsus, himself a living and transparent image of Christ, continued the work: at the very beginning of the Congregation, together with the great Gennaro Sarnelli, he preached a year of favor from the Lord. He would do the same in the years that followed, as a missionary, pastor, bishop, and doctor of mercy. This impelled him to renew moral theology and the celebration of the sacrament of penance. He revitalized popular piety, especially devotion to the Eucharist and to Mary, finally offering a type of prayer that is really a mystical dialogue.

The whole nineteenth century was inspired by Alphonsus. As his works spread among seminaries and the people of God, the Church conquered neo-Jansenism. In 1865, Léon Gauthier could attest: "The writings of Saint Alphonsus smoothed the way to the confessional, replacing both wrath with a smile and the step-father with a father" (cf. *Etudes littéraires pour la défense de l'Eglise*, Paris, 1865, p. 488). Over the course of the last two centuries human consciences have rediscovered Christ and once again have perceived truth as the norm for moral and spiritual life.

After Alphonsus, there has been a host of Redemptorists who have professed the *viva memoria* of Christ: Clement Hofbauer, John Neumann, the humble yet great Peter Donders, and so many, many others. I believe that the Congregation today is solicitous to conserve in new forms of the apostolic life this same authentic "profession" of Christ.

Now, to apply this idea to the present celebration: I am convinced that during my seventy years as a Redemptorist, the Congregation has encouraged me and shown me how to profess the Lord, beginning at Ciorani, then at Pagani, Cortona, Sant'Angelo a Cupolo and, since 1947, at Rome. What can I say? I have tried to accomplish something. But, I can see still so much mediocrity within myself! If there is anything good, it is not my accomplishment, but rather comes from God, from Christ and—I say this without any sense of empty piety—because the Mother of Jesus has helped me countless times in my life. I thank her, but I thank even more Jesus Christ, the Holy Spirit and God the Father. Finally, I am grateful to the Congregation, which has formed me in this piety and in this truth.